Expert Witness

A Defence Correspondent's Gulf War

1990–91

Frontispiece The Author at Qaysumah airbase, near Hafar-al-Batin. (Note the package of *Independents* lying, quite by chance, at his feet!).

Expert Witness

A Defence Correspondent's Gulf War
1990–91

CHRISTOPHER BELLAMY

Brassey's
London • New York

First English edition 1993

Christopher Bellamy has asserted his moral right to be identified as author of this work.

UK editorial offices: Brassey's, 165 Great Dover Street, London SE1 4YA
Orders: Marston Book Services, P.O. Box 87
Oxford OX2 0DT

USA orders: Macmillan Publishing Company, Front and Brown Streets, Riverside, NJ 08075

Distributed in North America to booksellers and wholesalers by the Macmillan Publishing Company, NY 10022

Library of Congress Cataloging in Publication Data
available

British Library Cataloguing in Publication Data
A catalogue record for this book is
available from the British Library

ISBN 0 08 041792 2 Hardcover

Typeset by Solidus (Bristol) Limited
Printed and bound in Great Britain by
Biddles Limited, Guildford and King's Lynn

We were fond together, because of the sweep of the open places, the taste of wide winds, the sunlight, and the hopes in which we worked . . . We lived many lives in those swirling campaigns, never sparing ourselves: yet when we achieved and the new world dawned, the old men came out again and took our victory to re-make in the likeness of the former world they knew . . .

T.E. Lawrence ('of Arabia')
Seven Pillars of Wisdom[1]

**For Scotland,
and all who helped
1987–91**

'Horizons reaching cold and blue . . .'

Contents

PART III – 'SUCH A VICTORY AS THIS'

Acknowledgements

Many of the people whose company I enjoyed and whose personal and professional help was crucial during the events of 1990–91 are mentioned in this book and to them I extend my warmest thanks. I shall only thank in addition those whose help was directly related to its production. They are Kristina Ferris, the *Independent*'s graphics editor, for allowing me to use the excellent graphics produced by her department; Richard Dowden for the use of some of his photographs and the picture desk for their cooperation. Special thanks must go to Andreas Whittam Smith and Matthew Symonds, Editor and Deputy Editor of the *Independent*, whose approval of the project made it all possible.

I must also thank Brigadiers Brian Dutton and Tim Glass, successive Directors of Public Relations (Army) in the Ministry of Defence and their staffs for all their help. Thanks too to the Director of Military Survey (MOD) and the Controller of Her Britannic Majesty's Stationery Office for use of the situation maps produced by the General Staff Map Section and shown collectively at the end of Chapter 6 (© British Crown Copyright 1993/MOD).

I am also grateful to Colonel Philippe Peress, the French Military Attaché in London, for helping me to decipher French military acronyms; to the Ministry of Defence Whitehall Library and the staff of our own library at the *Independent*, who were of constant assistance. Tim Ripley helped with orders of battle and the JSTARS photographs, which form the first continuous picture of a great battle unfolding in its entirety ever recorded.

I also thank the staff of Brassey's publishers, particularly Jenny Shaw and Brigadier Bryan Watkins, for their sympathetic treatment of a complex and, ultimately, sizeable book, and especially Bryan for making many useful suggestions and improvements.

Writing the book whilst continuing to work as a journalist was tricky, as the world continued in its convulsions, and I thank my wonderful wife Heather, who I married a year after the war, for all her support and understanding. She listened to this story 'of Antres vast and Deserts idle'. And, as in *Othello*, it seems, 'such a tale would win my daughter, too. . . .'

Note on Timings and Borders
Unless otherwise stated, all timings in this book are Saudi local ('Charlie'), three hours ahead of Greenwich Mean Time ('Zulu') and eight hours ahead of US Eastern Standard Time (Washington). The borders shown are *de facto*. Borders in the Arabian Peninsula are the subject of much dispute. During the crisis, many maps showed 'neutral zones' which had ceased to be valid. The Saudi border was often shown with jagged steps in the centre, not matching the *de facto* delineation on the ground.

List of Figures

List of Plates

Frontispiece The author at Qaysumah airbase

1. US Secretary for Defense briefs journalists in Riyadh, 8 February 1991
2. Press briefing Riyadh, 12 February 1991
3. Colonel Hervé Longuet describes the laser guidance pod for the AS-30 missile
4. Al-Ahsa – French officers
5. RAF Special Forces Chinook helicopter, 3 March 1991
6. Loading JP-233. Muharraq, December 1990
7. Sidewinder missiles. Muharraq, December 1990
8. F-117A 'Stealth' fighter at Khamis Mushait airbase
9. Scud missile on MAZ-543 Transporter-Erector-Launcher, near Prague 1992
10. Scud missile, showing vanes to direct the thrust. Near Prague 1992
11. Iraqi SA-6 surface-to-air missiles incinerated on the Nasiriyah-Basra road, March 1991
12. *Al-Hussein* missile erected
13. RFA *Fort Grange*
14. Checking the map on a Sea King helicopter before flying north over the Gulf
15. Sunset over the Gulf: a Sea King on RFA *Fort Grange*
16. Royal Scots by their Warrior Infantry Fighting Vehicles
17. Royal Scots on training in the Gulf
18. British Gunners of 4th Armoured Brigade
19. Lieutenant General Gus Pagonis has his stars pinned on by General Schwarzkopf and his own son
20. Brigadier Hammerbeck talking to his soldiers before the land battle

Chronology

1979
June–July   Saddam Hussein becomes President of Iraq. Purge of top ranks
                   of Ba'ath Party.

1980
22 September   Iraq invades Iran. Beginning of first Gulf War.

1981
7 June   Israel destroys French-built Osiraq nuclear reactor near
                   Baghdad.

1982
Summer   First use of tear gas in *Ramadan* offensive.

1983
July   First extensive use of lethal gas – Mustard – in *Val Fajr 3*
                   offensive.

1988
28 March   Iraqi forces use chemical weapons against Kurdish town of
                   Halabja.
18 July   Iran accepts UN Security Council Resolution 598 calling for
                   ceasefire, withdrawal of troops to an internationally recognised
                   border and a commission to decide responsibility for the first
                   Gulf War. First Gulf War ends.

1989
15 September   Farzad Bazoft, *Observer* journalist, arrested in Baghdad.

1990
10 March   Farzad Bazoft condemned to death for spying. Hanged
                   15 March.

22 March	Dr Gerald Bull, artillery genius, designer of a range of 'superguns', murdered outside his Brussels flat.
28 March	British Customs seize US-made 'Krytron' capacitors at Heathrow, bound for Iraq, in the mistaken belief that they were nuclear bomb triggers.
10 April	British Customs at Teesport seize steel tubes destined for 'Project Babylon', the supergun project.
14–15 July	Arab Foreign Ministers meet in Tunis. Iraqi Foreign Minister Tariq Aziz accuses Kuwait of syphoning oil from the Rumailah oil field.
31 July–1 August	Kuwaiti and Iraqi representatives meet in Jeddah. Kuwaitis unmoved: talks break down.
1–2 August	At 22.00–23.00 GMT on 1 August (01.00–02.00 local on 2 August) Iraqi forces cross into Kuwait.
2 August	UN Security Council passes Resolution 660 demanding Iraqi withdrawal and calling for negotiations to resolve differences.
4 August	EC imposes economic sanctions on Iraq.
6 August	UN Security Council Resolution 661 imposing sanctions on Iraq.
8 August	US 82nd Airborne Division deploys to Saudi Arabia. Operation *Desert Shield* is underway. Saddam Hussein annexes Kuwait.
11 August	First British warplanes – Tornado F3s – fly into Saudi Arabia. Operation *Granby* is underway.
15 August	Iraq reaches agreement with Iran, renouncing claims to Iranian territory. Releases 24 divisions for KTO.
25 August	UN Security Council Resolution 665 authorising 'necessary measures', including military action, to enforce sanctions.
27–31 August	Author visits Gulf with Tom King, UK Defence Secretary.
28 August	Iraq annexes Kuwait as its 19th Province.
14 September	UK announces it is sending 7th Armoured Brigade to Saudi Arabia.
5 October	US Defence Secretary Dick Cheney says Iraq now has over 350,000 troops in Kuwait and that 25 countries have contributed to Allied military deployment, now totalling 300,000 personnel.
26 October	CIA Director William Webster says Gulf cannot be secure as long as Saddam Hussein rules Iraq and that destruction of Iraq's arsenal may be necessary. Pentagon announces up to 100,000 additional troops and 700 tanks will be deployed in Middle East by the end of the year.
8 November	President Bush orders deployment of a further 200,000 troops to Gulf. Saddam Hussein sacks Chief of the General Staff Gen Nizar Khazraji; his replacement is Saddam's son-in-law, Hussein Rashid.

8–14 November	Author with Royal Navy in Gulf.
15 November	Iraq announces deployment of a further 250,000 troops to the KTO.
22 November	Britain announces enhancement of ground forces to a full division, 1st (British) Armoured, with the addition of 4th Armoured Brigade and divisional troops.
29 November	UN Security Council resolution 678. Authorises use of 'all necessary means' to force Iraq to withdraw from Kuwait if Iraq does not do so by 15 January.
7 December	Iraqi Parliament agrees to free all foreigners held in the country as parts of 'human shield'.
13 December	Saddam Hussein replaces Defence Minister Saidi Tumah Abbas with Lt Gen Abd al-Jaber Khalil Shanshal. Announces setting up of 370 civil defence training centres and orders building of air-raid shelters.
17 December	President Bush meets Allied ambassadors, stresses that no-one wants war but that a partial solution is unacceptable. British Ambassador and Consul, last diplomats in Kuwait, return to London. Foreign Office warns British subjects in the Gulf Region to be out by 15 January. Queen's Order enabling call-up of selected reservists signed: first time since Suez in 1956.
23 December	US Defence Secretary Dick Cheney and Chief of US Joint Chiefs of Staff Gen Colin Powell end five day inspection of US forces in Iraq. They report that Iraq has 500,000 troops in KTO and that US forces are ready to fight. Mr Cheney says coalition may soon have no other option than to use military force.

1991

2 January	Nato Defence Planning Committee authorises deployment of aircraft from Belgium, Germany and Italy to south-east Turkey.
8 January	US Secretary of State James Baker and Iraqi Foreign Minister Tariq Aziz arrive in Geneva.
9 January	Baker and Tariq Aziz meet for six-and-a-half hours. Aziz refuses to accept letter from President Bush to Saddam Hussein. Saddam Hussein says Americans will swim in their own blood if war starts. Author arrives in Riyadh.
14 January	Iraqi Parliament votes to go to war rather than accept UN demands.
15 January	Deadline for Iraqi withdrawal from Kuwait passes.
16–17 January	02.38, local time, on 17 January US AH-64 Apaches cross into Iraq to clear a way through the air defences. At about 03.00 F-117a Nighthawks hit strategic targets. White House spokesman announces 'The liberation of Kuwait has begun.' The operation is called *Desert Storm*.

17 January	Iraq launches first Hussein missiles against Israel: Tel Aviv, Haifa. One also fired at Dhahran, but brought down by a Patriot ABM – the first time in the history of war a ballistic missile has been successfully intercepted.
18 January	US aircraft attack Iraqi missile launchers.
20 January	First missile attack on Riyadh. Saddam Hussein says so far he has only used part of his war-making capacity. In the first broadcast since hostilities began, he threatens to use 'all the means and potential God has given us'. One of the missiles penetrates Saudi defences. The search for 'Scud' launchers is stepped up.
22 January	Concern at relatively high losses of RAF Tornados as fourth aircraft is lost to enemy action. But RAF has already changed tactics because attempting to close down airfields is pointless.
23 January	First big success for British Special Forces: SBS cut fibre-optic cable link to missile sites.
25 January	Iraq releases oil into Gulf.
26 January	US bombers stem flow of oil with precision attack on manifolds.
28 January	Iran informs UN that Iraqi planes have flown to Iran, where they are being interned.
29–31 January	Battle of Khafji.
3 February	Allies claim air supremacy and sea control. Reports that Allied air raids have released small quantities of chemical weapons fall-out.
7 February	Reports that Iraq has set fire to oil wells in Kuwait.
8 February	US Special Forces inserted into Iraq.
9 February	US officials report 20 per cent destruction of key Iraqi equipment in KTO.
13 February	US aircraft destroy air-raid shelter in Baghdad, believed to be a 'command' or 'leadership' target. In fact, at least 400 civilians die. Allies re-examine targeting priorities.
14 February	Allies have destroyed more than a third of Iraqi tanks, artillery and armoured vehicles in KTO.
18 February	'Reconnaissance by battle' begins with artillery raids along Kuwait border.
22 February	President Bush gives Iraq until 17.00 GMT (20.00 local) on 23 February to begin immediate and unconditional withdrawal or face ground offensive.
23 February	Orders for ground forces to eject Iraq from Kuwait. 1,685 out of 4,200 Iraqi tanks, 1,485 out of 3,000 artillery pieces in KTO reported destroyed. 50 percent.
24 February	At 04.00, attacks launched directly at Kuwait by US and Arab forces. At 05.30 the French 6th Light Armoured Division attacks on extreme left flank. By 08.00 US 101st Air Assault

	Division has launched the largest helicopter assault in history. Ground operation is called *Desert Sword*.
25 February	British 1st Armoured Division passes through breach created by 1st (US) Infantry Division (Mechanised) and into enemy rear. Operation *Desert Sabre*. US 101st Air Assault Division has reached Euphrates. JFC(E) and JFC(N) pushing into Kuwait itself. Baghdad radio announces leadership's agreement to withdraw in accordance with Resolution 660. US says Iraq must comply with all 12 Security Council Resolutions. Iraqi Hussein missile falls on Dhahran, killing 28 US soldiers and wounding 100. The worst single Allied reverse of the war.
26 February	Iraqi forces in full retreat. 21 Iraqi divisions no longer combat effective. Nine British soldiers killed when US A-10 mistakenly attacks two Warrior AIFVs.
27 February	Iraq offers to comply with three of the UN Resolutions (660, 662 and 674) on condition there is an immediate ceasefire. US Marines encircle Kuwait City, then seize airport. By afternoon, 29 Iraqi divisions estimated destroyed. President Bush announces that coalition forces will suspend attack at 05.00 GMT (08.00 local) 28 February. Gen Schwarzkopf reveals his plan. Estimated 50,000 Iraqi prisoners so far.
28 February	05.00 GMT ceasefire. UN Security Council meets to discuss further letter from Tariq Aziz in which Iraq agrees to comply fully with all resolutions.
1 March	US Embassy staff arrive in Kuwait. US 82nd Airborne Division identify Iraqi position which fights on, briefly – 1000 prisoners.
2 March	UN Security Council Resolution 686. Sets out framework for permanent ceasefire, requires Iraq to rescind annexation of Kuwait, accept liability for war damage, release all Kuwaiti and third-country citizens, return all property, cease hostile and provocative actions and release prisoners of war. A battle breaks out 30 km west of Basra. US 24th Infantry Division engages Iraqi convoy 30 km west of Basra. In two hours they destroy 187 vehicles, including 23 T-72 tanks.
3 March	Iraqi generals meet Gen Schwarzkopf and Lt Gen Prince Khalid at Safwan. They do not initially comprehend the magnitude of their defeat. Ceasefire terms agreed. As a token of good faith, a small number of prisoners to be released immediately.
5 March	Iraqi forces suppress revolt in Basra, Nasiriyah and Najaf. Allies observe with 'interest'.
6–7 March	Author returns to Britain.

11 March	Iraq renounces annexation of Kuwait.
13 March	President Bush says Iraq's use of helicopters against rebels violates ceasefire.
15 March	Gen Schwarzkopf sends warning that continued use of helicopters against rebels could jeopardise ceasefire.
3 April	UN Resolution 687 establishes terms for permanent ceasefire, including turning Iraq into a largely 'demilitarized state'.
5 April	UN Security Council resolution 688. Condemns Iraq's repression of its civilian population, including the Kurds, demands that Iraq ceases repression. Nato accuses Iraq of massive violation of human rights and demands it stops attacking Kurds.
7 April	Formal end of second Gulf War.
8 April	James Baker visits Kurdish refugee camp on Turkish border, calls for international response. EC endorses British proposal to create enclaves or 'Safe Havens' on Iraq–Turkish border. This becomes Operation *Provide Comfort* involving 12,000 US, British, Dutch, French, German, Spanish, Canadian and Turkish troops. Author flies to Incirlik, south-east Turkey to cover operation. RAF drops its first relief supplies.
9 April	UN authorizes UN Iraq–Kuwait Observer Mission (UNIKOM) to deploy in demilitarised area along Iraq–Kuwait border to monitor ceasefire.
10 April	US declares 'no-fly' zone north of 36th parallel over Iraq.
19 April	Author returns to Britain.
15 May	British decide to withdraw from Kurdistan.
21 May	Allied troops begin withdrawing to Kurdish protests.

1992

4 April	Iran launches first air-raid on Iraq since 1988 – first Gulf War ceasefire. One Iranian Phantom F-4 is shot down near Baghdad. Iraq resumes fixed-wing aircraft flights.
Late July	Intelligence sources report Iraq has 28 to 30 divisions, with forces rebuilt to about 40 per cent of pre-Gulf War levels, including an Army of 350,000 and 2,000 tanks and 2,000 artillery pieces, with 300 aircraft. A belt of defensive position, hems in the Kurds to the north. Up to five divisions, meanwhile, hem in Shi'a rebels in the south.
26 August	US achieves exclusion zone prohibiting Iraqi aircraft flying south of 32nd parallel. RAF send six GR1s and GR1as to reconnoitre Iraqi activity in the area under cover of the exclusion zone.
End of August	'Third River', canal between Tigris and Euphrates, completed.
27 December	US F-16 shoots down Iraqi MiG-25 over exclusion zone south of 32nd parallel. A second Iraqi aircraft flees to Iran. Iraq begins moving SA-2 and SA-3 missile batteries southwards.

1993

4 January	SA-2 and SA-3 batteries deployed south of 32nd parallel.
5 January	Iraqi aircraft make three incursions into exclusion zone: three, seven and 16 miles deep.
6 January	US supported by Britain, France and Russia gives ultimatum to Iraq to withdraw surface-to-air missiles within 48 hours; Iraqi aircraft should not fly south of the line and they should take no hostile action by, for example, locking on to or tracking Allied aircraft. Iraqis respond by saying they have the right to move forces anywhere on their own territory, including deploying their own air defences.
7 January	Movement of Iraqi missiles detected but it is unclear whether this is in response to ultimatum or routine.
8 January	Iraqi defiance of Allies continues right up to 22.15 deadline. However, at the last minute it appears that missiles are being withdrawn. US signals 'no attack imminent'. Iraq refuses to let UN planes, including those carrying weapons inspectors, land in the country.
9 January	US says Iraq has moved missiles out of no-fly zone south of 32nd parallel and has backed down in the face of Alliance solidarity. Iraq says it has not.
10 January	Iraq denies a UN aircraft permission to land. Hundreds of workers raid bunkers just inside Kuwait (part of the sprawling port of Umm Qasr) and remove weapons including four Silkworm anti-ship missiles, in order to retrieve them before UN deadline of 15 January.
11 January	Iraqi workers mount another raid into what UN says is Kuwaiti territory and begin demolishing warehouses. US, Britain, France and Russia protest. UN accuses Iraq of repeated violations of Gulf War ceasefire terms and warns of serious consequences if it does so again.
12 January	Iraqi workers return to continue demolition work on Kuwait warehouses.
13 January	Iraq says UN may fly planes into no-fly zone but too late to prevent Allied raid. Some 114 Allied aircraft launch night attack on four fixed sites at Tallil, Najaf, Samawah and Amarah and four mobile sites near Basra and Nasiriyah. Only the RAF, attacking Amarah, completely destroy their targets.
14 January	US despatches 1200 ground troops to Kuwait. White House says only half of bombs dropped the previous day hit their targets.
16 January	Iraq says UN inspectors may fly in but only from Jordan. UN rejects offer.
17 January	US launches attack on Zaafaraniyah nuclear facility with about

40 Tomahawk cruise missiles fired from USS *Cowpens*, *Hewitt* and *Stump* in the Gulf and USS *Caron* in the Red Sea. Target destroyed. Iraqis claim to have shot several cruise missiles down with AAA. US later says one of the missiles was responsible for hitting the Rashid hotel in central Baghdad, killing two women. Iraqi MiG-23 shot down over northern no-fly zone.

18 January — Allies attack again at dawn with 43 manned aircraft (29 attack and 14 support). Targets in southern no-fly zone missed on 13 January destroyed. US says air defence system in southern zone destroyed.

19 January — Four more incidents in northern no-fly zone after Iraqis reportedly lock on to US and British aircraft. Air defence sites attacked in return. US confirms it is sending carrier USS *John F Kennedy* to eastern Mediterranean, accompanied by two cruisers each carrying 120 Tomahawk cruise missiles. In a calculated gesture towards incoming US President Bill Clinton, Iraqis offer unilateral ceasefire.

20 January — 08.00 local (05.00 GMT) 'ceasefire' comes into effect. Later, Bill Clinton sworn in as 42nd President of the US.

Introduction

There are, and will be, many books on the 1991 Gulf War, the crisis which preceded it and its untidy aftermath. Why another? And why two years after the war? The aftershocks which resounded in January 1993, with two manned aircraft attacks and one massive strike with cruise missiles, are perhaps enough to answer the last part of that question.

This book looks at the war and its legacy from two perspectives: one, as an account by a military historian and student of the evolution of warfare, the other, as a journalist who was there as Defence Correspondent of a national daily newspaper. Hence the title. In so doing, I aim to add something useful to the other works on the subject. Like many people, I kept a very detailed diary during the war. It was obviously a unique historic event, so I recorded conversations, times, feelings, hunches, word for word. But that is only one of a hundred or so sources. My aim, call it crazy, call it over-ambitious, was to combine an academic approach, complete with footnotes, with first-hand experience. By doing so, I hope to mirror the Yin and Yang of the art of war: the combination of the intellectual and reflective with the outdoor, immediate, physical and practical.

I recognise the limitations of this approach. As the philosopher and strategist Karl von Clausewitz (1780–1831) knew, 'there can be no purely military evaluation of a great strategic issue ... nor a purely military scheme to solve it.'[1] The most extraordinary aspect from a military viewpoint was also a political one – it was a coalition war without precedent. To get a coalition of so many nations with different equipment, doctrines, cultures and religions, including former enemies, to stay together and fight together was a political and diplomatic achievement without parallel.

The mechanics of the war were also utterly extraordinary, though, paradoxically, nothing was a surprise. The great left flanking movement was utterly predictable – a strategic textbook manoeuvre. But that it could happen at all, in the real world, in 1991 and *still* take the enemy off guard, *that* was the surprise.

Partly because of accidents of terrain and climate, and the passivity of the enemy, it was exactly what US (and Soviet) military thinkers had worked towards. It was also the first time that Giulio Douhet's 1920s predictions about air power came true.[2] As predicted, command of outer space was instrumental in guaranteeing communications, pinpoint navigation and constant surveillance of the enemy. It was the first time great offensives – land and air – had been planned, amended, rewritten and even ordered to begin by computer. It was truly historic.

But even such a dry-eyed, scientific approach cannot be divorced from the author's own experience. He was personally drawn into the development of US military thinking and study of the operational level of war in the 1980s. When the Gulf crisis erupted in August, 1990, he had just finished a PhD thesis on the Russian and Soviet view of future war – thanks, in part, to some US Army funding.[3] To see a war with many of those characteristics unfolding was therefore a bizarre experience: a paradigm of future war long foretold in Soviet and US writing, yet fulfilled even more perfectly in the near-sterile, broad vastness of the desert. The enemy was perfectly uncovered, enabling the vision of war dominated from the air and from space to be played out in near-perfect conditions – although the weather was unusually bad for that part of the world that year.

Many of the other books about the war were, understandably, written immediately after it, while memories were still fresh and public interest high, but before some of its secrets even began to be known and before the victors' patience with Iraq's continued defiance and mendacity snapped, leading to renewed attacks in early 1993. By standing back, the author had hoped to identify errors and misperceptions and to give a more complete picture of what happened than would have been possible had the book been completed sooner. For example, the Allies claimed to have destroyed all Iraq's nuclear facilities during the air bombardment of the country. Not until the beginning of October, 1991 – when many books on the war had been published, or were close to publication – did UN inspectors discover that the main hub of Iraq's nuclear weapons programme was Al Atheer, 60 miles south of Baghdad, of which the Allied Command was unaware and which escaped serious damage during the war.[4]

Soon after that, in November, it emerged that large numbers of depleted uranium rounds had been fired, which still lay in the desert: a hazard to those attempting to clear Kuwait, while those lying in Iraq might even be a potential source of fissile material for the Iraqis.[5] In April, 1992, for the first time since the war, the Iraqis put fixed-wing combat aircraft into the air again, in defiance of the ceasefire, and moved SA-2 and SA-3 surface-to-air missiles north of the 36th parallel, which they had been forbidden to cross.[6] Iraqi military power, not as badly damaged as the Allies had thought, was stirring again.

In July we heard that the Iraqi Armed Forces had probably been restored to about 40 percent of pre-war strengths, which made an interesting comparison with Allied war objectives, explored below. The Iraqi Army and Air Force were attacking the Shi'a Marsh Arabs in the south, which provoked renewed Allied action. On 26 August the UN Security council declared a 'no-fly' zone south of the 32nd parallel, in order to enable reconnaissance planes to operate in safety while surveying the situation on the ground.

And, at the end of August, 1992, the great 'Third River' between the Tigris and Euphrates, which also helped drain the marshes was completed. It was a vast geo-strategic project in the best Iraqi tradition, and a concrete expression of Iraqi ingenuity, determination and resilience. They were recovering from their defeat.

Then, at the very end of 1992, seeking to test the resolve of the West, particularly America, as President Bush's Administration gave way to that of President Clinton, Iraqi fixed-wing aircraft pushed into the no-fly zone declared in August. On 27 December, a US F-16 shot down an Iraqi MiG-25 – the other Iraqi aircraft fled to Iran. At the same time, the Iraqis moved more SA-2 and SA-3 anti-aircraft missiles a few tens of kilometres south of the 32nd parallel. On 6 January, 1993, the Americans, supported by the French, British and Russians, gave Iraq 48 hours to withdraw them. The Iraqis moved them, but it was unclear whether they were withdrawing them as demanded or whether this was a normal procedure. If the missiles were not withdrawn, the Allies would launch an attack, probably against the missiles themselves and their associated radars but also, perhaps, against command and control facilities and airfields. The Allies and Iraq were closer to fighting again – a miniature 'Gulf War III' – than at any time since March 1991. Then, at the last minute, Saddam Hussein backed down – or so it appeared briefly. On 10 January, Iraq refused to allow UN aircraft to land and hundreds of Iraqi workers swarmed across the disputed border with Kuwait to recover Iraqi weapons. They returned on the following two days, while the UN warned of dire consequences. Then, on 13 January, Allied patience snapped. US, British and French planes attacked air defences in the southern no-fly zone. The night attack was not as successful as hoped, but the main aim was to teach Iraq a 'short, sharp lesson' about respecting the no-fly zone. In parallel, Iraq continued to impede UN weapons inspections. On 16th it insisted that the inspectors should fly in from the west, avoiding the no-fly zones as it could not guarantee their safety. A 'proportional' and appropriate target was again selected – the Zaafaraniyah nuclear facility, and on 17 January over 40 cruise missiles fired from ships in the Red Sea and the Gulf headed for the target. In an extraordinary coincidence, one, possibly hit by anti-aircraft fire, landed miles from the target, right in front of the Rashid hotel, the headquarters of the foreign press corps, killing two civilians.

The next day manned aircraft again attacked the air-defence targets in southern Iraq, by day. This time, they closed the air defence system down.

These three attacks were a powerful 'aftershock', two years after the 1991 war. From the point of view of the writer, there was something to be said for waiting to produce this account. Iraq then declared a unilateral 'ceasefire' to begin on 20 January, to coincide with the beginning of President Clinton's Administration in the US. It was unclear whether the ceasefire would hold, or whether the aftershocks would continue. But it was a good point to draw this account to a close.

The two years after the war also saw a progressive reduction in the Iraqi 'body count'. The initial estimates of over 600,000 Iraqis in the Kuwait Theatre of

Operations were rapidly revised downwards, to below 400,000, but that still did not explain the discrepancy between the number of prisoners taken by the Allies, the number estimated to have escaped, and the total estimated Iraqi strength at the start of the Allied air campaign on 17 January 1991. Gruesome pictures of incinerated Iraqi bodies contributed to the view that there had been colossal numbers of Iraqi dead. The military authorities consistently refused to give any official estimate of the number of dead and wounded, saying they did not want to get involved in 'body counts'. The sentiment was laudable but the result unsatisfactory as historians would like some sensible estimate of the casualties on both sides in any war. The absence of any reliable estimate of Iraqi casualties combined with the picture of aweful (as well as awful) *material* destruction on the roads north of Kuwait city reinforced the impression of indiscriminate slaughter facilitated by high technology.

The Allied air campaign had concentrated on destroying equipment – principally armour and artillery, not killing men, and many Iraqis had fled. The higher estimates of Iraqi dead varied from 40,00 to 100,000. Lt Gen Charles Horner, the US Air Commander, estimated a more modest 25,000 dead, while the lowest estimate, a year after the war, was 15,000.[7] Then, two years after the war a former Defense Intelligence Agency analyst, John Heidenrich, who had been in the DIA during the campaign, revised the estimate downwards again, to some 1,500 in the air war and a maximum of 6,500 in the ground campaign. His evidence, cited in a 20-page article, used interviews with Iraqi prisoners-of-war, the standard three to one ratio for wounded to killed in action, and other analytical tools. In their swift advance from 24 to 28 February, the US forces found and buried only 577 Iraqi corpses.[8] A British Surgeon told the author that the two field dressing stations which served both the British 1st Armoured Division and the collapsing Iraqi Army each cleared less than 60 casualties, mostly minor, while large numbers of ragged, utterly demoralised and often leaderless prisoners were taken throughout the British area of operations (see Chapter 6). 'Given the usual casualty ratios of three wounded for each dead combatant, one would have expected to see thousands of casualties in the four days of the advance if the subsequent casualty estimates were to be believed', he said.[9]

Of the 71,000 prisoners taken by the Allies in total, only 2,000 were wounded. John Heidenrich estimated the total at 750 to 1,500 dead from the 37-day air campaign and 2,250 to 4,500 wounded, with an absolute maximum of 6,500 dead and 19,500 wounded in the ensuing four day ground campaign. He estimated civilian deaths at less than 1,000.[10] Although forces other than the Americans – for example, the British, reported scenes of carnage, the number of bodies found ties in with these estimates. As a senior British officer told the author soon after the war, many more dead could have disappeared, in collapsed trenches. There were also deaths at sea and most of the casualties from the air bombardment would have been cleared away before the ground campaign was launched. Nevertheless, the author's colleague, Patrick Cockburn, visiting Iraqi communities after the war, also reported a small proportion of men missing. If Mr Heidenrich's estimate errs on the low side, the author believes it could be in the right order. If so, it casts doubt on the wisdom of the Allies' decision to stop the fighting so quickly, in part because they feared accusations of 'butchery' (see Chapter 7). The real body count will never be known but if the revised estimates are correct, it is a testimony to the technology, strategy and planning of the Allied operation that it achieved its goals with much less bloodshed than in any comparable campaign. The Iraqis were under orders to withdraw as the Allied ground offensive got underway and that order may have saved tens, perhaps hundreds of thousands of lives, Iraqi and Allied.

The author's overall impression of the 1991 war is reflected in Clausewitz's dictum that 'the maximum use of force is in no way incompatible with the simultaneous use of the intellect.'[11] The Allied Forces triumphed over an Iraqi Army which, whatever its limitations and however much it was overestimated undeniably had more 'combat experience' of a major recent war in that theatre. The Allies' actions were based on peacetime procedures, military thought and study, and training. The whole operation, led by the Prussian figure of General Schwarzkopf, reminded the author, above all, of the triumphs of the elder Moltke and the Prussian/German General Staff in the 1860s and 70s. Or perhaps of the younger Moltke and the Schlieffen Plan – executed in 1914, but not taken quite far enough. It was a very Prussian operation – militarily brilliant, but ultimately let down by politics, or politicians.[12]

It was also a very *Russian* operation. After years of studying the Soviet military system as a potential adversary, it would be surprising if US and British generals had not been impressed by parts of it, and imitated it, consciously or subconsciously. It was the first war fought by US and British generals who explicitly recognised and thought in terms of the operational level, the level between strategy and tactics, the level at which great campaigns are orchestrated. At the time, I remarked on the similarity to the great double encirclement at Stalingrad. The use of artillery was very Russian. It was the first war in which the US and UK made extensive use of multiple rocket launchers. The commander of the artillery of the British 1st Armoured Division described the division as an OMG (Operational Manoeuvre Group – a Soviet nostrum), and the arrangements for finding and allocating targets as a 'reconnaissance-strike complex' – a Soviet term.[13] At the beginning of the ground war, the US 1st Infantry Division created a breach and the powerful 1st British Armoured Division – the OMG – was pushed through – exactly as the Soviet Army would have done it.[14] In the deployment before the ground war, XVIII Corps passed through VII Corps, leapfrogging ahead, out to the West – a Soviet move – passing one corps through another – which the Americans had never emulated before. A year later, I was discussing the matter with the Russian (as he was then, the USSR having disintegrated) military attaché in London, an artilleryman. 'I discussed this with General [Rupert] Smith. It was pure Soviet', he said. 'Manoeuvre of fire, not of troops.'[15]

Furthermore, Operation Desert Storm and especially Desert Sword, the ground component, were the most cerebral campaigns ever fought. Technology, surprise, operational skill, heuristic and academic training: taken together, they represented the triumph, above all, of *intellect*. Everything was thought through to an astonishing degree. As someone with an academic approach to these matters, the author was nevertheless surprised, awed, humbled, by the steel edge of the commanding intellects – General Schwarzkopf and Major-General Rupert Smith, in particular. To take an intellectual approach is therefore not to lose any of the drama, the colour, the awesome uncertainty and sense of history unfolding which all who were involved felt during those days.

To envision the character, scale, pace and appearance of a future war during a long period of peace is an awesome exercise. Especially if it is to be utterly different from any previous war. After Iraq's invasion of Kuwait on 2 August 1990, large scale military operations on a classic, almost text-book pattern, suddenly appeared likely. It was a bizarre, self-fulfilling prophecy: a desert Cannae planned by computer. The huge mechanized battles, the 'surgical' use of air power, crushing fire from massed heavy artillery and Multiple Launch Rocket Systems, the deadly grasp of encirclement, the identification and destruction of targets in 'real-time', the long-awaited perfection of 'AirLand battle'. For decades these ideas had been the preserve of staff officers and a few dedicated specialists. And this war was, in a horrible way, an 'improvement' on the vision. The sterile desert was a plainer canvas, a cleaner sheet, than the crowded and overpopulated counterpane of Europe, where such operations had been expected to take place.

But there is another way of looking at it, as a major in 101st Air Assault Division has pointed out in a comparison with the Battle of Omdurman in 1898. Omdurman, like the Gulf War, was won by a highly disciplined force using the latest technology against an inferior enemy which foolishly choose to fight on their terms. As the Lancers' charge which followed Omdurman was the last hurrah of a system of warfare already obsolete, so, perhaps, was the great armoured sweep of VII Corps and the air-mobile leap of XVIII Corps through southern Iraq. It was 'the final echo of Third Army's great wheel across France [in 1944].'[16] The Iraqis played into the Allies' hands by engaging them in the kind of war at which the Allies were best, and in a perfect environment for it: large-scale, 'high-tech' mechanized operations in the desert. The next war will most likely be against someone who will emulate the North Vietnamese or the IRA – someone far cannier – or even against anarchy and thuggery on our own streets, as the events in Los Angeles in April 1992 portend.

Nor was the campaign representative of one against a determined enemy, neither in the air – where virtually no fighter opposition was encountered, nor on the ground. By and large, the Iraqi Army did not want to fight. If they had fought with even the determination of the Argentinians in 1982, it would have been very different. That is not to say the AirLand Battle would not have worked or that the Allied armies, with supplies and ammunition for 60 days' fighting stacked behind their left flank, would not have won. But the effect on public opinion and confidence in the pampered democracies of the West would have been interesting, to say the least.

The Allies had developed their vision of future war in the context of an unlimited collision between the two former world systems. But it is debatable whether it would have worked in that context. It *did* work in the context of limited war – war limited by its political objectives – the kind of war most likely in the future.

Writing on this question in 1989, the author formed the conclusion that large scale organised force was only likely to be used either to keep the peace or in the event of a 'criminal' appearing on the international scene – a delinquent dictator going berserk. The international community will probably feel the need to retain sufficient military power between them to restrain and control a renegade power, exactly as they did during the Gulf War. Wars of this type must not be confused with 'low intensity warfare'. They may require large-scale military operations in the classic form, to seize and secure vital areas. The encirclement of Kuwait, which rates alongside Cannae (216 BC), Khalkhin Gol (1939) and Stalingrad (1942–43) as one of the most perfect encirclement battles of history, underlines this. Such battles, limited in their political aims, and even in the proportion of national resources deployed, may nevertheless be extremely violent. The population of Western democracies will be intolerant of protracted or bungled operations. They have to be swift, with one's own casualties kept to a minimum. As in surgery, the greater the precision required, the sharper the instrument, the finer the laser needs to be.[17]

From the time of Napoleon onwards, the tendency was to wage war more and more unrestrictedly, involving entire societies and culminating in the demand for 'unconditional surrender' of Germany in the Second World War. But future large-scale military operations, if, regrettably, they are necessary, will be more like those of Prussia's Frederick the Great (1712–86). Frederick never intended to destroy France, Austria or Prussia as a state or lay waste their territory. He abhorred the idea of 'a war of the people' or a 'nation in arms'. War was for professionals. It was limited war but, make no mistake, the individual battles were bloodbaths.[18] In retrospect, the Gulf War was like that. It was never General Colin Powell's intention to destroy Iraq, merely to cut its military machine back to a manageable level. To remove it from the state it had occupied, but to leave it strong enough to counterbalance Iran. General Tom Kelly, the US Director of Operations, tells us:

> On 5 August I found General Colin Powell [Chairman of the US Joint Chiefs of Staff] sitting in his office in the Pentagon staring out of the window and tapping his teeth with a pencil. 'Some problem, Sir?' I asked. 'No problem, Tom', he told me. 'I'm just thinking about the endgame. How do we finally deal with Iraq? We can't leave them with nothing – we have to balance Iran. It would look best to me if we allowed them an army of about 100,000 with something like a thousand tanks.' That was Colin Powell on 5 August 1990, the sharpest man and best commander I know.[19]

The Allies did not achieve that objective, overestimating the damage they had done to the Iraqi forces. But the concept had all the calculation – some might call it cynicism – of the Age of Reason. It was classic, Frederician limited war.

Clausewitz had recognised the distinction between wars 'to exterminate the opponent, to destroy his political existence' and wars waged to weaken the opponent sufficiently so one could 'impose conditions at the peace conference', as early as 1804.[20] But even so, Clausewitz denied that limited aims justified limited effort. In the later years of his life Clausewitz broke the alternatives down into two pairs. War was waged to defeat the enemy completely in order either to destroy him as a political organism or to force him to accept any terms whatever. Or, it was waged to acquire territory in order to keep the area conquered or to bargain with it in the peace negotiations. His Note of 10 July 1827 distinguished between war 'to *overthrow the enemy* – to render him politically helpless or militarily impotent, thus forcing him to sign whatever peace we please; or *merely to occupy some of his frontier districts*, so that we can annex them for bargaining at the peace negotiations'.[21]

The 1827 definition of overthrow had softened a little since 1804. The 1991 Gulf War was certainly not to 'exterminate the opponent, to destroy his political existence', but it was perhaps intended to facilitate imposing terms. It was also waged to acquire territory. Kuwait was to be kept. Southern Iraq was merely the route to accomplish operational manoeuvre. It was not intended to be kept as a bargaining counter, merely an expanse in which forces could manoeuvre relatively freely.

With hindsight, had the Allies decided to use it as a bargaining counter, they could perhaps have imposed more severe and intrusive terms on Iraq. Had they sought to make Iraq more militarily impotent, that might also have helped.

The 1991 Gulf War thus spanned several of Clausewitz's categories of war, but clearly fell short of a strategy of overthrow. This was to be limited war, switched off the moment predetermined objectives had been achieved, in its purest form.

But the ability to fight the Second Gulf War (the First was between Iraq and Iran from 1980 to 1988) did not derive from any conscious decision to maintain a superb instrument of limited war. Whether anyone can afford to maintain such an instrument, just in case, as well as strategic defences on the one hand and forces for 'low intensity' warfare on the other, is a crucial question in the new world order. As subsequent involvement in Bosnia showed, general purpose forces designed for mid- to high-intensity conflict may be just what is needed for 'aggravated peacekeeping'. But the ability to fight the 1991 Gulf War derived from an earlier paradigm – the need to repel a Warsaw Pact invasion of Europe. Mercifully for the Gulf States and the West, Saddam Hussein timed his aggression against Kuwait to coincide with a new trust between East and West, yet before the instruments of the Third World War had been dismantled. He really got it wrong. But it was in the perceived need to fight the former Warsaw Pact and Soviet Union – and in the consequent study of Soviet military art – that the technology, planning and operational art of the Second Gulf War were forged.

As a member of the press, I naturally formed some views on the handling of the news media during the war, its approach and aftermath. Within the limits of operational security, I believe that the military command did everything it could to help. I was never short of anything to say. Some of the material I filed which could not be used, because of lack of space, appears in this book. If I was ever frustrated, it was not by any shortage of information at my end but the fact that so much excellent material was being filed from Washington, London and our numerous correspondents in the field that I could not have most of the newspaper to myself. Sometimes I was slightly exasperated by the fact that news appeared on the US TV Cable News Network (CNN) before I could get it to my newspaper, and that sometimes there was a tendency to follow CNN. This did not happen very often, however, and people soon tired of CNN's constant and self-congratulatory coverage

– which continued even when there was nothing worth reporting. It was the first big war in which reporters could communicate directly with their organisations using satellite dishes – a potential hazard in forward areas, where satellite aerials were prohibited, as the enemy could home in on such broadcasts.

The Allied war effort probably benefitted from the efforts made to help the media. One aspect of the 'Hail Mary' deception plan – the need to persuade the Iraqis that the main attack would come in the East and from the sea – was helped by the media getting that mistaken message across, as General Norman Schwarzkopf acknowledged in his final war briefing. The point is not 'the public has a right to know'. The point is that, as the RAF's *Air Power Doctrine* points out, 'the conduct of war is affected by group passions, cohesion and determination. A significant war effort cannot be sustained by a democratic state in the face of public hostility or indifference.'[22]

The best briefer, inevitably, was General Schwarzkopf. He knew exactly what he could say, what he wanted to say, and what he could not. He had the best view of what was going on. And he did not have to ask anybody else's permission. He fought to ensure that campaign news broke in Riyadh first, rather than in Washington or London. Whenever his busy schedule permitted, he talked to the press personally. Less senior spokesmen did not have the whole picture. It was not that they were being evasive or devious, but usually that they just did not know. General Schwarzkopf realised that in 1991 public information (PI) was not just a sideline. With the need to maintain public awareness and support, and to keep the coalition strong, PI had become *one of the principles of war.*

Inevitably, also, that raised the question of preserving journalists' independence and impartiality. Some of the US reporters – and one or two British – seemed to take the view that 'impartiality' meant hostility towards and suspicion of the military, who were trying very hard in very difficult circumstances. On one occasion I was criticised for appearing too friendly on television with one of the British spokesmen. After two months working together, was it surprising we called each other by our Christian names?

Most of the UK press were in no doubt that Saddam Hussein was an evil dictator with some very unpleasant weapons, who was responsible for all kinds of atrocities and who had invaded a neighbouring sovereign country. We felt sorry for the Iraqi soldiers and civilians who had been dragged along with his schemes. But war is war. While the war lasted, 'impartiality' did not mean giving aid and comfort to the enemy. I wanted to understand what was going on, and to do that I needed detail, and to report it as far as I could. We all knew a lot more than we reported. Many of us knew the dispositions for the 'Hail Mary' plan pretty well exactly, but no-one, to my knowledge, reported them from the theatre. That was not a function of censorship by the military, but of our own professional ethics. If, on the other hand, we had discovered that British troops were being sent into battle with inadequate training, equipment, poor leadership, or had been let down in any other way, and that senior officers or politicians were about to risk lives unnecessarily, then we would have been very impartial indeed.

PART I

The Storm Clouds Gather

1

Three Campaigns to the Sun

'Hello, Christopher, it's Robert Fisk in Dhahran.'

It was 3 am, Riyadh time (midnight UK time) on 17 January 1991. I had not quite got off to sleep.

'I'm getting calls from **-****-***s on the newsdesk about air strikes on Baghdad. I have quizzed them closely. What has been heard is anti-aircraft *fire*. I am urging *extreme* caution. It could be an exercise.'

'Absolutely,' I said. The previous day the Pentagon had been leaking 'tomorrow morning', which made Robert – a hardened Middle East and war correspondent – and me think it wouldn't be.

'I'll call you back.'

A few minutes later, he did. 'The BBC are saying "explosions".' Still not sure.

I telephoned the *Independent* in London. Bobby Block, a night news editor, who later sent some excellent despatches from Kuwait and Bosnia, answered.

'Fitzwater has confirmed it,' he said – Marlin Fitzwater, the White House spokesman. And then, in the magisterial tone which Americans can convey on such occasions, '*The liberation of Kuwait has begun*. Can you file 100 words?'

Then the air-raid siren went. The continuous tone that meant imminent attack – aircraft or Scud missiles. There was supposed to be a general warning first, a warbling tone, but they only once got it right during the whole war. It turned out to be a false alarm. The following day, I learned that two Iraqi planes had been detected – possibly trying to defect, or lost, heading for Khafji. But it was good practice, and there was no doubt that war had started.

As the siren wailed, I dictated 100 words over the telephone, describing what was happening. That takes, I suppose, about two minutes. Somebody started banging on the door. They were telling everybody to get across to the 'shelter' – in fact, a conference hall attached to the Intercontinental hotel – which offered little, if any, extra protection, and was reached along a plate glass passage which would have multiplied, rather than diminished the effect of a nearby explosion.

'Okay, okay, I'm coming' I said. I finished my 100 words, picked up my gasmask and some supplies for the morning, and joined them in the hall. There were urns to provide hot water for tea and coffee, but the plugs had not been attached. As the hotel handymen began affixing the plugs, we listened to the radio. There were Western journalists and businessmen, and Saudis in their traditional costume. There was one RAF officer in the hotel, who was obliged to don his full nuclear, biological and chemical warfare (NBC) suit – we called them 'doom suits' – olive green with velcro straps all over the place. With everyone else in civilian clothes or dressing gowns, he looked rather silly. I had already decided that inside a strong building we were unlikely to be splashed with lethal droplets, and that inhaling vapour was the only likely hazard if there was a chemical strike nearby. But he had to obey orders.

The first reports indicated little Iraqi resistance to the air attacks. Eventually, they sounded the all-clear, which was also flashed across the television screens. The hotel manager, a young American, said a few words, saying that they were trying to get things organised so that future alerts were as trouble-free as possible. But for the moment, he said 'just don't call room service'.

So this was my war.

* * *

Before I go any further with my story, it is important that we should take a close look at the military characteristics and backgrounds of the principal contestants and have some understanding of their operational philosophies during the period leading up to the war.

> The Arabs of Iraq respect nothing but force and to force only they will bend ... [but they bear little resentment or it wears off quickly]. They seem indeed to accept the situation, admit that they were beaten, bow to superior force, and bury the hatchet until a good chance comes of paying off the score.
>
> *Lieutenant General Sir Aylmer Haldane, 1922.*[1]

Modern Iraq was the creation of British policy, following the defeat of Turkey in the 1914–18 war. It was formed from three *vilayets* of the Ottoman Empire: Basra, Baghdad and Mosul. The first two comprise delta lands peopled by Arabs. Basra *vilayet* included Kuwait – one basis of the Iraqi claim to it. But Mosul *vilayet* in the north – Iraqi Kurdistan – differed notably. In 1920 Iraq came into being as an independent state under British mandate, although until 1926 it was uncertain whether Mosul would remain in Iraq or Turkey. The borders drawn up at the Cairo conference in May 1921 have largely endured to the present day. However, the Iraqis have consistently objected to the unratified UK–Turkish Convention of 1913 being used as the basis for the autonomy and frontiers of Kuwait. A British-Kuwaiti agreement of 1899 had given Kuwait British protection in exchange for British control of its foreign relations. The draft 1913 Convention recognized Kuwait as an autonomous *gaza* of the Ottoman Empire.[2]

Modern Iraq has an area of 434,924 square kilometres, and in 1988 had a population of 17,060,000. One third of its area is covered by the southern and western deserts: the former formed part of the Kuwait Theatre of Military Operations (KTO), the latter was the site for Scud missile attacks on Israel. Water is the controlling factor in communications, especially the two great rivers, the Tigris and Euphrates which, like the Nile and the Indus, formed one of the cradles of civilisation. One of the first illustrations of troops using considered tactics and technology specifically designed for military purposes is on the Standard of Ur, a beautiful box in the British Museum, dating from about 2,500 BC. The archaeological site, Ur of the Chaldees, lay near one of the main Iraqi airfields in the KTO, and in the path of the final Allied advance.

The British had begun building installations in Mesopotamia during the First World War to support their campaign against the Turks, especially Basra. Arriving in 1920, to suppress a nationwide revolt, General Haldane recalled:

> The first thing that struck me as we approached Basrah was the size of the place, which exceeded by far anything that I had pictured ... Indeed, we seemed to have arrived on the outskirts of a miniature Liverpool, the creators of which had not only provided for the necessities of the vast force which overcame the Turks, but had prepared for a development of the country such as might not be attained for half a century.[3]

Haldane also grasped another point which was to be crucial in 1991. 'The flatness of the country ... allows little to be seen from the deck of a river steamer ... I soon came to the conclusion that the best way to gain a bird's eye view of a Mesopotamian battlefield is from an aeroplane, as the outlines of the trenches held by either side can easily be traced.'[4]

After the suppression of the revolt, the RAF offered to keep the peace from the air. Churchill, as Secretary of State for War, had been an enthusiastic supporter of the idea, 'the Air Force to be the principal force or agency of control while the military and naval forces on the ground and river would be an ancillary power.'[5] At the time many considered it 'a capricious notion, too venturesome to call for serious consideration.'[6] But the RAF got their way. And in the same year, 1920, an Italian officer, Giulio Douhet, was compiling a book on air power which suggested that air forces could win wars – and not just little colonial wars – virtually alone, at any rate, as the principal striking force. And it was over this same open, sandy and rocky expanse that, 70 years later, in 1991, technology finally caught up with Douhet.

Oil was found in Persia in 1908, increasing the strategic importance of the Shatt-al-Arab waterway between Iraq and Iran. In 1938 the Anglo–Iranian Oil Company (now British Petroleum) and the Gulf Oil Corporation of the United States struck oil in Kuwait, although Kuwaiti production did not begin until after the Second World War, in 1947. Kuwait may have the world's largest oil reserves, and, since the oil lies near the surface, it is especially easy to extract. By 1961, almost 40 per cent of the UK's oil came from Kuwait. On 25 June 1961 the Iraqi Prime Minister, Major General Abdul Qarim Qasim formally revived the Iraqi claim to oil-rich Kuwait.[7]

A Stitch in Time ...

There was little hard evidence at that time of Iraqi military movement, but there was a division in southern Iraq with a mechanised brigade at Basra. On 29 and 30 June intelligence reports confirmed the movement of reinforcements – especially armour – towards Basra, 50 kilometres from the border.

What followed highlights the disproportionate value of timely action and the old adage that what a battalion can do today will require a brigade next week, and so on. On 30 June the Sheikh of Kuwait declared a state of emergency and mobilised his own, 2,400-strong army to face Iraq's 60,000. The previous day Britain had ordered the 30,500 ton aircraft carrier *Victorious* and the 22,000 ton commando carrier *Bulwark*, with 600 Royal Marines on board, to Kuwait. The latter was already in the Middle East and would be off Kuwait within 48 hours. It was, and 42 Commando Royal Marines duly landed by helicopter near Kuwait City on 1 July. A squadron of Hunter ground-attack aircraft was put on alert at Bahrain and within a week (7 July), 24 Infantry Brigade Group, with three infantry battalions and elements of two armoured regiments, was in position on the Mutla Ridge, north of Kuwait City. Within another week, the British force was 5,000 strong, a strong reinforced brigade group with land-based airpower and carrier aircraft. The British handled the situation sensitively, keeping their forces out of Arab eyes, on the edge of Kuwait city, and staying in constant touch with the Sheikh. The aim, as the then Foreign Secretary, Lord Home put it, was 'a force big enough to ensure the independence of Kuwait, but no bigger than that.'[8]

Qasim delivered a speech in Baghdad on 14 July, but by now international support for Kuwait was growing. Early in August 1961 the Arab League announced its intention of deploying a protective force to Kuwait and as this force deployed the British withdrew. Qasim was overthrown by an alliance of nationalist Iraqi Army officers and the Ba'ath Party in February, 1963. The Iraqis recognised Kuwaiti independence in October. If they ever had a claim, based on the extent of the Ottoman Empire, they renounced it then.

Qasim denied that Iraq was ever serious in its military threat to Kuwait. The Iraqis do not seem to have undertaken any large-scale military movements. But the British could not be sure, and naval forces alone, although they appeared on the horizon between 08.00 and 09.00 on 1 July, were not enough. A British brigade was just enough to deter an Iraqi division. The author of a paper on the subject in 1974 wrote 'the Iraqis could too easily have sent an overwhelming armoured column racing into the City of Kuwait 60 miles from the Iraq border, in just a few hours. The British then would have faced the far more difficult task of throwing the Iraqis out, of undoing a *fait accompli*.'[9] Seventeen years later, the UN found itself in that unenviable position, with vastly stronger Iraqi forces, experienced in war.

NEBUCHADNEZZAR WITH SCUDS

The rise of Iraq as a military power of concern to the US and other Western states was a function of the First Gulf War of 1980–88, and owed a lot to the West's attempts to bolster Iraq as a counterweight to what was seen as the more extreme Islamic state of Iran. With hindsight, the new threat to stability in the Middle East was the West's own creation. But while the First Gulf War was on, it had seemed the lesser of two potential evils. By its creation, the West gave a new twist to Marx's 19th century warning about the proliferation of new weaponry and military technology. Marx and Engels had been horrified at the thought of 'Genghis Khan with the Minié rifle, the railway and the telegraph'. Now, Nebuchadnezzar was to get chemical weapons and Scuds.

Iraq's geo-strategic position constrained it to concentrating on the development of its ground forces. Whereas Iran has 1990 kilometres of coastline, Iraq has only 16, and is thus almost completely land-locked. Iran has five naval bases, some out of range of Iraqi aircraft: Iraq has only two, Umm Qasr and Basra, and they are almost on the Iranian border and within reach of Iranian artillery. Historically, Iran has thus identified more with the Gulf and the Sea, Iraq with the 'fertile crescent'.[10]

1968–80: Iraq's Military Build-up

On its accession to power in 1968, the Iraqi Ba'ath party began a military build up as a precaution against Iran. The number of tanks and Armoured Personnel Carriers (APCs) doubled from 600 of each in 1970 to 1200 and 1300 respectively in 1975. Aircraft, on the other hand, only increased by 10 per cent. Almost all the new equipment came from the then Soviet Union. And with the Soviet equipment came Soviet advisers, who remained in Iraq in strength up to the 1991 war. But, contrary to what some have supposed, their influence was limited to working the equipment and to the creation of an organisation appropriate to that equipment – not to teaching doctrine and operational art. Iraqi divisions, for example, were 10,000 to 15,000 strong – Soviet style. But tactics, like rank badges, remained very British. 'World War II *Brit*', a US intelligence officer insisted, during the 1991 war. By that he meant extremely cautious, defensive, two-up-and-one back. He was not flattering the Iraqis.

During 1975–76, Iraqi arms purchases declined, but in 1977 Iraq was able to turn once more from internal problems to match Iran's build-up. Between 1977 and 1979 Iraq purchased more advanced weapons, weapons which would later be used in the 1991 war. These included 450 T-72 main Battle tanks, several dozen 122mm and 152mm self-propelled howitzers, TU-22 bombers, Mi-24 Hind attack helicopters and Il-76 transport planes. Iraq also ordered 40 Mirage F-1 fighter-bombers from France in 1977.[11]

In 1979 and 1980 Iraq placed an order for 100 AMX-30 tanks and 100 Gazelle and Lynx helicopters with France, part of a move to reduce dependence upon the Soviet Union in some specific areas and possibly to reduce Soviet leverage.

1979: Overthrow of the Shah. Saddam Hussein Assumes the Presidency

The overthrow of the Shah of Iran in 1979 and the establishment of an Islamic republic led to a rapid deterioration of relations between Iraq and Iran. It also threw Iran's Armed Forces into total disarray, with 85 senior officers executed between February and September 1979 and hundreds more, including most at brigade-commander level, imprisoned or forced to retire.

These traumatic events coincided with the assumption of the Presidency of Iraq by Saddam Hussein, in July, 1979. He had already been in effective control for eleven years, since July, 1968, but holding the office of President seems to have inspired – or coincided with – a new confidence and aggressiveness.

September 1980: Iraq Invades Iran

On 17 September 1980, President Saddam Hussein of Iraq abrogated the 1975 Algiers agreement and said he would exercise full sovereignty over to the disputed Shatt-al-Arab waterway. Five days later, on 22 September, Iraqi aircraft bombed Iranian airfields and on the following day ground forces, five divisions, invaded Iran on three fronts. Iran retaliated in kind, but the Iraqis pushed on to capture Khorramshahr and seize some 10,000 square kilometres of Iranian territory. But the Iraqi advance was halted after stiff resistance at Susangerd. By this time, newspapers were comparing the casualties and positional nature of the conflict to the First World War.[12]

After the initial phase, Iraqi positions were largely static which made resupplying them correspondingly easier. Roads were built to carry supplies, particularly artillery ammunition, right up to the front line. Huge 'pantechnicons' carrying ammunition would queue up right behind gun positions, according to those who witnessed Iraqi operations. They only managed to sustain First World War levels of ammunition expenditure – 200 to 300 rounds per gun per day – by this means. In a conflict against a fast moving enemy, this would be impossible. If the enemy had air superiority or even parity, such piles of ammunition would present a lucrative and spectacular target.[13]

September 1981–August 1982: Iraq on the Offensive

In September 1981, an Iranian offensive succeeded in pushing the Iraqis back over the Karun river and relieving the besieged oil centre of Abadan. In December, Iraq and Saudi Arabia signed an agreement on a common border and dividing the diamond-shaped neutral zone that had been established in 1922. When the later Gulf crisis erupted in August 1990, many of the available maps still showed this diamond-shaped area causing some confusion.

During the first part of 1982, the Iranians continued their counter-offensive, recapturing Khorramshahr on 24 May. On 13 July, Iran launched another offensive attempting to capture Basra. During April and August the Iranian oil terminal at Kharg Island was bombed.

March 1983: The 'War of the Cities' – Overture

In March and April 1983, Iraq carried out a series of attacks against civilian targets in Iran, the antecedent of the so-called 'war of the cities', although this term is used to refer to the missile exchanges from March 1985 onwards. The missiles were Soviet SS-1s, Nato codename 'Scud', which were to become a household word. During 1983 Israel and the US also accused Iraq of importing equipment from Europe for a chemical warhead plant near Samarra. During 1984, Iran and Iraq began to extend the conflict by attacking other nations' ships in the Gulf. When, in May, Iran attacked Kuwaiti and Saudi tankers, Saudi Arabia responded by shooting down an Iranian fighter plane over the Gulf. Iran captured the Majnoon islands in March although there were few territorial gains during 1984.[14]

1984: Iraq's Defensive Complex

Faced with huge Iranian numerical superiority, the Iraqis developed a complex web of defences, in a belt some 20 kilometres thick. My colleague Major-General Eddie Fursdon, then defence correspondent for the *Daily Telegraph*, described the scale and extent of the battlefield in a number of fine despatches. Because there was virtually no cover in the desert – as in Saudi Arabia, Kuwait and adjacent Iraq, everything had to be spread out more than usual and dug in or protected by sand revetments – banks, or 'berms'. Tar poured straight onto the sand provided instant roads to move equipment across this over-sized battlefield.

The Iraqis also flooded an excavation to create a huge man-made moat, 24 kilometres long and one wide, probably to shield Basra. At the southern end it expanded into a 10 kilometre wide lake by the end of 1983. The Iraqis were very good at digging and sculpting the landscape. Such was the scheme developed by the Iraqi Army in 1983–86 and employed, though in a less grandiose fashion, in 1990–91. The battlefront during this period is shown in Figure 1.1.[15]

So important did the humble bulldozer become that captured specimens were displayed as trophies of war. The commander of the Iraqi III Corps, Major-General Maher Abed al-Rashid ordered special patrols to destroy Iranian earth-moving equipment.

The Missile War

Iraq had received its first Scud-A missiles in 1975, and had small numbers of Scud-Bs, range about 300 kilometres, at the beginning of the war. The first Scud-Bs were

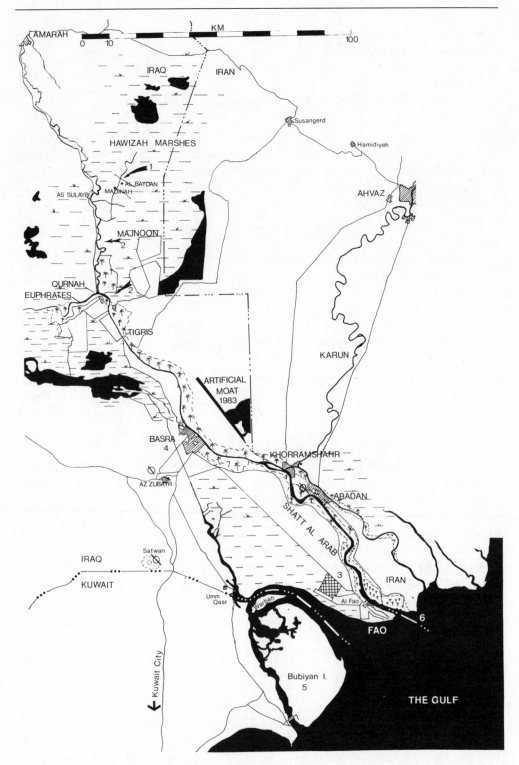

Figure 1.1 The Southern Front, Iran–Iraq War, 1980 onwards.

KEY
1. Iranian offensive against Majnoon Islands, February, 1984. First use of 'human wave' tactics. Recaptured by Iraq 25 June 1988.
2. Iranian offensive, March 1985.
3. Fao Peninsula. Al Dawa ('Dawn Light') offensive, 9 February 1986, takes the peninsula from Iraq but bogs down elsewhere. Iraq launches offensive to retake the peninsula, 17 April 1988 and recaptures Fao on the following day.
4. Basra. Iran launches Operation Ramadan, 12 July 1982 in an attempt to take the city. Iran's first invasion of Iraq. Other offensives following in March 1985, December 1986 (Operation Kerbala IV), January 1987 (Kerbala V) and February 1987 (Operation Ya Zahra – end of Kerbala V).
5. Warbah and Bubiyan Islands. In 1981, Iraq claimed the islands, a year after reasserting territorial claims on Iran. Subsequent Kuwaiti support for Iraq during the First Gulf War defused this territorial issue until August 1990.
6. Thalweg Line. The riverine frontier that follows the median line of the deepest channel. Under agreements of 1914 and 1937, the Thalweg Line formed the basis of the frontier between Iraq and Iran along the stretch of the Shatt al-Arab opposite the Iranian ports of Abadan and Khorramshahr. In 1975, the line was applied to the whole waterway under the Algiers agreement but repudiated by Iraq in 1980 on the outbreak of war.

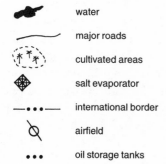

water

major roads

cultivated areas

salt evaporator

international border

airfield

oil storage tanks

fired on 27 October 1982. Three missiles were fired that year, and 33 the next, rising to 193 in 1988. The Scuds were first used against cities near the border: Dezful, Ahwaz, Khorramabad and Boujerd. The regular Scud could not reach Tehran, which is about 500 kilometres from the border. Iran acquired its Scuds from Libya in late 1984 and early 1985, firing 14 that year, rising to 77 in 1988. In March 1985, the attacks on civilian targets intensified into the 'War of the Cities'. By this time, the Iraqis had fired about 200 missiles, killing 1500 people and injuring 7,000. During the entire war, it is estimated that 875 surface-to-surface missiles were fired. When the War of the Cities resumed in 1988, another 2,000 people were estimated killed. This was a relatively small number, but between 25 and 60 per cent of the population of Tehran fled to the comparative safety of the countryside, underlining the disproportionate effect of missiles as weapons of dislocation and terror, rather than for use against hard military targets.

In August 1987, Iraq announced that it had test fired a new missile with a range of 650 kilometres. This was the *al-Hussein*, based upon Scud-B but developed with the assistance of Egypt, East Germany and, possibly, North Korea. It had a smaller warhead than the basic Scud and hence a longer range.

Although this claim was at first dismissed by Western analysts, Iraq does indeed appear to have fired five of these weapons on 29 February 1988. The *Hussein* is widely believed to have been a modification of 300 Soviet Scuds, delivered in 1986.

Their range could be extended either by reducing the warhead weight from the standard 800 kilogrammes to about 250 kilogrammes, or by adding extra fuel tanks – or both. The first *Husseins* fired in 1988 appear to have been plain Scuds with smaller warheads. The missiles fired at Israel and Saudi Arabia in 1991 were of a similar type.

In March and April 1988, about 190 *Husseins* are reported to have been fired at Iran. They could just reach Tehran from Iraqi territory. In April 1988, a further enhancement of Scud, *al-Abbas*, with a maximum range of 900 kilometres, was also fired.[16]

1986: Iran on the Offensive

Returning to the land battle, during 1986 Iran opened up a second, south-western front in its drive to capture Basra, landing troops on the Fao (Faw) peninsula in February. Iran was unable to capture Basra but began to bombard it with artillery from July. Iraq responded by launching crippling attacks on Iranian oil installations.

During 1987 the threat to other nations' shipping in the Gulf became more pronounced as a Soviet freighter was attacked by an Iranian patrol boat and the US Frigate *Stark* was hit by Iraqi planes with the loss of 37 lives. In July, the US Navy began to escort Kuwaiti-registered tankers through the Straits of Hormuz and in August the UK, French and Italian governments agreed to send Mine Counter Measures Vessels (MCMVs) and escort vessels into the Gulf. In December, 34 merchant ships were attacked either by Iraqi aircraft or by fast patrol boats manned by Iranian Revolutionary Guards, the so-called 'boghammer' threat, which has led to navies up-gunning their major surface combatants with small-calibre, rapid firing guns.

August 1988: End of the First Gulf War

In April, Iraq recaptured the Fao peninsula, after two years of Iranian occupation. However, in the north-east of Iraq Iranian troops advanced into the Kurdish Autonomous region. Iraq's response was to use chemical weapons against the town of Halabja on 28 March, killing an estimated 5,000 people with nerve gas. On 3 July, the USS *Vincennes* provoked an outcry by shooting down an Iranian airliner.

Iran accepted UN Security Council Resolution 598, calling for a ceasefire, on 18 July 1988. Finally, on 20 August, 1988, the UN succeeded in getting Iran and Iraq to agree to a ceasefire, and a 350-strong UN Iraq–Iran Military Observer Group (UNIIMOG) took up positions on the border between the two countries. Peace talks began on 25 August and although they soon reached an impasse over the Shatt-al-Arab waterway, discussions continued under UN auspices. Even by 18 July, the Iran–Iraq war ranked as the longest conventional interstate war of the 20th century. Estimates of military and civilian casualties went up to and beyond a million dead on the two sides, with at least as many wounded.

The war had dragged on for eight years and had only ended in an inconclusive draw because of Iranian obstinacy and ineptitude on the one side and Iraq's use of chemical weapons and foreign help on the other. Iraq had only managed to capture one sizeable town – the Port of Khorramshahr – after a battle lasting a month. If any lessons could be drawn, they were, first, that the Iraqi use of armour was slow and unimaginative – in part, because most of the tanks did not have radios, to prevent them acting in an cordinated fashion if they decided to mutiny. They were mainly used dug in, as artillery. The Iraqis were less prepared to suffer casualties than the Iranians, though far more so than any Western army. Elite troops – the Republican Guard Force Command (RGFC), whose main function was to protect Baghdad, and the regime, were kept out of the fighting until a late stage – a precedent for 1991 which proved particularly valid. It was not deployed at the front at all until 1984, and scored some successes in the last months of the war. The performance of the Iraqi air force was poor, in spite of even less competence on the Iranian side. Many aircraft were sent to Jordan, out of range of Iranian attacks. Iraqi forces fought better on their own territory than on that of Iran, and chemical weapons were successful in dislodging well dug-in Iranian troops.

When a state starts a war and does not win, its failure is usually attributed to over-estimation of its own strength. But, as one analyst argues, in Iraq's case this may not have been so. Iraq's grand strategy 'did not fail because its military power was insufficient for the attainment of national goals, but because it did not ask more of it.'[17] Aircraft, armour and chemical weapons were not used with the determination they should have been. The extreme passivity and tardiness of the Iraqi forces in 1991, their failure to grab chances within their grasp, followed the same pattern.

Chemical Warfare

One noteworthy lesson concerns the Iraqi use of chemical weapons. It was cautious, incremental and carefully limited. Iraq did not use chemical weapons until it had signalled its intentions with tear gas and then issued repeated warnings. Exactly when the first attack took place is not known but we do know that they used non-lethal tear gas in the *Ramadan* offensive in the summer of 1982. Even this attack is reported to have interrupted the operations of an entire Iranian division – which may well have encouraged the Iraqis to make further use of chemical weapons. In July, Baghdad radio warned that there was 'a certain insecticide for every kind of insect,' and lethal mustard gas may have been used in December, 1982.

It took the Iraqis a long time to develop an effective chemical warfare force. The first extensive use of gas was to block the Iranian *Val Fajr-3* offensive in July 1983. They attempted to use mustard gas against Iranian forces high in the mountains but failed to take into account the fact that mustard gas is heavier than air. It flowed downhill, causing considerable Iraqi casualties. Such experiences were likely to induce extreme caution in the handling of poison gas.

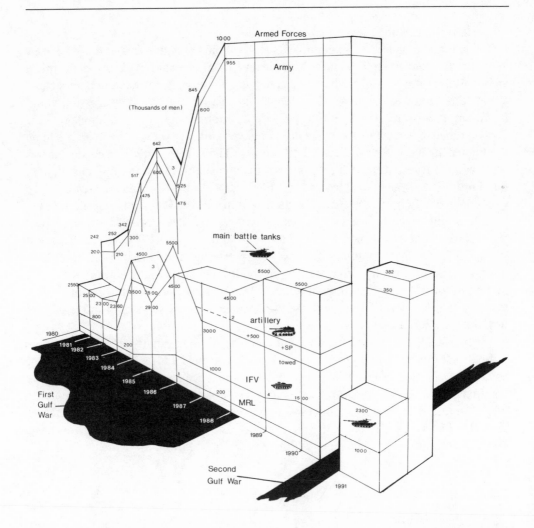

KEY
Figures from the *Military Balance*, 1980–92. The points plotted represent the estimate for June/July of that year, recorded in the Balance issued the following autumn. The figures are purely quantitative, and reflect old equipment going out of service as well as new coming in, and losses in battle.

1. 1986 was the first year IISS estimated the number of MRLs: earlier Balances just list the types.
2. 1988 was the first year IISS quantified SP artillery separately – 500 pieces. Henceforward these are shown on top of the towed artillery strengths.
3. This sharp drop may reflect battle losses, reorganisation and new counting criteria. The general trend may have been more continuous.
4. Armoured infantry Fighting Vehicles as defined in the CFE Treaty: effectively, Soviet BMP. The large number of Armoured Personnel Carriers, wheeled IFVs (e.g. BTR-60, M-113, Panhard M-3) is not indicated. In 1990 these were estimated at 7,100, or rather more than the total number of tanks.

(Source: *The Military Balance*)

Note
July 1992 assessment of Iraqi strength: Army 350,000 men, 2,000 tanks and 2,000 pieces of artillery.

Figure 1.2   Growth of Iraqi military strength 1980–91 (based upon contemporary estimates).

A further increase in the scale and frequency of chemical weapons attacks was heralded by another warning in September 1983, that 'modern weapons … not used in previous attacks for humanitarian reasons' would be used. During 1983, the news that Iraq was using chemical weapons began to leak out. During 1984, as chemical weapons were used more and more extensively, they may have begun to use nerve gas as well as large amounts of mustard. In June 1984 Maj-Gen al-Rashid spoke of 'scything the Iranians down like ripened wheat' – then interpreted, correctly, as a veiled reference to chemical weapons.

When the Iranians did not heed them, Iraq used poison gas only on vital sectors of the front only and even then when there was really no other way to check the Iranian offensives. As a former British military attaché in Baghdad put it, 'when they did it with the Persians it was to cope with mass attacks on a very narrow front. They used them at a distance. But they took no chances themselves.' Only 2 per cent of Iranian casualties overall were due to chemical weapons, even though the Iranians were not trained or equipped for chemical warfare. With hindsight, Iraq's failure to fulfil its threat to use chemical weapons in 1991 does not seem so surprising.[18]

1981–89: External Assistance for Iraq

When the First Gulf War started, in 1980, the Soviet Union suspended arms exports to Iraq, although they resumed in mid-1981. By the end of that year, there were reports of the arrival of quantities of Soviet armaments including 200 T-55 and T-72 tanks and more advanced SA-6 surface-to-air missiles. In January 1983, another order yielded T-62 and more T-72 tanks, MiG-23 and MiG-25 fighter-bombers and more SS-1 Scud-B surface to surface missiles. 100 of the highly accurate but short-range SS-21 missiles were also ordered, but it is unclear whether they were actually delivered. During the war, Iraq managed to increase its order of battle. The increasing strength of Iraqi forces and equipment during and after the First Gulf War is shown in Figure 1.2.[19]

Between 1982 and 1989 the Iraqis ordered 1,000 Soviet T-62 and Chinese T-59 tanks, BMP-2 infantry fighting vehicles and MT-LB artillery command post vehicles. All these systems appeared in the Kuwait Theatre of Operations. During the 1980s, Iraq ordered, in all, about 40 major conventional weapons systems. Convinced of the value of artillery by their experience in defending against the Iranians, they ordered 100 Astros-II multiple rocket launchers (MRL) from Brazil and 300 Egyptian versions of the Soviet BM-21 MRL. Self-sufficiency was clearly an Iraqi aim. Before the 1990 invasion of Kuwait, the Iraqis claimed to be building their own T-72s, known as *Assad Babil* – 'Lion of Babylon'. They certainly made certain components, including their own gun barrels, although they were some way from building complete tanks. And they were self-sufficient in a wide range of ammunition – a lesson Saddam Hussein may have learned in the winter of 1975, when, on his own admission, the Iraqi Army had to suspend operations against the Kurds because of 'a great shortage of ammunition'.[20]

Nuclear Ambitions and Development

Although the first Gulf War was over, Iraq's acquisition of long-range weapons did not lose the momentum it had gained during those years, either. On 5 December 1989 the Iraqis test-fired *al-Aabed* ('the Worshipper'), a 48-ton, three-stage satellite launch vehicle from al-Anber Space Research Centre. Al-Aabed was believed to be a separate development from the 2,000 kilometre range military missile, *Tammuz-1*. The evolutionary pattern of Iraqi missiles is uncertain. In August 1989, the big defence complex near al-Hillah, 60 kilometres south of Baghdad, was devastated by a huge explosion, reportedly killing 7,000 people, including Egyptian military advisers and engineers.[21] It was to this facility that Farzad Bazoft, the Iranian working for the British newspaper *The Observer*, was drawn – an assignment that cost him his life.

Iraq was believed to be serious about acquiring nuclear weapons as long ago as 1981 when, on 7 June, the Israelis sent F-16 fighter bombers 650 kilometres to bomb the Osiraq nuclear research facility outside Baghdad. That set the Iraqi programme back several years, but Iraq began to rebuild it, using West German technology and French and Egyptian labour, much expertise and critical components being purchased with the profits from Iraq's oil.[22]

The subsequent course of the Iraqi nuclear programme only became apparent in 1992, after UN inspectors were given powers by UN Resolution 687, adopted in April 1991, to uncover the extent of the nuclear programme and supervise its destruction. Before the 1991 war, it was known that the Iraqis had attempted to buy 33.9 kilogrammes of plutonium from Italian arms smugglers in 1984, although they were the victims of a confidence trick. It was known that during 1987–88 Iraq acquired specialised equipment for making the centrifuges necessary to enrich uranium, and that in 1989 Iraq had attempted to acquire steel with a high nickel content whose main use is in uranium centrifuges.

But it was only in October 1991, some months after the end of the war, that seized documents revealed the '*Los Alamos*' of the Iraqi programme, *Al-Atheer*, 100 kilometres south of Baghdad (Figure 1.3), which escaped largely untouched by bombing during the war. The Iraqis had been pursuing their goal of building a bomb along two parallel tracks. On the one hand, a team led by the British-trained Jaafar Dhia Jaafar was using Iraqi expertise to duplicate the technology of the 1940s Manhattan project, which produced the uranium bomb used at Hiroshima. The Manhattan system relied on machines called calutrons to separate the Uranium-235 needed for a bomb from natural uranium. The information has been readily available in university text-books but vast amounts of money are needed to build large numbers of calutrons. Iraq had the money, from its oil revenues. Eight calutrons, each with a three-metre diameter magnet were found at Tarmiyah, north of Baghdad. Another 17 were under construction and there were plans for a further 65. If these plans had come to fruition, the Iraqis would have been able to produce 25 kilogrammes of U-235 a year, enough for at least one nuclear bomb.

On the other track, they were buying foreign equipment and knowledge to help

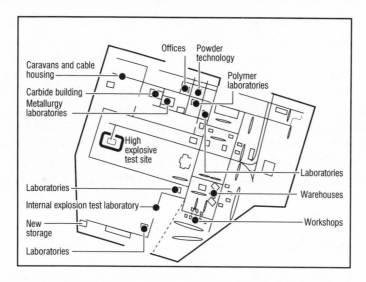

Figure 1.3   Al-Atheer nuclear research facility. (Source: *The Independent*)

develop more modern systems for obtaining weapons-grade uranium. At a third site, Thuwaitha, south-east of Baghdad, the UN found hundreds of tons of uranium ore and an experimental plant for producing plutonium, calutron magnets and components for high-speed centrifuges, the high-technology route.

The UN inspectors were given 'unprecedented and unique powers of investigative and destructive pursuit.'[23] They discovered that the Iraqi nuclear programme had involved about 10,000 people, had been going on for ten years – since the destruction of Osiraq, had cost around $10 billion and was, in the words of David Kyd, the International Atomic Energy Authority (IAEA)'s Director of Public Information, 'on the brink of success.' They discovered that Iraq had been three to four years away from a nuclear weapon when the war started. In June 1990, *The Military Balance* had assessed (correctly, as it turned out) that Iraq was 'unlikely to be able to produce nuclear weapons for several years.' The Allies knew of two points in the triangle, Thuwaitha and Tarmiya, and bombed them to destruction. Thuwaitha was the focus of the first post-war IAEA inspection, from 14 to 22 May, 1991. But they appear to have been unaware of Al-Atheer, and it escaped unscathed apart from a hit on the cafeteria.

The 11th IAEA inspection from 7 to 15 April 1992 focused on Al-Atheer, the centre of the Iraqi effort to 'weaponise' nuclear devices. Buildings were either filled with concrete or demolished using high explosives. These included a high-explosive test bunker, a 15,000 square metres 'casting' or 'metallurgy' building, a carbide building and a reinforced concrete control room. The team found presses of the type used to make the conventional explosive charges to compress nuclear material to critical mass. According to Mr Kyd, the buildings 'incorporated technical features in the design which made them suitable for handling enriched uranium, for example in the ventilation system. Our objective was not to leave facilities which would make it easier for the Iraqis to continue their programme....' He added that these were 'custom-tailored buildings with features to make it difficult for satellites to monitor the activity taking place within them.' For this reason, Al-Atheer had escaped Allied attention although virtually all the other buildings the IAEA had visited up to that time had been 'virtually destroyed by aerial bombardment.'[24]

In the three to four years before perfecting a nuclear device in 1994–95, Iraq could probably have developed a suitable missile delivery system – and it has large numbers of suitable aircraft. Iraq's problems would not have ended with manufacturing the first 'bomb'. More than one bomb is needed to make a state an operational nuclear power and to develop a fully fledged, scientific weapon – with a known yield – it needs to be tested. However, even a 'fizzle' from an imperfect device, equivalent to a couple of thousand tons of TNT, or a terrorist device could have given Iraq the ability to wreak untold damage on a city.

Creating the Chemical Arsenal

Although Iraq was three to four years from a nuclear weapon, it had, as shown, a proven chemical warfare arsenal. Iraq first acquired small stocks of chemical weapons from the USSR in the 1970s and may have conducted some chemical warfare training supervised by Soviet and Egyptian officers. In 1975 it approached the Pfaudler company in the US for help in building a 'pesticide' blending complex. When the company's officials reached Baghdad, it became clear that the Iraqis wanted a huge facility for making agents regarded as outdated for agricultural purposes. But they were regarded as precursors of nerve-gas. When Pfaudler pulled out, the Iraqis approached ICI, which immediately recognised the potential of what was being asked for and refused to negotiate further.

The first Iraqi chemical weapons facility was probably Samarra, 100 kilometres north of Baghdad. By the start of the 1980–88 war, Iraq was probably producing some mustard gas there and was building two pilot plants able to produce nerve-gas. After the initial use of tear-gas in the First Gulf War, a massive effort to increase chemical stockpiles seems to have begun in mid-to-late 1981. By 1983 there was enough mustard, probably produced at Samarra, to begin to deliver it at the battlefront. Iraq also acquired the equipment and chemicals to make nerve-gas, the so-called 'G-agents' – Tabun (GA) and Sarin (GB). These G-agents only act for a few days, and burn off even more quickly in desert heat. But while present, they act almost instantaneously through exposed skin and eyes.

In 1984, a new research facility was set up at Salman Pak, 56 kilometres south of Baghdad. The facility was then expanded to work on other chemical and possibly biological weapons. At about the same time, a new facility to produce mustard gas, Tabun and Sarin was created at Samarra. It occupied about 26 square kilometres, and comprised numerous protected facilities, defended by troops and SA-2 anti-aircraft missiles. Production probably began in 1983 and by 1985 large amounts of mustard gas were being produced. Production of Tabun began in 1984 and Sarin in 1985 or 1986. Another chemical warfare facility was set up at Fallujah, 65 kilometres west of Baghdad, in the late 1980s. Some reports said this could produce Sarin and the persistent V-agent, VX. These reports also indicated that Fallujah was the main centre for filling shells and rockets with nerve-gas.

Most of the technology and equipment was obtained from Austria and West Germany. Production expanded from about ten tons of chemical weapons of all types per month in late 1985 to over 50 tons a year later. In early 1988, Iraq was credited with producing 70 tons of mustard gas a month and six tons each of Tabun and Sarin. After the end of the war, production efforts expanded. By 1990, Iraq was credited with being able to produce large amounts of VX and up to 2,000 tons of Tabun and Sarin a year, but these reports needed (and need) to be treated cautiously. However, the high priority Iraq gave to chemical weapons is attested by the presence of Hussein Kamil Hassan – Saddam Hussein's son-in-law and cousin – at the head of the Ministry of Industry and Military Industries, responsible for chemical and biological weapons production.[25]

A Biological Threat?

Reports of Iraqi biological weapons development need to be treated even more cautiously. Biological weapons are natural organisms and are therefore, on the face of it, easy to manufacture. They can be grown in a kind of soup in simple facilities. But storing them and preventing their escape is difficult, and they are imprecise when used. They can easily infect the user. Biological weapons, theoretically able to devastate huge areas, can be grown in small laboratories. But the author has encountered no reliable reports of types of Iraqi biological weapons. Allied Troops in the 1991 war were inoculated against Anthrax and Bubonic Plague – two of the most suitable biological agents, and it seems reasonable to assume there was intelligence that the Iraqis had these available, though in what quantities and how delivered is unclear.

From mid-1989 to mid-1990 Iraq's attempts to acquire strategic delivery systems – the Abbas and Hussein missiles, plus the enigmatic long-range super-gun were well documented. Iraq deployed six al-Hussein launchers to an airfield close to an area commonly known as H-2, after the pumping station, in the western Iraqi desert, from where they could hit targets in Israel and Syria. The broad area is shown in Figure 1.4.

By this time Iraq had also acquired 100 G-5 and 200 GHN-45 guns from South Africa and Austria – the very latest field gun technology, enabling them, theoretically, to out-range any of the artillery which the United States could field against them. Both embodied the influence of Gerald Bull, the brilliant gun designer who was behind the larger 'supergun' project. The GHN-45s came first, in the early 1980s, followed by the G5s in the middle of the decade. The Iraqis had tried out South African ammunition and were so impressed with it they placed special orders. If these guns had been used correctly during the 1991 war they could have given the Allies a lot of trouble, and the Allies expected to face superior artillery of this type – as prophesied in their manual FM 100-5 (see page 22). But the Iraqis seem not to have deployed these new weapons in the Kuwait Theatre of Operations (KTO) at all – at any rate, very few, if any, were captured.[26]

Grounds for Over-Estimation

Hindsight is a wonderful thing, and it now seems obvious that the Allied command over-estimated the numerical strength, the competence and the drive of the Iraqi forces. However, there was no way of knowing that. An almost total lack of first hand intelligence from human sources (humint) – mainly because for 40 years the Western Allies had been devoting most attention to the Soviet Union – was at fault. If you pick up the chatter of 42 divisional HQs in the ether, you have to assume there are 42 *full* divisions – half a million men. Intelligence organisations also get much information from the open press, as the author discovered in his interactions with intelligence organisations during and after the 1991 war and the crisis in the former state of Yugoslavia. And the press, by its nature, tends to exaggerate. As a US officer said in one of the numerous Gulf War briefings attended by the author, 'there's half a million of them out there. And they've got *tanks*.' Wouldn't you assume the worst?[27]

KILLER INTELLECT

While Iraq was quietly arming, a rearmament of a different kind was in progress in the United States and, somewhat later, in Britain. It was a quiet, studious, even academic rearmament. But then, the elder Moltke, architect of the victories over Denmark in 1864, Austria in 1866 and France in 1870, had been known as 'the library rat'. It had three elements: AirLand Battle doctrine; recognition of the operational level of war; and a renewed respect for military history. And study of the main potential enemy at the time, the Russian and Soviet military system, had a crucial influence on all three elements.

A Bold and Realistic Reappraisal (FM 100-5)

In the late 1970s and early 1980s, the US Army and Air Force developed the doctrine known by the fused syllables of AirLand Battle, under the direction of General Donn A Starry of the US Army's Training and Doctrine Command (TRADOC). AirLand Battle was enshrined in the document *Field Manual (FM) 100-5*, issued in 1981 and approved by both the US Army and Air Force. It was often confused with a more futuristic study, *AirLand Battle 2000*, also dating from that era. But during the 1980s that was superseded by *Focus 21* and *Army 21*, both of which aimed to provide a framework for equipment planning into the next century. But AirLand Battle was the current Army and Air Force doctrine, set out in the current manual.[28]

The original idea was to make the most of high technology to defeat numerically superior Warsaw Pact forces in the event of the Third World War erupting in Europe. A smaller force can defeat a larger one if it can move more rapidly, striking first at one point, then at another. But dropping light forces ahead of the main body is little use without high-speed equipment on the ground, like the M1A1 tank and the Bradley Infantry Fighting vehicle to link up with them quickly.

The helicopter bridges the gap between ground and air since it is largely freed from the constraints on ground movement – mines, obstacles, bogs and cliffs – yet can take advantage of ground cover. The extreme example of this is the OH-58 Kiowa helicopter with its spherical sight mounted on top of the rotor blades, so that it can spy out the land with everything else hidden behind the sinuosities of the ground. The helicopter multiplies commanders' ability to do what they have always dreamed of: keep the enemy off balance, go round his flanks and attack him from all directions. The principle was well understood by the Mongols, who were nearly always so numerically inferior to their opponents. Yet there were continuous reports of vast Mongol hordes, because they moved about so fast that the same force would appear in several different locations.[29]

Landing lightly-equipped airborne forces to seize vital areas as stepping stones for heavier ground forces was nothing new. Parachute and glider-borne troops had often been used this way in the Second World War. But they were too lightly equipped to hold on for long in the enemy rear against heavy armoured counter-attack. The Soviet Marshal Mikhail Tukhachevskii (1893–1937), one of the leading advocates of airborne forces, realised this and inspired all kinds of attempts to beef up airborne troops with armour and mechanical transport.[30] But the helicopter was the ideal solution. It is a powerful anti-tank weapon in its own right. And whereas airborne troops, once dropped by parachute, have their feet for mobility and a rifle or machine gun for firepower, helicopters can continue to move, in accordance with a rapidly changing situation, and can carry powerful armaments of their own.

The US Army and Air Force trained to fight a much more competent and tougher enemy than the Iraqis were to prove. The 1982 edition of *FM 100-5* warned that the US Army:

> must be prepared to fight highly mechanized forces typical of Warsaw Pact or Soviet surrogates in southwest or northeast Asia. In the areas of greatest strategic concern, it must expect battles of greater scope and intensity than ever fought before. It must anticipate battles fought with nuclear and chemical weapons.[31]

The description, in the former theatre, fitted Iraq. And the prospect of desert war was noted. 'Combat in vast, arid regions over extended frontages will require imagination and skilful adaptation.' And then, citing Sun Tzu, the Chinese strategist and philosopher of the 5th century BC, '"Rapidity is the essence of war; take advantage of the enemy's unreadiness, make your way by unexpected routes and attack unguarded spots".'[32] And the manual underlined the value of military history in establishing a framework for thinking about military operations, citing Ulysses S Grant's Vicksburg Campaign of 1864 as an example of a 'well conceived, violently executed offensive plan.'[33]

Its Impact on the Desert War

The manual also predicted that the US would be called upon to fight in desert conditions for many reasons – 'strategic location, natural resources, assistance to an ally, and deterrence of aggression, to name a few.' The Allies came to Saudi Arabia for all of these reasons. They fought by the book. It is worth studying what the book said about desert war.

> Armor and mechanized infantry forces are most suitable to desert combat; however, airmobile forces can also be advantageous. For the initial lodgement, airborne forces are valuable. Army and Air Force air may support airborne and airmobile forces in bearing the brunt of the fighting until heavy forces arrive . . .
>
> Desert conditions can vary radically. The unequalled visibility and flight conditions of a clear day may be ruined by a raging sandstorm that can halt all military operations. Long periods of drought are interrupted by sudden rains that bring flash floods and mud but little relief from water shortages. Large areas of generally excellent trafficability are interspersed with insurmountable mountains, dunes, impassable ravines, bogs and sand seas. The availability of water will be a prime factor in planning and executing desert operations . . .
>
> Flat desert areas have a significant effect on military operations. Because the terrain does not canalize large forces, large-scale use of mines and obstacles becomes necessary. The lack of prominent terrain features severely increases the problem of land navigation . . . Key terrain in the classic sense loses its importance to smaller units . . .
>
> Because of the sparse vegetation, concealment in the desert is more difficult than in many other environments. Concealment, however, is not only possible, *it is absolutely necessary*. To survive on the desert battlefield, forces must use camouflage nets, pattern and mud painting, covers for reflective surfaces and similar methods. In general, easy observation and long fields of fire make undetected advances and withdrawals extremely difficult.
>
> Deception measures of all types (feints, ruses and decoy equipment, for example) become mandatory for success. Troops should move at night or during sandstorms while maintaining strict communications security. Long-range engagements place a premium on accurate gunnery at maximum range.[34]

Airborne forces did indeed provide the initial lodgement, rapidly backed up by heavier armour. The Iraqi defences in occupied Kuwait and the Allied conduct of the war bore out all the points above. The absolutely crucial problem of navigation – knowing where you are, where your friends are and where the enemy is – would be largely solved by a combination of satellite navigation systems and air surveillance. This was a vital enabling factor, without which operations could not have gone anywhere near as smoothly.

Deep Battle

The really pivotal aspects of AirLand Battle doctrine are the stress on deep battle, electronic warfare, airspace coordination, concentration, surprise, speed and audacity.

> AirLand Battle doctrine takes a nonlinear view of battle. *It enlarges the battlefield area, stressing unified ground and air operations throughout the theater. It distinguishes the operational level of war – the conduct of campaigns and large-unit actions – from the tactical level. It recognizes the non-quantifiable elements of combat power, especially maneuver, which is as important as firepower.*[35]

Generals Powell and Schwarzkopf did indeed enlarge the battle area – far beyond what many people expected – and unified ground and air operations were characteristic of the campaign.

Deep battle supports the commander's scheme for manoeuvre by disrupting enemy forces in depth. In either attack or defence, timely and well-executed deep strikes against enemy forces not yet in contact with one's own ground forces are essential. The main means of executing this deep attack are air forces and artillery, while the corps level is the focal point for intelligence collection and distribution.

The theory of deep battle was first enunciated in the 1920s and 30s by military theorists in the UK, Germany and Soviet Russia. It meant the simultaneous attack of enemy forces throughout the entire depth of their deployment, making optimum use of the ranges of available systems – aircraft and airborne forces striking deepest, then the longest-range artillery and so on.[36]

The Operational Level of War

This discussion of deep battle was inseparable from recognition of the operational level of war. Until probably the Russo–Japanese War of 1904–05, armies usually manoeuvred strategically to a battle which, in itself, was tactical. But the extension of battle-fronts and the increased duration of battles gave rise a new level. Multiple armies in contact over hundreds of kilometres and for weeks on end mounted complex operations which, although not strategic, in′ that they could not of themselves defeat the entire enemy force, were clearly more than tactical movements as previously understood. The term *operativ*, as opposed to tactical or strategic gained ground in the German Army, and was adopted by the Soviet Union from the late 1920s. Deep battle: coordinating fire support on a vast scale, pushing units forward one after another, implied a concept of the operational level of war.

But not until the 1980s, fuelled by constant study of the Soviet military system, did recognition of the operational level become widespread throughout the US and then UK forces. But by 1985, a British General, Sir Martin Farndale, could preface his remarks to a military audience by saying 'Gentlemen, I am talking about the operational level of war'.[37] And the British also recognised that, preoccupied with small-scale, battalion-sized actions in a hundred scraps across the world, they were neglecting to teach their generals – or potential generals – how to fight big battles. So in 1986 the Army Board approved the establishment of the Higher Command and Staff Course, based at the Staff College, but designed for those who would exercise brigade command, or the equivalent in other services, and above. One of the first directors of this course was Major-General Rupert Smith, who would command the 1st (British) Armoured Division in the 1991 Gulf War. To hear how he planned to fight his division, on a narrow front, in great depth, was to hear the style and feel the mental edge of a Fuller or a Tukhachevskii, a Triandafillov or a Guderian.[38] And in 1989 General Sir John Chapple, then the Chief of the General Staff, signed the preface to *Design for Military Operations – the British Military Doctrine*. He recognised that some would say this was 'not the British way', and that defined doctrine would act as a straitjacket. 'To them I would say that as a nation we have had no shortage of original military thinkers. Also, the modern battlefield is not the place where we could hope to succeed by muddling through.'[39] Like *FM 100-5*, and perhaps inspired by it, *Design for Military Operations* also included historical examples, from Marlborough – a quite remarkable General – through to the Soviet Vistula-Oder Operation in January, 1945.

The intellectual regeneration of the British Army owed something to the brilliant work of the late Brigadier Richard Simpkin, author of *Race to the Swift*, published in 1985.[40] In one of the most profound books on war since Fuller, he, like the Americans, stressed speed, violence, and the use of the exponentially increased firepower of modern weapons as the enabling force to permit manoeuvre. But perhaps he did not emphasize enough the other side of the coin, whereas the Americans did: manoeuvre enables you to concentrate your firepower even more destructively.

One of the best ways to start a depth battle and keep it going is to hurl an especially well-armoured and resilient formation through a hole in the enemy forward defences, to throw him off-balance and keep him reeling as other blows come in from the main forces, while air power pounds the enemy everywhere. It is an idea as old as war, but it was the concept of the Soviet Operational Manoeuvre Group, first reidentified in 1982 and the subject of much anxiety – and imitation.[41] The circumstances in which it might have been decisive in that precise form and those colours have now passed into history, but the Russians might have gained some gratification in seeing it work with a British division passed through a breach created by a US division, and turning to tear at the vitals of a stunned Iraqi Army. A starved rat introduced through an incision into the abdomen of a strapped-down and concussed victim is an unpleasant, but accurate analogy.

Study of the Soviet system also revealed that officers could and should expand their intellectual horizons beyond those of a first university degree. So many of the Soviet officers whose outpourings we analysed were Candidates and Doctors of Military Science – a bit below and a bit above our PhD, respectively. The British had nothing comparable: the Americans were making a constant effort to keep the pen intertwined with the swordplay. I had joined the British Army in 1973, when efforts were being made to recruit graduates. As an undergraduate being sponsored through university by the Army, I met considerable hostility from other officers. I remember somebody, I forget who, saying that there was no example of graduates exercising high command in war. Years later, I realised that was wrong. One Oxford man – admittedly he had not taken his degree, but people did not bother in those days – *had* exercised high command. Field Marshal Sir Douglas Haig had seen the British Army through its only 'first division' contest, during the First World War. He had been in command from 1915–1918. For some of that time, Britain had provided the main effort, virtually alone, after the collapse of Russia and the weakening of France, in 1917–18, against a major continental power, Germany. But he had gone down in history as one of the most unimaginative and pig-headed generals of all time, though some scholars disagree.[42] General Colin Powell, who had gone on to obtain a Master of Business Administration, and General Norman Schwarzkopf, who had a Master's Degree in Guided Missile Engineering, will go down rather differently. And among their staff, there was a leavening of highly trained specialists, down to the expert on photographic imagery who decided that the hundred square kilometre grid of holes detected in front of the advancing XVIII Corps were not a minefield, after all.

The Future of Land Warfare

During the 1980s I was lucky enough to be associated with these developments in US doctrine and US military education and training. Evolving AirLand Battle doctrine was crucial to a book I wrote between 1984 and 1986, *The Future of Land Warfare*. It was essential to keep as up-to-date as possible with US Army doctrinal thinking, and TRADOC were most helpful. In 1985 I was invited to share ideas with the US Army Command and General Staff College at Fort Leavenworth, Kansas. I was impressed to see that they had a degree programme called 'Master of Military Art and Science' – MMAS – although this was a vocational degree and I doubted whether civilian institutions would accept it.

I had to give a presentation on 'The future of land warfare', which I concluded by saying I thought that future lay largely in the air. One of the students was incensed, interpreting this to mean that I proposed handing over all command and control to the US Air Force, which was not what I meant at all. But traditional boundaries would have to be made flexible. You might have an Air Force officer in command of – or exercising operational control over – huge land forces. But then, that would have come as no surprise to the RAF in the 1920s.

By now, it had become apparent to me that I, also, must obtain a PhD. One of my American colleagues, Bruce Menning, a Professor at Leavenworth, suggested I should examine the Russian and/or Soviet view of the character of future war. I obtained funding with American help and eventually began my formal research at Edinburgh University in October 1987. My studies soon led to the conclusion that the Russians believed that, in the future, a single air-space operation could create conditions where ground forces became almost an auxiliary, and that high precision weapons could do as much damage to enemy forces as nuclear weapons had been

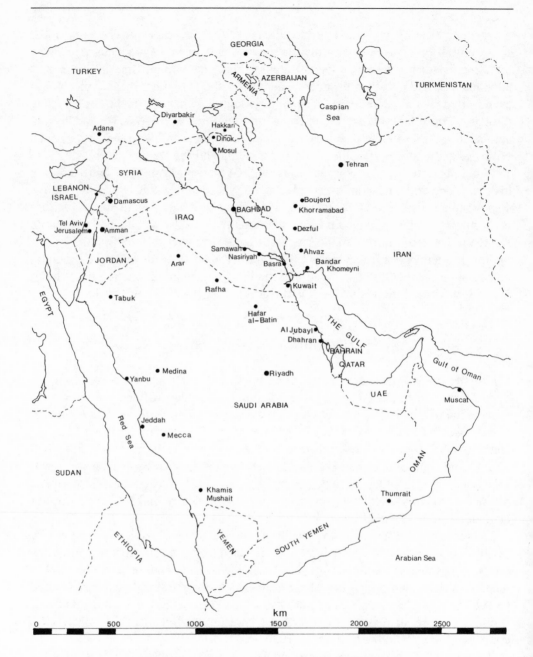

Figure 1.4 Iraq, Saudi Arabia and the Middle East.

required to inflict when the delivery means were less accurate. Automated (compu-
terised) command and control was also central to their discussions. And a whole new
generation of weaponry was on the horizon: lasers, charged and neutral particle
beams, high powered microwaves. I finished my research in April 1990, and joined
the *Independent* as Defence Correspondent. A lot of people were sceptical about the
need for Defence Correspondents. The Berlin Wall had come down, peace was
breaking out all over the place, after all . . .

Well, Russian military studies would still be of use coping with the break-up of the
Soviet Empire. But what of those vast plans for wide-ranging encirclement
operations, OMGs, AirLand Battle doctrine, the operational level of war, deep battle
– continuous, relentless, day and night – the possibility of using air power to paralyse
and control the enemy as never before, conferred by precision guided munitions and
satellite surveillance – an air-space war, as the Americans and Russians had both been
discussing?

But then, they say, 'no plan survives contact with the enemy'.[43]

And the enemy was about to reveal himself . . .

SADDAM HUSSEIN

Ultimately, Saddam Hussein's dominance of Iraqi strategy worked in the Allies'
favour. He made mistakes that no military man would have made, and he was an
obvious focus for public hostility and ridicule. For the media, he was the classic
dictator, the personification of all that is evil. It was far easier to focus Allied public
opinion against him than against 'Iraq' as a country. Westerners often said they really
liked the individual Iraqis they met, and there was real sorrow that so many were later
killed. But Saddam was the perfect villain. One day in Riyadh, during the war, a film
crew went to interview Saudi women – not the easiest thing to do. One, clad in black
from head to toe, was happy to be interviewed.

'And what do you think of Saddam Hussein?'

'Well . . . I think he should be killed. But first, he should be *tortured for a hundred
years* . . .'

If you had asked the same question about Philip of Spain in Elizabethan England,
you would probably have got a similar answer.

Yet Saddam's personality is complex. At the beginning of the war, it was forecast
that the psychology of the dictator would be of supreme importance. In dealing with
a democracy, on the other hand, political and economic considerations may be
primary.[44]

Psychiatrists were unanimous that Saddam was not mad. Like the Nazi war
criminals tried at Nuremberg, they were spectacularly normal in terms of mental
health. They just had three characteristics: overwhelming ambition, no ethical
standards, and strongly developed nationalism. And without the support of large
numbers of 'normal' people, the Nazis could not have produced the war effort – and
suffering – that they did.

The closest any reports come to diagnosing mental illness are accounts of Saddam's extreme fears, for example, his anxiety that US satellites might be able to read his writing. This may be understandable, however, in the light of the intelligence reports he received from the US up to three years before, on the Iranian Army's positions.

Saddam shared many characteristics with Hitler and Stalin. Like Hitler, he was an unsuccessful student who withdrew into a fantasy world. Saddam found the excitement of politics and terrorism a welcome change from the tedium of school. Like Stalin, he was capricious and unpredictable in his favour and disfavour. He would frequently pause over execution lists, lighting his cigar, and changing his mind over names as he read them.

His fondling of the head of a captive British boy, which outraged the Arabs even more than it outraged Westerners, is an expression of a typical characteristic of dictators. It is sadism – it has no aim but transforms a feeling of impotence and inferiority into the show of omnipotence. That is probably what happened when he was under economic pressure but saw that defenceless Kuwait was at his mercy.

Saddam was born in 1937 of a relatively humble Sunni Muslim family in Tikrit, north of Baghdad. He was brought up by an uncle, an army officer, who beat him frequently. He became familiar with guns from the age of ten – a possible reason for his fascination with the unlikely supergun project. He had already murdered one of Abdul Qasim's supporters when he was selected to form part of an eight-man hit squad to kill Brigadier Qasim. The attempt was bungled, but Saddam's role was later exaggerated, with claims that he had provided covering fire enabling the others to escape. He escaped to Egypt, but the Egyptians refused to fund his political ambitions. In 1963, Qasim was overthrown and three years later, aged 29, Saddam became leader of the secular Ba'ath Party. In 1968, when Hassan al-Bakr became President in a bloodless coup, Saddam became head of the presidential security service. A reign of terror, with show trials and public executions followed. He soon became vice-president, responsible for the expansion of the Iraqi Army and its chemical warfare resources.

In 1979 he quietly took over as President of Iraq. Soon after coming to power he 'discovered' a plot against him. During the televised trial which followed, 21 members of the party were found guilty of treason and Saddam invited other members to form the firing squad. It was a clever way of consolidating his power, getting rid of his enemies and making the Party, not just himself, look responsible. In his first presidential speech, he had said 'I will not call on my comrades in the command or on my brothers the people to do anything I would not do myself'.[45] Like Hitler and Stalin, he was physically brave, and not afraid to get his own hands dirty.

Saddam proved a poor strategist in the First Gulf War. It frequently led to disaster – as Hitler and Stalin had also insisted on taking personal command, with sometimes unfavourable results. After the Iraqis lost Khorramshahr in 1982, Saddam told a West German interviewer that he had executed two divisional commanders. 'This is something very normal in all wars', he said. He was 'an indifferent strategist, prone to dramatic but often simplistic responses to complex problems. Against this must be balanced a high degree of personal courage and single mindedness in pursuit of his chosen ideal'.[46]

Much about Saddam is explicable. His ruthless treatment of the Kurds, for example, may be because in the early days it was the Kurds who presented the major challenge to the insecure Ba'ath Party.[47] He fought an eight year war with Iran yet suddenly gave up Iraq's few gains so he could move 24 divisions south, to counter the new threat from the Allies. He threw away a whole Army in the KTO, but he did not care about them. He cared about the Republican Guard, and many of them escaped. He is pragmatic, and an opportunist. His overriding ambition is to be the head of the Arab world, and like other dictators, he does not care a jot how much of his own nation's blood, or anyone else's, he spills to get there.

There is also something very Arab about Saddam's brinkmanship. We Westerners find the practice of haggling very difficult. If something costs £6.99, I either pay £6.99 or do without it. In any street market in the Middle East, you haggle. You expect to get down to perhaps a third of the original price. If you turn and walk away, they will chase after you. 'All right, all right ...' So with Saddam. He may have genuinely not realised that when he was told 'get out by 15 January or else', they really meant it. And, like all dictators, he would assume that a dictatorship, ruled by terror, must be stronger than a society based on free speech and democracy. He expected the Coalition, and Western public opinion to crack. He was wrong.

In a serious study, there is no place for mysticism. But, on a light-hearted note, the prophecies of the 16th century French seer, Nostradamus, are of interest. Nostradamus's quatrains feature a number of forecasts of a great war in the 1990s and a 'third Antichrist', which his interpreters take to mean one after Napoleon and Hitler. I do not believe that Saddam is the 'third Antichrist'. However, I was struck by some of the quatrains. A dictator with a name like Magus or Alus seems to be implied. In the original French, the word *main* (hand) appears repeatedly, as if Nostradamus is trying to spell his name:

> *His hand finally through the bloody Alus,*
> *he will be unable to protect himself by sea.*
> *Between two rivers he will fear the military hand.*
> *The black and angry one will make him repent of it.*[48]

The 'land between the two rivers' is Mesopotamia. Could the 'black and angry one' be a stealth fighter?

2

Don't Go Home

April–December 1990

It was 11 April 1990, about 6.30pm. I had been the Defence Correspondent for one week, and was about to leave the office. The Deputy Home Editor, David Felton, caught my eye.

'*Don't* go home,' he said. 'Something about an enormous gun being detained by Customs on the quay at Teesport – bound for Iraq.'

It was a story that would run and run.

Initial doubts that the one-metre diameter steel tubes, machined to exceptionally fine tolerances by Sheffield Forgemasters and Walter Somers, were destined to form part of a gun were soon dismissed. In fact, there were two different types of gun. HM Customs and Excise had seized eight segments of a 1000mm 'supergun' and one of a 350mm 'Baby Babylon'. It rapidly emerged that many tubes had already been exported, and after the 1991 war UN inspectors found a 'Baby Babylon', assembled, stretching up a mountainside at Jabal Hamrayn in Iraq, which had been test fired several times. But it was also soon apparent that the larger gun was an experimental system, perhaps connected with launching satellites into space, rather than an operational military system for firing projectiles. Of course, launching satellites also had profound military implications – if the Iraqis had had satellites they would have confounded the successful Allied plan for a vast, covert deployment of their ground forces.

The idea that the bigger gun could be used for weapons delivery was quickly ruled out. The calibre was larger than necessary. A gun of this size would be very inflexible: it could not be traversed and the only way of adjusting the range would be to adjust the explosive charge – resulting in inaccuracy. It could only realistically be aimed at one target – as the German 'High-Pressure Pump' or V-3, buried in the chalk of the Pas-de-Calais, had been intended to fire at London at the end of the Second World War. The moment such a gun was fired it would show up on seismometers the world over. There would be a crate of beer for the first Israeli pilot to lob a laser guided bomb down the barrel.[1]

Plate 1 US Secretary for Defense, Dick Cheney, briefs journalists in the Hyatt Hotel, Riyadh, 8 February 1991. Generals Colin Powell (*left*) and Norman Schwarzkopf (*right*) look on.
(*Photo: Author*)

Plate 2 Press briefing Riyadh, 12 February 1991. (*Left to right:* Richard Pile (*AP*), Hugh Muir (*Mail on Sunday*), Captain Joe Davis USAF, Chris Buckland (*Daily Express*)).
(*Photo: Author*)

Plate 3 Colonel Hervé Longuet describes the laser guidance pod for the AS-30 missile underneath a Jaguar attack aircraft.
(*Photo: Author*)

Plate 4 Al-Ahsa. French Air Force officers – *très chic*.
(*Photo: Author*)

Plate 5   RAF Special Forces Chinook helicopter, 3 March 1991. Note the bottled water!
(*Photo: Author*)

Plate 6   Loading JP-233. Muharraq, December 1990.
(*Photo: Author*)

Plate 7   Loading Sidewinder missiles. Muharraq, December 1990.
(*Photo: Author*)

Plate 8   F-117A 'Stealth' fighter at Khamis Mushait airbase, south-west Saudi Arabia.
(*Photo: Lockheed Corporation*)

Plate 9   Scud missile on MAZ-543 Transporter-Erector-Launcher, outside Prague, February 1992.
Some of these launchers were exported to Iraq.
(*Photo: Author*)

Plate 10   Scud missile, showing vanes to direct the thrust. Outside Prague, January 1992.
(*Photo: Author*)

Plate 11 Iraqi SA-6 surface-to-air missiles incinerated on the Nasiriyah–Basra road, 5 March 1991. (*Photo: Richard Dowden*)

Plate 12 Erected *Al-Hussein* missile on the rear of an *Al-Waleed* Transporter-Erector-Launcher. (*Photo: Duncan Lennox, Jane's Intelligence Review*)

Plate 13 RFA *Fort Grange* from the door of one of her Sea King helicopters.
(*Photo: Author*)

Plate 14 A Petty Officer aircrewman on board a Royal Navy Sea King from RFA *Fort Grange* checks
the map before flying north over the Gulf.
(*Photo: Author*)

Plate 15 Sunset over the Gulf. A Sea King on the after deck of *RFA Fort Grange*.
(*Photo: Author*)

Plate 16 A piper plays for his comrades of the Royal Scots as they stand before their Warrior Infantry
Fighting Vehicles.
(*Photo: Mike Moore/Today*)

On the other hand, as late as October 1990, when I discussed the matter with Intelligence experts in the US, they believed that three guns, trained on Tel-Aviv, Tehran and Riyadh could fundamentally shift the balance of power in the Middle East. Although their locations would be known – or would be as soon as they were fired – as a 'first-strike weapon' they could pour a stream of chemical shells or even a nuclear one through the air with almost complete certainty of delivery – more so than using aircraft, with more accuracy than the available missiles, and almost invulnerable to Patriot-type anti-missiles. The Americans added that they were exasperated by English legal red tape which prevented release of much of the information they needed to assess the military significance of the system.

This may have been the rationale for Baby Babylon, which had a slightly larger calibre than the V-3. In May, 1992 the parts seized by customs began what was probably their last journey, from the RAF airfield where they had been stored to the Imperial War Museum, the Royal Armouries and the Defence Research Agency's (DRA) armament establishment (formerly RARDE), at Fort Halstead. The latter would form a cheap but robust tunnel for ballistics experiments. IWM received the breech section of the 1000mm, weighing 44 tons; the Royal Armouries two pieces of 1000mm and the breech end of a Baby Babylon weighing 30 tons, while DRA got five 1000mm tubes. It was ironic, that the tubes should end up in the service of the nation whose expertise the Iraqis had attempted to buy.

There had also been a scare about Iraq's nuclear programme in January 1990 when a number of krytrons – high-speed capacitors of a type usable in nuclear warheads or in high-speed cameras to photograph ballistic phenomena – were seized at Heathrow airport. Iraq, it seemed, was clearly pursuing weapons and space development along several parallel tracks. Whether some of these would prove to be dead ends, whether the technologies would need substantial modification and adaptation – that was not really the point. The man seized was released in 1992 when it became clear that the krytrons were quite different from actual nuclear weapons components found in Iraq.

Another point was that super-long range guns of this type were the pet project of the late Gerald Bull, murdered outside his Brussels flat in March. Dr Bull had been the brain behind smaller guns – already known in the arms business as superguns – the Austrian GHN-45 and South African G-5, 300 of which had reached Iraq. Using ammunition of an improved shape and 'base bleed' technology, which employs a burning charge to fill in the vacuum which otherwise forms at the base of a shell and causes drag, these guns can fire 40km – 25 miles – without loss of accuracy.

Dr Bull had also agreed to supply Iraq with two other types of artillery piece, the 210mm calibre *Al-Fao* and the 155mm *Majnoon*, when he visited Iraq in February 1988. Assembly of these guns, designed specially for Iraq was completed in Spain and they were shipped to Iraq in late April 1988, prior to their appearance at an exhibition in May. Here, they were photographed by Christopher Foss, the authority on artillery and armour for Jane's Information Group. *Al-Fao* was estimated to have a range of 57 kilometres (over 30 miles) – the longest range self-propelled gun in the world.[2]

The Iraqis were clearly interested in long-range guns, and Dr Bull had been involved in something dark and secret. Whether the Israelis killed him for his association with Iraq, or the Iraqis killed him, believing that he was about to talk, was never discovered. The point was that when the Iraqis *next* did something spectacular, alarm bells would ring all over the world.

* * *

The immediate cause of the 1990–91 conflict between Iraq and Kuwait was the Rumaila oilfield which straddles the border. In mid-July 1991, Iraq claimed that Kuwait had stolen £1.3 billion worth of Iraq oil from this field. The Kuwaitis denied it, and in response Iraq cancelled £5.5 bn worth of loans received from Kuwait during the First Gulf War. A week later, Iraq and Kuwait agreed to talks in Jeddah, Saudi Arabia. They discussed oil pricing, disputed borders and the cancelled war loans. Then, on 1 August Iraq pulled out of the talks and at 01.00 hours, local time on 2 August (22.00 UK time) Iraqi columns crossed at multiple points along the border.[3]

Iraq was widely credited with having the fourth largest permanent army in the World although it may have been the fifth, behind China, the then Soviet Union, India and possibly Vietnam. The regular armed forces were estimated at a million of whom the vast bulk – 955,000 – were in the Army. Some 100,000 of these were massed on the Kuwaiti border with the Republican Guard (RGFC) in the lead. Kuwaiti forces numbered a little over 20,000.

* * *

According to US Defense Intelligence Agency reports released later, Iraqi forces had left their assembly areas late on 31 July and early on 1 August. These movements cannot have gone un-noticed by Western intelligence. The warning received has remained a controversial issue, as a British Airways Boeing-747 was trapped in Kuwait as the invasion was taking place. The Western embassies in Kuwait cannot have been unaware that an invasion was likely, but told Westerners to stay put rather than giving them the whole truth. With hindsight, this was the wrong action: in the first hours of the invasion the Iraqis were preoccupied with seizing key points and trying to trap the Emir, and had no interest in Westerners, who could probably have escaped.[4]

About 30,000 Iraqi troops including armoured brigades equipped with T-72 tanks were used in the main attack direct towards Kuwait City, a distance of about 130 kilometres. The Iraqis crossed the border at three points, using 350 tanks in total, including T-54/55s as well as T-72s. Some Iraqi units peeled off and occupied Abdaly, 130 km north of Kuwait City. Helicopters landed troops on Warbah and Bubiyan islands, key points at the head of the Gulf.

While the main armoured columns were moving down the road, Iraqi commandos crossed the bay in helicopters in an attempted *coup de main* to seize the Emir's palace. A DIA signal of 04.00 GMT (07.00 local) reported that fighting had continued

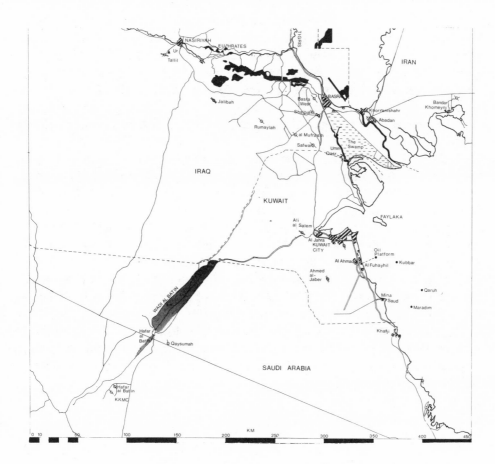

Figure 2.1   Kuwait and surrounding area.

and intensified at dawn. The Defence Ministry building had been attacked by Iraqi aircraft and runways at Kuwait International Airport were intentionally cratered.[5] A later report said 50 Kuwaiti tanks were counter-attacking towards the Emir's palace, and that the Kuwaitis might have shot down some Iraqi helicopters and had attempted to bomb the Iraqi columns on the road to Kuwait City.[6] The area is shown in Figure 2.1.

The Kuwaiti plan may have assumed that the Iraqis only intended seizing the disputed areas in the north of the country, and therefore concentrated on establishing a defensive line on the Mutla ridge. When the Iraqis surged on into Kuwait City, that plan was confounded.

DIA reports timed at 10.30 and 15.30 on 2 August *both* said there were *no* indications the Iraqis intended continuing into Saudi Arabia.[7] Either the view was later revised or the West felt it could not take any chances, as the risk of the Iraqis continuing their advance was widely quoted as the reason for the US and other Allied deployments.

Kuwaiti troops had been on alert for some time and readiness may have been affected because it was the start of the Arab weekend – Wednesday night. British servicemen, among 66 members of the British military advisory team in Kuwait on 2 August, also reported an amphibious attack of some kind south of Kuwait City. The Regimental Sergeant Major described how an Iraqi company arrived at the British quarters and how he was taken to see 'an Iraqi four-star General [full General] whom I assumed to be the commander of an Army.' The Iraqi General gave permission for the servicemen to collect their families, and they then became prisoners until the release of all hostages in December.

The Iraqis did not expect stiff resistance – some of the T-72s were reported tearing down the road at near-maximum speed, suggesting they were not fully loaded with ammunition. The temperature on that August day was over 40 degrees Celsius, so the high speed may have been necessary for survival. Even though Kuwaiti resistance was tougher than expected, the Army base at Al-Jahrah, west of Kuwait City was overwhelmed. But 'fairly fierce' fighting continued for the first 14 hours.[8] By the evening of Thursday 2 August, the Iraqis appeared largely in control of Kuwait City, including the Emir's palace and Central Bank, although fighting was still reported at Shuwaikh, north of the City. The Emir, Sheikh Jaber al-Ahmed-al-Sabah escaped by helicopter to Saudi Arabia, but his younger brother, Fahd, died defending the palace which was attacked by Iraqi jets. Kuwaiti jets shot down some Iraqi aircraft. In December, the author was shown a Kuwaiti Hawk in a hangar at Muharraq, which had flown to Bahrain after allegedly flying 15 sorties, but the extent of Kuwaiti resistance may have been exaggerated.

* * *

Kuwait was part of the six-nation Gulf Cooperation Council (GCC) defence pact, signed in 1981 with Saudi Arabia, Oman, the United Arab Emirates, Quatar and Bahrain. Like Nato, the GCC committed members to aid each other in the event of one being attacked but once Kuwait was seized there was nothing the others could do.

The immediate concern was that the Iraqis would carry on. By the end of Friday, 3 August there were reports that up to 100,000 Iraqis had come within five miles of the Kuwait/Saudi border. But over the weekend they dug in, consolidating their positions. However, the US continued to believe that there was an 'imminent threat' to Saudi Arabia – especially the vital oil fields lying along the coast, directly south of Kuwait.

The United Nations' Response

On 2 August the United Nations had immediately adopted Resolution 660 condemning the invasion and demanding Iraq's immediate and unconditional withdrawal. On 6 August they demanded restoration of the legitimate government and imposed economic sanctions. On 7 August the US announced an unprecedented move, agreeing to send several thousand troops in a joint operation with Egypt and Saudi Arabia. Egypt's 500,000 strong Army was the second largest in the Arab world after Iraq's. On 8 August, the British said they would also send forces, but implied these would be limited to sea and air, at least to start with. The US Operation was called – appropriately enough, DESERT SHIELD: the British, with typical lacklustre *sangfroid*, GRANBY. The British MoD later claimed, cleverly, that this was a most appropriate name as John Manners, Marquis of Granby (1721–70), had been a dashing and brilliant cavalry commander in the Seven Years' War, but I doubt that was in anyone's mind in August, 1990.[9]

As one would expect from reading the US Field Manual, FM 100-5, the first US troops deployed were from 82nd Airborne Division: a brigade of 4,000. The long Allied build-up had begun. At the time of the Iraqi invasion of Kuwait the Americans had the USS *Independence* Carrier Battle Group in the Indian Ocean, and a small squadron in the Gulf. A week later a second carrier battle group, based on the USS *Eisenhower* had reached the Red Sea while two more battle groups, based on the carrier *Saratoga* and the battleship *Wisconsin*, were steaming across the Atlantic.

Conflict Modelling

Initial assessments of the balance of forces were gloomy. The Pentagon's modelling division, Joint Chiefs of Staff (JCS) J8, had only turned its conflict modelling resources to Iraq about six months before. Two or three years earlier they had modelled a Soviet break out from Afghanistan towards the Indian Ocean. They had relied heavily on air-power and shied away from intervention on the ground. However, the terrain for that scenario was more favourable: B-52 bombers were used to block mountain roads. But in the Kuwait Theatre of Operations (KTO) there were no mountains – indeed, no natural barriers to speak of, except that it was framed on two sides by water. The first model of conflict with the Iraqis suggested that US troops, in smaller numbers, would be overrun. 'The broad theme was that we couldn't get behind the power curve' – the same problem that the British faced at Isandhlwana in 1879 and Custer at Little Big Horn in 1876. They would not be able to start killing them soon enough or kill them fast enough. Even then, experts doubted that air forces alone could defeat the Iraqis. But if the entire Iraqi Air Force were destroyed – an entirely feasible proposition in the Pentagon view – it would then be 'a rather long duck shoot'.[10] That view proved correct.

The Allied Build-Up Begins: A Lack of Human Intelligence

On 11 August, the British Joint Commander, Air Chief Marshal Sir Patrick Hine, appointed Air Vice Marshal Sandy Wilson to be Air Commander British Forces Arabian Peninsula, based in the Saudi capital, Riyadh. Once again, the RAF was in charge of British forces in this part of the world. The first priority was to defend Saudi

Arabia and to that end a squadron of Tornado F3 Air Defence fighters flew into Dhahran early on 11 August. The British build up, too, had begun. So had the Egyptian, with 3,000 troops arriving on 12 August.[11]

The next strategic milestone was 15 August, when Saddam Hussein reached an accommodation with Iran, against whom he had recently fought the murderous eight year war. He renounced his claims to former Iranian territory and began withdrawing from the small areas occupied. It was immediately clear this would release large forces for the KTO. But how many?

By this time, British Defence Intelligence resources, for so long preoccupied with the Warsaw Pact and Soviet Union, had been switched to concentrate on Iraq. Many of the 'Soviet experts', I discovered when I bumped into an old colleague at the Defence Ministry in Whitehall, had become 'Iraqi experts' overnight. Their knowledge of Soviet equipment was a help, but very little was known about organisation and tactics, and 'humint' – intelligence from agents and sources in Kuwait – seemed negligible. This proved a major weakness throughout the conflict. Sigint – listening in to Iraqi broadcasts, and 'national technical means' – spy satellites produced false readings. The main problem was that although you could identify a brigade headquarters, you had no idea whether that brigade was fully, or half manned, or scarcely manned at all. You had to assume it was fully manned, which explains why the Allies wildly over-estimated the number of Iraqis in the KTO.

Defence Correspondents are Briefed

It was at this time that I received the invitation to the first of many intelligence briefings at the Ministry of Defence. Briefings for Defence Correspondents, *only*. The thinking was that by using trusted defence professionals, with whom the MoD had a close – and personal – relationship, facts about what was happening could be disseminated without compromising sources, creating political embarrassment, or giving events a political 'spin'. People who knew the subject were also less liable to misinterpret things, and business could be done much more quickly because the MoD did not have to explain the difference between a brigade and a division and that a lieutenant general was higher than a major general, and so on. I later found that many journalists, particularly the Americans, felt it essential to give the source of any fact or allegation. The rules for the select group of defence correspondents were 'completely unattributable' – not even 'Whitehall sources' or some other euphemism. As defence correspondent of the UK's official newspaper of record, I was quite happy to say 'this is so, to the best of my knowledge and judgment'. Nobody needed to ask where I got the information.

The briefings followed a standard format, with the Deputy Chief of Public Relations, an Intelligence officer, sometimes an officer from a relevant service and, frequently, Major General Alex Harley, the Assistant Chief of the Defence Staff (Overseas), a Gunner officer, as I had been, who was one of the MoD's announcers during the war itself.

On 15 August, they told us that the deal with Iran released 24 divisions which had previously been tied up on the Iranian border, and which would now be available for action against the Allies. For the first time we were shown a breakdown of where the Iraqi forces were: 24 divisions of various types in northern Iraq, 24 in southern Iraq, and four infantry divisions and three armoured or mechanised divisions in Kuwait itself. These divisions numbered between 12,000 and 15,000 men each. The map also showed all the Allied forces in place, so in the next day's *Independent* the readers got an accurate picture of what was happening. It was the first of many elaborate graphics, converted from hasty sketches into immaculate artwork by the graphics department, who excelled themselves throughout the crisis and conflict.

The Iraqi Plan: Analysis

With hindsight, Iraq's military actions in the Kuwait Theatre of Operations (KTO) can be broken into three phases: the invasion in August, the period of deterrence from September 1990 to January 1991, and the defensive phase during Operation DESERT STORM in January and February 1991. The deterrence phase began as soon as the Iraqis had consolidated their hold on Kuwait and the Allied build-up in Saudi Arabia had begun. Throughout the autumn and early winter, Iraq's general headquarters built up a defence in depth not dissimilar in concept (though greatly inferior to) the Soviet defence of the Kursk salient in 1943. Iraq probably never believed that it could achieve a classic military victory over the Coalition forces. Nevertheless, deterring an Allied attack, achieving a stalemate, or even the conduct of a slow withdrawal inflicting heavy Allied casualties would, in their eyes, constitute an Iraqi victory. Throughout the deterrence phase, they conducted psychological operations emphasizing the risk of high Allied casualties, and the threat of weapons of mass destruction and terrorism.

The deterrence phase was partly successful. The Allies were reluctant to attack, and believed that a military operation might be costly, protracted and fought with chemical weapons. However, this Iraqi policy contained the seeds of the Iraqi defeat, as the Allies, in response, created forces so strong, that when deterrence failed, the Iraqis were crushed with unexpected ease. And because the Iraqi plan concentrated on defending Kuwait, forcing a war of attrition inside the country, it contained a 'self-imposed limitation' – most of the Iraqi forces were stuck inside Kuwait. The Allied command therefore had every inducement to adopt the indirect approach, and later did so, hammering the Iraqis against their own defences.[12]

With Tom King to the Gulf

At the end of August, I went with Tom King, the UK Secretary of State for Defence on a visit to the Gulf area. He was accompanied by Air Chief Marshal Paddy Hine, the British Joint Commander. Our visit coincided with the arrival of a second RAF squadron, this time Tornado GR1 fighter-bombers, at Muharraq, the military airfield on Bahrain. Before departure from RAF Lyneham, the press party had a couple of hours' refresher training in using the Nuclear, Biological and Chemical (NBC) equipment. We were each issued with two suits and the latest S12 respirator, which comes in four sizes. To check that it fitted properly, a pungent spray smelling of pear-drops was squirted in one's face. The Forces took the chemical threat extremely seriously. It was unclear whether the Iraqis actually had a chemical warhead for their *Scud*, *Hussein* and *Abbas* missiles, but no chances were being taken and, of course, there was always the chance of air attack.[13]

Mr King's VC-10 flew through the night. The next morning, for the first time, I saw the pinkish Saudi desert below. It reminded me of the sea, extending unbroken and uninhabited as far as the horizon. Occasionally, craggy escarpments rose out of the sand, like rocks from the sea. And from this height, the sand looked like beach sand patterned by rivulets of water. In reality, these were huge, wind-blown dunes, able to swallow heavy armoured vehicles. The Tornado F3 fighters proved surprisingly at home here. Instead of roaming high over the North Sea, they now used the same navigation system to find their way above the sea of sand. It was 28 August. We touched down in blazing sunshine at Dhahran. We were not bowled over by the heat, as we expected, when we left the plane, but then it was only 08.00. Later in the day, the heat hits you like a sword. Even if you are acclimatised, any kind of arduous work is difficult. To my surprise, Robert Fisk, our Middle East correspondent, was there to meet me – our first introduction.

The size of the King Abdul Aziz air-base was awesome. With hindsight, how very fortunate it was for the Allies that Saudi Arabia had so many vast and largely empty facilities, ready for use by a huge Army and Air Force. Virtually nowhere else in the world would have been as favourable for a long, measured but largely trouble-free build up. Either there would be no facilities, or they would be full.

There were few US soldiers: as soon as they arrived, they were moved out into the desert. But there were scores of helicopters belonging to the 82nd and 101st Airborne Divisions: Black Hawk combat assault helicopters, AH-1 Cobras, UH-1 general purpose and OH-58 Kiowan combat scouts with the distinctive ball above the rotors containing the sight, which could peer over terrain while the rest of the helicopter remained hidden. The British Tornados were shaded in shelters with corrugated iron roofs.

'*Don't* go forward of the aircraft', warned a Wing Commander, 'These aircraft are *armed.*' Their missiles were live, pointed in one direction, as if down a rifle range. 'This is operational flying,' one of the pilots added, telling us in confidence that they had flown close to the Kuwaiti border and locked radar on to Iraqi planes.

After a meeting with the air and air defence commander of the eastern Saudi region, Prince Turki bin Nasser, we flew on to Bahrain. The next day, we saw the 12 Tornado GR1s newly arrived at Muharraq. Unlike the silver grey, air defence F3s, these low-level ground attack aircraft were painted that pinkish fawn which merges perfectly with the desert, known as 'desert sand'. A line of RAF personnel, in the lightweight jungle camouflage designed for very different terrain, screened the aircraft. The new desert camouflage clothing would not be unveiled until the end of October, and they still carried the old 7.62mm Self-Loading Rifle, not the Army's stubby new 5.56mm SA-80. They also wore issue sunglasses. I took a photograph – my first to be published in the *Independent*, a source of greater satisfaction to me than any number of words. The firm which made the sunglasses telephoned the paper to ask for a copy for publicity purposes.

We also visited Oman, where the Nimrod Maritime Patrol Aircraft, helping enforce the blockade, were based at Seeb. Oman is an exquisite country, a real jewel on the Indian Ocean. A press conference was held at the British embassy in Muscat, which is perched beside a rocky cove, overlooked by an old Arab fort on the clifftop above. You expected Sinbad the Sailor to drop anchor any moment. We stayed at the Al-Bustan Palace hotel, dined on seafood and wandered along the private beach by the Indian Ocean shore. It's an ill wind . . .

We stopped at Riyadh on the way back, where I counted nine AWACS Airborne Warning and Control Aircraft, US and Saudi, and two EC-135 airborne command posts. That amount of airborne warning, command and control was enough to fight a war in Europe. But then, the Arabian Peninsula is the size of Europe.

Our take-off was delayed because Mr King had to fly south to Thumrait to see the British Jaguar squadron there. The Omanis were highly sensitive about the presence of these combat aircraft (as opposed to the Nimrods) and did not want the press anywhere near them.

The VC-10 sat on the runway in the 40 degree temperatures of a Saudi August afternoon, baking on the outside. Inside, it was air-conditioned. Eventually the time came to take off. The aircraft lumbered down the runway and very nearly reached the end before inching into the air. It seemed terribly close to the ground, bits of scrub still looking very near.

'We're gaining very little height,' said David Fairhall, my opposite number from the *Guardian*. We did not seem to be climbing at all. The heat coming up from the desert made the plane rock from side to side, and it looked as if a wing was going to scrape the ground. For a moment, I thought we were going in. Then, slowly, slowly, the plane lifted. Charlie Miller, the Press Association defence correspondent, who, like David, had spent decades travelling in military aircraft, looked worried.

'What's the matter,' said Chris Verey, the MoD's Deputy Chief of Public Relations, 'have you no trust in the RAF?'

'I'm still not happy', said Charlie.

But the ground was getting further away. Eventually, the desert turned that familiar shade of pink, as opposed to the light greyish-sandy colour it appears close to.

The hotter it is, the harder it is for a plane to climb, and the more runway you need. And it was *hot*. For me, it was probably the most worrying moment of the entire crisis, apart, perhaps, from one moment during the war . . .

The British Contribution

In the second week of September rumours began circulating that the British were going to send 'tanks', rumours reported by the BBC. People get very excited about tanks which, as a former artillery officer, I find surprising. They get even more excited when such rumours are reported by the BBC. I tried to keep an open mind. There was a good chance we might send 24th Airmobile Brigade, based at Catterick, which had helicopter-borne anti-tank teams – in fact, the sort of force which the French later deployed and which would be used so successfully as a flank guard. But I put forward an armoured brigade (including two armoured regiments and an armoured infantry battalion) as a front runner. On 14 September it was confirmed that 7th Armoured Brigade, with 120 Challenger Tanks, 45 Warrior Infantry Fighting vehicles, 24 M-109 Self-Propelled Howitzers, 16 armoured reconnaissance vehicles and 11 helicopters, and between 4,000 and 6,000 troops would be sent. The brigade is the smallest all-arms formation, embodying all the main combat elements in a balanced structure. It was the heaviest, most potent UK force to be deployed since 1945. After the announcement, Brigadier Brian Dutton, then the Army's Director of Public Relations smiled and summed it up. 'Proper job', he said. 'Proper job'. Indeed. This was a real military force – none of your 'low intensity' nonsense.

Later, on 22 November, it was announced that this force would be expanded to a full division of up to 25,000, with the addition of a second brigade, 4th Armoured Brigade, weighted more towards armoured infantry, and divisional troops and headquarters. Mid-November was the crucial time, when the decisions were taken to expand US and British forces to the scale which would be used in the war.

The Iraqi Deployment Increases in Size and Weight

By the end of August, the estimate of Iraqi forces in Kuwait had increased to 170,000. By mid-October the Iraqi defences had acquired the rough shape of the deployment they would retain until the Allied land attack on 24 February. There were now 11 divisions deployed in line along the southern Kuwaiti border and the coast, six divisions as a mobile reserve west of Kuwait bay and the Republican Guard as an operational reserve of 11 divisions on the northern Kuwaiti border and stretching up to Basra. Total, 28 divisions or, if they were all fully manned, over 300,000 troops. Reports of the Iraqis constructing a 'second defence line' at this time must have been inspired by the mobile reserve.[14] By the end of the month US sources estimated that 125,000 men were deployed to defend Kuwait and southern Iraq against attack from the sea.

A Visit to Washington: Further Assessments

How the quality of the Iraqi troops and leadership would stand up against Western professional soldiers, rather than Iranian old men and children, was always a complete unknown. At the end of October, I visited Washington under an obligation incurred before I had joined the newspaper. However, I was also able to use the visit to contact Net Assessment, the organisation whose job it is to assign quantitative values to qualitative judgments, and to ask them about the pressing issue of the day.

> One of the significant unknowns is the general quality of the Iraqi Armed Forces. My assessment is that the Republican Guard forces are quite good – that's seven divisions. There are another eight to 10 divisions in the regular army which are quite competent. After that the quality falls off quite quickly. Many of the assessments tend to exaggerate their capability. There are nowhere near 50 competent divisions [there were believed to be 55 in all]. I think there is a core of highly competent military forces, particularly in the defensive. I think the Iraqis would be a very tough nut to crack.[15]

Some people wondered whether the Pentagon was deliberately being highly pessimistic to mislead the Iraqis and as an insurance policy. But what they said squared with what the British were saying, and the Pentagon was soberly sceptical about the potential of the high-tech weapons on which so much reliance was placed. A year after the war, the initial assessments of high-tech weapons' effectiveness were severely downgraded. But even in October 1990, they had warned:

> One of the areas that makes the assessment very difficult is a real range of predictions of how high-technology weapons may work. If they work as advertised, they may well have a real impact: such an impact that the Iraqi structure may come crashing down. But it rarely works as advertised and even if it does I can't guarantee Iraqi collapse. I'm not confident that the Iraqis would collapse and if they don't you're talking about a force that's been trained for 10 years. Troops that have been through a couple of battles have a significant degree edge over troops that haven't been in combat before. That's not a trivial issue.[16]

Such was the sober assessment on which General Schwarzkopf based his planning.

* * *

In the middle of November, the US decided to increase their strength further, partly in response to a continuing Iraqi build-up. General Schwarzkopf later said he had made 'a very deliberate decision to align all these forces along the border with Kuwait', to convince the Iraqis that any Allied attack would be head-on, rather than the intended flanking operation. At exactly the same time, mid-November, the US announced a practice amphibious assault on the Saudi coast, playing on the well-known Iraqi fear of the Americans' awesome resources for amphibious landings.[17]

By 25 November, Iraqi strength in the KTO was estimated (the worst case, based

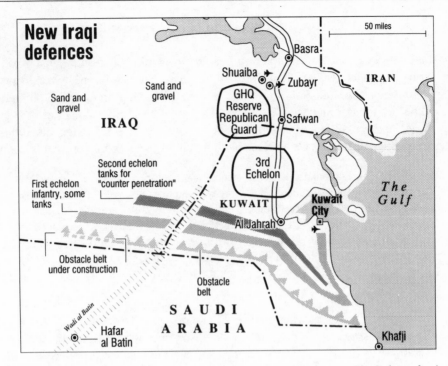

New Iraqi defences

50 miles

Basra

Shuaiba

Zubayr

IRAN

Sand and gravel

Sand and gravel

Sand and gravel

IRAQ

GHQ Reserve Republican Guard

Safwan

Second echelon tanks for "counter penetration"

First echelon infantry, some tanks

3rd Echelon

The Gulf

Kuwait City

KUWAIT

Al Jahrah

Obstacle belt under construction

Obstacle belt

SAUDI ARABIA

Wadi al Batin

Hafar al Batin

Khafji

Figure 2.2 Extension of Iraqi defences, November 1990. (Source: *The Independent*)

on the number of unit and formation headquarters) at 459,000 men, 3,700 tanks, 2,400 guns and 2,300 other armoured fighting vehicles. The unattributable MoD briefing on that day confirmed that the defensive line along the southern border was being extended. For 80 kilometres west of the Wadi al-Batin the ground was fairly flat sand and gravel – good going for armoured vehicles. Major General Harley reckoned the Iraqis might extend their line – which already ran 30 kilometres west of the Wadi – another 50 kilometres, as far as the more difficult ground. The Iraqis clearly felt some anxiety about this flank. Whereas earlier they might have assessed that political sensitivity would make the Allies reluctant to enter Iraqi, as opposed to Kuwaiti, territory, hardening international pressure might overcome these scruples.

A Battle of Encirclement? The Precedent of Khalkhin Gol

The question of disputed territory – Kuwait – as opposed to undisputed territory – Iraq – and the constraints this might place on military operations rang a bell immediately, with the US military, and with me. One of the most perfect battles of encirclement of all time was conducted by Lieutenant General, later Marshal, Georgiy Zhukov (1896–1974), against Japanese forces in the Mongolian desert, in 1939 – the battle for Nomonhan, or Khalkhin Gol. It was at the forefront of all our minds because two Soviet analysts had recently put it forward as a model for a possible 'defensive' strategy for the Soviet Union, and it had therefore attracted much

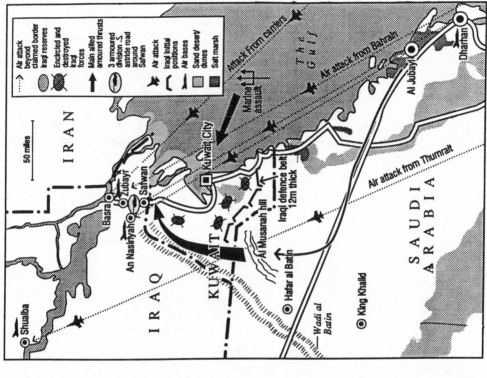
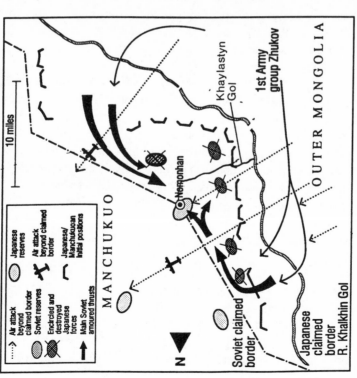

Figure 2.3 Similarities between Zhukov's operation at Khalkhin Gol, August 1939, and a possible operation against Iraqi-occupied Kuwait. (Graphic prepared for *The Independent* but not used, October 1990)

renewed attention.[18] But, in addition, the similarities with the situation in and around Kuwait were many and striking.

Soviet sources maintained that the Japanese had invaded a piece of the territory of Mongolia, their ally, east of the Khalkhin Gol river. In fact, the boundary was in dispute. Merely pushing the Japanese back to the original border of the territory which they occupied in China was not enough. There would still be a threat of renewed Japanese action. They had to be 'cut off and killed', to paraphrase the term later made famous in the KTO context by General Colin Powell.

But for political reasons, it was deemed unacceptable to cross into *un*disputed territory. Therefore, Zhukov's plan envisaged encircling the Japanese just inside the boundaries of the disputed area which they had occupied. Keeping it within those bounds made it strategically 'defensive', although in military terms it was a violently offensive battle. However – and here was an interesting precedent for Iraq, there was no such compunction about crossing borders in the air. Aircraft of both sides ranged far and freely, attacking reserves and air bases. It is difficult to heed boundaries in an air battle, after all.

The similarities between the Khalkhin Gol plan and a possible operation to prise Kuwait from Iraqi occupation are shown in Figure 2.3. In fact, as Iraq was a complete international pariah, reservations about entering Iraqi territory rapidly evaporated. The shape of the KTO, a parallelogram stretching up to the Euphrates, suggested a vaster, more geometrical, wonderfully simple plan. However, one of the key points of Khalkhin Gol remained: air strikes took place across the whole of Iraqi territory whereas land movements were limited to a defined section of it.

Zhukov had also faced problems operating in the desert, far from his supply bases, which mirrored those of the extended supply lines, through Saudi Arabia. Zhukov's attack was launched 560 kilometres from the nearest railhead, using a constant stream of trucks. Even timber for dug-outs had to be brought in, although this helped Zhukov's deception plan as it was arguably material for 'defensive' works. Water supply was a problem for both sides. The Khaylastyn Gol tributary, though of no tactical importance, was vital as the only water supply for the Japanese. It was a most instructive lesson, and I later received word that the US JCS planners were giving it serious consideration. We could not publish a detailed comparison in the newspaper, but I alluded to the similarities, which was picked up by Channel 4 News.

Above all, Khalkhin Gol, like Kuwait, was an operation fraught with political sensitivities, influences and implications. It had to be surgical. There could be no going off at half-cock, no slackening until the enemy force was amputated. 'To win decisively, even spectacularly, alone would suffice'.[19] Schwarzkopf and Powell had to do the same.

As we have seen, by mid-October 1990 the Iraqis had 11 divisions in the forward infantry line, a mobile reserve of six on the western border of Kuwait, level with Kuwait City and an operational reserve of 11 divisions on the northern border, stretching up to the Euphrates.[20] By 17 October 175,000 Americans, 100,000 Egyptians and Saudis, 10,000 troops from the other GCC countries and 5,000 each from France, Syria and Pakistan were in position, with 8,000 arriving from the UK.[21]

* * *

On 19 October, the British Ministry of Defence demonstrated the new desert camouflage gear, ordered at the outbreak of the crisis. More significant, perhaps, was the return of body armour as a general issue, for the first time since the 17th century. Most wounds in war – up to 60 per cent (especially in the desert) are caused by artillery and mortar rounds. The new combat body armour (CBA) would not stop a bullet but it protected the vital organs against fragments. The staff officers who briefed defence correspondents reckoned it would reduce serious casualties by up to 60 percent.[22] It had taken us 300 years to rediscover what medieval armourers had known so well. For a soldier in combat, steel, or Kevlar – layers of nylon bonded into armour – is preferable to wool.

* * *

By the end of October, US estimates of the number of Iraqis in the 'southern theatre of operations' (later the KTO) had reached 450,000. At the end of October, I visited the Primary War Headquarters (PWHQ) bunker at High Wycombe from which any operations would be controlled. It was the most modern command centre in Britain with the communications necessary to direct a distant operation. Air Chief Marshal Hine said he doubted whether one could ever say one had enough forces for a given job, and suggested that the balance on the ground was still very unfavourable to the Allies. They would, he said, depend very much on air power to redress the balance.[23]

November: I Visit the Navy

In the second week in November, I joined the Navy in Abu Dhabi, where three minesweepers were hunting for Iraqi mines. On Thursday 8 November, *Atherstone*, *Hurworth* and *Cattistock* sailed into the Shah Allum Shoal 100 kilometres from the Iranian coast and 400 kilometres from the nearest Iraqi port. An Iraqi ship had been seen two months before with hatches open and cranes trained outward in one of the main routes for Gulf shipping. At this time, the Gulf was eerily tranquil. The small press party joined the Naval squadron at Jebel Ali in the UAE, where HMS *London*, the British command ship, lay alongside with the US 7th Fleet command ship, USS *Blue Ridge*. At that time we were forbidden to disclose the name of the port, as the Gulf states were sensitive about their involvement being advertised.[24]

We flew out to the shoal in a Sea King helicopter from the Royal Fleet Auxiliary *Fort Grange*. It was incredibly noisy, yet strangely soporific – or perhaps that sensation was due to the customary lack of sleep which attended all such facilities, indeed, the entire crisis. I will always recall the Petty Officer aircrewman, wearing a Vietnam-war style bandanna, handling his 15 passengers like a skilled executioner, dropping them in a canvas loop onto the deck of a ship below ploughing through the water at 19 knots. En route for the Shah Allum Shoal we passed many oil rigs, bright yellow, unreal, like models. The water was different shades of blue, depending on the depth – down to 60m in most places. The weather in mid-November was like a blazing hot, dry English summer day. Exceptionally pleasant.

There was no sense of danger or imminent war. The biggest danger was the sea-snakes: metre-long, creamy-white, revolting creatures, related to cobras. One night, after a nocturnal and rather perilous rope-ladder descent from *Fort Grange*, I saw one illuminated in the black, warm, calm water of the Gulf.

The minehunters found no mines. War, I was already concluding, is bizarre. On the bottom of the Gulf, 60 metres down and 100 km from Iran they found a Zimmer frame, used by the elderly and infirm to help them walk. How it got there, nobody would ever know.

* * *

Before Christmas, we spent much time preparing material for use in the event of war. Always a lover of maps, I was determined that we should have the best available. Air charts, available from British Airways, were the best for most military purposes, and I obtained 1/500,000 and one millionth scale charts of the region. But these would not be adequate if there were house-to-house fighting in Kuwait City and I also persuaded the Ministry of Defence to let me have some 1/250,000 scale air charts, just in case.

December: To Riyadh and Muharraq: The Force Commanders Briefing

In the middle of December I was offered another visit to the potential theatre of war, this time with the RAF. It would involve visiting the Tornado and Jaguar force at Muharraq, the military airfield at Bahrain, and also a visit to Riyadh. We would be in and out of Saudi Arabia – a country for which it was (and is) notoriously difficult for journalists to obtain visas. In October Tom King, the Defence Secretary had come to lunch at the *Independent* and I had joined him, Andreas Whittam Smith, the Editor, Matthew Symonds, Deputy Editor, and Hugh Colver, Mr King's Chief of Public Relations, for a useful discussion. Mr King had said that if conflict broke out the best bet was to have one's men in place. Once conflict was imminent, it would be difficult, perhaps impossible to get flights and visas would be even more restricted. Therefore, I was delighted to find that when the RAF returned my passport before the Tri-star flight to Riyadh I had a Saudi visa dated 14 December valid for 'several journeys for three months' – up to 14 March 1991. What might happen in those three months? Perhaps God was kind to journalists. Or was it the RAF's kindness?

On our previous visit with Tom King we had travelled on a VIP flight – complete with alcohol – and not disembarked in Riyadh. This time, it was standard RAF fare and we stayed in transit accommodation in the Saudi capital. On arrival, we were met by an RAF policeman, a Scot.

'Welcome to Riyadh, gents,' he said. 'Put your watches back 400 years.' The humour of the British servicemen was finely honed – reflecting their operational readiness. The Saudi women, in their all-enveloping black garments, were known, affectionately, as 'bin liners'. The beautiful Arabic script, relegated from Omar Khayyam to road signs, was known, brilliantly, as 'wormspeak.' I reported this, and for so doing was dubbed an 'anti-Islamic writer' by one of the Arab newspapers. 'Send them his picture' was the response of my *Independent* colleagues.

In Riyadh, we were taken to the HQ, British Forces Middle East, to meet Sir Peter de la Billière, the British Forces Commander Middle East and Air Vice-Marshal William Wratten, his deputy and air commander.

On the wall, there was a beautiful mosaic of infra-red air or satellite photographs, over two metres square, showing Kuwait and adjacent Iraq and Saudi Arabia in pastel shades. It reminded me of ceramic tiles: slate grey, bottle green for the salt marshes, chalky white for the wadis – dry river beds, pale blue for the beaches, purple for the built-up areas and deep black for the sea. At a scale of about an inch to the mile every street, every runway, even an individual storage tank was visible and uncannily real. There could be little doubt that, in the event of war the Iraqi forces were perfectly uncovered. It was what airmen had dreamed of since Douhet.

Air Vice-Marshal Wratten clearly shared those dreams. 'There is now the opportunity for air power to stamp its mark on the combat arena,' he said. 'It has never in history been done only from the air. If it is done this time, it will be the first time. It is the overall gathering of air power which is unique. It is awesome in its scope, in its entirety, in its potential.' The way the Iraqis were deployed, he said, lent itself to the use of air power in this almost ideal, clear, antiseptic environment. The target arrays were 'almost entirely predictable and almost entirely static.' But he was concerned that, as so often in recent decades, we would not be able to make a clean break between peace and war. 'The defined status of any conflict is the first of the blurred edges that we'll encounter. That could be the first and the greatest of the uncertainties.'[25]

As it turned out, it was not. But, as discussed in the next chapter, the war was won largely from the air.

At Muharraq we met the commander of the British base, Group Captain David Henderson, whose crews took disproportionate losses, though still light by the standards of other wars, during the low-level bombing of Iraqi targets at the beginning of the air war. He later became staff officer to the Chief of Defence Staff. Group Captain Henderson was exceptionally helpful and friendly and briefed us extensively.

Muharraq was surrounded by five Rapier Surface-to-Air missile positions. We visited one in a superb tactical position on flat, reclaimed land jutting out into the sea. Towards land, 300 metres of open, flat sand formed a perfect, lethal approach. From the position, bathed in bright sunlight, the view was all sea and sky. Two men were digging in a cable connecting a machine-gun post to the sandbagged command bunker, a good 40 cm below ground to prevent stray splinters severing it. The RAF Regiment and Royal Engineers had made exemplary use of the available materials, notably oil drums (surprise!), filled with sand. Walls of oil drums, three thick at the base, then two, then one, formed blast walls round the command buildings at Muharraq and on the surrounding positions.

I was impressed with what I saw and wrote it up for the newspaper. Then I encountered for the first time the conflict between accuracy and professional inquiry and the needs of secrecy – a possible conflict I would have to bear in mind constantly over the next few months. It is something that every defence and war correspondent has to bear in mind. A former RAF officer, a colleague of mine, wrote in to say that I had given away useful military information to Iraq. He finished by saying he hoped my report 'was an ingenious piece of disinformation and not an ingenuous example of professional attention to detail.' It was certainly not the former, I had not given the number or exact location of Rapier positions, but I was hurt and worried by what I might have done.[26]

We flew back to Riyadh in a C-130 Hercules transport plane, a most remarkable aircraft. Inside, silvery greenish-grey pipes, reminiscent of the entrails of an alien in an H R Giger science-fiction movie, were everywhere. From the flight deck, I saw Riyadh again – hardly a city ready for war. There was no black-out (nor was there during the war). At over 100 km away its bright glow was visible. A small observation dome in the cockpit roof permitted all-round observation. Here and there, in the ocean-black desert, necklaces of lights glowed. Ahead, above the city, the sliver of the crescent moon, its points facing upward like Muhammad's moon on the flight to Medina. Behind, the constellation Orion, and all around, numberless stars, never seen with such brightness and sharpness as in the desert sky. No wonder the ancient civilisations of the Near East were mesmerised by the stars, a spectacular video show every night. I recalled the words of a hymn we had sung at school, 'Oh Lord of every shining constellation, that wheels in splendour through the midnight sky.' But better in the desert, much better. Gigantic, mystic, foreboding, the constellations wheeled.

From Riyadh, back to Britain. Should war come, I had a potentially vital advantage – a three month, multiple entry Saudi visa. I was tired, and the trip had been hard. On 22 December, the day we came back, we were due to have our office party. By the time we had been through Customs at the RAF base where we landed (it may have been Brize Norton – I cannot remember) it was getting dark, sleeting and very cold. For some reason, Her Majesty's Customs are far more pernickety with servicemen coming back from potential theatres of war at RAF stations than they are with civilians at civilian airports. The drive back was hazardous – I had had virtually no sleep for several days. But I made it home, and on to the party.

And I had that visa.

PART II

The Storm Breaks

3

Ticket to Riyadh

January 1991

It was an unsettled Christmas and New Year. On 29 November, the UN Security Council had adopted a resolution, 678, authorising the US, Britain and other allies to use 'all necessary means' – force – against Iraq to liberate Kuwait if Iraq did not withdraw by 15 January. It was 'one final opportunity' to comply with the Council's demands. On 17 December, the Queen's Order authorising the call-up of British reserves was signed, for the first time since the Suez crisis of 1956. It was a cumbrous procedure, designed for the Third World War and not the small number of specialists required to flesh out the regular forces in a limited operation like this. One of the lessons of the war was that there should be a more flexible procedure for call-out while still protecting reservists' jobs. But it was an indicator of how serious the situation had become. On 28 December, senior United States officials made it clear that President George Bush would launch a massive attack if Iraq did not withdraw by 15 January. This denied the Allies much scope for surprise but, politically, it was the only way to proceed.

Monday 7 January was the first serious day back at work. This would be the *Independent*'s first war since it had been founded in 1986. At 15.30, a large meeting convened. During the preceeding weeks we had discussed who should go where, and where the best place was for the Defence Correspondent. There was a strong argument, which prevailed at *The Times* and *Telegraph*, that Defence Correspondents, as newspapers' in-house experts and analysts, should remain in London, pulling together the strands from various sources and helping sort out the small amount of wheat from the very large amount of chaff that would be flying in all directions. It had even been suggested that I should go to Washington, since much of the military data would be released in briefings there. But Washington would be a scrum with two thousand other journalists, and I managed to bury that idea. From my own contacts with the MoD I knew that much of the news would also break in Riyadh first, at the Headquarters of US Central Command. And from Riyadh I could, and would, of course, go forward if necessary.

The British forces were also planning to form small 'Media Response Teams' (MRTs) with forces further forward. These would be fully accredited war correspondents, carrying the MoD 108 pass identifying them as such if they were captured, under military orders and wearing uniform. That idea appealed to me but it was not the place for the newspaper's defence specialist. One might see nothing (as effectively happened in the ground war), or fail to see the wood for the trees.

Riyadh, I had concluded, offered the best of both worlds. And it had good communications – including facsimile machines which I thought would be useful for transmitting sketch maps. Although I had little experience of journalism, I had learned very early that there is no point finding a story if you cannot file it. And I was, in any case, one of few people with a valid Saudi visa.

'I think we should get Chris out there asap,' said Matthew.

'How soon can you get out there?' asked Andreas.

'Can I have 24 hours? Say Wednesday?' I asked. There were loose ends to tie up and I might be there for a very long time.

'I'd rather you went sooner,' said Andreas. 'Tomorrow'.

Airlines had begun suspending flights to the region. It was important to get out there and dig oneself in. Although war was not expected for another week, one needed time to find telephones, make contacts, and so on. In fact, it was not possible to get a ticket for a flight before Wednesday morning.

In Riyadh I would be in an anchor position, while Robert Fisk and Richard Dowden, both experienced overseas correspondents, would rove alone. Phil Davison and Tim Kelsey were also forward, for the *Independent on Sunday*, then a separate paper, and Oliver Gillie would be in Bahrain, covering the RAF. I believe we had more correspondents 'in theatre' than any other British paper.

There is normally a sharp divide between the 'Home' and 'Foreign' departments on a newspaper. The management recognised that although a war in the Middle East was obviously a foreign story, it was also a political and domestic story of the greatest magnitude. Therefore, they would set up a special 'Gulf desk', with staff from both Home and Foreign. All stories would be filed to them.

Tuesday 8 January was a very full day. I had prepared a number of articles for use when hostilities broke out, which were put in a queue called 'Glass' ('in case of war break glass'). I briefed my colleague Will Bennett, who had done defence for the *Mail on Sunday* and would be acting defence correspondent in London while I provided analysis and advice, as well as stories from Riyadh.

In the afternoon there was an MoD briefing, which I attended.

'Welcome, gents. The last briefing before war.'

Arthur Murray, one of the press officers, greeted us jovially. There was now no doubt that it was just that. The atmosphere had changed perceptibly. The tone was different from before, almost as if a conscious decision had been made to impress us with the gravity of the situation. The Iraqis were now referred to as 'the enemy'.

Iraq was continuing to reinforce its troops in Kuwait and showed no signs of preparing to withdraw. There was evidence of a more skilful hand controlling the troop dispositions, possibly a new Chief-of-Staff, Gen Hussein Rashid (not the

General Rashid of the First Gulf War, who was now retired). The mobile armoured reserves were being concentrated to counter-attack any Allied penetration. The strategy was described as 'deter-delay-defend'.

Iraq now had 36 to 38 divisions, each notionally 15,000 strong, in the KTO. This compared with 22 before the August invasion. In the east, forces facing Iran had been reduced from 22 to 10. The total number of troops in the KTO was estimated at 590,000 with 350,000 (22 divisions) in Kuwait itself. There were 4,200 tanks and 3,000 artillery pieces in the KTO, of which 2,600 and 1,850, respectively, were in Kuwait itself.

We were also told that, since 20 December, Iraq had test fired two more Scud or Scud-derived missiles, one reaching 300 kilometres (basic Scud range), the other 800 kilometres – an *al-Abbas* or the prototype of a new type of missile.

I dashed back to the office and filed before resuming preparations to travel. When travelling with the forces I had naturally been issued with service Nuclear Biological and Chemical equipment. But operating independently of them, we needed our own. There was a shortage of military NBC kit – it was all needed for the forces and teams from industry who were there to provide equipment support – much of the equipment was new, and had been rushed into service. Heather Kerr, the Foreign Manager, who ran the entire, not inconsiderable operation, found some civilian chemical protection suits in the Midlands and Peter Macdiarmid, one of our photographers, who was also going to the theatre of war, was despatched to pick them up.

Heather produced my tickets and a very large amount of cash, in dollars. This was standard procedure. If things went badly, hotels had a habit of refusing to take credit cards. And sometimes you need to buy your way out of trouble. If your life is in danger, you need to be able to bribe a taxi driver to take you 500 miles across the desert dodging Iraqi patrols. My greatest concern was that I might be mugged before I reached Heathrow airport.

We gathered in the pub and drank a lot. Saudi Arabia is 'dry', so there was an additional impetus to the drinking. All day I had been conscious of a swelling wave of good wishes. Everyone had been so helpful and positive. If the same vibes were behind everyone else, Service and civilian, heading for the war from many countries – and they were – there was no way the coming enterprise could fail.

I flew to Riyadh the following day. My visa was apparently valid but it might only work in conjunction with a military trip. But there were no problems. The Saudi authorities were efficient and courteous. When I had been to Riyadh before, we had used the military side of the airport, where the exotic concrete lattice-work buildings were incomplete, full of plywood, dust and wires. But here, the civilian side, there were purple fountains, flowers and a lot of high-tech.

Beyond customs, the hall was filled with US servicemen and women in their rather ugly chocolate-chip camouflage. A name badge caught my eye, and looking up from it I saw a colleague of mine from Edinburgh, Lieutenant Colonel Andy Hulse – now a civilian, though in uniform – *Dr* Hulse. He was wearing his Ranger wings but no rank insignia. Andy had been one of the US officers attached to Professor John Erickson's department. Two Sovietologists meeting again in Saudi Arabia on the eve of a war. How bizarre. We were pieces of driftwood, bobbing along on the tide – or into the whirlpool – of great events. I told him where I was staying – the Intercontinental Hotel, but I never saw him again.

The Intercontinental was an ideal base. People are sometimes scathing about journalists' habit of fighting wars from five-star hotels but in the Middle East there is sometimes little alternative. It was possible to dial London direct, and there was a business centre with telex and facsimile machines. Most of the correspondents staying in the Hyatt Regency, where the briefings were held (apart from the French, that is), and I contemplated moving in there. But, with journalists and the military tripping over each other, the Hyatt was claustrophobic and with everyone trying to file at once there was a good chance that all the telephone lines would be jammed. The Intercontinental was much more pleasant and although it was a taxi-ride away from the Hyatt I kept a room there for the whole war.

The next morning I checked in with the British and US Joint Information Bureaux (JIBs) in the Hyatt. The first person I bumped into was Tony Geraghty, author of books on the SAS and other things, who was a RAF reserve press officer, dressed in jungle camouflage as a Squadron Leader. I knew him through our mutual contacts with the French Foreign Legion Association. We exchanged greetings, but then two French journalists appeared and Tony began rabbiting away in French, much to the confusion of the US officers whose knowledge of languages other than English was non-existent. It was a small world, and it was all here.

It was necessary to be accredited with the Saudis as well, but that could only be done in Dhahran, 400 kilometres (250 miles) to the north-east. 'You'll get a thing with crossed swords and a palm tree and lots of wormspeak on it,' said Nigel Gillis, the chief MoD press officer in Riyadh. Those passes proved extremely useful. I arranged to go a couple of days later. In the meanwhile, I followed my orders and 'dug myself in' in Riyadh.

Saudi TV had started broadcasting public information films about gas attack. In this rabidly male-dominated country, I was surprised to see them presented by a young woman, whom I assumed to be a doctor, whose hair was covered but was not wearing a veil. She had probably trained at University College Hospital in London or somewhere similar, judging by her accent and schoolgirlish mode of expression. 'Fuller's Earth is very good. They use it for chemical warfare in England. But if not, talcum powder will do . . .' Fuller's earth is used to absorb toxic chemicals. It is also one of the ingredients of talcum powder, because it absorbs all sorts of nasties, chemical or biological. The programmes, if rather funny, were very informative. The family was a rock-solid institution in Saudi Arabia, and it was the responsibility of heads of families to ensure that their kin knew what to do if the Iraqis started firing Scuds with chemical warheads, or any aircraft so armed penetrated Allied defences. I purchased a copy of *Brief Notes and Guidelines on Toxic Chemicals and their Effects, Air Raids and Siren Instructions*, by two Professors at King Saud University Hospital.[1] The first general air-raid practice occurred on 13 January. The Civil Defence Directorate announced the distribution of gas-masks to civilians, on payment of a deposit of 100 riyals (then about £20).

On 14 January, the day before the UN deadline, I headed for Dhahran. Dhahran is one of three towns, along with Dammam and Khobar, which have merged into a conurbation. I was due to fly but on arriving at the domestic flight terminal, it became clear that the plane was going to be at least three hours late, so I and a Canadian journalist decided to share a taxi instead. The Dhahran JIB was at the International hotel, right by the airport. I obtained my pass, number 2093, and stayed in faded Hollywood-style grandeur at the al-Gosaibi hotel, on the coast. So there were over 2,000 journalists in Saudi Arabia. The desert-camouflage pass, from the Saudi Ministry of Information, was exceptionally useful: Saudi troops and police treated it with great respect and one wore it everywhere.

The atmosphere in Dhahran was noticeably more relaxed than in Riyadh, which lies in the Saudi equivalent of the Bible-belt, if such a thing can be imagined. I heard that there might even be alcohol around, since the Saudi religious police had all fled, but there seemed no point in making any particular effort to find it. It had been pouring with rain for about three days, flooding the streets. This had also interfered with Allied training. I was given a lift by a Kuwaiti. 'No drainage system,' he explained. As I left him I said 'Don't worry, we'll get your country back.' It sounded so banal, but I could think of nothing else.

That night I made contact with the newspaper, as usual. Kristina Ferris, our graphics editor, faxed me two maps for checking. They were putting together the package for use 'in event of war ...' A page of background material which I had stored in 'Glass' was published the next morning.

The next day, 15 January, I tried to get the train from Dammam back to Riyadh but it had been fully booked three days before. I flagged down a car, thinking it was a taxi, but it turned out be a rich Saudi's limousine. No matter: he kindly gave me a lift back to somewhere where I could get a taxi. On the way we passed a gas-mask distribution point, where a military truck, piled high with crates containing gas masks was being unloaded. 'Before nobody cared. Now look at the lines,' he said. We passed rows of US military trucks also, heading north.

Everybody seemed to be getting out of Dhahran. They were heading for Riyadh, out of the way of any possible Iraqi land offensive, and beyond, to Jeddah, out of improved Scud range. The price of a taxi to Riyadh was 800 Saudi Ryals: 300 more than when I had come the day before. The dual carriageway, which had been virtually deserted, was more like the A1 or the M6, full of big cars laden with mattresses and household possessions. We made good progress until near the end. For a country awash with oil, it is extraordinary that there are very few filling stations on the Dhahran–Riyadh road. About 100 kilometres from Riyadh we had to stop at the only filling station for petrol. There were scores, perhaps hundreds of cars in the same position, queueing for petrol, including a US military truck.

'I thought you'd be heading the other way', I said.

'Looks like we ain't,' said a very large black US soldier who was attempting to direct traffic.

I attempted to engage two female US soldiers in conversation, a beautiful black lady top sergeant and a pretty white one. 'You British press? Are you gonna *interview* us?' said the latter. 'Going to the *bathroom* is an *experience*,' she continued. The facilities were somewhat basic, I agreed. At this point the traffic started moving again, and we bade farewell.

On my return to the 'Intercon' I unpacked my gas mask and fitted the canister. The next day, 16 January, dawned, still peaceful. The telephone rang. It was David Fairhall, my opposite number on the *Guardian*. Like the *Independent*, they had decided Riyadh was the best place for the Defence Correspondent: a neat balance – *Times* and *Telegraph* in London, *Guardian* and *Independent* in Riyadh. He was on about the last plane in – a Saudi flight. He had the same visa as mine, courtesy of the RAF in December. By now, the Saudis, no doubt overwhelmed by media, were more cautious. David explained he was a journalist 'like the BBC'. 'BBC ... BBC ...' they muttered. With those three magic letters, he was in.

That night there were British and US briefings. The Americans said that they now had 425,000 troops in theatre, a rapid and unexplained rise from the 370,000 made public a week before. Of these, 245,000 were Army, 75,000 in the US Marine Corps, 60,000 Navy and 45,000 Air Force. The Army and Marines had 1,200 Main Battle Tanks, 2,200 armoured fighting vehicles and, 1,700 helicopters. They also had 1,800 fixed-wing aircraft, a colossal number. B-52 Stratofortress bombers had been moved from Diego Garcia in the Indian Ocean to an 'undisclosed Gulf airfield'. The RAF drove the point home. There was 'more air power than has been seen ever in the lead-up to or start of any armed conflict,' their spokesman said.

The total Allied forces approached 700,000 against an estimated (over-estimated, as it later turned out) 590,000 Iraqis in the KTO, with 4,500 tanks (all but 1,000 of the Iraqi total) and just about all of Iraq's artillery – 3,250 pieces. The Iraqi Navy comprised 15 missile-armed fast attack craft, five of which had been captured from the Kuwaitis, and many smaller craft which could be used for minelaying.

The big shore-based Silkworm anti-ship missiles were a potential hazard to allied shipping. The US had at least 40 ships in the Gulf including the battleships *Wisconsin* and *Missouri*, each carrying 32 cruise missiles, and the carriers *Midway* and *Ranger*. There were also 25 US Navy ships in the Red Sea including the carriers *John F Kennedy*, *Saratoga* and *Theodore Roosevelt*.

I was not conscious of any greatly heightened tension or expectancy. We had been tense and expectant for weeks, of course. Perhaps I had become numb. Robert Fisk called me from Dhahran, and said the Pentagon had been leaking 'tomorrow morning.' I filed the story of my Dhahran trip, including the significant fact that the BBC's Kate Adie had been there, and went to bed. I heard some large aircraft roar overhead, but did not instantly make the connexion.

It was just after 03.00 local, midnight GMT, when Robert Fisk called from Dhahran. It was war.

The planning, objectives, progress and problems of the Allied air campaign, which had begun, are described in the next chapter. But life in Riyadh now took on a special quality, and rather than disrupt the narrative I shall describe what I heard and saw over the ensuing weeks.

17 January was Thursday – the Islamic equivalent of Saturday – so Riyadh was

very quiet. As expected, the attack had begun with F-117 'Stealth' fighters, F-15s and cruise missiles fired from US ships. The first priorities were surface-to-surface missile ('Scud') sites, anything that could oppose the Allied air attack – fighter airfields, air defence missiles and the whole air defence network – nuclear, biological and chemical weapons facilities and then overall command and control. The Iraqis had put up patchy resistance, and the initial Allied strikes appeared to have been highly successful. I filed a good deal.

At 0400 the next morning the telephone rang again. It was the Gulf desk.

'We are getting reports that Iraq has fired Scud missiles at Tel-Aviv, one of which had a chemical warhead, and that Israel has *responded* . . .'

'Responded?' My heart sank to the floor. If true, that might mean a nuclear warhead. It would certainly mean that Israel was in the war, and the coalition might crumble. For a moment, I felt Armageddon might be at hand. In a darkened hotel room, out of contact, not knowing whether the Middle East was about to be plunged into a nuclear war. 'And it was all going *so* well,' I wrote in my diary.

I filed 200 words on what the consequences of such an act might be. There was no answer from Dhahran – they were all down in the air-raid shelters. They had an alert, Riyadh did not. I unpacked the rest of my NBC suit, and checked the fit of my mask.

As day dawned, it became apparent that no chemical warhead had been fired at Tel-Aviv, that 16 civilians had been hurt, but only lightly, that eight missiles had landed, and that a Scud attack on Dhahran had been 'thwarted' – shot down. At this stage, the Americans were not saying with what, but it was presumably a Patriot surface-to-air missile (SAM). The Americans later confirmed this, making it the first time in the history of war that a ballistic missile had been successfully intercepted in combat.

The initial reports that one of the 'Scuds' had a chemical warhead probably resulted from the small size of the warhead on the *Hussein* version, giving it the necessary range to reach Israel. Possibly trained to expect the larger all-explosive warhead of the original Scud, the Israelis had to assume initially that a smaller explosion indicated a chemical head, in which the explosive just disperses the agent.

That afternoon I had my first encounters with the French and General Schwarz-kopf. General Roquejeoffre, the French commander, briefed the French press and those of us who understood French on their contribution to the air attack. I was struck by the French desert camouflage, which had a rather geometrical, almost cubist pattern with Mondrian-style blotches in a shade between brown and maroon. Christian Dior, probably.

General Schwarzkopf's briefings were impressive affairs. You could guess when 'Norm the Storm' was expected, as security round the Hyatt hotel was even tighter than usual. An enormous bear of a man, he was guarded at all times by three wiry bodyguards – secret servicemen, I supposed – in civilian clothes and blue baseball caps, who prowled around with rifles equipped with telescopic sights. The civilian clothes were presumably so they did not stand out too much (although the rifles were a bit of a giveaway). But here, everybody was in uniform, or, in the case of the

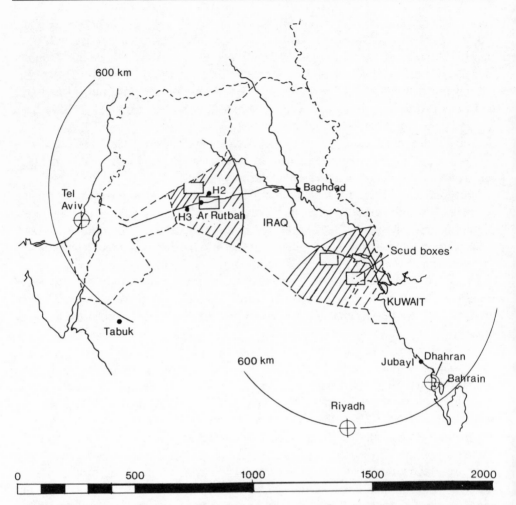

Figure 3.1   Scud launch areas (in relation to targets). Within the general areas in southern and western Iraq, the 'Scud boxes' targeted by Allied aircraft are also shown. Also shown is the 600 km maximum range of the Al-Hussein Scud derivative. The basic SS1 Scud could not have reached any worthwhile targets, except (if fired from Kuwait), Jubayl. Although Kuwait was believed to contain Scuds, none were found by the Allied forces when it was recaptured.

journalists, something not far off it, so they stood out a lot.

General Schwarzkopf said the Scud-derivative attacks on Israel had been militarily insignificant, but alluded to the problem which would dog the Allied air campaign – the difficulty of finding the mobile launchers, 'like needles in haystacks'. He said that three, targeted at Saudi Arabia, had been destroyed and another eight located. The hunt for Iraqi surface-to-surface missiles had always been top priority, but it would need more resources than planned. The Scud launch areas are shown in Figure 3.1.

The coalition air commander, Lieutenant General Charles Horner USAF, then showed us the first videos of successful precision attacks on Iraqi installations. The first two were by F-111s, the last three by F-117s. The bulk and ziggurat-like construction of the Iraqi bunkers was striking. If only the Babylonians and Ancient Egyptians had had concrete. Most dramatic of all was what General Horner called 'my counterpart's headquarters in Baghdad'. A laser guided bomb was dropped right down a ventilation shaft in the centre of the building, causing the corners to peel away, like a banana skin.

The night of 20/21 January saw the first *al-Hussein* attacks on Riyadh. The first alert was at 22.00 on the Sunday night, but the sirens could not decide what they wanted to say so we eventually wandered back to our rooms. I telephoned the JIB who confirmed that two missiles had been launched from Iraq, aimed at Saudi Arabia but that both had been shot down by Patriot missiles. I filed the information, by which time the hotel restaurant was shut, then telephoned Robert Fisk who gave me the Fisk instructions in the event of an air-raid. 'Don't go down to the shelter. Get up on the roof and see what's going on.' The siren went again at about 12.30. This felt more serious, and then there was the warbling tone – imminent attack. Donning the gasmask, I then heard four dull thuds in the distance, like doors slamming. These were probably Patriots. Hotel security men prevented people going outside. At 02.30 we were invited to a briefing at the Hyatt and told that six Scuds had been fired at Riyadh, that all had been engaged by Patriots and that the results were being analysed.

CNN then invited some people to see a tape they had just shot. It clearly showed the path of a flaming rocket motor plunging earthwards in a ballistic trajectory. It struck the ground and exploded with a pink flash. A second missile was then visible, and carried on despite Patriots exploding round it. The CNN crew thought they saw a third missile impact.

Later that early morning, President Saddam made his first personal broadcast since the war began, saying 'In the coming period the response of Iraq will be on a larger scale, using all the means and potential God has given us and which have so far been used in part'. Finding the rest of the missiles would divert the Allied air and special forces more than expected.

The streets were packed with troops and light armoured vehicles, probably a precaution against looting or protests from the 'third country nationals' (TCNs), the South-East Asians, Indians, Pakistanis and Bangladeshis who made Riyadh tick. It was unnecessary, and the TCNs were in business-like mood. The next morning, the man running the car-hire desk assured me that a missile had 'hit near Sulaymaniyah [district]', with more certainty than any of the official reports one had heard.

David Fairhall and I went looking for the site of the missile impact. At the JIB we found a Saudi warrant officer who quickly pinpointed the site of the 'hole'. 'The hole?' said Joe Davis, a USAF captain, who had also said he was going to buy shares in Raytheon, the Patriot manufacturers. 'Yes, I want to interview the hole,' I said.

It was not difficult to find the general area, and we then followed the traffic jams to the modest al-Alamiyah insurance building. The site was guarded by Saudi soldiers but on seeing the magic press pass they let me through. The hole was only about 500 metres from the AWACS aircraft parked at Riyadh military airfield – the old airfield nearer the centre of the city. The missile had come close to hitting a most significant target – but, naturally, one would not report that. At the back of the building there was a crater about four metres in diameter and one to one-and-a-half deep. A large hole gaped in the wall behind the crater and I could see right through to the front. Windows had been blown out and the walls round the windows looked punched-in. Yet only 10 metres from the immediate destruction the houses looked largely intact.

Two Americans in civilian clothes were examining the scene. I assumed they were CIA. 'Very light structural damage. No deep cuts,' one said. I was told that pieces of both a Scud-type missile and a Patriot had been found inside. The Patriot warhead breaks up into small steel cubes to cut through the target, and I saw one of the cubes. The crater was about the right size for a 8-inch artillery shell, which weighs about 200 pounds. This, I guessed, would square with the much reduced warhead size of the *al-Hussein* modification of the Scud, giving it extra range.

'Low altitude intercept,' said one of the plain-clothes Americans. So low, it seemed, that the warhead had come off and continued its course, maybe chased by a Patriot. It was not a frightening weapon – not with a conventional warhead, anyway. Sheets of corrugated iron lay haphazardly around, making the backyard of the building where the hole was look like a junkheap. 'It looked like that before', another onlooker said.

That night a Scud derivative landed in a well-known street in Tel Aviv. The Israelis clamped down very hard on film crews who tried to record the incident – and rightly so. Why were the Iraqis only firing a handful of missiles at a time? And why with small, conventional warheads? There was one grim possibility – these were only sighting shots. Once the Iraqis had got the range and line, they would go to 'fire for effect' with many missiles, possibly with chemical warheads. Reporting the exact fall of shot would only help them.

Targeting missiles is just like targeting artillery. The approximate range and bearing are found on the map. Fine-tuning is done, where possible, by observers who can see the target and the bursting shell. So with missiles. If it becomes clear that missiles are habitually landing short or left of the target, then the flight of subsequent missiles can be adjusted accordingly. The Iraqis also seemed to be firing at one target at a time, perhaps because the results of each salvo were being computed at a single centre.

A US officer later confirmed my hunch. 'If you say it's a couple of notches to the intersection of 1st and 8th Street, eventually if you live on 1st and 8th street you're going to have a serious problem.'

When adjusting artillery fire, high-explosive shells are used because they are easy to see and because the enemy will not know what is coming next. 'Fire for effect' could be conducted with chemical shells, and the Iraqis might be doing just the same with their Scud derivatives. The paper published this pessimistic prognosis, which I hoped would dissuade people from reporting the fall of shot, on 24 January. However, if the Iraqis were critically dependent on such information, one assumed they would have agents in the target cities to provide more reliable intelligence than that leaked through press ignorance. With hindsight, it seems that Iraqi intelligence was not nearly as good, or their intentions as ambitious, as we had feared.

Immediately after the war there was criticism of the Patriots' performance. They caused more damage by breaking up the Scuds over the target cities and by hitting the ground themselves, the argument ran, than if they had not been fired at all. The number of buildings which suffered damage in Israel roughly tripled after the Patriot defence was installed although individual cases were often less severe as the falling pieces were smaller.

There were three possible outcomes of a 'successful' engagement. The first and best was for the Patriot to detonate the incoming missile's warhead or completely destroy it. The second was where the Patriot would break the incoming missile into two or more pieces. The warhead – the heaviest and most robust part – would continue roughly on course and other pieces would also strike the ground at high speed. The third outcome, which seems to have happened in the incident described above, was when the Patriots homed in on pieces of a missile which had broken up either as a result of a previous engagement or of its own accord, and chased them to the ground. The risk of this was heightened because the US crews usually fired two Patriots at a time.

At first the Patriot operators could not distinguish between the front and back of missiles which had broken up on re-entry. Later the software was modified so that they could sometimes tell which was the back and which the part containing the warhead.

But Patriot was never designed to defend large area targets, and the effect of the missiles' high success rate in intercepting incoming Scuds was probably crucial to the maintenance of morale and in keeping the Allied coalition – that 'relatively fragile, complex enterprise', as Dick Cheney called it – together.

Immediately after the war, a sub-committee of the US House Armed Services' Committee met to examine how well the Patriots had worked, the implications of their performance for future anti-missile defences, and for the Strategic Defense Initiative (SDI). Richard Perle, a former Assistant Secretary for National Security Policy, said

> Patriot wasn't perfect, and it's true the Scud was a primitive device. Indeed, it was the very primitiveness of the Scud that permitted it to do so much damage as it did, even when intercepted. It is – it was – intended to defend military targets – in the first instance to knock down aircraft but, as improved in the 1980s, to defend military targets. Had it been used for that purpose, I think the results were really quite spectacular in terms of the number of intercepts, and if high accuracy was required to strike hardened targets, there's good reason to believe that most of the Scuds would have failed to achieve their military purpose. Obviously the debris did a great deal of damage in civilian areas.[2]

During the war the Iraqis modified their missiles, which may have enabled them to penetrate the US defences, killing 28 US soldiers when a Scud hit a barrack at Khobar city on the night of 25 February. Nevertheless, for most of the war the knowledge that Patriots were intercepting most of the Scud derivatives fired – 39 out of 41 fired at Saudi Arabia – was of disproportionate value to morale. 38 missiles were fired at Israel and two towards Bahrain and Qatar.

The first casualty from Scud attack occurred on 25 January when a missile crashed into the identification bureau of the Interior Ministry. One person was reported killed although later there were rumours that it was one *Saudi*, and that a large number of Third Country Nationals had also been killed. I was unable to substantiate this although there were reports of bodies being taken to hospitals in distant parts of the city. It was also the closest impact to the Intercontinental. Having been working late, I was having dinner in the restaurant at 22.40 when the waiters suddenly began ushering people out. A siren had gone off, although I had not heard it. Then there was a perceptible bang about a mile behind my left shoulder, to the north east – the direction of the unlucky building.

The Scud attacks became familiar, and their main effect was to interrupt sleep. After a week or so, people were getting very irritable. There was no set pattern although bedtime – around 23.00, and 03.00 to 04.00 in the morning – just after people had got back to sleep – seemed the most popular. The latter coincided with the main news broadcasts in the eastern United States (19.00 to 20.00), and that may have been deliberate. On 26 January, a US Intelligence officer forecast 'that guy's going to shoot prime time Superbowl Sunday.'

Life began to acquire a certain routine. I travelled frequently across the city, driven by Pakistani and Bangladeshi drivers. One morning, I noticed an AWACS taking off from the military airbase.

'Saudi one,' added my driver. 'It's going up to control the air battle . . .' he continued, authoritatively.

The media was making an expert of everyone.

Soon after my arrival, I heard a familiar language at a neighbouring table in the hotel. Russian. It was a Soviet delegation, and we made friends. They were in Saudi Arabia to set up an embassy, as part of a deal to allow the Saudis to fund Mosques in Central Asia in exchange for hard currency. On one occasion the Gulf Desk asked me to check a story about a number of Soviet military advisers still in Baghdad. My Russian friends told me that there were 155.

When the missile attacks started, they were the subject of interested conversation for the Russians, as for everyone else. Although the missiles were Soviet in origin, they always referred to them as '*rakety, SKAD*', using the Nato name that acquired universal currency.

On 31 January, I heard there was an opportunity for a correspondent to fly close to the front the next day, and instantly applied. I was selected. The report would be 'pooled', so anyone could use it – even if my paper did not. I booked an alarm call for 03.00.

Late at night I received a call from the newspaper saying that the Reuters news agency were reporting extensive Iraqi movements along the front, based on a pool report by a local newspaper reporter with the MRTs. He reported battle 'all along the front', and 100 Iraqi tanks destroyed. Dissecting what was said, it was clear that the reporter had blended the reports of Iraqi activity over the last three days of which the thrust to Khafji was a part and with all of which I was familiar, into one grandiose compilation. A pool correspondent at the front was likely to be three days behind with the news, which would have filtered down to him via the BBC. Because the Reuters news agency put several bells on the story, however, it was unfortunately taken seriously, in spite of my pleas to ignore it and my strenuous arguments that such reports, if true, would come from the high command and not someone with no military experience sitting in a fox-hole from where he could see nothing.

There was no time left to sleep. I checked in at the Hyatt and was taken to the unfinished, military side of King Khalid International airport. While waiting for the plane, I saw something very interesting. Four British soldiers: one captain and three without insignia. They were unusually tall, had dark, curly hair, and looked more like officers than ordinary soldiers, and even more like an Oxford boat crew. One captain, three soldiers – an SAS sabre?

The trip took me to Al Qaysumah, the main airfield near Hafar al-Batin. I saw the massive movement out to the left flank taking place, and reported the trip in terms designed not to reveal any crucial information. At the desert airstrip we visited I encountered a Royal Naval electronic warfare unit – an odd place to find the Navy, the middle of the desert. With hindsight, they were probably helping mimic the presence of the British division which had moved west to concentration area Keyes. The report was not checked or censored by the British military, who provided the facility, but in the event, was not published.

Dawn had still not broken when I climbed aboard an open-topped truck to drive out to a Hercules transport plane, one of the 'spokes' of the RAF 'hub and spoke' effort linking airfields, permanent and temporary, across the theatre of war. Two on this flight, nearer the front line, were permanent, marked on the air charts. One was a rough desert strip like unmade-up road. Flight Lieutenants Bill McBarnett, the pilot and Mike Wildeman, the co-pilot, of 47 Squadron, had been flying these routes for some months. Our talk soon turned, as it always does, to women. 'The most irritating and anti-social thing in this society,' one said, 'you can't talk to them, look at them.' But last week had been busy, as they completed moving 1st (British) Armoured Division to a 'new position', he said – from near Al Jubayl to concentration area Keyes, which was completed on 24 January.

The pilots were not only carrying the sinews of war. 'Shower gel for some girls in Jubayl', said Bill. The aircraft climbed fast, heading into the dawn. There is spare room on the Hercules' flight deck and a fine view through the perspex panelled front gives a splendid vantage point. A sergeant maintained a continuous supply of hot and cold running tea and coffee and, later, some splendid ready-prepared curries. But, at 6 am, not having slept at all and left the hotel at 3 am, coffee was in order.

As the plane climbed, so did the sun. The two pilots conversed continuously. They discussed what they would do if captured by the Iraqis. 'My number is 123456. What do you want to know?' one speculated on his reaction. 'Trouble is, if you told them, they wouldn't believe you,' said the other.

They told of the rain which had been a minor irritation. 'All the sand turns to this disgusting mud, which sticks, and there's this fog, which sits at about 300 feet.' Bill motioned with his hand to give the impression of a fog blanket.

As we reached the first airfield, near Jubayl it was getting light. The ground here resembles a spicy poppadum – exactly that colour – with dark flecks. Alongside the runway there were 'bladder tanks', large, soft bags waiting to be filled with fuel. The light at that time of the morning had that strange quality you associate with a thunderstorm.

'Last week, it was like the Somme', Mike said. 'People slopping about in galoshes. A real quagmire.' Here was a large medical facility, identical to the one in the TV series MASH, apart from the dominant colour – faded sand-yellow, not olive-green. The only other difference was the wall of sandbags round the base of each tent. There was also an airtight tent, in case of chemical contamination.

In a portakabin there was a supply of non-alcoholic Clausthaler beer, and a poster detailing the symptoms and treatment of the three main types of Anthrax, a favourite biological warfare agent against which Service personnel were being inoculated. They were also being inoculated against Bubonic Plague. 'Have you had your Bubonic Plague yet?', one young Flying Officer asked another. 'Not sure I want it', he said.

The next stage was at low level, about 250 feet, keeping just below the Iraqis' horizon. Now, they were not that far away. It was only 70 or 80 kilometres to the Iraqi border. Flying on, we could see vehicles moving up the tapline road, 'Dodge'. We followed it all the way to Qaysumah. Not many vehicles yet. The crew remarked on how empty it was. Perhaps the moves were complete, although later it becomes busier. 'Quite an interesting route, this. Tanks and armoured personnel carriers, all the time.' The flat, beach-like sand below was scored by armoured vehicles. 'It really suits the tank corps,' said Mike. 'It's extraordinary how they set themselves out. They draw patterns in the sand with their tracks.'

The intricate track plan resembled the curling lines on Celtic torques, brooches and bracelets. And that was not all. We saw a huge camp, smoke curling from between the tents. Seen from this height, in the distance, it looked like one of Alan Sorrell's drawings of a Celtic, Roman or Saxon town. We passed over rectangular revetted enclosures, stacked with green ammunition boxes and more bladder tanks.

Fuel, ammunition. The meat and drink of war. There were also more circular camps, with campfires again, like Wild West wagon circles. The desert is of immense extent: there must have been countless camps scattered across it. Dispersion was the key to their survival. Seeing it from up here, it was easy to understand how Iraqi troops might infiltrate between the vast, but still thinly spread forces deployed. And it was also easy to understand how knowing where the enemy is makes it easy to avoid him completely, enhancing the value of intelligence, and how speed in responding to that information gives one great freedom.

On the road, we now saw M-109 self-propelled guns on transporters, American by the looks of them, big, square trucks from Detroit.

We landed at a desert strip, known as LZ [Landing Zone] AH, passing low over a *sabkha* or dried-up lake, it surface partly cracked, and then braked sharply, hanging in the air, almost stationary, so it seemed. Then we touched down with a grinding, gnawing sound as the sharp stones met the rubber tyres. The rear door was opened as the aircraft taxied, still crunching ominously on the rough surface, but it came to no harm. The fastest turn-around the aircraft had done was three minutes, one of the crew told me. The engines kept running, to preclude any delay. All round, the desert glistened, the fine sand and chips of white stone, like a soft marble, reflecting the now hot sun.

By now, the road on to Qaysumah was busier. Towed guns, as well as self-propelled, travelling in the same direction [West–North-West]. I counted several battalions in all. 'Ever seen the M4 on a Friday night?' said Bill. At the next location, a permanent airfield, an aero-medical unit was practising loading casualties onto a Hercules. It was Al Qaysumah, the airstrip for concentration area Keyes, where the 1st (British) Armoured Division had just moved. Two weeks later, they would move to Assembly Area Ray, on the other side of the Wadi al-Batin, prior to moving to the staging area for the breakthrough.

At a distance, the red crosses looked almost black, giving the vehicles a Germanic appearance. There was a strong sense that these were young people of 1991, all around. Forget the sentimental claptrap about Tommy Atkins. These were indistinguishable from their civilian counterparts, save for the uniforms, and even the uniforms had been modified. Olive-green tee-shirts had become the standard wear for all ranks, male and female, with no distinguishing insignia. But they were very practical and becoming.

Some soldiers, mostly from Liverpool, had a large ghetto-blaster which was pumping out rap music, against which the officer giving the odd piece of advice had difficulty making himself heard. Their mood was surly, defiant, detached, almost contemptuous. But they got on with the job and looked as if they would have no compunction about killing the enemy in large numbers. They were wearing the distinctive American parkas with a dark brown check over olive-green. A valued trophy, no doubt. An American wandered past with a playing card, I think it was the Ace of Spades, tucked into the band of his 'Fritz' helmet.

On the last leg we flew high again. I saw two American A-10 ground-attack planes coming towards us, weaving from side to side, like hawks on a thermal. They passed to port, dangerously close, I thought, as if they were being aggressive, turned and dived together. Maybe they had scored some kills further north, and were jubilant.

Then we suddenly climbed. To starboard, I saw an eagle, sandy-yellow with black wing-tips. We had climbed to avoid it. 'Big as fucking helicopters,' said one of the pilots. 'They really lam into you if you hit them.' The eagle flew on, ignoring us, above the smoking camps, the clean, hard desert, as if he had seen it all before ...[3]

4

The Decisive Field: The Undivided Sky

January–February 1991

'To have command of the air means to be in a position to wield offensive power so great that it defies the imagination. It means to be able to cut the enemy's army and navy off from their bases of operation and nullify their chances of winning the war. It means complete protection of one's own country, the efficient operation of one's army and navy and peace of mind to live and work in safety. In short, it means to be in a position *to win. To be defeated* in the air, on the other hand, is finally to be defeated and to be at the mercy of the enemy, with no chance at all of defending oneself, compelled to accept whatever terms he sees fit to dictate. This is the meaning of the "command of the air".'[1]

'When I say the Air Force will be *decisive*, I do not mean to say the Air Force will be the *sole factor* of *victory* ... I go further and say neither will it be in future wars ... If, as I think, owing to resistance on the ground in the war to come, the Air Force will decide the war, will not the three Armed Forces have contributed to the victory? Will not all three of them have been factors of victory? If one of them should fail in its mission, could not victory have been lost? Only one thing could be said. The Air Force contributed *preponderantly* to victory.'[2]

General Giulio Douhet, 1921, 1929

Many of Douhet's specific prescriptions were wrong. Without radio and satellite navigation systems, computers and laser guidance, his vision of air war was conditioned by the inaccuracy of the bombing of the First World War – not even the Second. Ten bombers carrying two tons apiece could obliterate an area 500 metres in diameter. Ensuring that Italian aircraft could surmount the Alps to bomb beyond the mountain barrier was a problem. Military aircraft did not need exceptional performance – they should be based on civilian designs. Fighters and bombers needed the same range, speed and armour protection: only the balance between guns and bombs varied. The fragile, high-speed, immensely specialised military aircraft of the Second Gulf War, attacking specific military targets with great accuracy by night and day, were the antithesis of all his predictions. Yet for all the wrong reasons, they at last fulfilled them. Seventy years on, for the first time, the Air Forces crushed the will and ability of an entire nation and, even more remarkable, its armed forces in the field, to put up more than token resistance, thereby contributing *'preponderantly'* to victory.

Douhet could never have foreseen one crucial aspect of the Gulf War air campaign: the use of precision guided munitions (PGMs) – laser guided bombs (LGBs). First developed under a crash programme, early laser guided bombs had been delivered to the US Air Force in Vietnam. On 10 May 1972, 16 F-4 fighter bombers used 22 LGBs to completely destroy the Paul Doumer bridge in North Vietnam which had withstood successive waves of bombers using conventional 'dumb' bombs. During the Vietnam War, 25,000 LGBs were released, hitting 18,700 targets. The early systems were bulky, but their potential was clear. During the Second Gulf War, US pilots dropped 7,400 tons of precision munitions, out of a total of 88,500 tons. But that 8 per cent of bombs destroyed more than 50 per cent of the targets.[3]

However, the US Air Force maintains that the war still demonstrated 'the need to preserve large conventional bombers' ability to destroy large area targets.'[4] B-52 Stratofortresses dropped over 25,700 tons of bombs on area targets in the Kuwait Theatre alone, as well as on other airfields, industrial targets and storage areas in Iraq. The effect on morale was devastating, with between 20 and 40 per cent of Iraqi troops deserting their units before the ground offensive began.

Covert military operations began before launching the air campaign. On 12 January a number of helicopters were observed flying from occupied Kuwait to land at a Saudi military base. This led to reports of mass defections by Iraqi helicopter pilots. It later emerged that these were a joint UK/US Special Forces team tasked to capture Iraqi radar personnel to provide intelligence on Iraqi air defences for the coming air campaign.

The first air strike of the Second Gulf War was not by F-117 precision attack 'stealth' fighters, or by 30-year old B-52s, however. It was by Apache helicopters, *half an hour before* the bombing of Baghdad.

At 02.38, local time, on 17 January, eight AH-64 Apaches in two four-aircraft teams crossed into western Iraq to fire the first shots of Operation *Desert Storm*. They were to clear a corridor through the Iraqi air defences and knock out command and control systems. It was the classic application of what the Russians call 'integrated fire destruction of the enemy' – using every system for that at which it is best, in support of every other system. The Apaches could use the folds of the ground to hide and give them the advantage of surprise, well below radar level. They did not have to overfly the target area, exposing themselves to air-defence missiles. They could stand back and engage their targets again and again with Hellfire anti-tank missiles, 2.75 inch rockets and 30mm cannon. And, perhaps most important at this crucial point, they could return with accurate, filmed analysis of what they had done. They were not like cruise missiles, one-shot robots unable to confirm whether they had hit their targets. They cleared the corridor for subsequent 'fast-air' sorties by the F-117s against Baghdad and other strategic targets, and the Allied command knew they had succeeded.[5]

At 02.51, the first bomb of the war, a 2,000 lb laser guided bomb from an F-117 'Nighthawk' stealth fighter flown by Major Greg Feest hit a radar integrated operations centre 65 miles south west of Baghdad. Seconds later, other F-117s bombed selected targets in Baghdad itself. These were the headquarters and operations centres of: the Iraqi Air Force, Ministry of Defence, Intelligence Service, Secret Police, National Air Defence, Republican Guard and the Ministries of Military Production and Propaganda. They also hit command bunkers, communications and electrical power centres, military bases, bridges, an oil refinery, a railway yard and a Scud missile assembly factory.[6]

For the entire war, only F-117s were used to attack metropolitan Baghdad, because of their great accuracy and the strength of Baghdad's defences. According to an official US report, 'Baghdad was more heavily defended than the most highly defended Warsaw Pact sites in Eastern Europe during the height of the Cold War'.[7] Because of its tiny radar cross-section, the F-117 proved almost impossible to detect and the Iraqis would often not respond until their bombs actually exploded.[8] Although the F-117s represented only 2.5 per cent of the attacking aircraft on the first day, they hit over 31 per cent of the targets.

Some 40 Tomahawk Land-Attack cruise missiles were fired from US warships in the initial attack, a figure which had risen to 100 by the end of the first day.

The F-117 was a remarkable aircraft, designed by computer, its angular shape determined by the fact that the computers analysing the way that given shapes would scatter or reflect electromagnetic radiation could only cope with relatively simple polyhedrals. Once the computer found a polyhedral that would also fly, that was it. The result was sinister in the extreme, and its nickname Nighthawk – by coincidence also a Ku Klux Klan rank – was oddly appropriate, given its pointed head.[9]

Eighteen F-117s of the 37th Tactical Fighter Wing had flown to the Middle East on 19 August 1990, refuelling from KC10A tankers en route, and landing at King Khalid Air Base near Khamis Mushait in the extreme south-west corner of Saudi Arabia. It was a high desert location, 6,800 feet above sea level, bordered by mountains and well out of Scud range from Iraq or occupied Kuwait. It was 900 nautical miles from Baghdad. Khamis Mushait was strangely reminiscent of the F-117s' home base at Tonopah, Nevada and was soon christened 'Tonopah, East'. 1,500 US personnel, known as 'Team Stealth' worked there during the crisis and war. On 4 December 1990, 18 more F-117s from the 416th Tactical Fighter Squadron arrived, bringing the number at the start of the war to 36. Six more arrived after the Nighthawks' initial successes proved their worth, on 26 January 1991.[9] The Nighthawks represented only two per cent of the Allied aircraft, and they flew 1,271 combat sorties – less than one per cent. But they delivered 2,000 tons of precision-guided munitions, accounting for 40 per cent of all strategic targets attacked and achieving 75 per cent direct hits. No Nighthawk suffered as much as a scratch from enemy fire. At the start of the war, we believed there were only 22 Nighthawks in theatre. At the *Independent*, we marked Khamis Mushait on our maps, but did not show any aircraft there.[10]

The Iraqi defences were silent until the first bombs from the Nighthawks exploded, but then opened up a blind barrage of fire. Lieutenant Colonel Ralph Getchell, leading the first wave, described the skies as 'lit up like Las Vegas. But they didn't have a clue where we were coming from.' During the first 24 hours, 30 F-117s struck 37 'high-value targets'. It is claimed that this 'collapsed Saddam Hussein's air defence system and all but eliminated Iraq's ability to wage coordinated war. The concept of modern air warfare had been changed forever.'[11] Most of the 36 available F-117s, 48 F-15Es, and B-52s – flying all the way from the US at this stage – reportedly attacked all known nuclear, biological and chemical warfare sites at Mosul, Erbil, Kirkuk, Nineveh and Nimrud in northern Iraq and Samarra, Baghdad, Nippur, Lagash, Uruk, Ur and Basra in the south.[12] The B-52s attacked at low-level, having refuelled from tankers based at Milan.

It was believed the Iraqis had an 'early warning line' some way south of their front line and British aircraft were ordered to stay south of that until H Hour – midnight GMT, 03.00 local. British Tornados from Muharraq, Tabuk and Dhahran then attacked Iraqi airfields at low level with the specialised JP 233 runway cratering dispenser. Two Tornados, each armed with three ALARM anti-radar missiles, paved the way, like the US Apaches, firing their missiles before 20 more Tornados, each armed with two JP 233, attacked Iraqi airfields. They refuelled in the air, just south of the Iraqi border and in complete radio silence from VC10 and Victor tankers. They then descended to very low level – 200 feet – to delay the reaction of Iraqi air defence missiles and guns.

The next morning, in daylight, they would attack at 50 feet. Although taken by surprise, the Iraqi ground defences soon recovered.[13] Wing Commander Jerry Witts recalled delivering JP 233 on the first attack, without opposition, and heading for home

> It was some miles away to our right. All of a sudden there were a couple of orange explosions. They were totally silent. And the desert seemed to light up in a big orange flash. Then, milliseconds later, there was a wall-to-wall incandescent white curtain of light, which was barrage triple A [Anti-Aircraft Artillery] firing up into the air. I asked Adie [the Navigator] what was over there and he said an airfield. It was horrendous, it was solid – I could draw it better than I could describe it. I felt sorry for the poor buggers who were going through that.[14]

With 1,800 US aircraft in the theatre, and over 2,000 overall, there were 1,000 sorties in the first 14 hours – one every 50 seconds.

The Central Command Area of Responsibility (AOR) for air operations extended beyond the KTO, across the whole of Iraq. The cutting edge of the US fixed-wing aircraft consisted of 36 (later 42) F-117s, 120 F-15 fighters, 48 F-15E fighter bombers, 144 A-10 ground attack planes, known variously as 'Thunderbolt', 'Warthog' and 'Devil's Crucifix' – the latter because of their cruciform shape – 84 F-111 'tactical fighters' – in fact, precision bombers, 18 EF-111 and 48 F-4G electronic warfare planes, 249 F-16 fighter-bombers and some AC-, EC-, MC- and HC-130s, which were among 50 special forces aircraft, a number which also includes special forces helicopters. The remaining 1,000 US aircraft included over 300 tankers and the rest were transport planes.

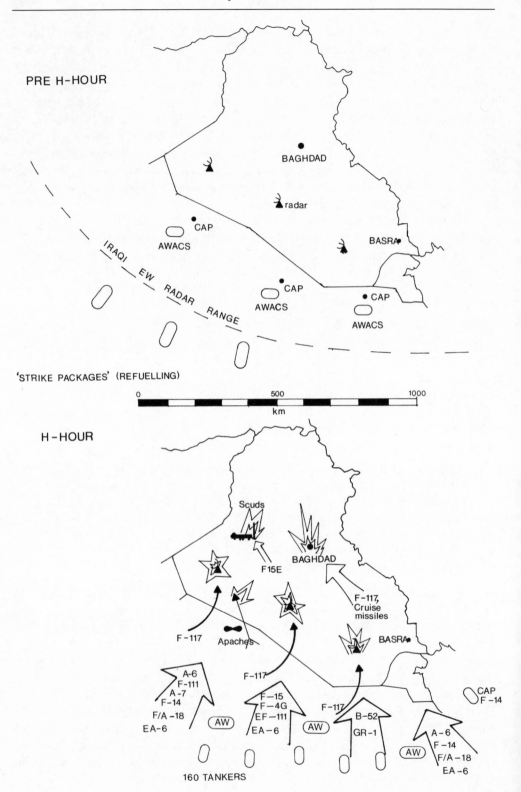

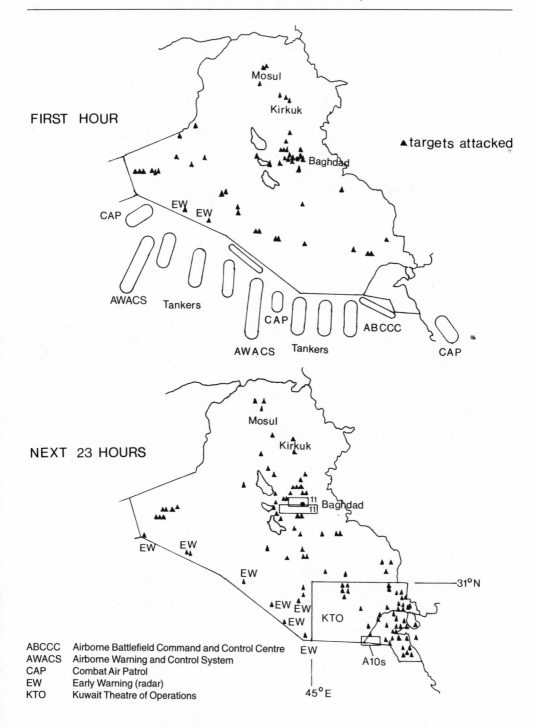

FIRST HOUR

▲targets attacked

Mosul

Kirkuk

Baghdad

CAP

EW EW

AWACS   Tankers

CAP

ABCCC

AWACS   Tankers

CAP

NEXT 23 HOURS

Mosul

Kirkuk

Baghdad

11

11

EW   EW

EW

EW

31°N

▲EW EW

▲EW   KTO

ABCCC   Airborne Battlefield Command and Control Centre   EW
AWACS   Airborne Warning and Control System
CAP   Combat Air Patrol   A10s
EW   Early Warning (radar)
KTO   Kuwait Theatre of Operations   45°E

Figure 4.1   The Allied Air Attack, 17 January 1991: the first 24 hours.

(Sources: Conduct of the Persian Gulf War. An Interim Report to Congress (July 1991; John
Boatman and Barbara Starr, 'Eyes of the Storm' *JDW* 4 May 1991, pp. 735–6)

The RAF deployed 160 aircraft of 16 different types. By mid-January the RAF had a squadron of 12 Jaguars, 45 Tornado GR1 fighter bombers including 6 of the GR1a reconnaissance variant, with 18 air defence Tornado F-3s, supported by 15 tankers – VC10s, Victors and a Tristar. They were later reinforced by 6 Buccaneer aircraft to designate targets for the Tornados with their laser marking equipment.

Saudi Arabia's air force included 42 F-15 fighters and 44 Tornados, which formed a useful addition to the Allied Force. There were also the other GCC air forces, and contingents from France, with 56 Jaguars and Mirages, Italy, with 8 Tornados and Canada with 26 F/A-18s (the latter only used for defensive roles). The complete Allied air order of battle is given in Appendix B.

Iraq's air force fielded 750 fixed-wing aircraft including nearly 50 MiG-29 Fulcrum and 30 MiG-25 Foxbat fighters, as well as 170 older fighters. The MiG-29, in particular, a splendid Russian fighter, was greatly feared. 70 Mirage F-1s could be used for either air defence or ground attack, and there were 90 MiG-23 Flogger ground attack planes, the Soviet equivalent of the A-10. As it turned out, after the first few days, the Iraq pilots put up no fight at all and 'voted for peace with their afterburners.'[15] Although first impressions were that they were running scared, it was soon realised, as more and more Iraqi aircraft took shelter in neighbouring Iran, that Saddam Hussein, recognising that the air war was lost, was saving his valuable aircraft to fight another day (see page 83).

The air campaign was complex and 'highly coordinated'. One Tornado F3 navigator, flying 'top cover' described seeing the Allied air armada converging on his radar screen. 'This was a mass raid from all sides, all levels, heights, everything, running up towards the boarder and aiming to cross it together in a blanket push. They reached a certain point, switched off their IFF [Interrogate – Friend or Foe?] and in they went.'[16]

Air-to-Air Refuelling (AAR) was crucial to Allied success, permitting heavily loaded attack aircraft to reach their targets. Had the Iraqis waged any sort of coherent air campaign, they would have made special efforts to destroy the vital and vulnerable tankers and Airborne Warning and Control System (AWACS) planes, without which many of the Allied planes could not have reached their objectives. On 20 February the defence correspondents were discussing the air campaign so far at the Hyatt. 'Imagine the effect of a few MiG-29s on that tanker force' was one comment.

The air campaign was divided into four overlapping phases: suppression of Iraqi air defences; the strategic bombing campaign against industry and command and control; interdiction – cutting off the KTO; and battlefield preparation and support. The Scud hunt came under the heading of the strategic campaign, but could equally be counted as a fifth phase. About 300 sorties a day were flown against Scuds, far more than expected.

Along with Scud missiles and nuclear, biological and chemical facilities, anything that might deny command of the air to the Allies was top priority. There were 60 Iraqi airfields with 600 Hardened Aircraft shelters, and there were estimated to be 7,000 Surface-to-Air Missile (SAM) launchers and over 10,000 anti-aircraft guns. With their unique JP 233 weapon, the RAF played a major role in attacking them. The airfields were huge, with plenty of spare space to provide redundancy in the event of damage. 'Upwards of three times the size of Heathrow', the British air commander, Air Vice Marshal Wratten said after the war. He also described the 'walls of triple-A' reported by the pilots on the first raids.

After the first three days, the RAF changed its strategy. Three RAF Tornados had been lost in action, though none to AAA. Air Vice Marshal Wratten later described the change in thinking:

> To take JP 233 against these airfields was not only unnecessary but unjustified. In consultation with the Centaf planners, I agreed that our best contribution would be in the form of harassment. We would not try to close down his airfields.[17]

Inevitably, there was press speculation that this was an admission of failure, but the switch made sense. Had the Iraqis put up a fight in the air and been able to use their surface-to-air missiles to full effect, the 'middle airspace' – 15,000 to 20,000 feet, used by the USAF would have been even more dangerous than low level, where the threat was from AAA gunfire. When it became obvious that the Iraqis were not going to put up their air force, low level attack still offered the advantage of surprise. However, now the Iraqis were waiting for the Tornados, so this advantage was lost.

In addition, the US anti-radar missiles, which homed in on radar emissions, and the EF-111 and F-4G jamming aircraft proved more effective than expected. The ALARMs were so effective that the Iraqis dared not turn their radars on, and when they did 'the effective jamming of the EF-111 negated their ability to track, acquire and target attacking aircraft ... one sign of their success was that after day four, all Allied aircraft operated with impunity in the mid- to high-altitude environment.'[18] As soon as it became apparent that there was little point in attacking operating surfaces from which the enemy was not going to operate and that flying in the mid-airspace was safer, the RAF also moved into it. At over 20,000 feet the aircraft were above the ceiling of all but 100mm and larger anti-aircraft guns.[19]

The Tornado GR1 was not, admittedly, an ideal medium-level aircraft and at that stage – 21 January – could not deliver laser guided bombs, so the attacks were less accurate. Their targets were changed to radar control centres, ammunition dumps, petroleum storage depots, power stations and Scud missile sites. This prompted the deployment of the Buccaneers to designate for the Tornados and, later, Sandra and Tracey, the two new Thermal Imaging Airborne Laser Designator (TIALD) pods.[20] The first joint sortie was by two Buccaneers and two Tornados from Bahrain, which hit a railway bridge over the Euphrates on 2 February.

On 23 January, attacks on Iraqi hardened aircraft shelters started, and on 24th a Saudi Arabian pilot, Captain Aueidh Saleh Chamrani, flying an F-15, shot down two Iraqi Mirage FC1s – the first double kill by a single pilot of the war. The F1s were carrying Exocet anti-ship missiles, suggesting they were either intending to attack Allied shipping or oil storage tanks, for which they are also suitable. By this time 15,000 Allied sorties had been flown.

The air campaign was calculated, methodical, meticulous and effective. After the war, General John Galvin, who as Supreme Allied Commander Europe was not directly involved but kept informed, described how the Allies dissected Iraq's command and control. Iraq was reckoned to have the fourth (or fifth) largest military establishment in the world and certainly the biggest and best prepared in the Middle East, as even the Russians acknowledged.[21]

We dismantled immediately his capability to control and direct it. He began using microwave communications – we took those communications off the air. He turned to troposcatter communications and we wiped out his troposcatter antennas. He turned to telephone systems and we took out all the telephone centrals. He then, finally, turned to small, brick style FM – frequency modulated – radio, on which he tried, unsuccessfully to command and control the organisation. He tried to fly his airplanes and we took him out of the air in matter of a few hours. He couldn't use even his small boats. We knew every move he made in the air and then, for the first time we were able to know every move he made on the land, because we had not only AWACS and JSTARS but we had radar capabilities to know all air movements and all ground

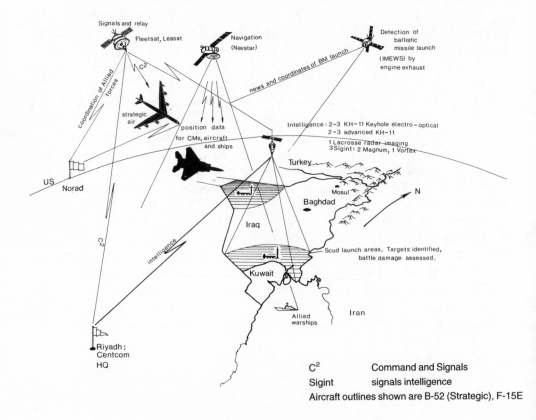

Figure 4.2 Satellites controlling the war.

(Sources: *Voyennaya Mysl'* 3/1991, p. 77; *JDW* May 1991, p. 736)

movements. We listened to practically everything, to just about everything he had to say and he couldn't communicate without our knowing it. All this is two things. This is organisation of our own force and dismantling of his.[22]

As expected this war was dominated from space, although one side had a total monopoly, and even then all the satellites did not work as advertised. The US had between 40 and 50 intelligence satellites. The KN-11 Keyhole electro-optical satellite had a resolution of several centimetres at 500 kilometres altitude. It was advertised as being able to take pictures so clear that a car registration number could be read, but the unusual amount of cloud meant that it was blind for days at a time. The newest satellite, Lacrosse, worked by radar so it was unaffected by light and cloud but failed to produce clear enough images. Ferret-D and Magnum monitored radio emissions, enabling their sources to be located and also intercepting the conversations. It was these satellites which provided the key to the assessment of Iraq's order of battle – and thus to the overestimation of Iraq's strength. The different satellites deployed are shown in Figure 4.2.

The electro-optical satellites made 14 passes over the theatre in a day, at intervals varying from 20 minutes to six hours; the radio-location satellites would make four to six passes, and the interception satellites 12. The data received from Ferret-D was processed at ground stations in Saudi Arabia. Landsat and Spot satellites-designed for the exploration of natural resources were also used, and produced the beautiful, pastel image I had seen at the British Headquarters in Riyadh. In concert with the high definition possible with the electro-optical satellites, these permitted constant monitoring of the changes in Iraqi deployment.

Satellite communications enabled the results of space reconnaissance to be transmitted to formations and units of the Coalition forces in one-and-a-half to three-and-a-half hours. At the Joint Command HQ a working group correlated the information from satellites with that from aircraft and 'humint' – agents and the Kuwaiti resistance.

IMEWS – Integrated Missile Early Warning Satellites – detected the launch of Iraqi Scud missiles earlier than was possible with AWACS aircraft, when they reached a height of 15 kilometres, or 30 seconds after launch. At first, this information had to be passed to the United States and took several minutes to come back to the theatre. Later, the system was modified and the information passed straight to Riyadh and Israel, and the Patriot batteries, which only took two minutes, and increased warning time from one to five minutes. During the war we noticed that the Scud alerts became more precise.

Satellites were also vital for communication: Fleetsat and Leasat, and for navigation. Fleetsat was used to pass information on aircraft from radar stations over the horizon in the forward zone back to the Joint Air Defence Centre in Riyadh, enabling aircraft and cruise missile flights to be monitored and corrected.

There were 15 Navstar satellites which enable forces on the ground to know where they were to within 16 metres. For centuries, knowing where you were and identifying friend from foe on the battlefield were the most difficult and unreliable factors. Now, every small unit could know exactly where it was and where friendly units were, even at night and in foul weather. Finally, there were at least two weather satellites. Apart from straight weather forecasting, which, as ever in war, proved extremely important, these were used to plot the changing areas which would be contaminated if, for example, chemical weapons were used against given objectives.

The Iraqis were sometimes able to deceive the US satellites and to conceal their missiles. Bad weather and, from about 22 February, smoke from large numbers of burning oil wells, hampered air and some satellite reconnaissance. The Iraqis could also have learned something of Allied operational plans from the pattern of satellite activity. For example, the low activity of the Fleetsatcom system bore witness to the low level of activity among naval groups during the first week of the conflict. But maybe only the Russians picked that up.[23]

The methodical progression of the air offensive also depended on accurate Battle Damage Assessment (BDA), while the coordination of 2,000 to 3,000 sorties a day without a single 'air-to-air blue-on-blue' – Allied planes crashing into or killing each other – depended on the creation of a computer-generated Air Tasking order (ATO). Recalling A.J.P. Taylor's description of World War I as 'War by Timetable', imagine redesigning the timetable for 2,000 to 3,000 trains every day, by computer, and changing it again at the last minute in response to changed circumstances and new intelligence. Targets in Iraq are shown in Figure 4.3.

On 26 January, we were briefed on Battle Damage Assessment (BDA) by a Colonel from General Schwarzkopf's Intelligence Office. It was 'deep background', a concept which the US journalists found difficult to understand. 'No tape recorders, no attributable or direct quotes', insisted the charming Lieutenant-Colonel Mike Gallagher, a Southerner. Many of the professional American military were Southerners, which gave the whole affair a slightly bizarre, *Gone With the Wind* feel. What followed epitomised the analytical spirit of 'killer intellect' alluded to in Chapter One – but that would have been no surprise to Robert E. Lee and his lieutenants, either.

The objective, our briefer said, was to bring down the opposition, not mere retaliation. This meant 'weaponeering' – designing a way of taking the target out. First of all, you define 'target sets' – command and control, military industries, and so on. There were 12 groups including leadership, bridges, oil, airfields, Scud missiles, biological and nuclear. In early February, as the ground war approached, a 13th 'battlefield preparation box' was added as number one priority. What was left over was then assigned to the other 12.

Within each target set, you selected objectives. If possible, they wanted to know how thick the walls were and who built it, so they could get the plans.

The choice of weapon is very important, but with certain weapons – for example, cluster bombs, one cannot easily see the effect. A flattened building is an impressive picture, but that may not be an appropriate way of taking out the target. It was harder to judge the effect on a target with the new 'surgical' weapons. 'But you can do yourself a favour if you totally understand the weapon and the target you're up against'.

The Central Command planners measured the success of their attacks by the response of the Iraqi logistic system, by what the Iraqis tried to replace, and by any

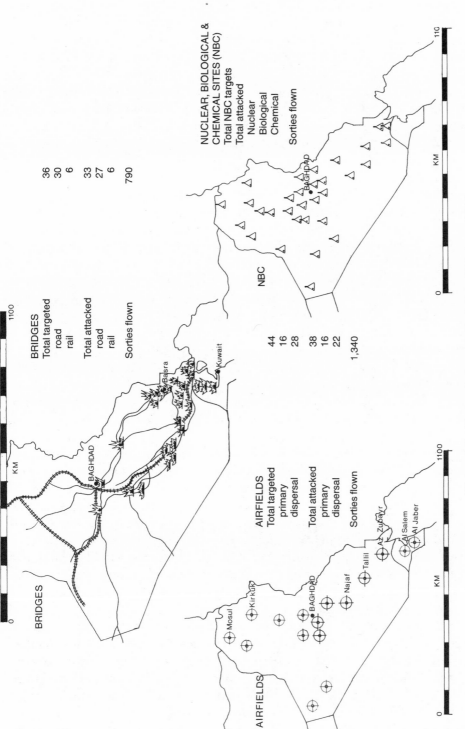

Figure 4.3 Targets in Iraq attacked up to 30 January 1991.
(Source: General Schwarzkopf's briefing 30 January 1991)

discernible effect on the morale of the Iraqi people. The initial assessments of target sets might have been wrong. If you have 100 targets in the set and identify 40 as 'key', and you then destroy those 40 and the set still goes on working, then you were wrong.

'Media is good', however, the Colonel added. The Americans learned of Scud launches from satellites, AWACS and their own pilots flying top cover over Iraq, and watched re-entry on CNN. CNN and Reuter were the first reports they had by which they could evaluate their own or the Iraqis' success or failure. Then came reports from pilots, then intelligence reports. 'The first reports will tell you that an event has taken place, the second that it has taken place but that you maybe haven't done as well as you thought.'

Lines of Communication were another target set. Bridges, we were told, seldom came in ones. 'These things usually come in threes'. Weaponeering a bridge was not easy. Do you want to bring a bridge down, by cutting the span which is relatively easily repaired, or cut it permanently, in which case you have to take out the abutments? And permanent bridges, liked by laser guided bombs, were different from pontoon bridges. 'Dumb bombs prefer pontoons.'

The shift from the air war to the ground war was subtle, a 'sliding time line', the Colonel said. Analysis of the effect of attacks on troops in the field was even more difficult than that of attacks on strategic targets, although this was probably the first time that a field army would ever be defeated, *preponderantly*, by air power. 'How do you shift from a facilities-oriented target base to BDA or an assessment of your abilities against troops? You can't just look down there and see people in fox holes – that just doesn't happen. *What has he asked for? Where does he go when he's hurt? Has he asked for people? Does he come together when he's told?* The first B-52 attacks on Republican Guard units had occurred, but the colonel was careful. 'It's too early to tell what kind of unit integrity exists.'

An important part of BDA was assessing the effect of cutting the logistic chain. Different sized formations could last different lengths of time, and if you cut the links between them you could work out the effect, from isolating battalions, brigades, divisions, corps, and, finally, the theatre command from the national logistic base. Divisions could last several days on their own stores, so cutting the link between corps and division was a high priority.

Runways were another problem. If the Third World War had happened in Europe, the Americans reckoned they could have repaired a runway in one-and-a-half hours. Although, in theory, the best mode of attack against a runway was straight along it, this made the attacking aircraft so vulnerable to triple A that a diagonal attack proved to be the best. But the US intelligence team was impressed by the Iraqis' ability to repair runways. 'Getting round the damage we're doing to fuel and ammo storage – that's difficult,' he said. 'And how do you determine the strength of the Air Force when he's hiding in bunkers – shelters equal to or better than any seen in Europe. Busting bunkers is a long process . . .' he added. 'The number of airplanes destroyed you know from shootdown. Everything else is speculation.'

The previous day, Friday 25th, there had also been reports that Saddam Hussein had executed some of his senior Air Force and Air Defence Force officers – about 135, they told us. The Americans took the reports seriously. 'Why am I doing that? Because he has a history of doing that. How does one individual maintain that kind of grip?'

Saddam was maintaining his grip.

Among the disciplines spawned by the new – or revived – cerebral school of war was 'craterology'. The US BDA teams had 'craterologists', who analysed photographs of US attacks and also the effect of the incoming Scuds. Against hard targets, you would expect a warhead with a relatively heavy case and correspondingly less explosive. But, as expected, the Scuds we had received had lots of explosive and little casing, creating greater overpressure in the surrounding area. A terror weapon. 'Look for very large blast marks. Buckling six feet up,' we were told. Comforting, that.[24]

By the end of the air campaign, coordination between Washington and Riyadh had become so good that a target found by a Pentagon analyst by 16.00 one day was destroyed by the next morning and a photograph of the damage would be on the analyst's desk when he reported for work (US Eastern Standard Time being 8 hours behind Riyadh time). This practice of close contact between intelligence analysts and those fighting the war is seldom practised in peacetime, but is learned in real war. 'I don't know how many times we have to relearn that', a senior US Defense Department official said.[25]

We received another briefing on the Air Tasking Order (ATO) in mid-February. The ATO depended on constant inputs from the Battle Damage Assessment people. Gentle touches to the rudder from General Schwarzkopf – 'put a little more emphasis here' – would have an effect two days later. The Night Targeting Cell, which included representatives of the other Allies, would reconcile the weapons needed with the targets requested. They would finish work at 04.00 to 05.00 each morning on the day before execution. Next came 'fraggers' – because they dealt with fragments of the operation – who tasked each type of plane. They then handed over to the 'stubby pencil guys', who would work out how much fuel was needed for each type of plane and whether the job was feasible. They programmed the Computer Assisted Force Management System (CAFMS), which generated the 250-page daily Air Tasking Order. About 150–200 people were directly involved in this process, a number rising to 300 if you count those counting bombs at all the bases. That afternoon, they finished their work, the ATO was published, and distributed to the air bases.

When a target was hit and it was assessed that the required damage was achieved, it was taken out of the ATO. Hundreds of 'intelligence-type analysts' were employed on this work. 'Are we hitting the right aiming points on targets?' was a key question. The Air Control Centre was the size of a ballroom, and General Charles Horner, the overall air commander, had daily meetings with up to 100 people present. A second room, called 'guidance and apportionment' had 50 people. There was one 'fragger' for each type of unit – F-16, A-10 and so on. The risk of damage to civilian targets was raised at the start of every briefing, to ensure that it was at the forefront of everybody's mind.

The ATO also included a number of undetermined missions allocated to Forward

Air Controllers. Each formation's movements had to be coordinated with the movements of AWACS, tankers, the Air Control Centre (TACC) and Forward Air Controllers. Air-to-Air refuelling was especially delicate. If too many aircraft were assigned to one tanker, by the time the last aircraft had refuelled it would be time for the first to refuel again.

The ATO also included an airspace control order, covering civil air traffic (although there was little over Saudi Arabia at that time). Another consideration was the presence of similar aircraft on opposing sides. 'We don't fly Mirages into an area where there could be enemy Mirages', we were told.

Each Allied Squadron had its own mission planning cell, a group of three to four pilots, on duty for two to three nights, to 'figure out what the frags were saying'. Then they would work out the time over target, the time it would take to get there and thus the take-off time. Pilots were briefed two-and-a-quarter to two-and-a-half hours before take-off.

Pilot reports were suspect as indicators of how well the aircraft had done against their targets. Cloud and smoke were likely to get in the way. But at least, at this stage, both sides on the ground were static. 'Only if we're going forward does it become fluid', the briefer stressed. Close Air Support (CAS) aircraft generally did not know where their targets were in advance, and all you could do was predict that there would be more sorties in one area than another. However, the attacking aircraft's flexibility was limited because, once fuzed, bombs could not be dropped below a certain height.

The air campaign also gave the CAS pilots the chance to hone their skills in real war before they had to integrate their efforts with the ground campaign. By mid-February, after 30 days of war, a pilot, a Lieutenant, could describe the learning curve.

'The first time I went out there it looked like a vast brown desert with scars in it. The second time I began figuring out what those scars might be, plus the FAC tells us what's in that bunker and what you're going at.'

'I see a turret sticking out of it, and I saw colour. I'm saying I improved my capability well over 100 per cent. Experience is the key to this. You know what to be afraid of. You don't lose fear, apprehension, but you know how high it can come, plus, as we attrit them, the SAMs, you can come down a little bit, get a little bit closer to your work.'

'The other thing you realise is that I'm flying in three miles high'.

At that height – 15,000 feet, – the tanks must have looked like ants.

'Exactly. A very good analogy.'

Sometimes, the pilots reported seeing targets off to one side and might be told 'we're already fragged x on it.'

The attacks on Iraqi troops resulted not so much in bomb cratering as in scars by troop emplacements, brownish-black in colour. And it was virtually impossible to tell what was Republican Guard and what was not, the pilots said. The SAM sites were huge – 'several acres'. The A-10s flew most sorties – perhaps two a day, with F-16s flying fewer and descending down to the B-52s, which, obviously flew least of all.

Some of the pilots, we were told, were terribly tired by this time, barely able to stay awake in briefings.[26]

Under these circumstances, is it surprising that on one occasion, 26 February, A-10s mistook British armoured vehicles three miles below for Iraqis? Or were the A-10 pilots, in particular, still too aggressive, loutish in their behaviour, even towards their friends, as I had observed on 1 February? 'Squadron commanders do not tolerate cowboy-ism. Air discipline's a big thing', we were told. Had it not been, and had the US and other Air Forces not been punctilious, consummately professional and, by the start of the ground offensive, well practised in real war, there would have been many, many more friendly-fire incidents.

Between 20 and 23 January, the Iraqis released quantities of oil into the Gulf from oil storage tanks at Al Fuhayhil and five moored tankers off the Kuwaiti coast. The crude oil from the tankers was heavier than that from the Sea Island terminal. The motives could have been sheer malice, the desire to impede a possible amphibious landing, of which the Iraqis were very afraid (although the discharge of oil would not have had much effect), to damage Saudi beaches and water desalination plants down the coast, or to provoke the Allies into a precipitate and therefore bloody assault. The desalination plants were designed to resist such accidents, but floating booms were installed as an extra precaution. Two such plants at al-Jubayl provided 250 million gallons of water a day, supplying three-quarters of Riyadh's requirements.

On 25 January, the US accused Saddam Hussein of an act of 'environmental terrorism.' There was outrage worldwide, perhaps best summarised by Prince Abdul Aziz bin Salman of the Saudi Ministry of Petroleum, Oil and Minerals, who described Saddam as 'the Lord of Death or the Lord of Disasters. He is definitely the father of destruction.' Experts estimated that the spill, coming from the five tankers and the offshore terminal at Mina al-Ahmadi, might be up to a dozen times – some estimates were 15 times – larger than the *Exxon Valdez* disaster in Alaska in March 1989.

Thwarting environmental catastrophe is one of the more promising future uses of military power. On Saturday night, 26 January, we received a foretaste of what might be possible in the future when US F-111 bombers with GBU-15 laser guided bombs attacked the manifolds – assemblies of pipes and valves – controlling the flow of oil from the storage areas on shore to the Sea Island terminal.

The following day, at 20.00, General Schwarzkopf told the story of the successful mission. He used sketches based on air photographs to overcome classification problems, a technique which General Powell in Washington had pioneered the previous week. I sketched them hastily, as in Figure 4.4. As in all military operations, luck had played an important part. During Friday, the US Air Force had consulted with oil experts, representatives of Aramco, the Saudi oil company, and Saudi environmental agencies. It had quickly become obvious that 'the best thing we could do would be to set the source of this oil spill on fire', General Schwarzkopf said. Oil was flowing from the Sea Island terminal itself and an oiling buoy further out to sea. That night, by chance, Allied forces detected an Iraqi vessel next to the Sea Island terminal and opened fire, setting it ablaze, stemming the flow from the buoy and much reducing the flow from the terminal.

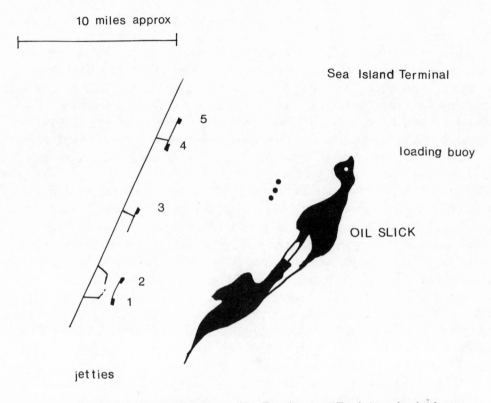

10 miles approx

Sea Island Terminal

loading buoy

OIL SLICK

jetties

a.   Situation 12.27 pm local 24 January 1991. (Based upon satellite photography, sketches
     used to reduce classification for General Schwarzkopf's presentation). Numbers 1–5
     indicate oil tankers, contributing to the slick.

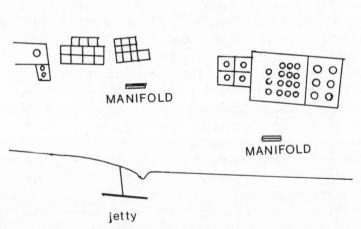

miles

0   5

MANIFOLD

MANIFOLD

jetty

b.   Circles indicate oil storage tanks of varying sizes.

Figure 4.4   Author's sketches of the attack on the oil manifolds.

Knowing the design of the two storage complexes and the manifolds lying seaward of them, the USAF learned that destroying the manifolds would stem the oil flow completely, although they could be repaired in about two weeks – important for post-war reconstruction. This was a consideration which, we learned from the British Embassy, was already exercising a powerful influence on Allied plans. General Schwarzkopf then showed video taken from the missiles as they did their *kamikaze* dives into the manifolds.

On 26 January, a huge fireball could be seen at the Sea Island terminal. The following day it had subsided and the smoke was a different colour, indicating that the oil was lower in the water. Some oil continued to pour out, as there was 13 miles of it in the pipes between the manifolds and the terminal. But although the slick was, by now, 35 miles long and 10 wide, the operation had stemmed the flow and been an unqualified success.

At the same Sunday briefing, we heard reports of Iraqi planes fleeing to Iran the previous day (26th). The Iranian government had said that any aircraft landing there would remain there until the end of the conflict. The next day, 28 January, 100 aircraft, including 39 combat planes, were reported to have landed in Iran – indicating a deliberate policy, not random defections. With hindsight, it seems that the aim was to conserve Iraq's Air Force – Saddam Hussein had used the same tactic in the First Gulf War, when he sent some of it to Jordan. The timing was no coincidence. USAF F-117s, F-111s and A-10s had started attacking Hardened Aircraft Shelters (HAS) on 23 January, quickly demonstrating that there was no hiding place for Iraqi aircraft in Iraq.[27] The GBU-27 900lb laser guided bomb with a hard, steel case proved particularly effective against HAS.

During the war as a whole, 122 aircraft flew to Iran, including 115 combat aircraft (24 Mirage F1s, 4 Su-20s, 40 Su-22s, 24 Su-24s, 7 Su-25s, 12 MiG-23s, 4 MiG-29s). At least one Adnan Airborne Early Warning aircraft – a most significant asset – also fled: the other two were believed destroyed on the ground. These included, the Iraqis 'lost' over 400 aircraft, including 35 fixed wing aircraft shot down in air-to-air combat (9 Mirage F-1s, 4 Su-7s or 17s, 2 Su-22s, 2 Su-25s, 4 MiG-21s, 7 MiG-23s, 2 MiG-25s and 5 MiG-29s). The remainder were destroyed on the ground.[28]

On 31 January, the UK agreed to allow RAF Fairford, Gloucestershire, to be used as a base for B-52 strategic bombers, substantially reducing the time for each B-52 mission. By 1 February, there had been 35,000 Allied air sorties, 19,000 of them US, and France agreed to let the B-52s overfly France, further assisting the giant bombers in their destructive missions.

A most important part of the 'air' war was waged by the two Navies prosecuting offensive operations against Iraq: the US Navy and Royal Navy. In every war scenario against the great continental adversary, the West won the war at sea, and so it was in the Gulf, spectacularly. The whole of the Iraqi Navy was destroyed, mainly by helicopter attack. In all, 34 combatants (seven Osa missile craft, six P-6 torpedo craft, seven inshore patrol craft, eight mine countermeasures vessels and six amphibious ships) were destroyed.

On 29 January, some RAF Jaguars detected Iraqi fast patrol boats off the Kuwaiti coast, probably part of the combined operation against the Saudi port of Khafji. There were probably 17 boats, ranging from large barges to 20 foot fast patrol craft, and all armed with missile launchers and machine guns. Lynx helicopters from three British ships, *Gloucester*, *Cardiff* and *Brazen* attacked the flotilla with Sea Skua missiles leaving two sunk or damaged and scattering the rest, which were then attacked by fixed-wing planes as they scurried for shelter.[29] I had worked on the early procurement of Sea Skua in the Ministry of Defence 13 years before, a missile designed to knock out medium-sized craft, and it was strangely gratifying to see it being so successful. For the next two days the 'Battle of Bubiyan Channel' continued. According to the British Joint Commander, it 'broke the back of Iraqi naval resistance' and led the Allied naval commander to declare Coalition sea control of the Gulf on 8 February. A year later, I visited HMS *Cardiff* on another trip to the Gulf and made the acquaintance of its pale grey helicopter, which had proved one of the most efficient killing machines of the war.

On 6 February, Sandra and Tracey, the two RAF TIALD pods for Tornado, arrived at Tabuk. On 9 February, they were declared operationally ready, further increasing the RAF's ability to strike targets with precision and thus releasing US aircraft such as F-15s and F-111s to go after Scud launchers. TIALD could either be used autonomously – enabling a Tornado to designate its own target, suitable for targets of opportunity, or to designate for other Tornados. It could keep the laser spot on a target at ranges from 5 kilometres for a tank to 30 kilometres for a power station. Because it has a thermal imager and a television camera, it can 'see' the target in different weather conditions, and it proved valuable for reconnaissance as well as targeting.

The first TIALD attack involved four sorties against Hardened Aircraft Shelters in the giant H3 airbase complex in western Iraq. On 11 February, two sorties took place against the Hachama rail bridge near Samawah, south of Baghdad. Six laser guided bombs caused severe damage to the structure.[30] On the third day of TIALD operations, 12 February, Air Commmodore Ian Macfadyen gave the regular press briefing in Riyadh, and revealed the existence of the new pods. The TIALD attacks from Tabuk are shown in Figure 4.5.

At 04.00 the next morning, 13 February, US bombers over Baghdad – presumably F-117s – struck a concrete bunker, one of five such fortifications, in the Amiriyah district of western Baghdad, killing an estimated 400 civilians, many women and children, who were inside. They were mainly members of the families of the Ba'ath party élite. The US said they believed it was a command centre, claiming to have intercepted messages from it. Troops had been seen leaving it, it was surrounded by an earthen berm, and it had a camouflage pattern painted on the roof. But journalists taken to inspect the scene said they saw no evidence of communications equipment or military use. After the war, it emerged that any important facility in Iraq was camouflaged and surrounded by barbed wire – including grain elevators, food storage and even the widely publicized baby milk factory. In fact, the camouflage generally worked against the Iraqis because the splodges of green paint made facilities stand out against the greyish-pinky-yellow desert. Was the attack on the Amiriyah shelter a genuine mistake? Had the Iraqis deliberately lured the Americans to attack it and then removed signals equipment as a callous ruse to create international opprobrium and discredit the Allied claims that they were able to conduct high precision bombing against military targets? Or was it, indeed, a 'command target', but of a broader kind?

On 14 February, I recorded in my diary that we had been told it was a 'leadership target'. Later, the briefer told us it was a 'command and control centre'. Perhaps a Freudian slip – the two categories were different. The leadership and its families were the top, ruling class of Iraq. I suspected that the attack might have been deliberate, even if women and children were put at risk. They were, after all, Iraq's future as well as present leadership. Or maybe they thought Saddam Hussein might be inside. A *leadership target. . . .*

US Signals Intelligence was so good that one doubted whether there could have been a mistake, unless the Iraqis were deliberately deceiving the Allies. Certainly, one ruled out carelessness.

The US ability to destroy individual targets with great accuracy had led the Iraqis to abandon using specially constructed shelters. After the Amariyah shelter incident, nine similar shelters were erased from US target lists.

Another setback to the Allies' punctiliously precise bombing campaign apparently occurred at 16.20 on 13th when three RAF bombs missed their target, a bridge at al-Fallujah, and one landed 800 metres to the right, in a market place. The Iraqis claimed that the incident happened on 14th, and that a Tornado was downed. The RAF said they attacked two bridges, one adjacent to Fallujah and one north of there, on 13 February, but had not lost a plane. They did lose one on 14th, attacking an airfield. 'It's just interesting that they're a day out and that they're claiming an aircraft', Niall Irving, the RAF spokesman commented. The aircraft attacked down the river to minimise the chance of civilian casualties, although the best chance of hitting the bridge would have been obtained by attacking along its axis. They showed the film taken by the Buccaneer designator aircraft. There were some direct hits on the bridge but two bombs fell short and one veered off towards the town. 'Three of the bombs didn't guide for one reason or another', said Group Captain Irving, speculating that the vanes at the back were not working properly. It was just one of those things. 'We fly a *long way* to drop those bombs', he stressed. 'Nobody wanted to waste them'. The frankness with which the RAF showed the film went a long way to disarming allegations that they were being devious or secretive, and was a valuable reminder that in war the surgical precision selected videos had suggested could never be completely guaranteed. 'It took a lot of knocking on doors to get it [ie. permission to show the film]. We spent most of the day working on it', he said.

Whatever the reason, the much more serious destruction of the Baghdad bunker was a setback to the Allies' image. On 14 February, it was suggested that as many as 100 of the 150 strategic targets remaining in and around Baghdad might be dropped. But after nearly a month of the air war, it seemed extraordinary that they were still trying to dislocate command and control. The emphasis was in any case shifting, towards isolating the battlefield and the destruction of Iraq's army in the field. In my diary, I recorded that there was 'division among senior US commanders as to whether to go on hitting Baghdad. To *me*, it certainly doesn't make sense. Surely the time has come to smash front line troops above all.'

The RAF TIALD teams attacked aircraft shelters at H2 and Mudaysis in central Iraq on 15 February, and at H3 on 16th. On 17th they switched to bridges, on 19th attacked ammunition dumps, and on 20th, as the ground offensive approached, switched again to airfields near the Kuwait border to impede the Iraqis from flying aircraft with chemical weapons down from northern Iraq.

On 18 February, some of us were taken by C-160 Transal, the two engined French version of the Hercules, to the French airbase at al-Ahsa. It lies east of Riyadh, and south of the main Riyadh–Dhahran road. And very French it was: very compact, very balanced, very neat. It was surrounded by small, sandy hills, which created an

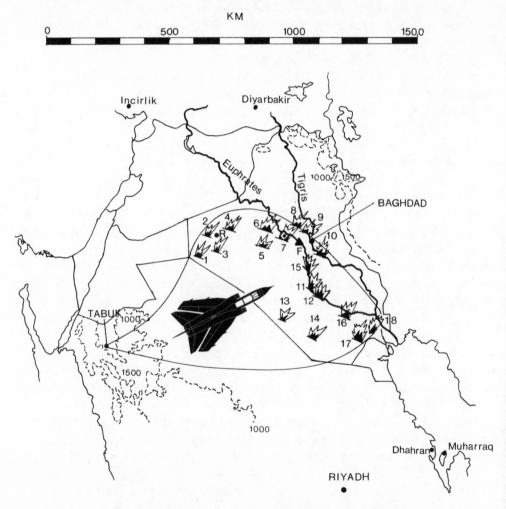

Figure 4.5   TIALD attacks from Tabuk, 10–27 February 1991.

(Source: GEC–Ferranti, *TIALD, The Gulf War* (1991), p. 33)

artificial impression of remoteness. There was a squadron of Mirage-2000 air superiority fighters, half a squadron of Mirage F1 CRs and some Jaguar reconnaissance planes to spy out the land and two squadrons of Jaguar attack planes. Neat sandbagged walls protected the radars, while the paths were all marked with white stones.

The French clearly thought they were not getting enough attention and had laid on the facility for the '*Anglo-Saxons*' – British and American press. They were most forthcoming, telling us the exact number of aircraft. We hoped, secretly, that we might get some of the fabled French rations, including a half-litre of wine. The food was, as expected, superb, but there was no wine in dry Saudi Arabia, not even for the French.

Colonel Hervé Longuet wore the eagle insignia of a US colonel: he was obviously

KEY

TIALD – Thermal and TV Imaging Airborne Laser Designator

 1. Ruwayshid
 2. H3 North-West
 3. H3 South-West
 4. H2
 5. Mudaysis
 6. Al Asad
 7. Ar Ramadi (road bridge)
 8. Al Habbaniyah
 9. Al Taqaddum
10. Ubaydah bin al Jarrah
11. As Samawah (road bridge)
12. As Samawah (rail bridge)
13. Wadi al Khirr
14. Ghalaysan
15. Hachama (rail bridge)
16. Tallil
17. Jalibah South-East
18. Shuaibah

F – Fallujah (bombs, *not* TIALD, went astray)
R – Ar Rutbah
Hachama is near Samawah

Dotted lines indicate high ground – 1,000 and 1,500 metres in northern Saudi Arabia and Iraq.
Outline is a Tornado Gr-1.

fed up with people not recognising who he was from the arcane French system of gold and silver bars. As well as these, the other French officers all wore the ubiquitous 'Saudi equivalent rank badge', with black crowns and stars on a leather tab – but then, everyone in Riyadh did as well, including General Schwarzkopf.[31] Among the French here, exquisite silk scarves and expensive sunglasses were *de rigeur*.

The 5th Tactical Fighter Wing, which flew the Mirage-2000s, had flown 1,000 hours or 400 combat air patrols, without seeing a single Iraqi aircraft. 'It's a bit disappointing to spend a lot of time in the air without seeing or doing anything,' said Lieutenant Colonel Stephane Abrial, its commander. He thought that when the ground campaign began, they might see Iraqi aircraft trying to engage Allied troops – but, in the event that never materialised, either.

None of the French Jaguars were lost to accident or enemy action, in part, the pilots believed, because they were two-engined. Colonel Longuet showed videos of French attacks on Iraqi hardened aircraft shelters with the AS-30 missile – a superbly accurate weapon – which dived into the doors.

If I had any doubts that the Allies had plans to use nuclear and chemical weapons, they were dispelled, as we were taken to the operations cell *'nucléaire'*, although its main preoccupation now was the possibility of chemical attack. The French NBC officer reckoned that 80 per cent of useful protection was in the mask: the same conclusion we had drawn.

Meanwhile, the air attacks had inflicted constant attrition on Iraqi ground forces. On 8 February, US Defense Secretary Dick Cheney had arrived in Riyadh to hear the Central Command assessment of how the air campaign was going. About 600 Iraqi tanks out of 5,500, including 4,200 in the KTO had been destroyed, and 400 artillery pieces out of 3,000 in the KTO. These assessments were fairly conservative. Those figures matched other reports of 15 to 20 per cent destruction of armoured vehicles. However, with damage to command, control and resupply and the Allies' total air superiority, the effect on the overall Iraqi ability to wage war was undoubtedly far greater. The next day, the estimate of systems completely destroyed was increased, to 750 tanks, 650 guns, and 600 other armoured fighting vehicles out of 2,600. Mr Cheney stressed that there was 'no magic trigger ... no 38 per cent destruction of tanks.'[32] At the time I wondered about 38 per cent – that seemed a pretty good trigger, actually.

There was a risk that the law of diminishing returns applied: the easy targets had gone: those which remained were more difficult. The ground offensive might be launched once the law of diminishing returns really began to bite. However, there was an alternative view, that the air campaign was more successful than expected. If it works better than you thought, carry on with it. Perhaps you can do it all from the air, after all. Perversely, the very success of the air campaign might lead to its extension, rather than its curtailment.

On Thursday 14 February, St Valentine's day, estimates of the key ground systems destroyed by air attack were increased to 1,300 tanks out of 4,200, 1,100 artillery pieces out of 3,000 and 800 other armoured vehicles out of 2,600 – nearly 30 per cent. The loss of the artillery, the main means of delivering chemical weapons, was particularly significant. Lieutenant General Tom Kelly, the Pentagon spokesman, described Iraq's military position as 'precarious'. The Iraqi troop casualties were 'very high' and the threat posed by chemical and biological weapons had diminished. 'While there is still a threat from that it is nowhere near as significant as it was at the outset.'[33]

The Allies had now flown 70,000 sorties, with 2,800 in the previous 24 hours, of which 800 were on targets in Kuwait and 200 on the Republican Guard. The Allies estimated they had cut the peacetime capacity of the roads in the KTO – estimated at 80,000 tons a day – by half. The US Army claimed to have cut Iraqi supplies by 90 per cent. By 15 February, 27 out of 31 main bridges on key routes were down. They had responded by putting pontoon bridges over the rivers or by building crude, earthwork dams. Allied aircraft had prevented the Iraqis from running supply convoys and the last attempt, had resulted in over 50 trucks being destroyed.[34] Reporters with the British troops now south of the Iraqi border reported devastating raids by US B-52s on Iraqi positions, which were not only seen but heard 30 miles away. Reports that 7-ton BLU-82B 'daisy cutter' bombs were being dropped on minefields and Iraqi defensive positions (these were not, as often erroneously reported, Fuel-Air Explosive weapons) and occasional Fuel-Air Explosive devices (although they were not used *en masse*, but held back as a possible form of retaliation against chemical attack) made it clear that the final preparations for a ground attack were underway.

The relative value of the strategic and tactical air campaigns is hard to assess, and Pentagon officials themselves were divided. One analyst, William M. Arkin, working for Greenpeace, has derided the role of the strategic campaign. He was able to inspect 13 of the 30 targeted leadership and command bunkers; 49 of the 170 command, control and communication sites, 16 of 20 oil refinery and distribution facilities and all 75 rail and road bridges attacked, and to compare US Air Force target lists with damage inflicted.

Mr Arkin concluded that much electronic equipment – computers and telephone circuitry – had been withdrawn from the concrete facilities, so that the Air Force only destroyed empty buildings. Powerplants near Basra were on the access and exit routes of many Allied air attacks and were therefore used as secondary targets, so they were hit repeatedly. Of more than 800 targets, perhaps 50 were misidentified. Attacks on oil storage sites were less effective than supposed, so that petrol was still cheap after the war. In spite of protestations that Saddam Hussein himself was not a target, Mr Arkin alleges that the USAF 'racked their brains trying to figure out how to kill Saddam, but they could not get it done. They just didn't have a clue where the Iraqi leadership was.'[35]

Pentagon officials disputed Arkin's view that the air campaign was efficient, legal, but largely irrelevant. 'Iraq was paralysed strategically and could not talk to, feed, reinforce or withdraw its Army. It was helpless and on its own, a situation in which individuals can survive, but not an army,' an Air Force Officer said. It was pure Douhet. One of the targeteers put it more strongly. 'If you don't believe the strategic air war affected the outcome of the Persian Gulf conflict, you just don't understand modern war. There are a significant number of people in uniform that don't understand that there has been a revolution in warfare.'[36]

The strategic campaign and the final tactical preparation overlapped and were interdependent. Two powerplants in the Basra area and a nearby switching station were pounded by non-precision weapons because they were earmarked to pump oil into the fire trench system designed as an obstacle to the Allied ground force. Because the Allies knew little about the system, they bombed all six generators. Later, when intelligence improved, F-117s were used on three consecutive nights to destroy the 23 junctions at major distribution points so that more oil could not be pumped in, while oil already in the trenches was set on fire.[37]

By 22 February, 90,000 Allied sorties had been flown. On Saturday 23 February, we were told 1,685 of the 4,200 Iraqi tanks in the KTO were reported destroyed, and 1,485 artillery pieces out of 3,000. Between 50,000 and 54,000 tons of explosive ordance had been dropped on Iraq and Kuwait.[38] There was no 'magic trigger' but 50 per cent was as good as any . . .

It later emerged that the Coalition had indeed fixed 50 per cent destruction of armour and artillery as the tripwire for the ground war – a figure exceeded by about 10 per cent, with F-111s with Pave Tack and A-10s with Maverick missiles accounting for about 1,000 armoured vehicles each. With this kind of accuracy, the traditional balance of forces on the ground required for a ground attack had changed from three-to-one to one-to-one.[39]

Reconnaissance by Battle

January–February 1991

The Battle of Khafji, from 29 to 31 January, was the first significant ground battle of the war and the biggest in Saudi military history up to that time, as the Saudi Joint Commander, Lieutenant General Prince Khalid bin Sultan, told us with some pride. Muhammad's battles, in the 7th Century of the Western calendar, had been small affairs, between a few hundred tribesmen, and the fighting which attended the creation of the modern Kingdom after the First World War involved only some hundreds of armed men. In 1902, King Abdul Aziz ibn Saud captured Riyadh by surprise with about 40 men and in 1913 broke the Turkish hold on the Hofuf area with 600 men, but individual battles were smaller.[1] When the Iraqis put a 'brigade minus' across the border, the Saudis wanted to defend their own territory and show what their Army and National Guard could do, and General Schwarzkopf was happy to oblige.

The Saudis had evacuated Khafji right at the start of the crisis, in August 1990, as it was within range of Iraqi artillery and chemical weapons. When the war started on 17 January, Iraqi artillery bombardment set the oil refinery alight. Leaving such a forward position virtually unoccupied was a normal defensive technique, probably pioneered by the Germans in the First World War when they had only light patrols covering the forward edge of their defences, leading to the 'forlorn loneliness of the front line'. Khafji was even lonelier – it was empty, apart from two six-man US Marine reconnaissance groups, and the odd TV crew, whose broadcasts brought Khafji's apparent emptiness to Iraq's attention. After two weeks of terrible pounding by the Allied Air Forces, and unable to respond, the Iraqi command felt it had to do something, even if the forces committed were doomed. At least they might win a few propaganda points – and they did gain a headline, though little else.

The Iraqi force that moved into Khafji at around 22.30 on 29 January was one of two thrusts by the 5th Mechanised Division. The western thrust, by 20 Mechanised Brigade, was struck by Allied aircraft in the desert and forced to disperse on the border or driven back beyond it. The main, eastern thrust was by 15 Mechanised

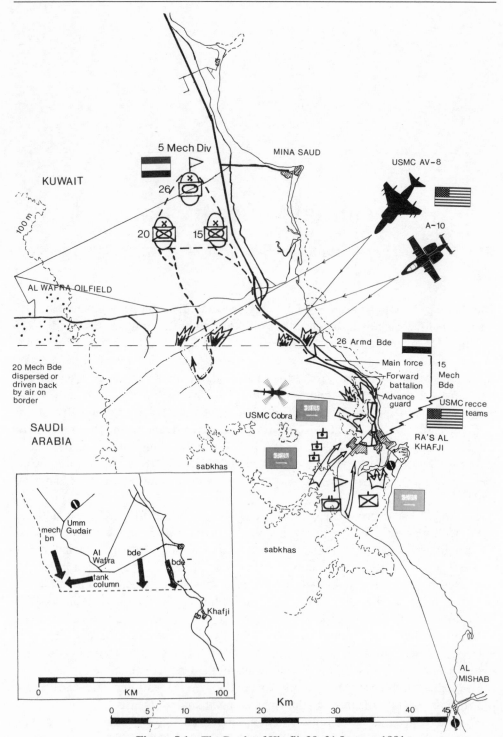

Figure 5.1   The Battle of Khafji, 29–31 January 1991.

(Sources: Briefings by General Schwarzkopf, Wednesday 30 January and General Prince Khalid, 8 February 1991)

Brigade, while 26 Armoured Brigade was held back, as most countries' military doctrine would expect, as an armoured reserve to exploit success.

Another two thrusts took place to the west, south of the Umm Gudair oilfield, where 11 US Marines were reported killed, the first Western casualties on the ground.

Analysing the battle of Khafji a week later, on 8 February, Prince Khalid showed how the 15 Mechanised Brigade broke down into an advance guard, forward battalion and main force. Behind this came 26th Brigade, which was destroyed by Allied air attack.

Prince Khalid indicated that the main military reason for recapturing Khafji immediately was to rescue the two US reconnaissance teams. They were also instrumental in the operation, as they continued to direct Allied artillery fire from among the surrounding Iraqis, while remaining undetected. It was also face saving. Inevitably, some of the press howled that the Allies had been surprised, but an armoured column of about 2,000 men and 50 tanks – 'a brigade minus', as Brigadier-General Richard Neal, the US Deputy Director of Operations and spokesman described it – can easily emerge from the clutter of several divisions and drive 15 kilometres very quickly. That is why you have defence in depth. The force which entered Khafji itself was about 600 men.

Once ensconced in a built-up area, the Iraqis were difficult to dislodge. General Schwarzkopf quickly decided that the Saudis should retake the town with Qatari help and US and British aircraft and artillery in support – A-10s, Jaguars, US Marine Cobras and 155mm guns. The Saudis and Qataris converged on the town late on 30th. The Iraqis beat back several attempts to drive them out, but the Allies entered the town at 07.30 on 31st and had largely retaken it by 13.00. Lieutenant General Khalid, who had also briefed reporters at the scene on 31 January, using a map propped against the remains of a BTR-60 Armoured Personnel Carrier, said the whole area 'had been cleared of Iraqi forces' by 13.45 hours, although artillery and rocket fire, including Brazilian-made Astros rocket launchers used by both sides, continued during the night.

One of the captured US reconnaissance teams was rescued at about 11.30 hours,

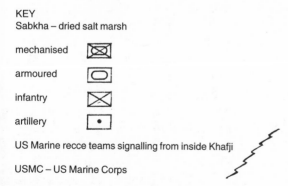

KEY

Sabkha – dried salt marsh

mechanised

armoured

infantry

artillery

US Marine recce teams signalling from inside Khafji

USMC – US Marine Corps

The move into Khafji was one of four thrusts. After the war, intelligence experts believed that the prime aim of these movements was simply to reconnoitre allied deployments south of the Kuwait/Saudi border, as the Iraqis by this time had no other means of finding out.

the other an hour later. Even then, there was the risk of more attacks. At about noon, another Iraqi incursion, with 80 tanks was seen moving south towards Khafji. Some reports said they had their turrets reversed, meaning that they might be trying to surrender. But this was apparently a ruse: they turned and fired on the Saudi troops screening the town.

Prince Khalid's maps, reproduced in Figure 5.1, indicated that the successful counter-attack had involved three Allied artillery batteries, a tank battalion and infantry company, although we were told that full details would not be available as they would compromise the Allied order of battle in the area. On 8 February, we were told that the Iraqis had lost 32 dead, 35 wounded and 463 Prisoners of War, plus 11 tanks in the town itself: the Allies lost 18 dead and 32 wounded. Aircraft also destroyed 15 other Iraqi vehicles withdrawing north, and US artillery may have destroyed another 17.[2] It was an intense little battle, but the Saudis were cock-a-hoop. The presence of the Saudi Army and National Guard – forces balanced so that neither might acquire political dominance – underlined the political nature of the operation. In this, as in the great operation to come, political considerations exercised constant influence. In the short term, the Iraqi incursion made the Allies jittery, suggesting that more attacks were in store. This resulted in the incorrect reports of large scale Iraqi movements on 31st (see Chapter 3).

The relative inaction of the ground forces inevitably led to some frustration, though more for the journalists, many of whom who had been deployed with a view to covering the ground offensive, rather than the air war which was best done from Riyadh – or Baghdad. On 23 January, Robert Fisk reported apparent chaos near the front, but with the number of armoured vehicles involved that impression was inevitable. Anybody who has dealt with armoured vehicles in mud on a military exercise expects to see the odd one bogged down.[3]

As General Powell constantly reminded Dick Cheney, 'We're not in the business of running an air campaign, stopping it, and running the ground campaign. There's a certain synergism, if you will, between air forces, ground forces, amphibious forces.' The air campaign, Mr Cheney said, might be more effective if ground action forced the Iraqis to move.[4]

An example of the overlap occurred on 26 January when the US Army made the first use of the new Army Tactical Missile System (ATACMS) in combat, against a surface-to-air missile site. The ATACMS operational test battery had been quietly moved from the artillery school at Fort Sill, Oklahoma, to Saudi Arabia in autumn, 1990. The ATACMS, fired from the standard MLRS launcher, could deliver 1,000 anti-personnel bomblets out to ranges of up to 150 kilometres.[5]

The plan for the ground war was a constant preoccupation, as it had been back home before the conflict started. Just after arrival in Riyadh, I had seen someone in the hotel restaurant with a book called *If War Comes: How to defeat Saddam Hussein*, by Trevor N Dupuy, a well-known and prolific pundit.[6] The book was based on testimony given to the Senate Armed Services Committee on 13 December.

Using his extensive database from military history, Colonel Dupuy had constructed some scenarios for a possible land battle. The first option, Operation *Colorado*

Plate 17 Royal Scots on training soon after their arrival in the Gulf.
(*Photo: Mike Moore/Today*)

Plate 18 British Gunners of 4th Armoured Brigade gun-cleaning after range firing with their M109
155 mm Self-Propelled Howitzer.
(*Photo: Mike Moore/Today*)

Plate 19 Lieutenant General Gus Pagonis, the logistical commander for Operation *Desert Storm* has his third stars pinned on by General Schwarzkopf and his son Captain G.W. Pagonis.
(*Photo: AP*)

Plate 20 4 February 1991. Brigadier Christopher Hammerbeck, Commander 4th Armoured Brigade, talks to his soldiers during the run-up to the land battle.
(*Photo: Reuter*)

Plate 21   Before the Ground War. The sinews of war along the tapline road east of Hafar-al-Batin.
(*Photo: Author*)

Plate 22   Tapline road ('Dodge') – US artillery (M-109) moves east for the 'end run'. (Shot from a
British Hercules C-130 aircraft).
(*Photo: Author*)

Plate 23   The Battle of Khafji, as explained by the Saudis (briefing by General Khalid).
(*Photo: Author*)

Plate 24   HMS *Gloucester* having destroyed a Silkworm missile with two Sea Dart missiles off the
coast of Kuwait.
(*Photo: Press Association*)

Plate 25   MLRS of the 1st US Cavalry Division engaging Iraqi positions.
(Photo: AP)

Plate 26   27 February 1991. British infantry take Iraqi prisoners during their advance through eastern Iraq.
(Photo: Reuter)

Plate 27 Troops of US 101st Airborne Assault Division during the great sweep forward.
(*Photo: Reuter*)

Plate 28 More Iraqis trying to surrender to the *Independent* (the Saudis got there first!).
(*Photo: Richard Dowden*)

Plate 29 Welcome to Iraq! Note the Allied recognition mark on the side of the tank.
(*Photo: Author*)

Plate 30 Safwan, South Iraq, looking west. Perimeter guard, US Army Bradley Infantry Fighting
Vehicle and Apache armed helicopters (*left, background*), 3 March 1991.
(*Photo: Author*)

Plate 31 Female military police corporal keeping onlookers away from the Iraqis. Safwan, 3 March 1991.
(*Photo: Author*)

Plate 32 The Author at Safwan, 3 March 1991. Behind, a knocked out T-55. On the skyline, just visible, Patriot air defence missiles.
(*Photo: David Fairhall*)

Springs, aimed to force Iraqi surrender by air power alone; the second, *Bulldozer*, was a frontal assault. The third was called *Leavenworth*, named after the US Army Command and General Staff College. Its name suggested it was a satisfactory War College solution. It was a very limited left flanking move, going just behind the Iraqi front line from the Wadi al-Batin, with an amphibious assault in the south of Kuwait and, most extraordinary, an airborne landing just behind the Iraqi front line. The fourth, *Razzledazzle*, was slightly less cautious, cutting into Kuwait further north, with an amphibious attack north of Kuwait City linking up with an airborne landing in northern Kuwait. During the waiting phase, we were told that the Bubiyan area was unsuitable for an amphibious attack, as it was so marshy.

Even the move of 1st (British) Armoured Division, acting as the hinge between the frontal assault and the great left sweep proved more daring than this. After the war, I assumed that Colonel Dupuy's analysis was one more ingenious piece of deception. The Iraqis expected the Allies to attack right up the 'slot' – the Wadi al-Batin, and to come from the sea, as in Colonel Dupuy's two favoured solutions.

On 30 January, I had breakfast with Jacques Girardon of the French newspaper *L'Espress*, who had just returned from the front. He had seen columns of trucks moving up the tapline road, with helicopters either side, like the cavalry screen in a late-19th century military textbook, and then turning off to the north. I also spoke to Richard Dowden on the telephone, who reported some Allied forces as far west as Raf'ha, 300 kilometres west of the western edge of Kuwait. 'It's all up there,' he said, 'further west than I thought'. I could only agree.

My Hercules flight on 1 February confirmed that the Allies were moving well west of Kuwait. That was no surprise in itself, but the fact that forces were as far west as Raf'ha produced a small diagram in the diary which accurately reflected the extent of the Allied encirclement. 'It could be the most spectacular battle of encirclement in history, equal to Stalingrad', the 30 January entry read.

On 12 February Geneviève Rossier, the Canadian Broadcasting Corporation radio correspondent in Riyadh, telephoned me, obviously upset. In her quest for French language interviews, she had spoken to a woman whose son was in the French Foreign Legion. The woman had confirmed that the Legion were with the US 82nd and 101st Airborne Divisions and would be moving into *Iraq* (not Kuwait), 'in a few days'. I was uneasy about discussing such matters on the telephone, but by now I had an accurate picture of the Allied deployments. To have the light forces – the French *Daguet* ('Gazelle') division and the two US Airborne on the flank was classical stuff. The analogy which instantly presented itself was Lieutenant General Issa Pliev's Cavalry-Mechanised Group on the flank of the Soviet offensive into Manchuria in 1945. I knew the French were on the flank, although I did not know they were subordinated to XVIII Corps. That Corps was in empty desert, offering clear space for a flanking manoeuvre, just as Pliev's mobile group had moved through the Gobi desert – an operation of which I had made a special study. And Pliev's flank guard had been an oddly heterogeneous force: wheels, tracks and hooves, just like XVIII Corps, with its heliborne infantry and fast, wheeled, AMX-10 armoured reconnaissance vehicles.[7]

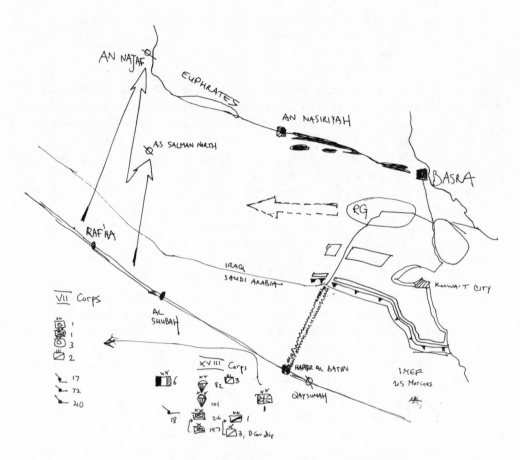

Figure 5.2   Author's sketch of possible battle plan, 13 February 1991.

That lunchtime I met a gloomy Robert Fisk, who was visiting Riyadh. He thought we were in for a prolonged, bloody battle, with chemical weapons and all the consequences of their use. He explained the plan as he saw it, and it made instant sense. It was wonderfully geometrical. The first movement, far to the west, from Raf'ha, would push towards As Salman airfield and An Najaf. It would cut off the entire quadrilateral bounded by the Euphrates and the southern Iraqi border. Like the rook on a chessboard, this would draw the Republican Guard out from their positions on the northern Kuwaiti border, making them more vulnerable to air attack and permitting a second Allied thrust, from just west of Kuwait, to take them in the flank. Finally, Allied forces would move directly into Kuwait from the south in concert with an amphibious assault. The last detail was wrong, and the sequence of the main moves was different, but it was a fair approximation to the genuine plan. The following day's sketch is Figure 5.2.

On 17 February, I spoke with an American journalist who had just returned from the desert well west of the Wadi al-Batin, where he reported three divisions of tanks

– the 1st and 3rd US Armoured and 1st British, presumably. 'It looked like the Oklahoma land rush', he said, 'seven lanes wide.' Because the great movement could not start until the air campaign began, in case the Iraqis found out, it had to be completed with considerable haste.

If I communicated this to the newspaper, there was a risk that someone excitable would print it. On 7 February, I had telephoned the office from the Interior Ministry press bureau which was on one side of the Hyatt ballroom, where all the briefings were held. In conversation I was asked, on the telephone, what the Allied battle plan was. 'This is an open line,' I said, exasperated. It was not even my hotel, but a Saudi Interior Ministry line. Eventually they got the message.

However, when the ground war started, we would need maps. Faxing sketches from the hotel was always a slightly nerve-racking business, as although I would never dream of divulging any military secrets, my maps had a rather serious appearance which was liable to attract interest and, as Kipling said, you have to 'make allowance for their doubting, too'. On a couple of occasions I passed the business centre and saw Saudi Military police sitting in there, as if they were monitoring communications. Saudi Arabia is not the place to get arrested for spying – or, indeed arrested for anything.

In the end, I telephoned Kristina, the graphics editor.

'*As a precaution*, can you prepare maps stretching out as far as Raf'ha', I said.

'Raf'ha? Where's that?'

'Out to the west.'

'Can't see it. Is it near Hafar al-Batin?'

'No, go left, left . . .'

'That's *miles* away.'

'Can you do it, please . . .'

Until the ground war, the secret was safe.

In his final briefing (*Appendix A*) General Schwarzkopf described the movement of the flanking force to the west as 'absolutely an extraordinary move' – the famous 'Hail Mary' play in American football. It could not begin until the air war had started, and the Iraqis' 'eyes' had been punched out. From then on, the Iraqis could not see what was happening and, even more important, would be unable to do anything about it, even if they could. The chances of such a move being unobserved were small, with the amount of dust generated by 4,500 trucks in use every day. Just one Iraqi patrol sneaking over the border might have realised what was happening. But those that did were intent on surrender, not reconnaissance. The Iraqis did have six infantry divisions, two armoured and one mechanised immediately west of Kuwait by 23 January, but these were heavily damaged by air attack and, in the case of the infantry, virtually immobile.

Like Khalkhin Gol, but ten times larger, this was an encirclement only possible – and a campaign won – by logistics. Incredibly ambitious, computer competent. Much has already been written on how that move, without precedent in the history of war, was done.[8] The logistics bases along the route were most important. General Schwarzkopf's logistics chief was Lieutenant General William 'Gus' Pagonis, whose staff expanded from three to 50,000 between August 1990 and the start of the ground campaign. General Pagonis was given 21 days to complete the move: he planned to do it in 14, and XVIII Corps, over 100,000 strong, with all its combat service support (for vehicle repair), supplies and ammunition, was moved in 16 days. In all, 350,000 troops, 2,000 tanks and several hundred thousand tons of stores – fuel, ammunition and spare parts – were to be shifted along just two roads leading west, enough for 60 days. As General Schwarzkopf later confirmed in his end-of-the war briefing, 'we wanted to have enough supplies on hand so if we launched this, if we got into a slugfest battle, which we very easily could have gotten into, we'd have enough supplies to last for 60 days. It was an absolutely gigantic accomplishment.'

The logistic support plan was in five phases. XVIII US Corps had been deployed first, starting on 9 August 1990. President Bush decided to send VII Corps to join it on 8 November 1990. The first phase of the logistic plan, *Alfa*, involved repositioning of supplies from Dhahran and al-Jubayl along Main Supply Route 'Dodge' – the tapline road – while simultaneously moving VII Corps to its tactical assembly areas. Huge logistics bases were built during December 1990 along Dodge near King Khalid Military City (KKMC) and along the other MSR, Sultan, just south of KKMC. These were designated Alfa, Bravo and Delta and were to hold all the supplies to sustain two Corps and those needed by the higher command – 'echelons above corps (EAC)'. This phase began in late November and lasted until the Allied air offensive started on 17 January 1991.

Phase *Bravo* involved moving the two US commanded Army Corps, XVIII and VII, to attack positions. This phase coincided with the beginning of the air offensive and lasted through January. Phase *Charlie* would be direct support of the ground offensive with the resupply of consumables: ammunition, fuel, water and food. It anticipated building new logistic bases – Hotel, November, Oscar and Romeo – deep inside Iraq, if the offensive were bogged down and protracted operations had to be sustained. *Delta* was the subsequent defence of Kuwait and restoration of facilities and services, Echo – redeployment to the US.[9]

There was constant speculation about the possibility of an amphibious assault on the Kuwaiti coast. On 4 February, the US battleships *Missouri* and *Wisconsin* opened fire with their 16-inch (406mm) guns on targets – Iraqi bunkers – in Kuwait. With a range of 40 kilometres, the 16-inch guns could put the shells, each weighing nearly a ton, into an area the size of a tennis court – 'a very accurate system'. It made sense to use everything available, and the battleships were ideal to destroy targets within about 25 kilometres of the coast. But in the popular imagination, the image of the battleships firing against the shore was associated with Marine landings. On 7 February, in Riyadh, there was an unattributable briefing on amphibious assaults, with maps and diagrams of how you do it. With hindsight, that was a subtle piece of disinformation. I filed a piece on the techniques of amphibious landings (unused), but some newspapers used the material, perhaps further convincing the Iraqis that the assault – or a big part of it – would come from the sea.

On 6 February the *Independent*'s Richard Dowden took the first four prisoners of the war to be captured by a Briton. He and Isabel Ellsen, a French free-lance photographer working for us, were driving down a road near the border when they were approached by four soldiers. At first they did not realise who they were. They turned out to be Iraqis waving the 'safe conduct' surrender notices which had been dropped in large numbers. Nervous – there are more graphic phrases –, Richard did not immediately think to disarm them. But he handed them over to the Egyptians, the nearest Allied force. They graciously allowed Richard, our Africa Editor in more normal times, to have first crack at interrogating them. It was a spectacular front-page 'splash', and a welcome boost to morale the next day.

There were constant rumours that the ground war was imminent – we expected it the night of 16th, but it did not start so soon or suddenly. It was delayed for three reasons: the bad weather, which reduced the effect of Allied air attacks or, just as crucial, assessment of their results; the difficulty of finding the Scuds and the resources thereby diverted; and the determination to wait until the Iraqi ground forces were close to collapse before risking a ground attack.

Nor was the start of the ground campaign a clear-cut event. My study of the Soviet military system had led me to expect a period of 'reconnaissance by battle' – *razvedka boyem* – aggressive, quite large-scale probing by forces up to battalion-strength on either side. The Iraqi defences resembled those of the Second World War, when preliminary probing attacks and reconnaissances in force over two to three days preceded major offensives. That is what we began seeing from 18 February. In addition, the increasing number of 'line crossers' – Iraqis coming over the border to surrender – was a useful source of intelligence. Confusion was a necessary – and desirable – part of the land-war build-up.

The British played a key part in the deception. Because the Iraqis based much of their military technique on British example, it was believed that they would pay special attention to what the British were doing. In mid-January, the British 1st Armoured Division moved west, from the positions where it had been training with the US Marines and providing the heavy armour which they lacked, to concentration area Keyes just east of the Wadi al-Batin.

It has been alleged that the British believed the US Marines would be too 'gung-ho' and risk unnecessary British losses, but British official sources have strenuously denied this. The British commander in the Middle East, General Sir Peter de la Billière, said in his account of the war that he had been concerned that the British would be involved at the point where the heaviest casualties were expected – the frontal attack – and that the British would therefore suffer disproportionately. Casualties were therefore a factor of *some* importance in his desire to move British forces westward, but he never mentioned this to General Schwarzkopf, he said because he felt the military and political arguments were sufficient in themselves.[10]

It was, again, a more subtle question, of where the particular qualities of the full British division could best be employed. On 6 December, the British Joint Commander, Air Chief Marshal Sir Patrick Hine, flew to Riyadh to try to persuade the Allied Command to employ the British division – heavily armoured and highly mobile – where it could best be used: for open, high-speed warfare in the desert, not to provide mobile pill-boxes for the US Marines. And, to put it another way, it was

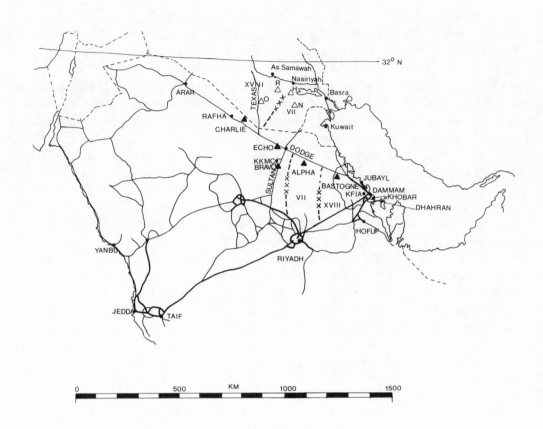

Notes:
The graphic shows the original positions of VII and XVIII Corps, and their approximate areas of responsibility after they changed positions and moved west. From 7 August 1990, 494 ships unloaded at Al Jubayl and Ad Dammam. 7248 incoming flights (commercial, C5 Galaxy and C-141 Starlifter) unloaded at Dhahran Airbase, KFIA and KKMC. Of these, 6,755 arrived at Dhahran.

Figure 5.3   The Theatre. Showing the up-to-date Saudi road network and and indication of the distances to be covered by logistic efforts.

(Sources: Zaki MA Farsi, *National Guide and Atlas of the Kingdom of Saudi Arabia* (1st edn., 2nd printing, February 1989); Lieutenant General William G. Pagonis, 'Good Logistics is Combat Power', *Military Review*, September 1991, pp. 28–29.)

a very strong division – 25,000 men and women, uniquely self-sufficient, more akin to one of the revived Soviet corps formations introduced in the 1980s – on which I had conducted a study while at Edinburgh University. Such a formation was ideal for an operational manoeuvre group. It would be inappropriate and constricting to subordinate a large British division to the US Marine command structure. Better give it to a massive higher formation geared to operational manoeuvre – to the US Army's VII Corps. Conversely, when the British contingent had only been a brigade, it *had* to stay close to the port of Al Jubayl because of its limited independent resources. When it was increased to a division, it could operate more independently, and new possibilities were opened up. An additional advantage was that the British and US Armies (as opposed to the US Marines) shared common Nato procedures. Brigadier Ian Durie, the UK artillery commander, later said 'it was good that we came from the same Theatre – Nato's VII Corps – that we spoke the same operational language.'[11]

Even after the air war had started, VII Corps equipment was still arriving by sea at the ports of Ad-Dammam and Al Jubayl. The number of trucks on the roads west increased and the Allies increased their use of the railway to Riyadh for supplies going in that direction to two or three a day, each with 75 wagons, to take the strain off the roads.[12] But for movement further out to the western flank, there were only two roads. The vastness of the logistic task is seen in Figure 5.3 and selected main movements, plus the preparatory artillery 'raids', in Figure 5.4.

XVIII and VII Corps began moving to their attack positions on 20 January and continued round the clock for two weeks. By 3 February their concentration was completed. There were only two routes: Dodge and Sultan. XVIII Corps – over 100,000 troops – had to travel over 800 kilometres, VII Corps, 550 kilometres. VII Corps alone had more than 7,000 tracked vehicles and 40,000 wheeled.

Under cover of the air attack, the lighter XVIII Corps was passed through the heavier formations of VII Corps and out to the flank as VII moved, north to the border. The Americans had never done anything like this before. VII Corps' marshalling area was south east of Hafar al Batin. The entire corps would have to move nearly 150 kilometres west, crossing Main Supply Route (MSR) Sultan and then 135 kilometres north to the border, crossing Dodge and the oil pipeline, which ran along the surface, on the way. To avoid massive traffic jams with XVIII Corps moving north and west while VII moved west and north, plans were made to construct a by-pass south and west of the King Khalid Military City. Engineers with heavy plant were committed to the project. Just days before the first convoys were expected to use the by-pass, unusually heavy winter rains turned it into a quagmire, and all efforts to make the by-pass serviceable failed.[13]

So the existing roads, converging on one cross-roads in Hafar al-Batin, would have to be used. The 318th Movement Control Agency (MCA) – a reserve unit – allocated blocks of time to each Corps to move on their designated supply routes, with a military police brigade controlling movements. At the peak of the movement, 18 vehicles a minute passed a single MP checkpoint on the northern route (hence my colleague's comment about 'seven lanes'). To do this with minimum disruption, the start times of convoys from as far away as Riyadh (Sultan) and Dammam (Dodge) had to be carefully planned. When the 6,000 to 8,000 wheeled and tracked vehicles of each of VII Corps' divisions approached the points to cross Sultan, checkpoints set up on the road leading north stopped all through traffic. They were manned by US Movement Control Teams (MCT) and US and Saudi Military Police. According to Colonel Peter Langenus, commanding 318th MCA,

> Civilian traffic, halted at these checkpoints, saw only huge, blinding sandstorms, preventing them from seeing what was masked by the storm. When the divisions finished the movement west they turned north to cross MSR Dodge. A new challenge awaited ... Parallel to and south of MSR Dodge is an oil pipeline running on the surface for hundreds of miles. Huge mounds of desert sand were bulldozed on top of the pipeline to create 50 separate sites to cross over the pipeline. After the thousands of vehicles of each division were channeled over the 50 mounds of sand they went on line to cross MSR Dodge. MCTs and military police halted traffic on MSR Dodge to permit the crossings which remained hidden under the natural and man-made *shamals* [sand storms].[14]

From there, there were virtually no roads leading north from Saudi Arabia into Iraq. Routes through the desert were marked for the supply trains to follow. They

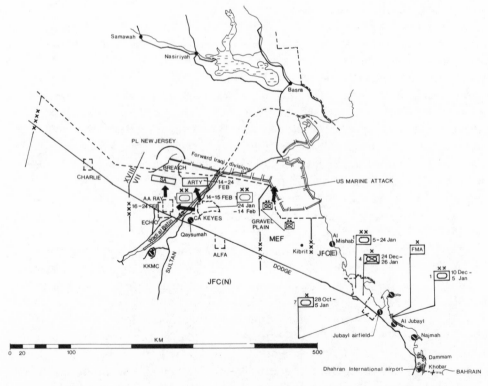

Figure 5.4   The Allied build-up prior to envelopment of the Iraqi forces, artillery raids and proposed breach for 1st (UK) Armoured Division

used chemical lights, bicycle reflectors and road signs. The routes were marked, northward, through the Saudi–Iraq border. The new routes then became the Main Supply Routes along which fuel, ammunition, water and food were carried on, as far as the Euphrates river.

> Never before had movement control been called upon to manage the simultaneous movement of two corps, while at the same time controlling the movement of thousands of trucks, tracks, planes and ships needed to sustain a force of more than half a million soldiers.[15]

During *Desert Shield* and *Desert Storm* 3,500 convoys moved 200,000 miles each day between them. A 32 million mile drive – over a third of the way to the Sun, in all. One was reminded of Field Marshal Alexander Suvorov, Russia's greatest general, asking a soldier, and the soldier, as usual, never lost for words:

'How far is it to the Moon?'

'For Suvorov, two campaigns.'[16]

For Powell, Schwarzkopf, and their thousands of staff, it would be three campaigns to the Sun.

The tracked vehicles were moved on Heavy Equipment Transporters (HETs), some from eastern Europe, with drivers contracted from South Korea, Pakistan, Bangladesh, Egypt and other Allied countries. 1,300 HETs and 2,700 other transporters took

KEY
AA   Assembly Area
Arty   area of Artillery Group raids, 14–24 February
CA   Concentration Area
FMA   Force Maintenance Area
JFC(E)Joint Forces Command (East) (Saudi, Kuwaiti, Omani & UAE)
JFC(N)Joint Forces Command (North) (Egyptian & Syrian)

KKMC King Khalid Military City
MEF   Marine Expeditionary Force (US)
PL   Phase Line
SA   Staging Area

¹ □ UK Armoured division

⁷ □ UK Armoured brigade

₄ ⊠ UK Armoured infantry brigade

⊠ US Marine divisions

Notes:
The map shows five main corps-level commands (from left to right) XVIII, VII, JFC(N), MEF and JFC(E), but concentrates on the positions of 1st (UK) Armoured Division prior to breakthrough. The logistic bases of 1 and 2 (US) Marine Divisions are also shown.
1st (UK) Armoured Division moved from CA Keyes during 14–15 February 1991 (move known as *Dibdibah Charge*) to AA Ray and the artillery raid positions (raids from 14–24 February). From Keyes, the division also conducted an exercise (*Dibdibah Drive*), with 1st (US) Infantry Division (Mechanised) from 4–6 February.

part in the operation. Some drivers were Philippinos, guided to their final destinations by Spanish-speaking Americans.

Bases Charlie (supporting XVIII Corps) and Echo (supporting VII, including the British) had to be set up in parallel with the movement of the Corps to the west. Charlie was far to the west and, for security reasons, could not be set up until the air campaign had started, so as not to alert the Iraqis prematurely. By the start of the Ground offensive, 24 February, there were 29 days' supplies of food and water, 5.2 days' supply of fuel and 45 days' allowance of ammunition. The Corps' daily requirements were estimated at 450 truckloads (9,000 tons) of ammunition for VII Corps and 400 truckloads (5,000 tons) for XVIII, and 400 truckloads or 2.4 million gallons of fuel for VII and 480 smaller truckloads or 2.1 million gallons for XVIII. These reflected XVIII Corps' lighter configuration and higher fuel requirements, because of its emphasis on high speed and airmobility. In order to economise on consumption of supplies, two plans were developed, the construction of roads following the two attacking corps and bringing in more supplies by sea if a port in Kuwait could be made available. Provisional logistic bases, Oscar and November, were to be set up 90 miles forward of Charlie and Echo, but because of the speed of the operation they were never fully set up. Supplies were merely dropped there for the Corps to pick up.[17]

To the east, the US Marines who were kept close to the sea for deception – the Allied Command wanted the Iraqis to think they might be at sea – and for ease of resupply, also accomplished unprecedented feats of logistics. On 28 December, they began stocking their base at Al Kibrit, south of the centre of Kuwait's bottom salient and level with Al Mishab. By 4 February, they had supplies for 17 days' combat. The Marines would attack the centre of the Iraqi forces occupying Kuwait, but exactly where was open to debate. On that day the two divisional commanders, Major General James Myatt, commanding the 1st Marine Division and William Keys, commanding 2nd, suggested to the Marine Commander, Lieutenant General Walter Boomer, that they should launch a two division breach – two divisions in parallel. To do this, a forward logistic base was needed, ideally between the two divisions' jumping-off points, in an area known, simply, as 'the gravel plain' (see Figure 5.4). Kibrit was 50 kilometres from Al Mishab, on the coast: the Gravel Plain was 130 kilometres further. In the search for an operational codename for a base to be constructed there, one Marine officer suggested *Al Khanjar* – the small dagger worn by Saudi adult males as proof of their manhood. A Marine artist quickly devised an image of a dagger plunged into the centre of Kuwait, where the Marines were going. The codename stuck.

On 6 February, Brigadier General Charles Krulak called on General Boomer. His logistic teams were ready to go and set up *Khanjar*, but if they were to set up a base for two parallel divisional assaults they would need to get going. General Boomer answered:

> 'We will make a two divisional breach of the Iraqi defences at these locations' and pointed to the breach sites on the west flank [of the southern salient]. It was a go![18]

Khanjar was vast, covering 11,280 acres. There were over 40 kilometres of blast walls ('berms', the term which became ubiquitous in the Gulf War, although the original fortress berm meant something else[19]). The ammunition supply point covered 780 acres, with 151 separate cells for Marine and Army ground and air munitions. The fuel farm was also dug in, holding 5 million gallons by the start of the ground war. The Americans also built two rough airfields, able to take C-130 Hercules. This vast forward base would supply two US Marine divisions and the Army's Tiger Brigade.

While *Khanjar* was being built, four-lane 'highways' were constructed from it to the Kuwaiti border. Known as the '*Khanjar* expressways', these were eventually extended into Kuwait, through the breached minefields and on, 65 kilometres into Kuwait following 1st Division and 40 kilometres following 2nd. As with the movement of VII and XVIII Corps, so the coordinated movement of the two Marine Divisions and the Tiger Brigade within 20 kilometres of the border of occupied Kuwait was described as 'phenomenal'.[20]

There were problems. Because artillery shells and propellant charges were loaded separately, by 28 January, VII Corps had 50,000 artillery rounds without charges and 50,000 mortar rounds with no fuzes. 2nd Armoured Cavalry regiment deployed without any ammunition in its vehicles because the shipping waivers allowing them to take ammunition from the US had not been granted before they left. On 17 January, when the air war started, 13 tank companies (squadrons), three Bradley mechanised infantry companies and 21 howitzer batteries were still stuck at the Saudi eastern ports. In November, there was a critical transport shortage, and 300 contractors' vehicles were hired from December to March to overcome it. By 27 January the bottleneck had abated with regard to personnel, with only 14,000 soldiers waiting to be moved inland but the movement of heavy tracked vehicles was still hampered by the lack of transporters. Two Bradley battalions deployed 400 kilometres across country on their own tracks, but this was grossly extravagant on fuel and wear and tear. Some 35 armoured, infantry and mechanised infantry companies were waiting in a queue to deploy. The last VII Corps combat units to arrive moved direct from the coast to their assault positions 400 kilometres inland without pausing.

There was widespread concern about the Allied powers' reliance on chartered ships under flags of convenience, although most fulfilled their contracted obligations fearlessly, even during missile attacks, while the soldiers were better protected in their chemical warfare suits. When Scud missile attacks on the ports started, two ships, the Bahamian registered *Coal* and the Kuwaiti *Trident Dusk*, refused to sail into the target area on 21 and 26 January, 1991. One was boarded by the US Navy and the crew and captain replaced.[21]

Once in theatre, British logistics covered the same distances as the rest of VII Corps. From Al Jubayl to the Force Maintenance Area was 350 kilometres. The British contingent comprised 400,000 tons of vehicles, munitions and other freight. Again, vehicles were hired from the 'host nation' – Saudi Arabia. Every day, a convoy 40 miles long left Al Jubayl, heading west. Major Kingham of the Royal Engineers supervised US labour to build the longest fuel pipelines since the Second

World War, the 'Pipeline Over the Desert (PLOD)', 95 kilometres long, with six pumping stations, from Al Jubayl.[22] Tragically, Kingham was killed in a traffic accident when PLOD was commissioned on 26 February, and it was named the 'Kingham Line' in his honour.

Only one Allied force came from a completely different direction – the French. Their debarkation port was Yanbu, on the Red Sea. Yanbu and Jubayl, huge ports with empty facilities ideal for debouching armies, were oddly symmetrical, and both under the Governance of Prince Turki, who entertained a number of the journalists to a delightful picnic in the desert on 17 February. Yanbu was seven days' sailing from Toulon and 1,700 kilometres from As Salman, planned as the most forward base of the 6th Light Armoured 'Daguet' ('Gazelle') Division. This was the distance from Paris to Bucharest, making the round trip equivalent to Paris to Cairo. The French deployed 300 heavy transport vehicles. French eccentricity apart, having one division supplied from a different direction made the load on Dodge and Sultan manageable.[23]

We were frequently told 'they're moving about', but with no details. It was another part of the general air of deception, so we would not take the snippets we knew as permanent. From what we knew of the formations involved, we assumed that XVIII Corps was still on the inside, to the east, when the ground war was about to start. Thus, one diagram published on 16 February and two on 25 February showed XVIII Corps on the inside and VII out to the west (see next chapter, Figure 6.3). On 25th, it became obvious that I had VII and XVIII Corps the wrong way round. 'A deception so perfect it even fooled the *Independent*'s Defence Correspondent', I consoled myself. The record was not put straight in the newspaper until 27 February, by which time the offensive was nearly over. Inadvertently, we may have contributed something to the deception plan although, then as now, I doubted whether the Iraqis had the time or staff to analyse the volume of information pouring out from the Western press.

From 24 January to 14 February, the British were in concentration area Keyes, whose airhead at Qaysumah I visited on 1 February. They had kept up radio transmissions from the east coast, to convince the Iraqis they were still there. Two days before the exercise Dibdibah Drive, which took place from 4 to 6 February, they stopped and broadcasted on low volume from the west. Then they began broadcasting loudly again, to simulate a move back to the east. The deception involved playing tapes of the training exercises of the previous two months back over the airwaves, including tape of artillery exercises. If the Iraqis had picked up the move to the west, they might now be persuaded that it was a training deployment. Bluff and double bluff.[24]

Special Forces, some based near Tabuk at a site 900 kilometres north-west of Riyadh, were also operating inside Iraq, primarily to target the Scud missile launchers in western and southern Iraq, but also to rescue downed Allied pilots. The British were usually inserted by helicopter, sometimes by Chinooks of the RAF Special Forces carrying their dune buggies or 'Pink Panther' open-topped Land Rovers. They also used motorcycles. I saw one of the four RAF Special Forces' Chinooks, in its distinctive spider's web camouflage, at Kuwait City airport after the ceasefire. The RAF Special Forces earned one DSO, one DFC and three mentions in despatches after the war. I was told that one RAF pilot took a Special Forces group 800 kilometres into Iraq, but landed in a minefield, blowing off his rear wheels. He managed to fly back with a bent aircraft, an exploit which might have earned him a DFC.

'The day the air war began,' General Neal said later, 'there were a lot [of Special Forces] out there. Two weeks ... it was a Special Operations theme park.' (Actually operations started on 20 January). The missile sites, mobile launchers and command and control systems were attacked either directly or designated for air attack. On occasions the Special Forces had to close with Iraqi troops and there was intense fighting. Four British SAS men died and four were wounded behind enemy lines. Of those who died, one was apparently killed by a ricochet and two others died of exposure on a long escape from pursuing Iraqis. Although superbly trained and hardened to survive against the elements, the SAS men were unprepared for the unusually cold, wet weather. Having struggled through mountains and swum the Euphrates, exposure may have struck.

Special Forces operations are the subject of much rumour, but, in contrast to earlier wars, they were disproportionately significant, notably because of their success against surface-to-surface missiles which helped keep Israel out of the war. General de la Billière, an SAS officer himself for much of his military career, has published remarkable details of the Special Forces operations. General Schwarzkopf was sceptical about their value, and General de la Billière said he 'steamrollered' the US general into using them. The first British Special Forces crossed into Iraq on 20 January. They had their first major success on 23 January when a team from the Royal Marines' Special Boat Service (SBS) landed by helicopter to cut a fibre optic cable just 60 kilometres from Baghdad. They dug down to find the cable while their two Chinook helicopters waited, engines running. They took the ground marker denoting the course of the cable to General Schwarzkopf, and this event seems to have significantly affected his attitude to Special Forces' operations. The US Special Forces were deployed on 8 February, but, better equipped, they operated much more openly. The British SAS operated in open-topped Land Rovers and on motorcycles or on foot.

According to the commander of a US F15E squadron, the SAS helped to identify one third of the 20 or 30 mobile 'Scud' (*al-Hussein*) launchers destroyed by his unit. The SAS used hand-held Global Positioning Systems (GPS) to pinpoint the targets and passed the information on to AWACS control aircraft, which in turn vectored in A-10s by day and F-15Es by night. But sometimes it took as long as 50 minutes for the attack aircraft to appear – by which time the SSM launchers might have moved. So the patrols increasingly took matters into their own hands, using Milan anti-tank missiles mounted on their Land Rovers. The SAS are credited with destroying several launchers by this method, especially when bad weather prevented aircraft finding the targets. The missiles, liquid-fuelled, needed time to prepare for launch and could not be moved far from roads. The SAS ambushed some convoys and found that small-arms fire was often enough to put the missiles out of action.

The US teams were deployed later, from 8 February. There was an obvious risk that US and British patrols would run into each other, so in western Iraq, the main area of operation, a demarcation line was established. The Americans kept to the north of the main Baghdad–Amman road (see Figure 3.1), 'Scud Boulevard' – the northern Scud box. The British kept to 'Scud Alley', south of the road.

One of the greatest reported successes was towards the end of the war, when a joint UK/US team found a group of 29 missiles poised to strike at Israel, and called in A-10s to destroy them. In Riyadh, we gained the impression that the Iraqi missiles were being destroyed by air attack. After the war it became increasingly apparent that the Special Forces were responsible, either indirectly, by pinpointing the missiles which could not be seen from the air or space when hidden under bridges or, more and more, by direct attack.

After the war, in summer 1992, the Iraqis claimed that Allied Special Forces had not destroyed any Scud launchers at all, listing numbers which, they said, they had destroyed themselves. It was an extraordinary claim, reported on the BBC's *Newsnight* programme.[25] Those numbers were not far off the various reports of Allied successes, and it seems likely that the Iraqis were refusing to admit that the Special Forces had been so successful inside Iraq.

The US and British Armies launched their first conventional 'land' attack on the Iraqis with artillery raids, beginning on 18 February and lasting for five days. The Royal Artillery – in which I had once served – hit 18 Iraqi positions on that day, aiming to kill 'high-value targets' and unmask enemy guns. Brigadier General Richard Neal spoke of 'reconnaissance and counter-reconnaissance efforts all along the border.' But, as part of the Allied deception plan, it was the Saudi–Kuwait border, not the Saudi–Iraq border, in order to keep the Iraqis thinking that the main thrust would be into Kuwait, not to the west.

According to Brigadier Durie, the UK artillery commander, these were 'Theatre orchestrated preparatory fireplans or "raids" ... to attack high pay-off targets, to confuse and deceive as to where the main attack was to come from, as well as to practise our fire coordination procedures.'[26]

While the UK division remained in area Ray from 14 February, the artillery stayed east of the wadi and moved up to the border on 17 February (see Figure 5.4). VII US Corps passed targets to all its artillery, including the British, with a time period in which they were to be attacked. The British refined the target data, where possible, by flying drones – small, unmanned aircraft. The original plan envisaged artillery going well beyond the border, behind a US reconnaissance screen, but this was abandoned for fear that these preparatory actions would get out of hand and, egged on by media excitement, the Allies would be dragged into a full-scale land war before they were ready. Instead, they stayed behind the border 'berm' or embankment.

Another reason for this reticence was the continued possibility that the Iraqis might withdraw from Kuwait and that there might be a negotiated peace, although the military commanders doubted it. For as long as possible, the Allies wanted to preserve the option of 'switching off' the conflict. Once Allied and Iraqi ground troops became entangled, that could be difficult. It is easy to forget, with hindsight, that right up to the start of the ground war, diplomatic negotiations continued outside the theatre.

To reduce the chance of being detected and hit by return fire, no British artillery battery was to remain in position for more than 15 minutes from first firing. This meant the 8-inch (203mm) M-110 batteries had to redeploy after engaging just two targets. A typical mission, fired on 21 February, involved 1,300 rounds – maybe one salvo from 12 MLRS and 18 rounds from each of 72 guns. Such a mission could be fired very quickly.

The first British raid, on 18 February, was fired by 32 and 39 Heavy Regiments, the latter with the newly procured Multiple Launch Rocket System (MLRS). US A-10 aircraft reported on the effectiveness of the opening salvoes. An A-10 reported three battery positions destroyed and a company of tanks damaged. The Iraqis did not return fire. Over the next five days, the British MLRS regiment, 39, fired five fireplans; 32 fired three, one with 39 in the 1st (US) Cavalry Division sector 40 kilometres to the east. The three Field Regiments (2, 26 and 40), fired four between them. One Iraqi divisional artillery commander, later captured, said that out of 100 guns, he had lost 11 to air attack before the ground campaign, but another 77 to artillery fire before his position was overrun by 4th Armoured Brigade. It was a measure of the devastating effectiveness of modern artillery.

On 20 February, US forces landed by helicopter in Kuwait and captured up to 500 prisoners. It was the first time that the US had admitted crossing the border with ground troops and the largest single Iraqi surrender so far. As Brigadier General Neal said that day, 'the border is broadening,' a humorous description of the subtlety of the transition to full-scale land operations. At 14.00 hours on 20 February AH-64 Apache helicopters and OH-58 Kiowas attacked an Iraqi bunker complex north of the border, 13 out of 15 bunkers were reported destroyed and 450–500 men – an entire battalion – surrendered to the helicopters. They had to summon transport helicopters to take the prisoners south of the border. The classic divisions between 'air' and 'land' power were clearly blurring: that action could only be described as 'taking and holding ground' in the classic manner.[27]

Equally extraordinary was the fact that none of the neighbouring Iraqi battalions fired in support of the one that surrendered. If each unit sat in its foxholes, staring fixedly to its front, with no attempt at mutual support, that would make the Allies' job much easier.

On 22 February, Baghdad radio announced that the 'ground battle' had been 'begun by the enemy'. Captain Ronald Wildermuth, US Navy, one of the Allied spokesmen, denied that a ground war had started, although, on their own admission the Allies were hurling four times as much artillery fire at the Iraqis as the British Eighth Army fired at El Alamein. We were told quite openly that Allied official sources would remain silent until Allied forces had seized their preliminary objectives – some possibly 240 kilometres from the Saudi border.

The same day, President Bush announced that the Iraqis had until 23.00 on 23 February to withdraw from Kuwait or face ground attack. The statement said that all

Iraqi units should be withdrawn from Kuwait in a week and from Kuwait City itself within 48 hours. President Gorbachev also proposed a new 'six-point plan for peace'. But the Iraqis showed no sign of withdrawing. Instead, we heard that they were setting fire to oil wells in Kuwait, after US pilots reported seeing a huge pall of smoke across the area. At first 140 were reported afire, then 179, out of 950 oil wells in total.

A Saudi unit, supported by the US Marines, carved a 60 metre wide path through an Iraqi minefield on the border, indicating that the 'reconnaissance in force' was continuing. On the far west flank, there was a skirmish near Nachez, the French start-line. Several Iraqis tried to cross into Saudi territory, BMP movements were reported and the Iraqis fired on Gazelle helicopters which strayed too far into Iraq. 'Nothing really serious but the enemy is really there'.

On the evening of 23 February we were told of atrocities and executions in Kuwait. 'This is a trigger – a convenient one, but probably true', my diary recorded. 'They're setting the place on fire, pulling in males aged from 13 or 15 – I think we're going tonight. There is an air of real expectancy. No question that the Iraqis will withdraw.' It also emerged that the RAF were now dropping laser guided bombs on airfields, something we had not heard before, (although in fact, as explained in Chapter 4, they had moved to these at the beginning of the month). That seemed another indicator: one last, big hole to immobilise enemy planes.

I waited at the Hyatt for much of the evening, with Nick Constable of the *Daily Star* and Chris Buckland of the *Express*, who were filing for the next morning's Sunday papers but there was no more news. I returned to the Intercontinental.

There was a Scud alert at 05.00 on Sunday morning, 24 February. At 06.00 Nick Constable telephoned. The ground war had begun, at about 04.00.

6

Desert Cannae

24–28 February, 1991

'Time will *implode* and strategic space will *explode'*
> General G. Forray, French Chief of General Staff.[1]

Sunday 24 February dawned with cloudy skies and light rain. At 04.00 the 1st and 2nd US Marine Divisions and two Saudi task forces launched attacks through the Iraqi obstacle system in Kuwait – the 'direct approach'. Operation *Desert Sword*, the ground campaign, had begun. Far to the west, the French 6th Light Armoured Division were due to be the first to cross deep into Iraq, the far west wing – the 'indirect approach'. General Forray said they were 'first across the start line', although General Bernard Janvier, the Daguet Division commander, did not order it to move until 05.30 because he was concerned about navigation errors and units getting mixed up, and preferred to move in daylight.[2] At the time, XVIII Corps HQ said they had crossed the start line at 04.00.[3]

Third US Army, comprising XVIII and VII Corps was to 'destroy the RGFC [Republican Guard Force Command] and restore the sovereignty of Kuwait.' XVIII Corps would move on the left to block Iraqi lines of communication from north-west to south east and isolate Iraqi forces in the KTO. VII Corps, on the right, on the Army's main point of effort, and supported by elements of XVIII Corps would destroy the RGFC. Arab forces on the eastern flank of Third US Army would 'destroy enemy forces in zone and prevent reinforcement of IZ [Iraqi] forces facing VII Corps.' Thereafter, VII Corps would block Iraqi lines of communication north of Kuwait City and, on orders, occupy it. At this stage, it was not known that the Iraqis would vacate the city and the plan was therefore to encircle it before, if necessary, assaulting the urban area – potentially the most bloody and costly operation.

Operations orders at this level are remarkably cerebral:

> VII Corps intends to conduct a swift, continuous and violent air–land campaign to destroy the RGFC while minimising friendly force casualties. Aim is to make IZ

KEY
b – border posts
a – anti-tank (platoons)
120 – 120mm mortars

RAMa	*Régiment d'Artillerie de Marine* (Marine Artillery Regiment, French regular Army)
RD	*Régiment de Dragons* (Dragoon Regiment – sometimes erroneously referred to as Cuirassiers)
REC	*Régiment Etranger de Cavalerie* (Foreign Legion Cavalry Regiment)
REG	*Régiment Etranger de Genie* (Foreign Legion Engineer Regiment)
REI	*Régiment Etranger d'Infanterie* (Foreign Legion Infantry Regiment)
RHC	*Régiment d'Helicoptères de Combat* (Combat Helicopter Regiment – 5 Squadrons)
RICM	*Régiment Infanterie Chars de Marine* (Marine Tank Regiment – RICM originally stood for *Régiment Infanterie Colonial de Maroc*. (The acronym was kept and the new name tailored to fit)
RIMa	*Régiment d'infanterie de Marine* (Marine Infantry Regiment)
RS	*Régiment de Spahis* ('Spahi' Regiment – originally North African light infantry)

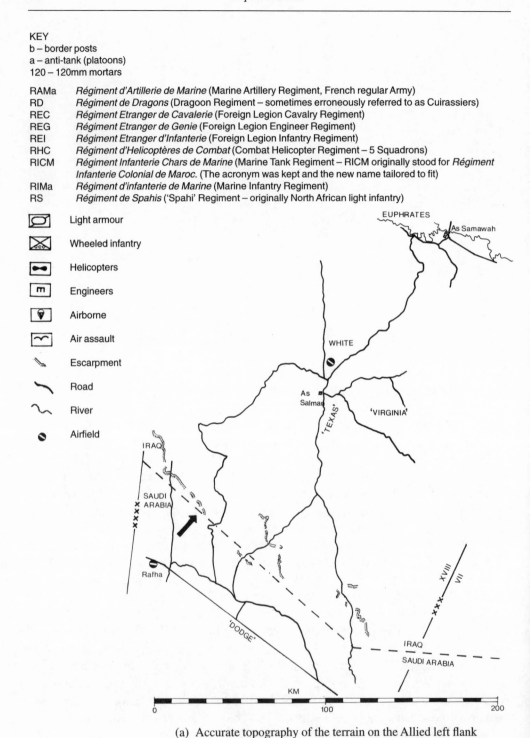

(a) Accurate topography of the terrain on the Allied left flank

Figure 6.1   Seizure of Nachez, 23 February 1991 and attack of French 6th Light Armoured Division.

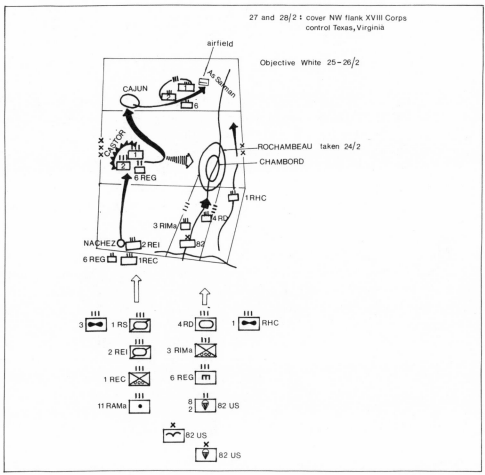

(b) Schematic of advance of 6th Light Armoured Division (based on a map in *Kepi Blanc*, June 1991)

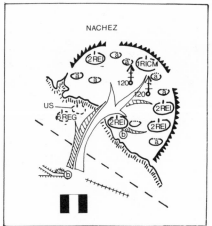

(c) Nachez Bridgehead, 22–23 February

forces move so that they can be attacked throughout the depth of their formations by ground fire, manoeuvre and air. In initial phases the Corps is to get maximum combat power moving towards the RGFC in minimum time.[4]

The Allied and Iraqi dispositions are shown at the end of the chapter in Figure 6.8 and the Allied plan and details of the Iraqi deployment in Figure 6.9.

XVIII Corps was to reach the Euphrates as fast as possible and prevent the Republican Guard Divisions from escaping – and to prevent other forces moving from outside to their rescue. VII Corps would perform a shallower movement, and destroy them. However, there was the risk that the Iraqi armoured divisions still in Kuwait would move west, to cut the vast – and vulnerable – supply trains stretching out behind VII Corps. To protect them against that eventuality, there was the British 1st Armoured Division, the hinge between the direct frontal assault and the swinging door on the left.

It was a classic double encirclement. VII Corps was the inner encirclement, XVIII Corps the outer, while three smaller corps (Arab Joint Forces Commands North and East and the US Marine Expeditionary Force) held the Iraqis' attention with a frontal assault. Every encirclement itself has two fronts – it can be attacked from within or without. The British 1st Armoured Division was thus the inner front of the inner encirclement.

The Daguet Division's mission was set out in XVIII Corps' 600-page Operation Order. It was to attack, open and clear the Main Supply Route Texas, a straight, metalled road across the desert to the Euphrates; to destroy enemy forces – the Iraqi 45th Division; and to seize Objective 'White' – As Salman airfield. Texas was XVIII Corps' axis and artery.

The Daguet Division included three regiments of the French Foreign Legion (1st REC (light armour), 2nd REI (infantry) and 6th REG (engineers), known as the *Groupement de Marche de la Légion Etrangère* (GMLE), French Marines and other Army troops and a brigade of the US 82nd Airborne Division. The Foreign Legion formed the western group: the 82nd, French Marines and Cuirassiers the eastern. The Daguet division was to seize the bridgehead Nachez, above an escarpment just north of the border, on the eve of the attack, and then to proceed to its first objective, Rochambeau – named, appropriately, after a French General who helped the Americans in the War of Independence. Here, the road winds a little before descending to the Iraqi defence lines, 40 kilometres inside the border, as shown in Figure 6.1(a).

The western group had occupied Nachez by 20.00 hours on 23rd. The next morning, two regiments, stretched out over 12 kilometres, led the eastern group up 'Texas'. 'Like a Grand Prix', one soldier recalled. The attack on Rochambeau began at noon, as in Figure 6.1(b).[5]

Meanwhile, by 08.00, the largest helicopter assault in military history had begun. Over 300 attack helicopters of the US 101st Air Assault Division, the 'Screaming Eagles', burst into Iraq along six air corridors, a 'bold, audacious action' to reach the Euphrates by spectacular bounds. They had been delayed by fog, but moved from 13 strike zones about an hour after dawn, led by Apaches flying 50 feet above the ground, carrying Hellfire anti-tank missiles. They carried 2,000 troops and 50 High Mobility Vehicles and light howitzers with them, plus tons of fuel and ammunition. Another 2,000 troops crossed the border on the ground. They were heading for a cradle of civilisation. 'Where life was created is where lots of it is fixing to end,' said one sergeant. 'I think it's a damn shame.'

The speed and violence of the American attack overwhelmed the stunned Iraqis, who did not put up much return fire. It produced one of the war's most horrible images as Iraqi infantry fled their bunkers, filmed on video 'like ghostly sheep flushed from a pen'.

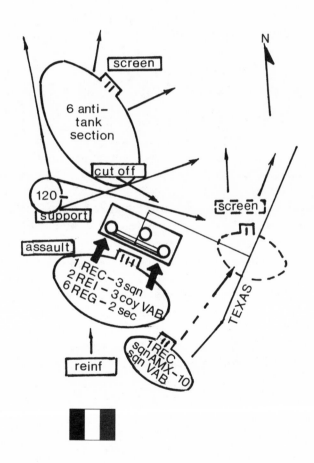

Notes

VAB – *Vehicle d'Avant Blindée* (Forward (light) Armoured Vehicle). Wheeled and equipped with HOT anti-tank missile – since seen in Bosnia.

1 REC equipped with AMX-40 vehicles.

Other abbreviations and acronyms as for Figure 6.1.

Figure 6.2   Attack on As Salman airfield, 28 February 1991 – detail

> One by one they were cut down by attackers they couldn't see or understand. Some were literally blown to bits by bursts of 30mm exploding cannon shells. One man dropped, writhed on the ground and struggled to his feet. Another burst tore him apart. A compatriot twice emerged standing from bursts. As if in pity, the American Army attackers turned and let him live ... the officers play the tapes and a hush falls over the room. Even hardened soldiers hold their breath as the Iraqi soldiers, big as football players on the TV screen, ran with nowhere to hide. These are not bridges exploding or airplane hangars. They are men.[6]

This is what we military theorists call the 'indirect approach'.

On the east coast, the Saudis breached the barrier very effectively, as did the two Marine divisions coming from the west of Kuwait's southern salient. At 04.00, with 3rd and 4th Marine Regiments leading, the 1st US Marine Division attacked across a minefield with a row of concertina wire beyond it. Once across, they were fired on by dug-in T-55 and T-62 tanks, but the Iraqis only fought for a few minutes. To the west, the 2nd Marine Division, supported by the US Army's Tiger Brigade, launched its attack at 05.30 hours. General Schwarzkopf later described this as 'an absolutely classic military breaching of a very, very tough minefield–barbed wire–fire trenches–type barrier'.

Although the Marines came under artillery fire crossing the second of two defensive barriers, they breached both. General Schwarzkopf said the operation was 'Textbook. I think it will be studied for many, many years to come as the way to do it.' At first, as it was all along the front, the weather was bad, with heavy wind, rain and clouds, hampering air support. 'God, we need some fuckin' airplanes ...' an American officer was reported as saying in exasperation. But by midday, the weather had cleared and by nightfall, 20,000 Marines had come through the two breaches in two Iraqi defensive lines, with little resistance and no casualties. Over 3,000 Iraqis, including an Army commander, had surrendered by nightfall and the Marines had advanced 20 miles towards Kuwait City.[7]

Immediately, the Allies encountered problems with the number of surrenders. The Marines reported 'they just keep coming and coming. I didn't know they had that many to give'. The main problem soon became gathering enough trucks and buses to ferry the prisoners to holding centres in Saudi Arabia.[8] The French to the west estimated 5,500 in the first ten hours (to 14.00) while there were 'many hundreds more north of our positions with white surrender flags'. By night-time, there were at least 10,000. On the left, the French attacked Rochambeau with 155mm artillery, MLRS and then AMX-30 tanks. As they advanced, the Iraqis stood up, surrendering. They took 83 prisoners in a few minutes. 'More and more prisoners. Nobody foresaw the enormity of this problem, still less did they foresee the effect it would have on the rate of advance,' says the French account.[9] 'Time is needed to neutralise the enemy, search their positions, disarm them, assemble them, push them towards the rear ... squads or sections [about 10 men] are quite simply swamped. We should have left a certain number where they were because we were in the middle of an attack and all objectives hadn't yet been taken.'

At 17.00 General Janvier decided he could not continue along his main axis, Texas,

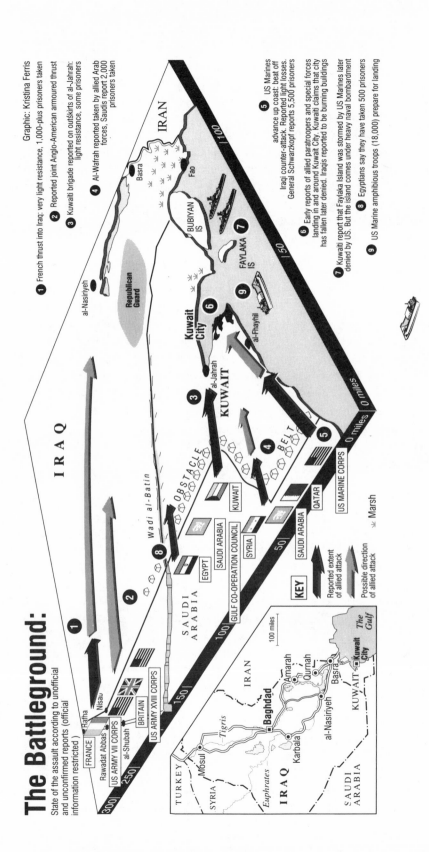

Figure 6.3 Graphic published 25 February 1991, showing the success of deception: XVIII and VII Corps counterposed (*The Independent: Graphic by Kristina Ferris*)

because of the prisoner problem, and, as darkness fell at around 18.00, took the opportunity to resupply his force. General Schwarzkopf said that by now the Allies were worried about the weather. During the afternoon, he had begun to hear stories of unspeakable atrocities in Kuwait City, as well as a report that the desalination plant had been destroyed. The plan had been to launch the remaining Allied forces – VII Corps in the centre – the next morning, but he decided to launch them immediately.

At this stage, the Marines were making progress through their breach and another Egyptian/Arab force and Saudi force were launched. This maintained the impression that the Allies were doing what the Iraqis expected – a head-on assault. At 16.00 I called the British JIB in the Hyatt to see what was happening.

'I'd get over here like a rocket, Chris.'

'What time?'

'I'd get over here like a rocket . . .'

Intense security and evasive telephone talk meant it was Norm the Storm. He was ebullient. 'We're going around, over, through, on top, underneath,' he said. The ground war was 'progressing with dramatic success, while contact with Iraqi forces had been "light".' I had duplicated copies of a sketch map of the theatre, stretching west to Raf'ha and north to Al Kufah, with roads and other features in some detail, so that I could sketch movements accurately at speed. I faxed one, which was used in preparation of the next morning's graphics. It was clear the French were heading towards Nasiriyah. Not realising at that time that the corps had been switched over, XVIII and VII Corps are shown counterposed, with the result that the airborne divisions (which we knew to be part of XVIII) and the British Division (known to be part of VII) are in the wrong places.

On the afternoon of 24th, 1st and 3rd US Armoured Divisions, 2nd Armoured Cavalry Division, 1st Infantry and 24th Mechanised were all launched, as shown in Figure 6.10.

The one formation held back was 1st British Armoured Division – the equivalent of a Soviet 'Operational Manoeuvre Group'. The rest of VII Corps had to advance rapidly through and past the first and second layers of Iraqi defence. Without adequate flank protection they could be cut off. 1st British Armoured Division's mission was to protect the flank of VII Corps by destroying the enemy's tactical reserves. These were described by General Schwarzkopf as 'tough fighters that we're worried about'.

The division was to be inserted through a breach made by the US 1st Infantry, a classic OMG insertion procedure, and then swing east, gobbling up the soft entrails of Iraqi forward divisions and attacking the harder tissue of the armoured reserve, 12 Armoured Division. The image of devouring the enemy was popular in the First World War, and was to recur. If not disabled by indigestion, the division could then help the rest of VII Corps engage the Republican Guard. Because it had two difficult jobs, the US 1st Infantry Division (Mechanised) would create the breach through which the 1st British Armoured Division was passed, to help it on its way.

The 19 February op-order foresaw three possible outcomes. The first was that, as planned, 1st British would have a 'clear run out of the breachhead' – what the

Russians call, in the OMG context, a *chisty proryv* – 'clean break'. The second was that the enemy would close on the breachhead line and the division would have to fight its way out. The third was that the enemy defensive position would prove deeper than anticipated and that the division would have to continue the breakthrough battle. The British brigades only learned that 'G-day' – the ground offensive – would begin on 24 February, two days before, ie: on 22nd.

The decision to launch VII Corps early meant bringing 'H' Hour forward 14 hours. The advantages of automated command and control immediately showed themselves. Orders were sent over the computer system, not on paper, although paper orders were kept as a back up. The VII Corps orders were rewritten and issued, over the computer screens in 35 minutes flat.

The first the British knew of the change was a message: 'look at your screens. Bad news coming in'. 'It was quite an adventurous thing to do. Not the sort of thing you get many marks for at a staff college,' mused Major General Rupert Smith, the British divisional commander.[10]

General Smith's design for battle embodied the 'deep-battle' concepts which had been studied by thinking soldiers since the 1920s. 'The British Army had to be in at the kill,' he later told an expert audience. 'Therefore I had to fight in such a way that we could endure – lots of little fights, fast.' There was no chance of lateral reinforcement from another division or corps (the Arab Joint Forces Command (North), to the east). He decided 'to deploy and fight in depth, not breadth. Only I could reinforce success ... the force ratios were such that the Allies should concentrate on a few axes and go in deep.' The enemy had powerful artillery, which out-ranged that of the Allies. Therefore, I could focus the power of the division rather than mass it, conduct business on a very narrow frontage ... attack the enemy in such a way as to prevent him firing and moving ... easily *digestible* objectives for the brigades.'[11]

The deep battle scheme had much in common with Soviet 1930s deep battle theory, notably in the way that units and formations were self-contained at each level. General Smith relied on his two brigades to deal with the objectives they were given. There was a divisional reserve group, mounted on tank transporters, ready to come fresh to the battle if needed. There was also a divisional reconstitution group. After each action, each brigade would be reconstituted to 90 per cent of its original combat power. If a company was badly knocked about, it would have been possible to replace it completely. 'We never suffered the casualties to prove whether this idea was a starter or not', General Smith said later. 'But we certainly had the ability to isolate formations. On the first night the brigades were completely cut off from divisional logistics.' To sustain the division in this long run, resupply routes were built behind it, heading right for the final objective. A 'route development battle group' was formed to protect that road. If the enemy had counter-attacked in the flank – the British fully expected to be on the receiving end of the Republican Guard coming from the north – they would have known exactly where the vulnerable resupply vehicles were, not scattered about across the desert.

Like all the Allied divisions moving through Iraq, the aim was to destroy enemy forces, not capture ground. There was no ground of any tactical significance whatever. It was like war at sea or in the air. The Iraqis' attempts to hold ground were, as General Smith put it, 'like an airman trying to defend a cloud.'

And, as at sea and in the air, it is equipment that destroys the enemy. Men and women are there to operate it. 'I was fighting my equipment, I was not equipping men,' said General Smith. 'Men were an *embarrassment*. They had to be *fed*, they were *casualties waiting to happen*.'

The British artillery exemplified the 'firepower not manpower' philosophy. As General Smith said, there was 'little point having MLRSs and A10s if you are not using them accurately at their full range. So, for these reasons, I grouped medium reconnaissance and air elements under the CRA [Commander Royal Artillery] to fight the depth battle.' To manage the difficult task of engaging depth targets while on the move, the CRA, Brigadier Ian Durie, devised a system similar to the Soviet 'reconnaissance-strike complex' which we had all studied in the mid-1980s, though without the automation. The 'Artillery and depth fire organisation' managed air support and electronic warfare as well as traditional artillery fire support, and all sources of intelligence and target acquisition with everybody working closely together. The artillery Group even controlled the reconnaissance regiment, the 16th/5th Lancers. 'This arrangement was designed to ensure that we could look for, identify and attack the GOC's [General Smith's] key targets in the divisional depth battle. In the event, as the battle developed, the lack of integral target acquisition assets and the speed of the Divisional advance, combined with the lack of response from the Iraqis, meant that we were never able fully to exploit the concept. Even so, we were credited by the Corps headquarters as being the division most capable of exploiting the divisional battle in depth.'[12]

Before 1st British was inserted, the US 1st Cavalry Division made a feint to the right along the Wadi al-Batin, which coincided with Iraqi expectations. Feints to confuse the enemy were a standard feature of any OMG insertion, and were illustrated in the graphic which we published, not knowing how close to the real thing it was, as 1st British moved through the breach. The original portrayal of an OMG breakthrough, the version we published and what actually happened on the night of 24/25 February are shown in Figures 6.4–6.6.

Learning that the launch time had been brought forward, at about midday on 24 February, Brigadier Durie had hurriedly to re-work the fireplan, reducing it from an hour to 30 minutes. Several targets were now 'unsafe' – there were friendly forces on them – and there was a serious risk of mistakes. All 60 batteries had to check the fireplan carefully: the last thing anybody wanted was to begin by blasting away one of their own units. The shorter fireplan was also influenced by fears that unexploded bomblets would impede rather than accelerate the advance. It had been discovered that between five and ten per cent of the MLRS bomblets did not explode on impact. With the Americans, Brigadier Durie agreed that the fireplan would begin at 14.30, prior to an 'H-hour' for the US 1st Infantry Division's forward move of 15.00.

The British planned to carry all their Main Battle Tanks and engineer equipment – the most critical equipment – forward on tank transporters. However, changing the

Artillery support for OMG insertion (postulated). DC, Dummy Concentration: TZ, Tactical Zone, up to 30 kilometres wide. 1. Several probing attacks to discover weak points in enemy defence: 2. Main forces punch hole through tactical zone; 3. OMG waiting silently in concentration areas up to 50 kilometres behind Soviet FLOT; 4. BM27s put down remote minefield to protect flanks of penetration; 5. 2S5s (range up to 28–29 kilometres) and 203 mm gun (up to 30 kilometres) fire at targets throughout gap; 6. Other Army and Front artillery engages other targets such as anti-tank weapons likely to threaten flanks of penetration; 7. OMG inserted with massive artillery and air support; 8. The OMG has now moved into the enemy operational depth; based on a tank division, the maximum range of its own artillery (2S3s) is some 24 kilometres; 9. 240 mm self-propelled mortars attached to OMG smash difficult targets close to and threatening it, up to their maximum range of 12 kilometres.

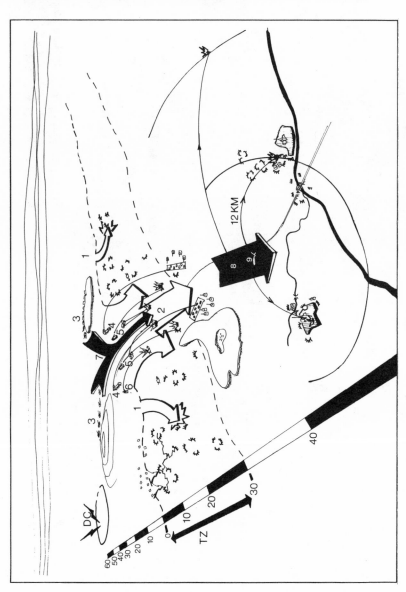

Figure 6.4 Schematic of possible OMG insertion, 1985.

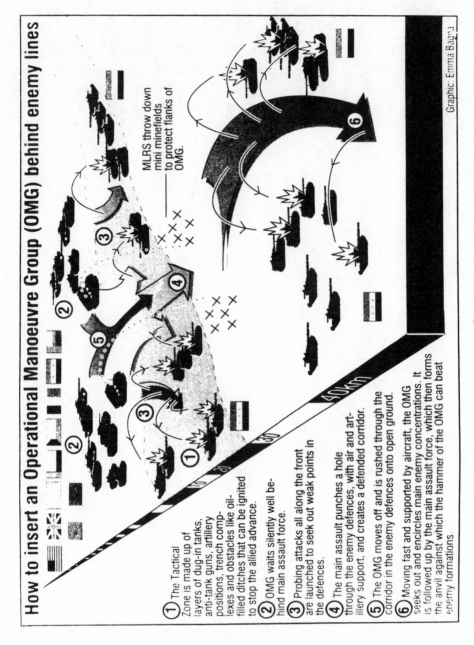

Figure 6.5 Graphic showing possible insertion of Allied 'OMG' (published in *The Independent*, 25 February 1991).

start-time also meant that most of these had to drive forward under their own steam. The British occupied a forming up point, with three Egyptian brigades to the east of them.

The US 1st Infantry Division forced a breach with 16 lanes. Two, D and M, were the main routes for non-tracked vehicles, at least 15 metres wide with a hard surface, and up to two kilometres long. C, G and K were lanes for tracked vehicles, not extending beyond the obstacle belt itself. Priority Two were lanes A and P, return routes for non-tracked vehicles, then R and O, the return routes for tracked vehicles. By last light they had advanced 15 kilometres, with no casualties. During the night, the British guns moved forward, ahead of the manoeuvre brigades.

By mid morning on 25th – 'G+1' – as discerning people in Britain saw our graphic in the morning paper, 1st Infantry had nearly completed the bridgehead. With little Iraqi reaction and no sign of their armoured reserves closing on the bridgehead, as might have been expected, General Smith ordered 7th Armoured Brigade through the breach to attack the deep northern objective, Copper North. They worked their way through the breach, through and round the gun positions, and were on their start-line by 15.00, the same time as the US 1st Infantry began their break-out. In fact, 1st Infantry did not overtake 7th Armoured Brigade until it was secure on its first objective and the battle switched to 4th Armoured Brigade in the south. This and subsequent British objectives are shown in Figure 6.7.

Meanwhile, on the far left, the French had begun moving again, towards objective 'White', As-Salman airfield. Had it not been for the Global Positioning System, the French reckoned they would have got lost during the night. At 11.00 the Legion was ordered to take the airstrip. Between 13.00 and 14.00, as the British were moving towards their first objective, Allied aircraft attacked As-Salman far to the west. Now they were in Iraq, they could have a drink, and they did. By 16.00, the Legionnaires were two and a half kilometres away, watching fascinated as artillery fire came down on the concrete runways. 'Like thunder when you can feel the shock wave on your face', one Legionnaire said. The engineers breached the perimeter wire with Miclics – an American version of the Bangalore torpedo, an explosive hosepipe, and the 1st REC regiment drove through, splitting into three and securing the airfield. A few kilometres away, the Spahis had taken objective Bordeaux, a crossroads south of the airfield, while the Marines and other French troops occupied the crests also to the south of the airfield.[13]

By the morning of 25th (see Figure 6.11) the 101st Air Assault Division had leaped forward again, from its base 'Cobra', and successfully arrived on Highway 8, the main road from Basra and Baghdad along the Euphrates. During the night, under cover of darkness and driving rain, their UH-60A Black Hawk helicopters had landed darkly along the Euphrates. The Egyptian corps in JFC(N), attacking Kuwait's southern border between the salient and the Wadi al-Batin, launched a breaching operation at 04.00 on G+1, the second day. It had taken its first main objective by late afternoon. On the east coast, JFC(E), comprising Saudis, Kuwaitis, Omanis and men from the UAE countries, were moving up towards Kuwait City, though delayed by fog and, as ever, vast numbers of Iraqi prisoners of war.

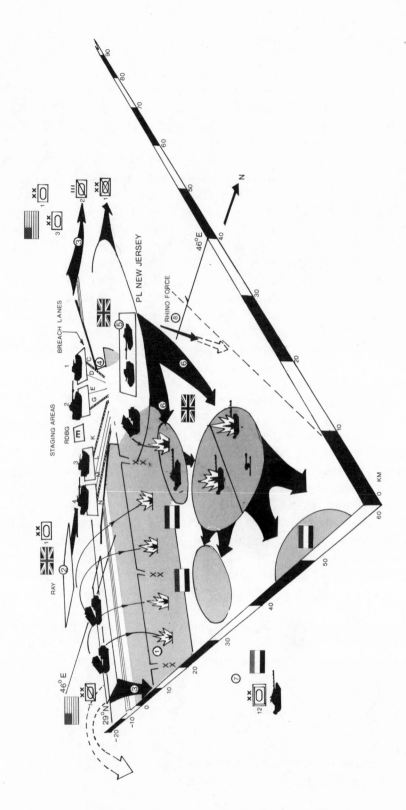

Figure 6.6 What actually happened on 25 February 1991. Insertion of 1st (UK) Armoured Division.

KEY

1. Tactical zone, made up of obstacle belt (first 10 km), behind which are divisional positions (15 km deep).

2. 1st (UK) Armoured Division (OMG) waits silently behind main assault force.

3. Probing/diversionary attacks by 1st (US) Armoured Cavalry Division (East) and 2nd (US) Armoured Cavalry Regiment (West). Artillery raids have added to the uncertainty as to where the breach will be made.

4. Main assault by 1st (US) Infantry Division (Mechanised) punches a hole through the enemy defences, with air and artillery support, and creates corridor.

5. 1st (UK) Armoured Division moves through the breach prepared by 1st (US) Inf. Div (Mech) with 8 lanes through the enemy defences and onto open ground.

6. 1st (UK) Armd. Div, advances into enemy depth, seeking out and attacking enemy formations. 4 Armd. Bde moves on the southern axis, 7 Armd. Bde on the northern one.

7. 12th (IZ) Armoured Division, the main Iraqi tactical reserve.

8. Rhino Force, the deception force, uses vehicle movement, dust creation, dummy radio transmissions and artificial noise to simulate movement of the advance guard of an armoured force in column. This force takes up station on a flank parallel to the divisional axis, simulating the movement of a noisy armoured column with slack radio discipline. The force includes an artillery observation post party which can broadcast a false fire plan but can also call for protective artillery fire if the force is attacked. On encountering the enemy, Rhino Force is to withdraw under cover of smoke and artillery fire. Large Area Smoke Screen (LASS) vehicles can simulate extra dust.

RDGB – Route Development Battle Group
PL – Phase Line

Shading indicates the entire depth of the tactical zone, both obstacle belt and depth of divisional positions. Depth is measured from the beginning of the obsteacle belt, which begins about 5 km in from the border berm (illustrated).

---------- – Northern edge of British sector (see Figure 6.7).

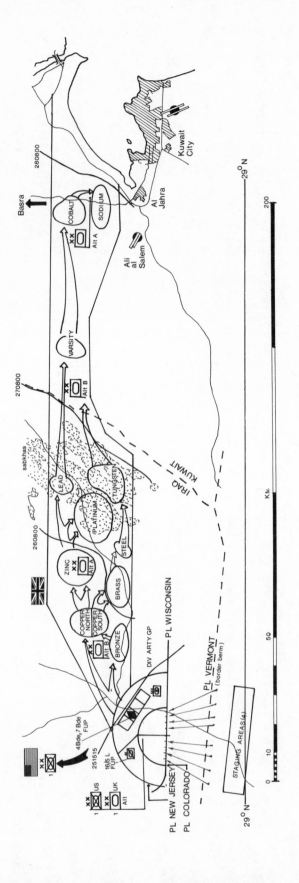

KEY

FUP – Forming Up Point

16/5L – 16th/5th Lancers (reconnaissance regiment)

Alt – Alternate divisional headquarters, which leapfrogged forward

Six figure groups – Date time groups: 251515 is 15.15, 25 February etc. All times are 'Charlie' (local). 280800 was cease-fire.

Objectives named after metals are known groupings of Iraqi forces. Note the great size of the objectives. 12 (IZ) Armoured Division is on objective Platinum.

Figure 6.7 Attack of the 1st (UK) Armoured Division. Having passed through the breach created by 1st (US) Infantry Division (mechanized), the Division swung right, behind the Iraqi forward defences, to engage the tactical reserves.

By the end of 25 February, seven Iraqi divisions were reckoned to be destroyed and 25,000 prisoners taken. The spearpoint of the US Marine 'Corps' – Marcent – was ten miles from Kuwait City. And, as a British official report later commented:

> One of the most remarkable features of that second day was that the Iraqis had still not grasped what was happening to them. They continued to believe that the greatest threat was from the south where 1st (US) Cavalry Division's feint attacks into the Wadi al-Batin had been so successful. The Iraqis continued to be unaware of VII (US) Corps' vast left hook which was gathering momentum to the north-west of Kuwait.[14]

By the next day, Tuesday 26th (see Figure 6.12), Saddam Hussein had given the order to withdraw from Kuwait, a surprise announcement on Baghdad radio late on 25th. But Iraqi heavy armour was effectively trapped by the rivers and marshes to the north, the bridges over which were down, and the Allied forces closing, unexpectedly, from the west. The 24th US Mechanised Division, which was completing a huge 200-mile sweep towards Basra, encountered 57 T-72s – the Iraqis' better tanks, probably belonging to the Republican Guard – heading west along Highway 8, and destroyed them all.

However, by this time the rapid advance of XVIII Corps had been interrupted as violent wind and rain got in the way of helicopter resupply. The following day, they had begun to outrun their fuel supplies and medical support as they ran into the Republican Guard from the left flank. They might have faced another serious obstacle, as Brigadier General Neal later reported:

> Just before the attack [on 24th] one of the problems we ran into was we flew an RF-4 [Phantom reconnaissance plane] over an area that the XVIII Airborne Corps was going to have to attack up in the northern part, and all of a sudden we got this picture back and it looked like an enormous minefield 10 miles by 10 miles square. That's an extraordinary number of mines. We just discarded this right away but other people who were smarter than us looked at that and said 'you can't just discard this. They're going to attack through this area – it's an enormous minefield.'
>
> It took us about an hour to figure out – this was right before the attack – that what we really were looking at was a gigantic seismographic place where the oil guys go through and punch holes in the ground and they're very evenly spaced – just like you'd find in a minefield, this enormous area, one hole right after the other. In an overhead picture it looked like a minefield. It took a real good imagery guy to read it out and decide that what we were looking at was one of these seismographic areas.[15]

There could be no doubt of the cardinal importance of trained specialists.

The 24th Infantry Division made what General Schwarzkopf called an 'unbelievable move' across into the Euphrates valley. By the 27th they were at the huge airfield at Jalibah, with three runways, destroying aircraft on the ground including some MiG-29s. 'We're outrunning fuel, we're outrunning medevac,' warned a major as he left for another mission. The 101st had also reached the Euphrates and were moving east along both sides of the river. According to Brigadier General Ed Scholes, the Deputy Commander of XVIII Corps, the Iraqis were still surprised to be attacked by Allied forces coming from the west three days into the war.

It went awfully, awfully fast. I think it's pretty obvious when you see the situation of our enemy. He is pretty disorganised, pretty confused. I think the key has been the speed and size of this operation, that really caught him totally by surprise. To be on the Euphrates, to block him and then to turn east to destroy his forces. Even the Republican Guards were shocked.[16]

In order to resupply the Corps, 230 Saudi trucks, each carrying 8,000 gallons of fuel, were running into a rear supply point every day. The entire Corps consumed about 2 million gallons a day.

Near the Kuwait border, the US Tiger Brigade had attacked, supporting the Marines. On the second day, as the attacking formations converged, the Brigade commander Colonel John Sylvester became concerned that the Syrians were getting too close to his left flank and that the Tigers might get Syrian T-55 tanks in their sights by mistake, and warned them accordingly. It was a constant problem.[17]

Some 16 hours after crossing the start line, and 100 kilometres into Iraq, the 1st British Armoured Division command and artillery communications and targeting nets broke down. 'If you wish to undertake offensive actions rapidly . . . then commanders need to be able to collect the information they need at that level. Gathering information from superior or flanking formations was difficult. If you want to conduct high-tempo operations in great depth you need information collecting equipments in reserve,' said General Smith. The speed of the British advance had out-paced the ability of its information-gathering resources to keep up. 'The equipments were inadequate – too slow. Neither were they hard enough,' he added. The official British report later confirmed that 'the Division also lacked a fully effective integral airborne surveillance, reconnaissance and depth target acquisition capability – the long-serving Midge drone proving unreliable and unable to provide real-time information.' The result: 'we abandoned the depth battle.'[18]

Brigadier Durie agreed. 'With no depth target information from Allied airborne reconnaissance means, now all dedicated to support the Corps main effort [against the Republican Guard], with drones and Army Air Corps helicopters unable to fly in the conditions, and with sound ranging never able to keep up with the speed of the advance,' he reallocated the Depth Fire General Support Group to a more modest role behind 7th Armoured Brigade.[19]

But the divide between 'depth' and 'contact' battles was, in any case, becoming blurred, and the artillery remained highly effective. The new British L15 155mm round was particularly deadly, and the Americans were 'endlessly impressed'. It was reported to be three times more lethal than earlier rounds, because of its multi-role fuse which allowed it to be programmed to burst on the ground or in the air at varying heights. Against troops in the open, airburst is by far the most efficient and lethal form, and the overpressure from the burst, never mind the efficient fragmentation, could cause severe concussion to troops nearby. On one occasion, 40 Field Regiment RA was, unwittingly, the first British unit to reach an Iraqi position during the night. At first light they saw the Iraqis 300 metres away and opened up with their machine guns while preparing to fire over open sights, when the Royal Scots Dragoon Guards charged through the Iraqi position from the south.[20]

The speed of the British Division's advance was limited as much by the slower elements – the old FV-432 Armoured Personnel Carriers, for example, and by the huge number of prisoners-of-war – as by enemy action. Also, the reconnaissance troops' older, lightly armoured vehicles of the CVR(T) series were unsuited to fast operations in open country.

Even so, the Iraqis were stunned by the speed and direction of the British attack. The only enemy guns which were not destroyed were captured in the Wadi-al-Batin area, the 'slot' where they expected the attack to come from, facing south. By 06.00 on 27 February, after 39 hours, the British had destroyed three divisions, destroyed or captured 264 tanks and 213 guns and taken 7,024 prisoners.[21] (See Figure 6.13.)

On the morning of 26 February, we were told that the Allies had not yet reached the Kuwait City limits, although they were closing. That night we were told that 21 Iraqi divisions were 'combat ineffective'. That did not mean they were all dead, wounded or prisoner, but they had broken up, many were disarmed, and others were just running.

The situation on the morning of 27 February is shown in Figure 6.13. The US Marines had encircled Kuwait City and controlled all access but the politically significant task of 'liberating' Kuwait city was left to the Arab forces of JFCN and JFCE. The Marines had encircled the airport, but had held off during the night because of the danger of firing at each other. 'We weren't in a hurry. We didn't have to have the airport by sunset last night ... I suspect it will be clear very early this morning,' we were told early on 27th. Meanwhile, the 101st to the west had established firm positions on the Euphrates and switched their effort to attacking the Republican Guard.

We were well briefed on the momentous events of the ground war as they unfolded. Brigadier General Neal would brief us at 07.00, when he came out of the war room after an all night shift, as well as in the evening. On the night of the 25th, I had dinner with some colleagues at the Gulf Royal Chinese Restaurant, and we heard that a Scud had fallen on Dhahran, killing at least 12 soldiers and injuring 25 more. We later learned that 28 had been killed and a further 100 wounded. The Patriots had not been launched to intercept it, apparently due to a software bug. Maybe our luck was beginning to run out. . . .

There was nothing one could do, absolutely nothing. We left at about 23.30, and passed a coachload of Chinese waiters who were waiting until we were thrown out before they could be sent home. 'The persistence of the normal is strong,' as Barbara Tuchman, the historian, wrote of the Black Death. Indeed. We returned to the Hyatt, when there was another Scud alert. By the time we reached the basement, the all-clear sounded. Afterwards, we chatted in someone's room until about 01.00 in the morning. On the way back to the 'Intercon' in a taxi, I was stopped by Saudi military police for a random check – the first time it had happened in the entire war. Now the Allies were clearly winning, the Saudis were getting more repressive.

On 26th, we received the first accounts of the early progress of 1st British Armoured Division. They were given by Colonel Barry Stevens, a former tactics instructor at the School of Artillery, Larkhill. Colonel Stevens perhaps misjudged the mood of his audience. We received the first reports of the tragic error by US A-10 pilots, when they attacked Warriors of 4 Brigade, killing nine British soldiers. It was an utter tragedy, although there could have been hundreds of tragedies like it. How many were there in the First and Second World Wars, do you think? In April 1942, RAF Hurricanes were demonstrating their ground attack prowess on Salisbury Plain. Five machine-gunned their targets – the sixth attacked a spectator stand in error, killing dozens of quite senior officers. That got a small paragraph or two in *The Times* on 30 April. The only reason I know is because my brother-in-law was born that day and we bought him an old copy of the paper for his 50th birthday.

As the Allies advanced, they had to deal with hundreds of Iraqi dead at a time. In the desert – anywhere – you cannot leave bodies lying around. It is a health hazard, apart from anything else. You bury them, recording the position and, if time permits, any identification, for others to trace them later. That is what the Geneva convention requires, and the Allies used their Global Positioning System to record the positions of the mass graves accurately. That is war. It also treats the dead with some respect. Colonel Stevens alluded to this practice.

'You mean you're *burying* them? Just *burying* them?' whined an annoying female US journalist.

Colonel Stevens was understandably annoyed at her naivété.

'I am not here to discuss the pornography of war . . .'. He stormed off.

I sympathised, but perhaps it was not the best way to deal with such questions. With that and first reports of the British deaths from friendly fire, the atmosphere became strained. People got very upset. Généviève Rossier said 'I can't stand this . . .' and left. The next day, by contrast, General Schwarzkopf, for whom everybody had colossal respect, explained the same Allied actions in straightforward terms. There were no complaints, not a murmur.

27 February was 'a slow day' for us. 'Waiting for briefings to gear up,' I recorded. 'Delayed several times: 17.30 – 18.00 – 18.10 – 18.20 – 18.30 . . .'

Meanwhile tanks of 1st and 3rd (US) Armoured Divisions had continued to attack the Republican Guard throughout the night. In spite of the continuing rain, the US had a pivotal advantage with their thermal imaging sights and kept firing. The remnants of the RGFC were driven back into the Basra pocket. Iraqi soldiers abandoned their vehicles and escaped on foot. The Iraqis had begun fleeing from Kuwait City the previous day, and had been slaughtered as they fled north carrying their pathetic booty of video recorders, television sets and some hostages, a massacre known as 'the road to Basra' although I was told that the worst destruction was on the road to the north east, out towards Bubiyan. On 27th, a Pentagon official said: 'Kuwait City is not under Iraqi control. That is clear.' The Arab forces were in the process of securing it. This followed the large-scale tank battle around the airport in which an Iraqi division lost over 100 tanks to 1st US Marine Division. Pockets of resistance remained along the Mutla ridge and the northern border of Kuwait.

On 27 February, 1st British Armoured Division crossed the northern extremity of the Wadi al-Batin into Kuwait. Brigadier Cordingley recalled 'At 9.30 am I entered Kuwait from Iraq and stopped to celebrate with a cup of tea. This seemed a typically

British thing to do.' They occupied objective Varsity by 12.30, which the Iraqis had evacuated. The division was warned of two possible future tasks. Either advance south to clear the Wadi al-Batin or east, to cut the Basra–Kuwait road. Since the 1st US Cavalry, who had been feinting up the Wadi had been withdrawn south and then pushed through the same breach through which 1st British had been inserted, that seemed an ignominious task. Nor was it ideal for a fast moving armoured division. But by late afternoon that looked the most likely task. Then, at 20.30 hours, the division was warned that it would most likely be advancing east. At 22.30 General Smith issued new orders. 'Attack east to cut routes from Kuwait City to prevent [the] Iraqi Army from retreating North.'[22]

By this time, everyone was terribly tired. 'Because of the risk of inadvertent "blue-on-blue" engagements as the divisions bumped into each other,' Brigadier Durie recorded, 'the Corps plan that had 1st Armoured Division swinging north was abandoned. Then the plan that we should open a Main Supply Route south … [through the Wadi-al-Batin] was also scrapped; lastly we were ordered to cross into Kuwait to be ready to fight north or east as required.'[23] It was in this condition that British tanks from 4th Armoured Brigade fired on Royal Artillery air defence vehicles of 7th Armoured Brigade. Brigadier Durie said they fired across their brigade boundary, an allegation denied by the 4th Armoured Brigade Chief of Staff.[24] However it happened, everyone was exhausted: two men were lucky to escape with burns, albeit severe. Tiredness was affecting men's judgement.

The division's advance had taken it across the Wadi al-Batin, the most prominent geographical feature in the area. Two years later, on 24 February 1993, the British announced the battle honours to be awarded. Some units could claim the theatre honour, 'The Gulf': those in the division's long advance, 'Wadi al-Batin'. It was a permanent landmark – after all, the boundaries of Saudi Arabia, Iraq and Kuwait might alter one day, and it had a rather exotic sound to it. There was also the battle honour 'Western Iraq'. There were only two groups I could think of who would be bidding for that: the SAS and the SBS.

But the wording of battle honours was the furthest thing from anyone's mind on 27 February 1991. Back in Riyadh, we got word that the 'sink' – the C-in-C, General Schwarzkopf, would speak at 21.00 (local). It was clearly going to be an event of some significance and I warned the paper to that effect. We were three hours ahead of London, so that worked in favour of filing stories for the paper.

The briefing was 'mind-blowing', as I recorded in the diary, although we did not expect anything so final or comprehensive. General Schwarzkopf revealed how he had reduced Iraq from the fourth or fifth largest military power in the world to a position in which it could not even threaten other states in the region after four days of ground fighting with just 79 US dead since 17 January.

He appeared from the war room to give a 'complete briefing on the operations'. Now that the Allied forces had reached their final objectives, there was no reason to conceal their positions or the operational art and strategy of the campaign any more, he said.

Concisely and rapidly he detailed one of the greatest campaigns in military history, a masterpiece of planning and deception at every level, which he had commanded.

He spoke showing a keen intellect, a dry sense of humour, a deep humanity, compassion for the dead and their families, disgust for the atrocities in Kuwait, of which he refused to speak in detail, and, only now that defeat and victory had been assigned, contempt for his adversary, Saddam Hussein.

Asked his opinion of Saddam as a military commander he said 'he is neither a strategist, nor is he schooled in the operational art, nor is he a tactician, nor is he a general, nor is he a soldier. Apart from that, he's a great military man'. I later thought that some of our home-grown 'strategic studies' experts should muse on those thoughts.

General Schwarzkopf described the low Allied casualties as 'almost miraculous. It will never be miraculous to the families of those people but it was miraculous.'

He would not speculate on the number of Iraqi casualties – nobody would, horrified by memories of Vietnam 'body counts' – but admitted that in the Iraqi units in the front line there had been 'a very, very large number of dead'.[25]

What General Schwarzkopf said is shown in Appendix A. My job was to get it in the next morning's paper. This was the commander of one of the greatest battles of encirclement in history – live. I took a taxi back to the Intercon, and contacted the office at 22.00 local, 19.00 in the UK.

It was Mark Rosselli on the Gulf desk.

'The boss classes were very impressed with the briefing [they had seen it on CNN, live]. The good news is you've got 1500 words. The bad news is we need it in one hour ...'

It would take nearly half an hour to file 1500 words anyway. 'Get copy to call me in half an hour,' I said.

I had followed the General's description of the campaign on my photocopied sketch maps. I penned the first few paragraphs, the trickiest bit. Then I would talk it through from my sketches and notes.

They were delayed getting back, because the satellite telephone links were all jammed with people trying to file.

'Somebody fast, please ...' Our copy takers are all fast – 1,000 words in 15 minutes. As the copy tumbled over the telephone, it would be stored, and I would get the occasional word count. '697....1239....1461....1513'

'Finished'.

'It's just what we wanted. We saw it coming through,' Mark said.

At midnight, Saudi time – 21.00 UK time, I put the 'phone down, ordered dinner and several bottles of Moussy non-alcoholic beer, and collapsed. After two months of alcohol-free war, you could convince yourself that the non-alcoholic stuff was the real thing.

I fell into a deep sleep.

The next morning, I woke at about 08.00. There had been a ceasefire, the radio said. At 08.00 Saudi time, 05.00 Greenwich time, midnight Washington time. The magic 100 hours had appealed to President Bush. There had been a sense of finality about General Schwarzkopf's hour-long final briefing the night before but I was still mildly surprised by the speed of the Iraqi collapse. I had thought the final battles would be hard. Hard they were, but sporadic and never prolonged. And incredibly free of Allied casualties, although the risk of disaster was never absent. There were about 200 Iraqi tanks in one, revetted position, two artillery battalions in another, but serious opposition had disintegrated. The position of Allied forces at ceasefire is in Figure 6.14.

'They've stopped too soon,' I growled to myself – an instant, visceral reaction.

Had they?

THE PENCILLED MAP ALIVE WITH WAR:
JSTARS PICTURES OF THE GROUND WAR FROM THE AIR

Never before in the history of war have the movements of forces in a great land battle been visible in their entirety. These radar pictures were taken from a US E-8 JSTARS – Joint Surveillance Target Attack Radar System – aircraft. The success of the operation depended on near 'real time' data from a handful of aircraft including the E8, the TR-1 high altitude reconnaissance plane (usually referred to by the US Air Force as the U2), and the RF-4C long-range Phantom.

The two JSTARS aircraft were built by the Grumman Corporation round Boeing-707 airframes and were still under development when pressed into service in the Gulf War. JSTARS has a huge, 7.3 metre antenna for its sideways looking radar mounted beneath the aircraft, combining a moving target indicator (MTI) mode with a synthetic aperture radar (SAR) for identifying targets. This allowed it to detect troop movements and even surface-to-surface missile sites. Sometimes the moving imagery was confusing. In one of the frames a 'vee' can be seen in the north – Iraqi forces moving into blocking positions, with three units dispersing to the north-west. In the south a thick return from the radar proved to be concertina wire blowing in the wind.

The two JSTARS aircraft flew alternating 12-hour shifts throughout the war. They and the U2s proved that satellites were not always the best means of surveying enemy activity. Satellite orbits are highly predictable, whereas high-flying aircraft are flexible and can provide more detailed information more quickly. Satellites did, however, play an important role in Battle Damage Assessment (BDA).

JSTARS proved ideal for tracking ground forces on the move, as the pictures show. Airborne and naval activity was monitored by E3 Airborne Warning and Control Aircraft (AWACS), of the US and Saudi Air Forces, US Navy E2C Hawkeyes and P3C Orions. The USAF also had Airborne Battlefield Command and Control Centres (ABCCCs) mounted in EC-130 modified Hercules aircraft to relay battlefield information to the attack aircraft waiting overhead.

These pictures are the manifestation of a matching of military theory and practice of which military theorists and historians have long dreamed. They bring to mind the words of Sidney Keyes' *Timoshenko* (1942). 'And in a rage of love, and grief, and pity, he made the pencilled map alive with war.'

PLATE A.24 FEBRUARY (G-DAY)

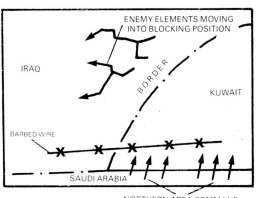

ENEMY ELEMENTS MOVING
INTO BLOCKING POSITION

IRAQ

BORDER

KUWAIT

BARBED WIRE

SAUDI ARABIA

NORTHERN AREA COMMAND

* Lower centre: Northern Area
  Command force in breeching
  operation.

* Heavy lateral return near
  the bottom is barbed wire
  blowing in the wind.

* Upper right. Iraqis moving
  into blocking positions,
  interdicted by Allied air
  strikes.

PLATE B.25 FEBRUARY (G +1)

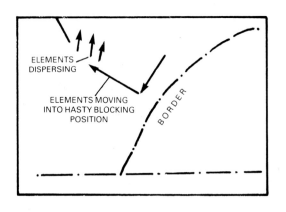

ELEMENTS
DISPERSING

ELEMENTS MOVING
INTO HASTY BLOCKING
POSITION

BORDER

* Enemy moving NW into blocking positions.

* These were engaged on the move and destroyed.

* Note. 3 elements dispersing on north side of the road.

PLATE C. 26 FEBRUARY (G +2)

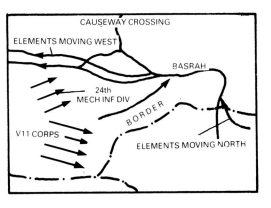

1st (UK) Armd Div.
* Lower left: VII Corps in attack of Republican Guard. 1st (UK) Armd Div. in south.
* Traffic in KTO moving north towards Basra
* Traffic from Basrah moving west on two parallel routes south of Euphrates.
* 24th Mech Inf Div moving to interdict routes.
* Top (centre), traffic moving north across causeway.

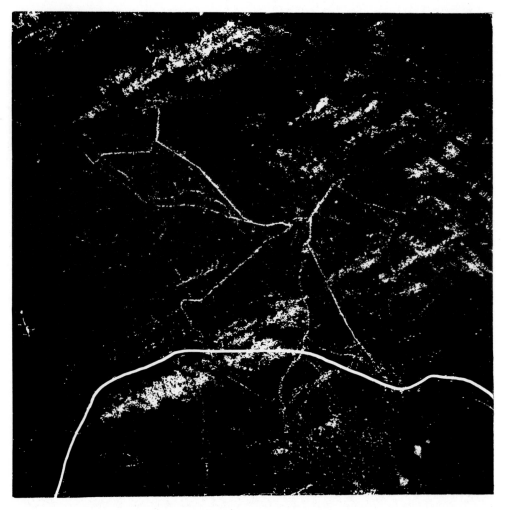

PLATE D.26 FEBRUARY (G +2)

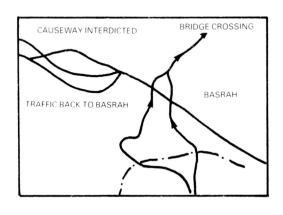

* Magnified detail of Plate C.

* Causeway interdicted, traffic blocked.

* Traffic flow is back to Basra along the two parallel routes.

* Some traffic crossing Euphrates at Basrah.

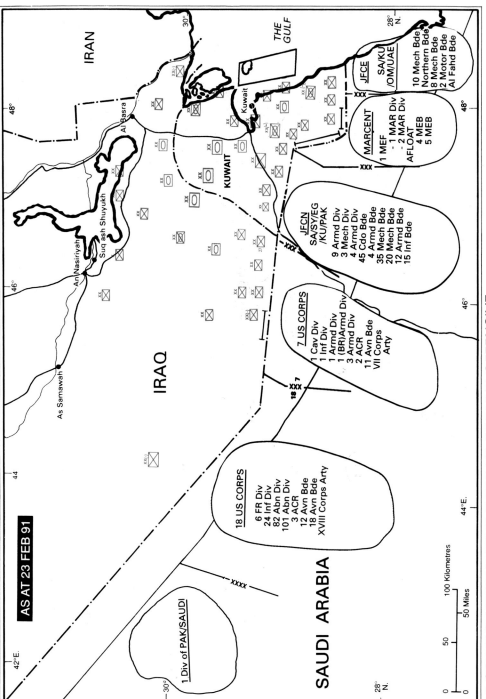

6.8 STATE OF OPERATIONS PRIOR TO GROUND OFFENSIVE

AS AT 23 FEB 91

IRAN

IRAQ

SAUDI ARABIA

KUWAIT

THE GULF

Al Basra
An Nasiriyah
Suq ash Shuyukh
As Samawah
Kuwait

18 US CORPS
6 FR Div
24 Inf Div
82 Abn Div
101 Abn Div
3 ACR
12 Avn Bde
18 Avn Bde
XVIII Corps Arty

7 US CORPS
1 Cav Div
1 Inf Div
1 Armd Div
1 (BR)Armd Div
3 Armd Div
2 ACR
11 Avn Bde
VII Corps Arty

JFCN
SA/SY/EG
/KU/PAK
9 Armd Div
3 Armd Div
4 Armd Div
45 Cdo Bde
4 Armd Bde
35 Mech Bde
20 Mech Bde
12 Armd Bde
15 Inf Bde

MARCENT
1 MEF
- 1 MAR Div
- 2 MAR Div
AFLOAT
4 MEB
5 MEB

JFCE
SA/KU
/OM/UAE
10 Mech Bde
Northern Bde
8 Mech Bde
2 Motor Bde
Al Fahd Bde

1 Div of PAK/SAUDI

100 Kilometres
50 Miles

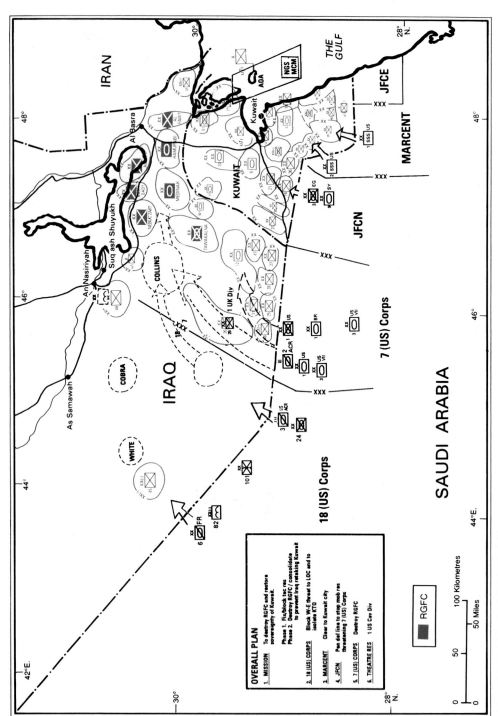

6.9 OVERALL ALLIED PLAN

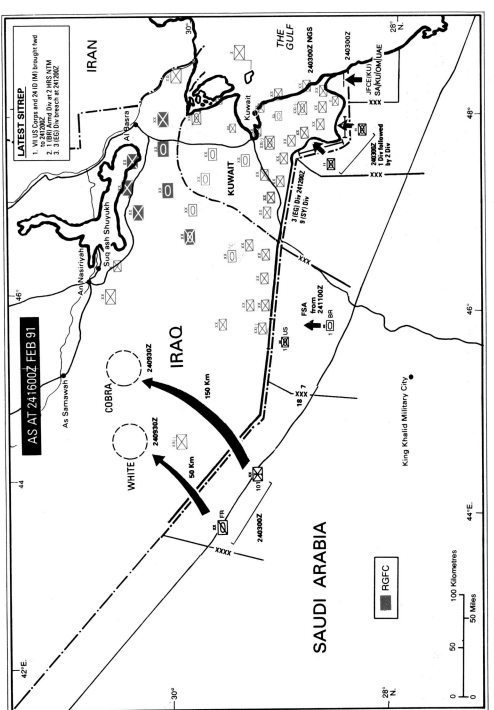

6.10 SITUATION PM 24 FEBURARY

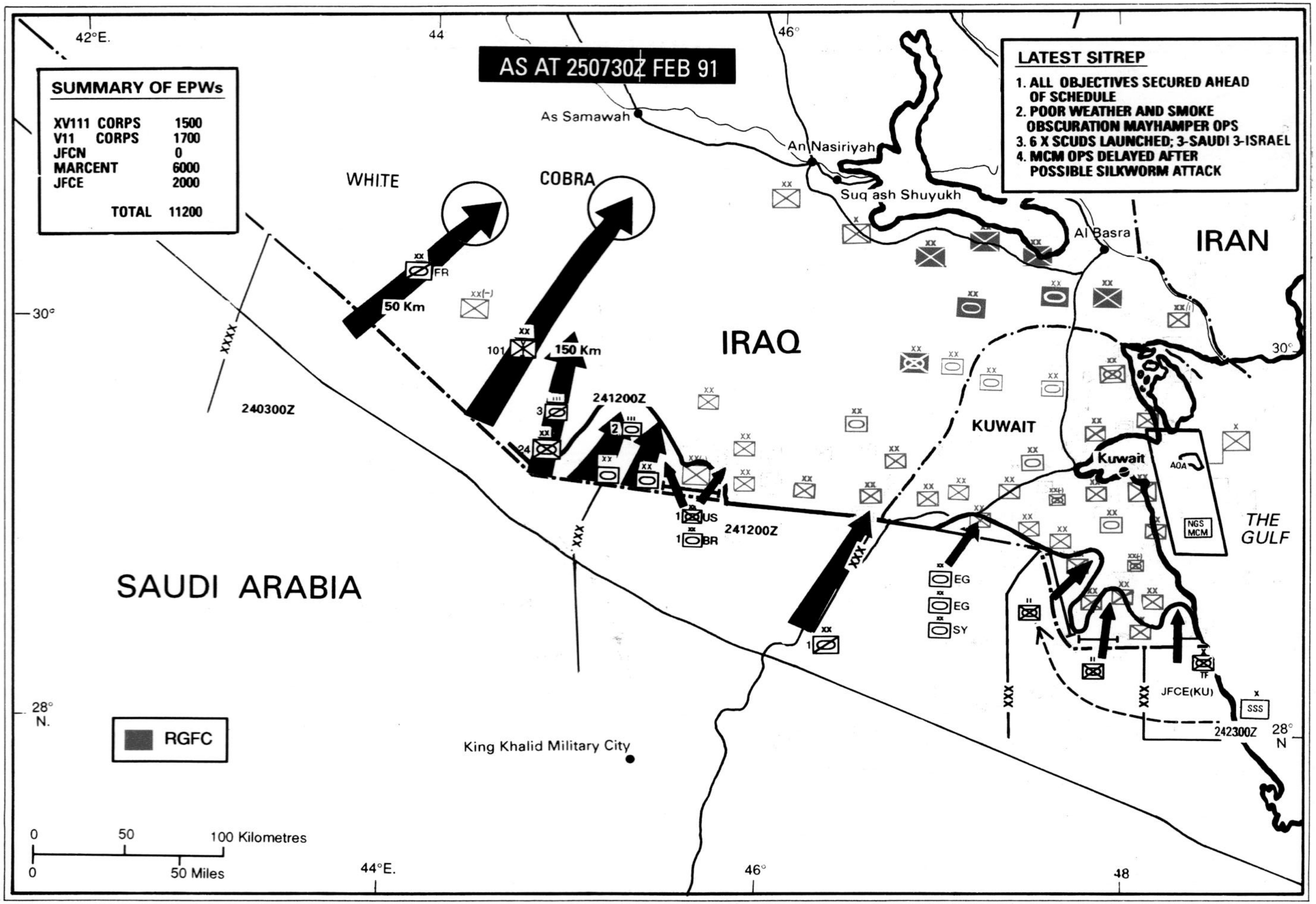

AS AT 250730Z FEB 91
SUMMARY OF EPWs
XV111 CORPS 1500
V11 CORPS 1700
JFCN 0
MARCENT 6000
JFCE 2000
TOTAL 11200
LATEST SITREP
1. ALL OBJECTIVES SECURED AHEAD OF SCHEDULE
2. POOR WEATHER AND SMOKE OBSCURATION MAYHAMPER OPS
3. 6 X SCUDS LAUNCHED; 3-SAUDI 3-ISRAEL
4. MCM OPS DELAYED AFTER POSSIBLE SILKWORM ATTACK
IRAN
IRAQ
KUWAIT
SAUDI ARABIA
THE GULF
As Samawah
An Nasiriyah
Suq ash Shuyukh
Al Basra
Kuwait
King Khalid Military City
WHITE
COBRA
50 Km
150 Km
240300Z
241200Z
241200Z
242300Z
JFCE(KU)
RGFC
0
50
100 Kilometres
50 Miles
42°E.
44
46°
44°E.
46°
48
30°
28° N.

6.11 SITUATION AM 25 FEBRUARY

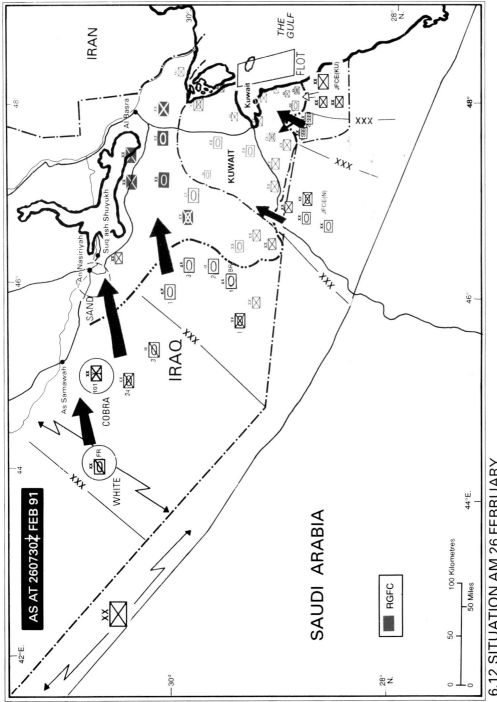

6.12 SITUATION AM 26 FEBRUARY

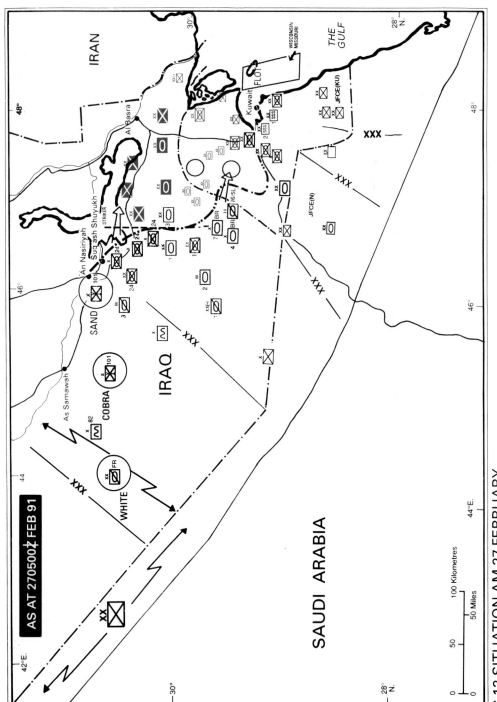

6.13 SITUATION AM 27 FEBRUARY

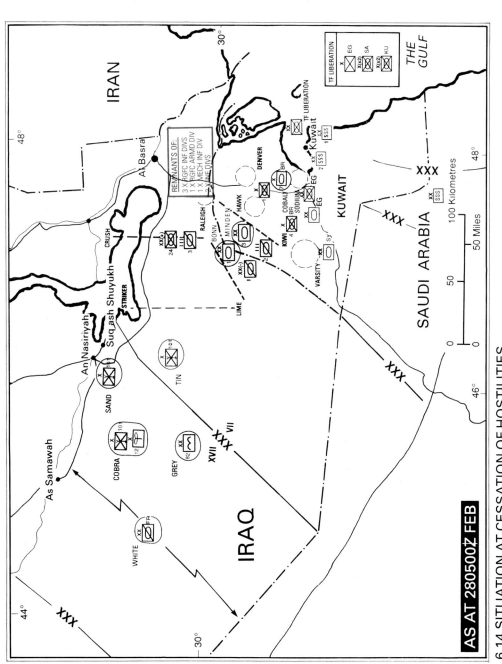

6.14 SITUATION AT CESSATION OF HOSTILITIES

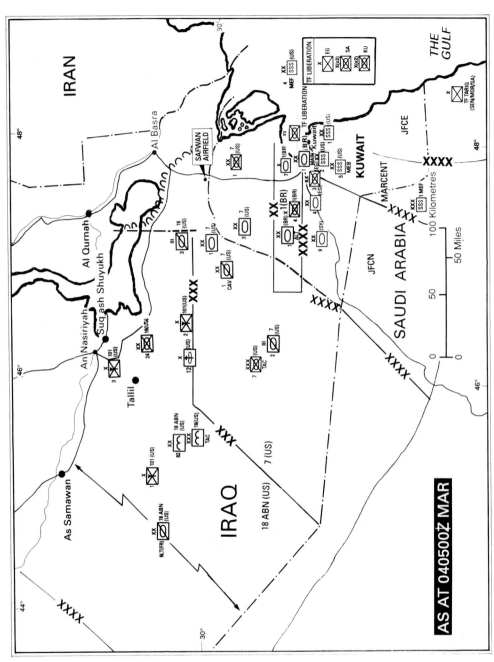

7.1 SITUATION 4 MARCH 1991

Field of the Cloth of Gold

March 1991

There was never any chance that the Allies might 'go on to Baghdad'. Baghdad is a city with a million more people than Rome, and to suggest that the Allied forces, their lines of communications extended by the time they reached the Euphrates, could have gone straight north is ridiculous. But the Allies might have been able to complete their encirclement of Basra. They did not.

Shortly afterwards, I believed this was a mistake. There was an uprising in Basra, which the Iraqis moved to crush with considerable success. Had the Allies pushed north, cutting Basra off completely, that might have allowed the flames of revolt to take hold. But did the US really want a Shi'a state in southern Iraq?

On the evening of 27th, President Bush summoned his advisers. He had a victory, and it is probable that he wanted to call a halt because to continue to destroy the Iraqi Army would lead to accusations of butchery. The Allies had also been incredibly lucky. At any moment, there could be a disaster. And the effect of a single reverse on a well-informed public which had got used to negligible casualties would be traumatic. To settle for victory and withdrawal was probably seen to be the best course. Although not primarily inspired by any fear of accusations of vindictiveness, this too may have been a contributory factor.

There was also the morale of the troops. Brigadier Cordingley was typical of thousands of Allied servicemen:

> Finally we had arrived in an area where vehicles, bodies and other military wreckage lay strewn around us in every direction. I was immensely relieved that we had achieved our aim with so few casualties but I also had a doubt about the sense of recommencing operations against an enemy that was clearly defeated.[1]

The British were among the first on the scene of the massacre at Mutla Ridge. The main attack on the fleeing Iraqi columns, possibly taking hostages with them, occurred on 27 February. The vehicles were stopped, their engines still running some days later. Susan Stein, a BBC camera operator, said the smashed columns were incinerated. This led to speculation that the Allies had used fuel-air explosives but in practice, if you hole a few petrol tanks, it only takes one more round to set the whole lot alight.

As noted in Chapter 6, the forces were very tired, and some formations were at the end of their supply lines. The British Chief of Defence Staff, Marshal of the Royal Air Force Sir David Craig, later told some defence correspondents that 'we didn't want any more Mutla Ridges'. But at the time, the British recommendation was to continue for another 12 or 24 hours.

On Wednesday night, General Powell contacted General Schwarzkopf on the secure telephone. What transpired is the subject of controversy. General Schwarzkopf later told a British TV interviewer that his recommendation had been 'continue to march'. He said he could have 'completely closed the door and made it a battle of annihilation'. But Brigadier General Neal was there when General Powell telephoned, and told several people that General Schwarzkopf had said 'the mission is complete'.[2] When the witnesses of that telephone conversation heard General Schwarzkopf say he had recommended they 'continue to march', they became angry.

The mission was *mostly* complete. Kuwait was liberated, but the RGFC was not totally destroyed. VII Corps had come round the Iraqi flank, aiming directly at the Republican Guard, but some of the Guard had slipped away. Aircraft, not ground forces, were inflicting most destruction on the RGFC. Another factor, often forgotten is that Basra is surrounded by marshes, and there had been unusually heavy rain. The desert where the Allies stopped was ideal for armour: the terrain around Basra was not. Tragically, but unavoidably, the Allies had inflicted most destruction on the forward, Iraqi Army units, because they did not want to be hung up on the wire but get through and on with the manoeuvre war fast. But the Republican Guard, due to receive its dose of destruction later, evaded it in part.

Also, there were reports as early as 26th that two Iraqi divisions had withdrawn north of Basra, having escaped across pontoon bridges. The Coalition forces did not have bridging equipment with them which would enable them to pursue the Iraqis north, across the Euphrates and marshes, following the destruction of the bridges in the air campaign. Another age-old lesson of war. If you destroy the enemy's lines of communication, that can also inhibit your use of them for pursuit. And the Allies' requirements were more exacting than the Iraqis'.

Overthrowing Saddam Hussein's régime and fanning insurrections in Basra and elsewhere was not part of the military mission. In the end, what contributed most to the Iraqis' ability to put down that revolt was not surviving tanks and members of the Republican Guard, but an omission in the Allies' ceasefire terms, allowing the Iraqis to continue to fly helicopters.

Nor would a formal ceasefire have guaranteed an end to the fighting. It would have taken some time for the orders to percolate down to Iraqi units, particularly as the Allies had, deliberately, destroyed their command and control structure. One of the problems with tearing out the command and control system is that when the enemy decides to surrender, he cannot communicate that order, either. Allied formations were told to be prepared to resume offensive operations if necessary. On 2 March, a big battle took place between 24th (Mechanised) Division and 140 Iraqi tanks at Rumaila airstrip 30 kilometres west of Basra. If the Allies had second thoughts about stopping too soon, this could have provided a pretext for resuming operations.

The speed of the Allied advance had also left pockets of Iraqis behind them. For several days after the ceasefire, the Allies were fully occupied 'policing up' the battle-field, as Iraqis came out of their dug-outs well behind the forward Allied positions.

There is an element of delay in the complex business of stopping a military operation. A good boxing referee does not wait until one party is beaten senseless or dead before stopping the fight. He can see the way things are going. That is what happened with the Iraqi forces in the KTO. And it was, after all, a 'limited war'. I later decided that, on balance, the Allies had stopped at about the right time. The enemy was broken, we had the victory, we should not push our luck – we had pushed it far already, and what happened next was an internal matter for Iraq.

President Bush was also influenced by the symbolic figure of '100 hours' for the ground war. The way everybody seized on the expression suggests he was right. He decided to announce a ceasefire to be effective from midnight, Washington time, 08.00 local. General Schwarzkopf signed his order to the theatre forces at 03.30, Riyadh time.

News of a possible ceasefire had reached the fighting formations in Kuwait and Iraq shortly after midnight, on 28 February. 1st British Armoured Division, on objective Varsity, were not expecting to move before 08.00, and were about the get some much-needed sleep. At 04.00 they were told to be on Cobalt, their next objective astride the Kuwait–Basra road, by the time the ceasefire came into effect at 08.00. They got there, with half an hour to spare.

North of Kuwait, 24th Mechanised Division and 3rd Armoured Cavalry regiment reached phase line Crush, 50km west of Basra. In the pocket – still a big pocket – there were remnants of three Republican Guard infantry and one armoured division, plus three regular army divisions. The Allies controlled Safwan, and the country around Az Zubayr, but not Az Zubayr itself.

The Allies had pressed home their assault right to the end. 'This was rapid warfare in its finest hour. Great speed. Superb leadership,' Brigadier General Neal said after the ceasefire. On 27th, at about 16.00, the Allied command estimated that they had knocked out 29 divisions. The following morning, after the ceasefire, the estimate had risen to $40\frac{1}{2}$ out of 42. That estimate – implying only one and a half divisions surviving – later proved excessive.

The final battle of the main campaign involved the US 24th Infantry Division against some 200 Iraqi tanks west of Basra. Two brigades of 24th had advanced with astonishing speed, passing Tallil airfield and east, through phase line 'Striker', 100km west of Basra to 'Crush', 50 kilometres west. The battle, as they moved towards 'Crush', was taking place as General Schwarzkopf spoke on Wednesday 27th. Offensive operations continued on the northern border of Kuwait, west of Safwan, and just west of Basra. Allied aircraft made a point of pursuing the Iraqi T-72s. 'We aggressively made a point of pursuing those tanks to the limit,' General Neal said.

There was confusion about how much Iraqi equipment was escaping. On Wednesday afternoon, we were told the Iraqis were having difficulty getting out of the pocket to the north because all the bridges were down. 'It's like trying to take a ten-pound bag and squeeze it through a one pound hole right now ...' But, General Neal added, 'there's also a lot of them escaping to the north and to the west.'[3] The Euphrates is so shallow in places that the Iraqis were able to escape across earthen embankments built below the surface of the water. Three Republican Guard divisions, Hammurabi, Medina and Tawakalna (*'Tawakalna ala Allah'* – 'Trust in God'), were lined up in a protective screen west of Basra.

The situation was confused and delicate, but the main operations were certainly over. The situation a few days after the main operations ended is shown in Figure 7.1. Many of my colleagues began packing, intending to move to Kuwait City, where the main political and human interest was focussed. As a military specialist, I remained in Riyadh, where plenty of interesting information and analysis of the war was coming out. Others began to go home, but, oddly enough, I had no wish to return to Britain at all. Much that was of great interest and importance to me was still to come.

At 02.00 on Saturday 2 March the 'phone rang. It was Nigel Gillis at the British JIB. 'Would you like to be one of two British pencils to be at a significant event in the desert [later today]?'

We always talked in riddles on the telephone. General Schwarzkopf was going to meet the Iraqis to thrash out the details of implementing the ceasefire. How to ensure the forces did not come into conflict, prisoner-of-war exchange. As a historian, one recalled the Japanese surrendering to MacArthur on board USS *Missouri* in 1945, or Keitel's representative, von Friedeburg, meeting Montgomery on Luneburg Heath. The *Missouri* was here in theatre, off Kuwait, and I fancied that they might ask the Iraqis to meet them there, but that would be a little too triumphant. It was to be Safwan, just inside Iraq.

The two British 'pencils' were David Fairhall and myself: the two 'heavy weight' British papers with Defence Correspondents here. We were later augmented by David Mason of the Press Association, a valued colleague and friend. I went to the Hyatt at 05.30, but we were then told that the meeting had been postponed for 24 hours.

Late on Saturday, the UN Security Council adopted UN Resolution 686, setting out the precise measures which Iraq had to carry out before a formal ceasefire was declared. Baghdad radio said Iraq accepted the resolution.

Meanwhile, on 1 March, the 82nd Airborne Division had identified an Iraqi Army position which surrendered after a brief fire-fight, yielding 1,000 prisoners. On 2 March, a major battle had broken out 30 kilometres west of Basra known as the 'battle contact at Rumaila'. One platoon reported a massive Iraqi convoy moving north-west towards Baghdad, and that it had fired a couple of rounds. 24th Infantry gave permission to return fire, at ranges between 1,000 and 2,000 metres. Army artillery and 20 US Cobra and Apache helicopters joined in. In less than two hours, they destroyed 187 vehicles, including 23 T-72s. About 70 Iraqi troops were taken prisoner, many as they tried to flee, some on foot, others driving.[4]

Sunday 3 March started at 01.45. It was the standard military performance of 'rush to wait'. I took a taxi to the Hyatt.

'You going somewhere, Sir? Dhahran?' asked the driver.

'A bit north of there. Kuwait . . .'

One still had to be a bit security conscious.

We boarded a coach at the Hyatt at 03.00 and waited outside Riyadh military airfield in the cold, dark early morning for an 05.00 flight in the ubiquitous, reassuring Hercules.

The sun came up outside the portholes at about 06.30. We landed at Kuwait City in the grey of the early morning, made greyer by the smoke from burning oil wells. Everything was grey, as if one had stepped into a black and white movie, with shades of Eisenstein. The airfield had only been recaptured four days before, and was an indescribable mess. The control tower, grey and blackened by fire, the mutilated wreck of the British Airways Boeing 747 trapped there on 2 August – only the logo on the tail was recognisable. And in the distance, oil fires. The effect of the ominous black cloud was claustrophobic. But it also had a terrible grandeur.

Desolation and destruction, which I had never witnessed before on this scale, have a terrible beauty. It was just awe-inspiring. Wreaked by the fiendish ingenuity of man and the vengeance of nature abused, it had a fabulous quality.

From Kuwait City airport the blazing oilfields to the south evoked a scene from Tolkien's *The Lord of the Rings*. The edge of Mordor.

A US helicopter landed close to a charred building, blowing black flakes and grey dust all over the place in a hot wind. The concrete runway was pock-marked with the scars from exploding cluster bombs – a weapon of devastating regularity. Each bomblet had made a hole the size of a soup bowl and the scars from the fragments were spattered in a semi-circle a foot or so to one side: a pattern repeated perfectly dozens of times for yards and yards.

We boarded a Chinook helicopter, which flew north across Kuwait bay. On the other side, we flew over the lethal symmetry of battlefield architecture. There were trenches running east-west, line after line of them. Neat fire bays projected forward from the trenches and, here and there, angular ravelins – arrowheads – stuck out. From low over the battlefield you could see not only the fire trenches but the entrances, like rabbit holes, to the underground portion. Around the edges, the foxholes were squared off with sandbags or bricks.

And there were rectangular revetments for tanks and round ones for guns. They were mostly empty, the oblong ones quickly bulldozed into shape from the surrounding sand. The Allied pilots had learned to attack from an angle, through the holes in the back. The round revetments looked like neat moon craters. A Soviet D-30 field-gun, perfectly positioned on its three-pointed star base to give a 360-degree field of fire was blackened like the skeleton of some strange bird, roasted to destruction. Many of the revetments were completely burnt inside, as if someone had gone across the battlefield with a giant cigarette, burning holes in the sand, picking out each gun position. That is, more or less, what the Allies had done.

The 50-mile deep defensive belt was a strange anachronism, I thought. It would have been impenetrable in two dimensions. In three dimensions, it seemed totally irrelevant. I could now see how pilots flying over the trenches in the First World War had quickly formed the impression that air power could completely alter the character of war.

The Rawdatayn oil-field burned most spectacularly of all. Had Hieronymus Bosch or Dante seen this in their nightmares? The wells roared like bunsen burners – big bunsen burners. The Chinook flew over one and banked as I looked through the open port. The heat came up – so fierce was it that I had to move back.

We followed the main road from al-Jahra to Safwan. There were many civilian cars, totally wrecked, but some, I suspected, dating from before the war. Tanks and guns had been swept off the road. Some trucks had been thrown on their sides. It was the classic wreckage of war, reminding me of Soviet Second World War paintings. I did not see the densely packed carnage of the 'road to Basra' shown on television – an officer told me the worst of that was on the road to Bubiyan.

I think we skirted round the point where the road crossed the Mutla Ridge – maybe that was deliberate, though I would doubt it.

We landed south of Safwan, one of a long line of Chinooks parked beside the runway. Surprisingly, the runway looked quite intact.

'I thought we were supposed to have blasted all the airfields?'

'Well, we gave this one to the Saudis, because it was close to them,' said an officer. He suggested that the Saudis had not made a very good job of it.

To the West lies a craggy escarpment, bristling with radars. What looked like an entire brigade – I later learned it was a full division – was guarding the airfield. To the South, facing due North, was a battery of Patriot anti-missiles, just visible behind the horizon. The 1st Infantry Division – the 'Big Red One' – were an impressive outfit. Bullshit that would have made Patton proud. They told me that the Americans had appeared on top of the escarpment, like the Zulus in the film *Zulu*, and sent two Apaches forward, to persuade the Iraqis to vacate the airfield. At first, the Iraqis, whose intelligence had been grotesquely flawed throughout, and who were not expecting the Americans from the west, thought that the Americans might be trying to surrender to them. They were soon persuaded otherwise.

The Allies meant to impress the Iraqis with the reception on that Sunday morning and impress they did. But the hardware and panache were not just to overawe – although that was very important. Three miles away, the Republican Guard were in defensive positions. To the north-west, we saw smoke. 'One of the targets we hit yesterday,' said an officer – 2 March – well after the de facto ceasefire.

At 11.30 two Apache helicopters moved slowly up each side of the road from the south in the rocky desert, just inside Iraq. Behind the helicopters came Bradleys with white banners bearing the red crescent streaming above them. They were escorting eight Iraqi officers in two US Army vehicles. All vehicles bore the Allied identification marks: an inverted 'V' (Arabic number 8) and orange plastic sheeting on the roof. The requirements of camouflage and identification are pretty mutually exclusive. In conventional war, the needs of identification tend to become overriding. That is why for hundreds of years armies went into action in brilliant colours. Half a mile away, on a misty morning, you might just be able to tell if they were friend or foe.

The red crescent banners were beautiful, flying in the crisp, clean desert air, as they would have at a meeting between Saladin and Richard I, or the Field of the Cloth of Gold in 1520 when Henry VIII met the French. Medieval banners on futuristic armoured vehicles and venomous, insect-like helicopters. All the ingredients of a science fantasy. But this was Star Wars come to life, after all.

The Iraqis had driven to a spot about three miles to the south having skirted round the Allied positions in civilian cars. The Americans met them, transferred them to their own vehicles, and escorted them in.

The huge frame of General Schwarzkopf, commander of Operation *Desert Storm*, was granite stern on the day that was the pinnacle of his military career. I suspected it was a bit theatrical, but then soldiers are very theatrical. His secret service bodyguards had changed into US desert camouflage, though without hats.

Major General Jabir Alsabah, the Kuwaiti chief-of-staff, embraced General Schwarzkopf, thanking him and the United States for the war effort. 'There's nothing to thank us for. It's been a team,' General Schwarzkopf said. The British Commander, Lieutenant General Peter de la Billière, was there as an observer. He was guarded by Royal Marines, who had not been involved in the land operation but had come direct from Kuwait City where they had helicoptered in to secure the British Embassy. They looked even smarter than the Big Red One, in desert camouflage and green berets, a combination no-one had seen before.

The Iraqis were shown into a search tent. General Schwarzkopf, in his punctiliousness, reminded me of a Spanish General in a Velazquez painting. 'I don't want them embarrassed. I don't want pictures of them being searched.' General Schwarzkopf himself was searched first. Even a knife or a syringe carried by one of the Iraqis could have spelled death for the Allied commander. Suicide missions were still on the cards.

The Iraqi team comprised two lieutenant generals, Sultan Hashim Ahmed, Chief of Staff at the Iraqi Defence Ministry and Saleh Abbud Mahmud, commander of the Iraqi III Corps. They were accompanied by Major General Khalid Husayn Ali, although he did not join them at the conference table. There were also four brigadiers, a colonel and two naval officers – the latter to tell General Schwarzkopf where they had laid sea mines.

Only a very limited number of people could witness the discussions, and David Fairhall and I agreed that David Mason, as the agency man, should go inside. He later told us what transpired.

The talks took place in three tents joined together, at a plain wooden table. There was a video machine in the corner, and mineral water, coffee, Houmus and crisps were provided. The meeting lasted less than two hours and General Schwarzkopf and Prince Khalid did almost all the talking. They agreed that on signature of the permanent ceasefire, the Allies would withdrawn from Iraqi territory and all Allied and Iraqi prisoners would be released. The Iraqis said they had 41 Allied prisoners of war. General Schwarzkopf said the Allies had 60,000 and were still counting,

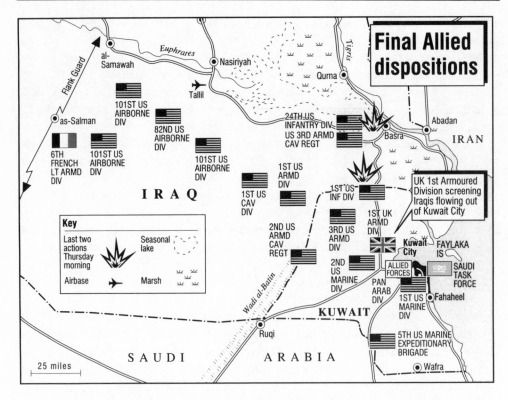

Figure 7.2   Allied deployment 2–3 March 1991, showing position of the two post-Ceasefire
clauses on 2 March.
(Published in *The Independent*, March 1991: graphic by Kristina Ferris)

which flabbergasted the Iraqis. They had no idea what had been happening. As a token of 'good faith' a small number of prisoners were to be released almost immediately.

The two sides agreed on measures to prevent contact between armed units – in effect, a ceasefire line. The Iraqis agreed to provide exact details of the position and composition of their minefields on land and sea. When they left, one of the Allied officers was clutching a map, which may have had some such details on it.

Flights of Iraqi fixed wing military aircraft were prohibited. The Iraqis asked General Schwarzkopf if they could continue to fly helicopters, because they needed them for relief work. He chivalrously agreed. It was a mistake. The Iraqis later used helicopter gunships in their repression of the southern (Shi'a) and northern (Kurdish) uprisings. If there was ever a lesson of the Second Gulf War, it is that, having achieved a great military victory at great expense, and got the enemy in your hand, you do not go soft on them at the conference table. There, a tough policy costs nothing – but mistakes cost a lot.

At 13.20 the delegates emerged and went to General Schwarzkopf's tent. 'Not part of the programme,' a major told me. At 13.40 hours the Iraqis emerged and were escorted to their vehicles. The proceedings degenerated into a dusty scrum as reporters pursued the delegates in search of quotes. A pointless exercise: I had more than I could use. I took photographs. The Iraqis were quickly away. General Schwarzkopf, a little less stern, walked back to a rostrum. 'I am very happy to tell you that we have agreed on all matters, including control measures to ensure that armed units of the Coalition do not come into contact with armed units of the Iraqi military,' he said.

The jovial and rather large Prince Khalid, looking a little absurd in his tank helmet, also made a speech. General Schwarzkopf was overheard muttering out of the side of his mouth 'Don't tell 'em anything.'

There was a satellite telephone dish set up right outside the conference tent, but the queue to file was very long and I would have time to get back to Riyadh, I thought.

We were given a lift back to the helicopter. Nearby, there were two T-55 tanks, lying in a hollow, marked off by white tape and guarded by a US soldier. There was always a risk of unexploded ordnance.

'I'm sorry, Sir, I can't let you go any closer. What happened, by the way?'

I told him that the Iraqis had agreed to all the terms. There was a smile, a perceptible sense of relief in his face.

Eventually, the Chinook took off, and headed back over the desert and Kuwait bay. The water by the harbour was slimy and green. From a distance, Kuwait looked like any other modern city, now bathed in sunlight, tall white buildings on a beautiful bay. There was some wreckage in the dock area. One of the big cranes was flattened, as if by a giant, angry fist. Ships in the harbour looked dead, as if they had been ransacked and left there for months. On the shoreline, just behind the beach, were foxholes and trenches – well-positioned to repel attack from the sea. They were squarely cut into the dunes as if a giant hole-punch had been used. There were similar defences along the other side of the bay as well. I suspected that the Allied casualties would have been much higher if they had attacked across this coastal killing-ground.

Further into the city, each piece of open ground was covered with more round revetments and angular foxholes, this time for anti-aircraft artillery and missiles. Taking this place would have been no joke if the Iraqis had chosen to defend it. But the anti-aircraft guns and missiles had already been removed. Here and there, individual buildings had been smashed – precision bombing, probably. Traffic was now flowing along the broad streets. One white pick-up truck was flying a Kuwaiti flag. For some, the nightmare was over. For others, who had been – or were thought to have been – on the wrong side, it was beginning.

We arrived at Kuwait City to find that the promised Hercules was not there to pick us up. This was an airfield recaptured from the Iraqis four days ago, and there was no obligation on anybody's part to take us anywhere. We could have been stuck there for days. In itself, that was no problem, but we had to file. A war-shattered airfield, with unexploded ordnance about, waiting for planes that never came with the clock ticking towards deadline. It began to be a nightmare. We found two Saudi Hercules that were going to Riyadh, but not yet. Eventually, one of the pilots turned up and told us there was an American Hercules round the corner, on the other side of the airfield. We sprinted across, a kilometre or so to the north-east. I had made no special effort to get fit, but suddenly found I was fitter than I had been for years. We piled into the plane and the US Air Force gave us MREs. They were much maligned, but these Meals Ready to Eat were just what one needed. Bags of carbohydrate, bags of energy, bags of fruit juice. I think I managed to write most of my story on the way back.

I reached the hotel at about midnight – nearly a 24-hour day, and grabbed the telephone.

It was Teresa Poole, one of our foreign news editors, who later became correspondent in Bangkok and Hong Kong.

'I'd have filed four hours ago if I could have, believe me.'

'Don't worry,' said Dr Poole, reassuringly.

The dateline was 'Safwan, occupied southern Iraq.'

The next day Heather, our Foreign Manager, telephoned to say that ITN had chartered a plane to fly from Dhahran on Wednesday 6th. They needed a plane to carry huge amounts of kit, but there was spare space for passengers. Would I like to get on it? I was still in two minds about whether to leave or not. Others had already gone. Mark Laity, the BBC radio defence correspondent, who had been in Saudi since before Christmas, who did a magnificent job and had missed out on the Safwan experience, flew home with the RAF. Géneviève Rossier had gone to Dhahran and on to Kuwait. Things were winding down, and I supposed that one should get out while the going was good. It was not possible to get out on scheduled flights. If I did not take the ITN charter flight, it might be another week. I attended a background briefing at the Hyatt. An old Saudi appeared, followed by his four young wives. They had no doubt been in Jeddah, and were coming back. During the war, Prince Khalid had exercised a protective effect on the Westerners. Now, the religious police began to reappear. The old Saudi Arabia was reasserting itself. At some point – it may not have been until the Tuesday, 5 March, I resolved to go. We were continuing to get good information on the insurrection flickering in Iraq, and I filed on the Tuesday.

We were told that troops loyal to President Saddam were using tanks, artillery and other heavy weapons to suppress the uprisings, the most substantial being in Basra, Nasiriyah and the Holy City of Najaf.

At first, there were reports of crowds in Basra and large numbers of vehicles parked in a chaotic state. This might have been a result of the Iraqi Army's disordered retreat, rather than a sign of rebellion. At this stage, Brigadier General Neal said, he was still more interested in the whereabouts of Iraqi forces than whether or not the mayor of Basra was still in charge.

Later, we heard that in Basra there had been engagements between tanks, though firing their machine guns rather than their main armament. 'We started seeing problems in Basra before the ceasefire was signed,' our briefers said. 'We couldn't get a handle on it. Then there were significant indicators of civil unrest. We watched it with curiosity more than anything else.' About two brigades – 4,000 to 5,000 men and 200 tanks of the regular army and Republican Guard – faced each other across Basra, split into small groups.

Asked if the Allies were giving any aid to potential opponents of Saddam Hussein, we were told: 'not officially, no.' One group of Iraqi soldiers and civilians had approached a US Army unit and asked for some of the arms and equipment the Americans had captured from the Iraqis to be returned to help overthrow the government. 'We're sticking out of this,' the US Army said. 'They're doing real fine all by themselves right now.'

Early on Wednesday, I took a taxi from Riyadh to Dhahran, arriving at about 10.30 for a 15.30 flight. Checking all the TV equipment in for the flight took forever. There were ITN, BBC, ABC, CNN ... and eccentric print journalists. Richard Dowden, who had been right forwards with the 82nd Airborne Division, was supposed to be on the flight, but did not make it. Phil Davison, who had gone into the breach with the US Marines, was there, looking remarkably fit, complete with his tin helmet, body armour and web equipment. The journalists were mostly male – though there were some women. It was rumoured that somebody had tried to smuggle a Kalashnikov rifle – a spoil of war – onto the plane, but was, obviously, caught by security.

The plane was delayed over landing fees. The airport staff would occasionally break for prayers. At one point, some people began making fun of the Saudis' devotions, which was a very stupid and dangerous as well as disrespectful thing to do. I had come to respect the Saudis, especially their legal system. You could leave your car open; there was no vandalism, graffiti, or thuggish behaviour. I was going back to all that.

Eventually, at 17.00, the plane took off. Jeremy Thompson of ITN said a few words. Then we were out of Saudi airspace, and out came the champagne cocktails. Most of us had not had a drink – the alcoholic variety – for two or three months. Our livers had shrunk nicely. We had all been on difficult and, in some cases (not mine) dangerous assignments. Quite soon, the effects of the alcohol became pretty apparent.

A report in the *Daily Mirror* later suggested that the plane had to divert to Rome because the passengers had become a flight safety hazard. The official reason was that, because of the long delay at Dhahran, the crew were in excess of their licensed flying hours.

At Rome, we passed Italian immigration quickly, muttering '*shokran, shokran*' – Arabic for thank-you – to the Italians. Someone flagged down an Italian police car, thinking it was a taxi. Rome was a good halfway point between Riyadh and London – to fly straight into the soggy, oppressive green of southern England would have been too much. We were taken to a hotel in the centre, booked in, and sat round the bar, drinking lovely cold Italian beer. The war was won. It was an historic experience. I am sure that some inhibitions were shed that night.

PART III

'Such a victory as this'

'The next greatest misfortune to losing a battle is to gain such a victory as this.'

Wellington
(As recorded in S. Rogers, *Recollections*, 1859)

8

Midnight Express

April–May 1991

Immediately after the Iraqi defeat at the end of February, Saddam Hussein moved his few remaining armoured forces towards – though not into – Baghdad, to help shore up his régime. Apart from the 35 tanks assigned to each infantry regiment, the only high-speed manoeuvre forces surviving were two mechanised brigades. Rebellion flickered and died in Basra. Meanwhile, on 5 March it was reported that Kurdish guerrillas had attacked the headquarters of the Iraqi 24th Division in the northern town of Dukan, as armed resistance spread from the Shi'a south to the Kurdish north.

Large contingents of Kurdish fighters were reported close to the main cities of northern Iraq which were 'on the verge of insurrection'. Massive demonstrations took place in Irbil and other, smaller cities. The northern uprisings were not directed primarily at the Iraqi Army, but at Ba'ath party officials. The problem with the Kurdish uprising was that it was not aimed at overthrowing Saddam Hussein within the accepted framework of Iraq, but, insofar as any coherent aims could be identified at all, at the creation of an independent Kurdish state, which would be regarded as a threat by the US and Britain's Nato ally, Turkey, as well as by Iran and possibly the then Soviet Union.

I arrived back in Britain on 7 March. After the bright light and wide open spaces of the desert, the mouldy appearance and clutter of England was depressing. It was good to see my colleagues at the office, but it was difficult to settle. People were friendly and 'demob happy' – I had missed a celebration at the end of the war which had gone down in history as 'The Mother of all Lunches'. The newspaper's coverage of the war was generally acknowledged to be excellent, although, as for all news organisations, it had been cripplingly expensive. But the world refused to stop turning. I had some time off, and we began to find out new information about the war.

On 18 March there was a report that of the 88,500 tons of munitions dropped on Iraq, 70 per cent missed their targets.[1] If that was true, the remaining 30 per cent did a very good job. The assessment of destruction of Iraqi forces in the KTO was revised to 3,700 out of 4,280 tanks and 2,600 out of 3,110 artillery pieces. That still left 580 tanks and 510 guns, an assessment later modified to 800 of each – a significant number, which escaped. And it was the best equipment that got away. What the Allies saw – T-55s, D-30s – was mostly old junk.

On 15 March, General Schwarzkopf demanded an end to the use of Iraqi helicopter operations against rebel forces in northern and southern Iraq. But the Iraqis had been allowed to fly them by the ceasefire terms, and to impose a new restriction was politically impossible. The following day, the US Army put out the first of the burning Kuwait oil wells. It was expected that the rest would take 18 months to extinguish: in fact, it took less than a year. The last of 732 blazing wells, which had engaged 27 firefighting teams, was extinguished on 6 November, 1991. Meanwhile, there was another incident on 20 March when a US F-15 shot down an Iraqi Su-22 which was flying, in violation of the agreed ceasefire, over Tikrit in northern Iraq.[2]

On 3 April, the UN Security Council accepted Ceasefire Resolution 687, guaranteeing the inviolability of the Kuwait/Iraq border and establishing a demilitarised zone between Iraq and Kuwait. It decided that Iraq should unconditionally accept the destruction, removal or rendering harmless, under international supervision, of all chemical and biological weapons and all stocks of agents and related sub-systems; all ballistic missiles with a range greater than 150 kilometres, and, within 45 days, the formation of a Special Commission to carry out immediate inspection of all Iraq's biological, chemical and missile capabilities. Restrictions on the import of foodstuffs were lifted, but Iraq had to cooperate with the International Red Cross in tracing third country nationals and Kuwaiti citizens still unaccounted for, and had to undertake not to commit or support any act of international terrorism. Finally, the resolution warned that the Security Council would take such further steps as might be required for the implementation of the resolution and to secure peace and security in the area.[3]

By the beginning of April, the Kurds, having attempted a rebellion, were in wholesale retreat towards the icy mountains on the Iranian and Turkish borders, pursued by the Iraqi Army. Some were mountain people, used to the conditions but others were from towns like Mosul, and unaccustomed to the rigours of the mountains. They also lacked the strong village organisation that helped the mountain dwellers survive in hard conditions. Many had fled in nightclothes, and were pathetically ill-equipped to face conditions that would faze professional mountaineers. As usual, television crews first brought their plight to public attention, and political action followed.

I was due to go back to Kuwait, with the Navy, to cover their continued mine-clearance operation. Then the RAF hinted that they might take a few journalists with them if they were called on to drop supplies to the Kurdish refugees. The operation was delayed, and I planned to go with the Navy. On Sunday 7 April, I was invited to have dinner with Heather, the Foreign Manager, in Acton. At 22.30 the telephone rang, a message from my sister, telling me to call Air Commodore Mike Barnes, the RAF's Director of Public Relations.

'Chris, we're going. Can you get to Lyneham by five o'clock in the morning?'

I checked with Godfrey Hodgson, the Foreign Editor, and we agreed that dropping supplies to the Kurds was the better story. I did not have my car with me, and Godfrey said to get a cab – to Wiltshire. Heather very kindly offered to drive me. Rather after 02.00, we joined the M4 and headed for Wiltshire.

The same day, 8 April, the British Prime Minister, John Major, announced his plan for 'safe havens' for the Kurds in northern Iraq. Whether the Iraqis would take to having slices of their country turned into semi-autonomous regions, and whether the Turks and Iranians, who also had large Kurdish populations, would approve, was uncertain.

The propeller-driven Hercules and tin shacks at Lyneham reminded Heather of her early days of air travel, in the 1950s. Before dawn, Fat Albert – the nickname of the Hercules – was in the air again, on a $6\frac{1}{2}$ hour flight to Incirlik, the NATO airbase adjacent to Adana. The F-111s had bombed from there in the war. Now, it was a life-saving mission. Four 100 kilogramme 'containers air cargo', with 'Kurdish relief' chalked on them were stacked in the back of the cavernous aircraft, plus a Land Rover and trailer. The most immediate requirement was shelter from the freezing rain and wind – a killer – and they had already flown out ten tons of blankets, nine of plastic sheeting and 6,000 man days of 'compo' rations. Those are high calorie rations to keep soldiers fighting fit, and would sustain refugees for many times longer. 'They'll be sprinting up the mountains,' joked one of the RAF crew.

Depending on the conditions, they would either drop the supplies by parachute or fly very low and push them out without parachutes. The former option was the only feasible one. The terrain on the Turkey–Iraq border is like the mountains on the Moon. The peaks, brown and jagged, rise to 12,000 feet, with valleys at maybe 4,000 to 5,000 feet above sea-level. The first aircrew we met spoke of 'breathtaking terrain and fearsome conditions'.

Operation PROVIDE COMFORT (US) or HAVEN (UK) involved about 3,700 US personnel, with British and French help. Based in Turkey, a NATO country, it came under US European Command, unlike the Gulf War, which was fought by Central Command. When we arrived at Incirlik on 8 April, the British had made their first relief drop, after pinpointing two groups, one of about 4,000 people, huddled in a mountain valley. The RAF had been there for just 24 hours and planes, including ours, were still arriving. Supply drops were taking place on both sides of the Turkey–Iraq border, and the border was 'difficult to define anyway'. The operation contained many lessons for future relief missions in dangerous, war-torn areas – such as that being contemplated in Bosnia as this book was completed, and which I later accompanied as the British troops deployed in October and November, 1992. Governments pressured into action to help mitigate scenes of appalling suffering faced a tough choice, summarised by an RAF officer. 'You could come in and set up your forces and miss a week of feeding people. Or you can go straight in but have no infrastructure.'

At this stage, the aircraft were flying at 3,500 feet above the mountains, releasing the cargo by parachute. They aimed to drop the supplies where it would take the refugees about 20 minutes to reach them, rather than risk them landing on the people

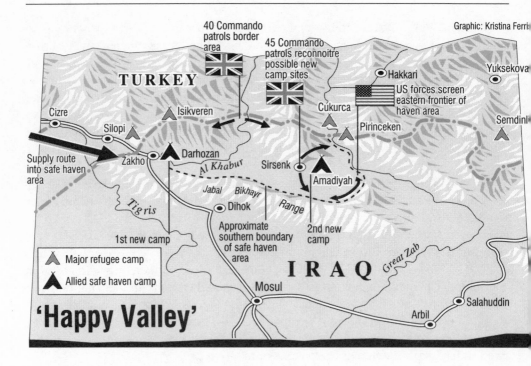

Figure 8.1   Iraq, north of the 36th parallel and Allied operations on the Turkey/Iraq border,
April–May 1991.
(*The Independent*: graphic by Kristina Ferris)

they were meant to save. Some Kurds were, unfortunately killed when supplies fell
on them. Besides the dangers of flying in the mountains, there was the danger that
the Kurdish refugees and Peshmerga guerrillas, not recognising the aircraft, would
think them hostile and shoot at them. US A-10s were acting as pathfinders for the
Hercules, and also to defend against possible Iraqi attacks from air or ground,
although the Iraqis were a little way to the south.

On 10 April, the US warned Iraq not to use its ground or air forces, including
helicopters, anywhere in the Kurdish areas of the country. American policy had
changed to create *de facto* enclaves for the refugees in northern Iraq and to protect
aid workers and Allied Forces helping them. Iraqi air activity – including helicopters
– was prohibited north of the 36th parallel, an area including the cities of Mosul and
Arbil. The area is shown in Figure 8.1. But Iraqi forces were not expected to
withdraw from that area, just to keep away from the refugees.

In the British headquarters at Incirlik we saw a list of Iraqi positions. Most Iraqi
forces in the area were dedicated to counter-insurgency operations. These included
I and V Corps. Some regular infantry was in the mountainous terrain north of the 37th
parallel, including the 10th and 38th infantry divisions. The 10th was one of a number
of divisions that fought in the KTO, and was reported to be operating severely under
strength. It appeared that the Iraqi Army was pushing the Kurds northwards, right up
into the mountains, and were in places less than a mile from the refugee camps. On

9th, a French aircraft was believed to have dropped supplies to the Iraqi Army by mistake. 'There are a lot of nasties on the other side of this ridge,' an RAF Hercules pilot told us – the Iabal Bikhayr ridge, 10 to 15 kilometres inside Iraq. Five divisions – 33rd, 44th, 38th, 54th and 10th – and three brigades – 121st, 701st and one unidentified – were north of the 36th parallel, with groups of Iraqi forces north-east and north-west of Zakho, which had anti-aircraft guns around it, and an Iraqi division further east, in the valley below al-Amadiyah. Al-Amadiyah had been Saddam Hussein's northern summer palace – like the British in India, he went to the hills in the hot summer.

There were also Iraqi Special Forces units providing Baghdad with intelligence on refugee movements – the only way the Iraqis could verify what was happening, as they could not fly any aircraft. The Iraqi SF groups probably infiltrated the refugee columns.

One had nothing but admiration for those Hercules crews. Their mission was complex, tricky and dangerous. On 9th, I flew with a US Hercules of 61st Tactical Airlift Squadron, based in Arkansas, although the flight crew had come from Mildenhall, Suffolk. The flight included four US Hercules and two French aircraft, with A-10s as pathfinders and F-15s and F-16s as the overhead air umbrella. The plane left Incirlik mid-afternoon and followed ground features closely. 'The weather's pretty good over the drop zone,' said the pilot, 'It's a go.' The aircraft climbed to 10,000 feet to clear the mountains as it approached the Iraqi border, vicious, serrated edges just below. The drop would take place from 2,500 feet above the valley floor. Peaks loomed out of the clouds on both sides, and to starboard a huge wall of ice loomed. Just north of the border were coloured dots – refugee encampments and the occasional car. We had heard there were 200,000 Kurdish refugees already in Turkey and 150,000 waiting on the border, with another 300,000 on the way north. From 2,500 feet I could not see people but I could see cars. They seemed to have abandoned them close to the border when they ran out of petrol or because the roads tailed off into mountain tracks. 'Some of those cars are in real precarious situations on top of ridges. You wonder how they got there,' said a USAF officer.

The target was a collection of 200 cars incongruously strewn across a high valley just inside Iraq. The American system was to let the cargo slide down rollers and out of the back of the plane under its own momentum. The British had teams of Royal Army Ordnance Corps soldiers to manhandle it out, giving greater speed and precision.

The release apparatus failed to work. A look of horror flashed across the sergeant's face and he pulled on a static line to release it manually. For a second, nothing happened, then – a click. For a second the cargo – 700 Meals Ready to Eat – did not move. Then it began to slide, accelerating down the rollers and away. The sergeant moved to the back and gave a thumbs up. In spite of the delay, the stores were nearly on target.

On another occasion I flew with the RAF. The hard, brown rocks of the higher peaks, with no vegetation, looking like sharp slabs of Christmas pudding where they were covered in snow, were the same. Near the target, Cukurca, there was cloud over the mountains, and cloud and mountains do not mix. You do not descend through cloud when there might be a mountain below. A US A-10 radioed that there was a hole in the cloud, about two miles west of Cukurca, and the Hercules followed. Seeing the window of opportunity, the Hercules dived with an agility surprising for such a normally stately beast. I had my camera, and it suddenly weighed a ton as the 'G forces' induced by the dive multiplied its weight. Every crew member looked out of the cockpit for looming mountains as the aircraft spiralled through the smoky chasm and out below the cloud. Ahead of us a ridge loomed, and the pilot threw the engine controls beyond the limit to get us over.

There were three sites, two of them huge, with tens of thousands of people and one with 2,000 – about 100,000 in all. We dropped most of the stores to the largest encampment. Then the aircraft climbed rapidly to 11,000 feet, the minimum safe altitude in that area. The crew were utterly drained. 'That was hard work,' said Flight Lieutenant Max Burton, the pilot. Who said fighter pilots have all the fun?

Adana was a relatively western city. I really liked the Turks, especially their belief in *Kismet* – Fate – which made any attempt at safety precautions pointless. One day, we took a taxi from Incirlik back to town and the driver stopped for petrol, puffing away at a lighted cigarette as the fuel poured in a few inches away.

The base for the British effort was moving east, to Diyarbakir. There had been calls for more use of helicopters because of the dangers of dropping supplies from aeroplanes, and the supplies could be taken closer to the people who needed them. A helicopter operation had to be based closer to the refugees.

I and some colleagues – Chris Jenkins from the *Daily Mail* and Gavin Cordon and Tim Ockenden of the Press Association – hired a car. As we moved east, the faith in *Kismet* became more apparent. People flashed their lights when they saw we had been so stupid as to put ours on *before it was actually pitch dark*.

The route was fascinating. There were crusader castles, guarding the route which followed the southern Turkish coast and then turned south into Syria. I had not appreciated until then that those castles were 'line-of-sight', one from the other, so that they could signal. The road ran north of the Syrian border and then crossed the Euphrates at Birecik. It was one of the few bridges over the Euphrates that was still standing, someone joked. On the other side, there were cave dwellings dug into the steep escarpment.

Before Diyarbakir, there is a high plateau. Tough little Turkish, then Kurdish children, barefoot at the side of the road waved and some saluted, assuming that Westerners must be military. There was a NATO listening post, surrounded by lights and wire. 'Don't even think about taking a photograph. Hide all cameras,' said Chris. This was NATO's south-eastern and wildest border. Turkish impatience with journalists and their habit of not giving the benefit of the doubt was legendary.

Night was falling, and through the doors of the small huts across the plain, fires could be seen glowing a warm red. This was another world – Kurdistan.

Diyarbakir is surrounded by high black basalt walls. After the antiseptic quality of much of Saudi Arabia, this was the real Middle East, which Marco Polo and

Tamerlane would have recognised. The children would chase the cars, and it was surprising that there were not frequent casualties. The streets were filled with market stalls and produce from the immensely fertile area around. It was exciting and fascinating.

Journalists, aid workers and the military were rapidly swamping the facilities of Diyarbakir. We found a small hotel eventually, although there were only two telephones – a recipe for disaster. We tried to check into the Caravanserai, a magnificent and exotic place round a courtyard, but the US Military had booked every room. They were moving in next week, and wanted it and its communications clear.

We knew the RAF were in Diyarbakir airfield, but getting to them was a problem. The Turkish guards were polite, but needed all kinds of permission to let us in and we kept going round in circles. Eventually, a bus pulled up on its way out of the base with Americans on board. Recognising an officer's rank, Chris Jenkins buttonholed him.

'Excuse me, major . . .'

It helps to notice that sort of thing. Many of our journalist colleagues were lacking in such diplomatically useful knowledge. Through his intercession, we gained admittance. Although the RAF were on the airfield and delighted to see us, it was always difficult to get in.

On the airfield, a tented town was springing up, which reminded me of scenes from *Henry V.* Brown American and British olive-green tents mushroomed across the airfield. The American camp was still in some disorder. Half a mile on, the British camp had a Union flag flying and a delicious smell of fried breakfast greeted us. The British soldiers had found a tortoise – there were many on the airfield, which they adopted, and were trying to get it to mate with a tin helmet. But I also saw crates of NBC kit. If the Iraqis got nasty, they had shown no compunction about using chemical weapons on the Kurds, even though they had not used them in the Second Gulf War. The following day, the Union flag was gone. The Turks, very particular about their sovereignty, had told them to take it down.

On 15 April the Turkish governor of the Diyarbakir region gave a press conference in a tea-garden below the basalt walls of old Diyarbakir. He said they would take 18 journalists by helicopter to Silopi, a centre for Haj pilgrims which was being converted into a camp for 'asylum seekers' – 'refugees' is a technical term conferring certain legal rights. We flew in a Turkish police Black Hawk helicopter past the slow, muddy waters of the Tigris, which, like the Euphrates, rises in Turkey, then south into the now familiar crags.

The Turks had been criticised for not doing enough to help the 'asylum seekers', but the Turks had a problem with Kurdish irredentism themselves, and they seemed to be trying. They had called in specialist doctors from Dicle and Firat universities with emphasis on the key areas – paediatrics, gynaecology. They were putting up 600 tents a day, and we wandered round the stores at Silopi, full of intravenous drips. The governor said Turkey should not be left alone to solve this problem 'because our country has become the target of so many refugees in the last eight to ten years –

Bulgarians, Rumanians, Iranians (some 300,000) . . .' He reckoned another 600,000 to 700,000 refugees from Iraq would end up on both sides of the border. There were 160,000 in appalling conditions in Isikveren alone. And then, interestingly, he went back into history. 'We like people. Throughout all history, slaves that have escaped from Africa, Princes and Kings who escaped from England, the Jewish people who escaped from Europe [from Spain, after the *Reconquista*] have sought refuge in Turkey throughout the ages. We are continuing this tradition. However we want everybody to help those people so we can give them assistance quickly.'

It seemed obvious that refugees – asylum seekers – call them what you will – were going to be one of the great international – and, therefore, security issues of the 1990s. What happened subsequently in Croatia and Bosnia reinforced that view.

There was a growing sense of activity at Diyarbakir. There were US C-5 Galaxies and C-141 Starlifters, cream-coloured trucks from the German Red Cross, brilliant white UN trucks, an Israeli C-130 Hercules in desert camouflage with a star of David beside the elegant flag of the Red Crescent, a Swedish Hercules with a triple crown and a German C-160 Transal with a black Maltese cross. There were also brightly painted local trucks, lined up outside the airbase, which took supplies by road. And there was a Russian Il-76 Candid, in white and grey. So many old enemies, working together. One American sergeant said they had even dropped Soviet Army greatcoats donated by the Russians. Russian greatcoats would be useful in those mountains.

I flew on a Chinook mission into the border area. Flying from Diyarbakir to Hakkari, there was no sign of life whatever among the peaks towering to 12,000 feet. Then, suddenly, there was Hakkari: two carpet factories and a Turkish Commando base in a valley at 5,000 feet above sea level.

To the Turkish soldiers who serve at Hakkari, it must seem like the end of the earth. Giant, crossed assault rifles, sculpted from wood, formed a bizarre and dryly humorous gateway. The CH-47 Chinook touched down to refuel before flying on to Cukurca to collect relief supplies for Kurdish camps further up the mountains, across the broad and transparent border. The Turkish Commandos, in pale blue berets and snow camouflage smocks – off-white with bright turquoise splodges – looked weather-beaten, exotic, hard as the rocks among which they stood. There had been several erroneous reports of UN troops in the area, because of the Turkish blue berets' similarity to UN headgear. But these were Turks, guarding Turkey. Some of their colleagues had been killed by Kurdish 'terrorists', they said. The élite commandos stood guard while ordinary Turkish soldiers and local Kurds loaded up the Chinook in which we had arrived.

'If they start bunging mortars in the back, let us know,' said the RAF loadmaster. There had been such incidents, when the Turkish Kurds had tried to smuggle arms to add to the firepower of the camps, using relief transport. The supplies included a large number of plastic shoes, tins of some sort of unappetising lard, sacks of potatoes, packets of pasta, bundles of blankets and tents. Many Turkish soldiers did not like the Kurds but they gave the feeling that they were doing something right, working fast and with good humour beneath the beating rotors of the Chinook. As the helicopter took off, the down-draught threw up a hail of stones and slivers of rock, sending the commandos, conscripts and correspondents diving for cover.

We helped load the helicopter. It was an amazing place to be. John Ingham, from the *Express*, suddenly said: 'Do you ever say to yourself "I actually get *paid* for doing this?"'

'All the time,' I said.

Waiting for the helicopter to return, I saw an A-10 appear over the jagged peaks to the south-east. The 'Devil's Crucifix', and so it must have appeared to Iraqi tank crews two months before. Now, it was on a mission of mercy, and seemed to be enjoying it. From the west, a stately procession of three Hercules appeared, American by the look of them – no refuelling probe. The A-10 swooped, turned and waggled its wings to say 'follow me'. Then it dived for the far side of the mountains – its mercy target.

I flew on the second Chinook flight to a well organised dropping point. We landed on one side of a stream, with a refugee encampment on the other, smoke from the fires making it look like a Red Indian village. 'Don't go too far away – we may have to get out of here in a hurry,' warned the loadmaster. There was always the possibility that they would rush the helicopter, although this lot seemed well disciplined. The Kurdish men waited until summoned forward. They had obviously had a hard time, but did not look as if they were starving.

A Turkish officer and a Peshmerga guerrilla fighter tried to speak to me in sign language. 'He needs a tent,' said the Turk. I indicated that the canvas sausages being unloaded were tents, and we bade farewell.

The helicopter returned to Hakkari, while another followed, carrying six casualties, two men, two women, one barefoot – not a good idea in these icy heights, a toddler and a baby on a drip. They radioed ahead, and soon after we touched down at Hakkari, a Turkish helicopter ambulance flew round the side of a mountain and transferred them to the Red Crescent hospital at Silopi.

By the time we got back to Diyarbakir, a vast airfield, it was dark. Our Ministry of Defence escort had disappeared, although, as he was a civilian, the Turks took no notice of him anyway. Wandering around military airfields at night without an escort is a bad idea. Especially in Turkey. But we found our way out without being shot.

Diyarbakir was a fascinating place. One day the local Kurds had a demonstration against what Saddam Hussein was doing across the border. It got out of hand and we heard reports that some people had been shot. We got on very well with the aid workers, who would maintain the relief effort once the military had begun to establish the infrastructure.

The First Secretary at the British Embassy in Ankara, Janet Douglas, was in Diyarbakir to help the British efforts, whether military or civilian Relief Organisations. I think there can only have been about 20 telephone lines out of the city, as getting through to the paper was a nightmare. She had a splendid new mobile telephone, a very valuable possession.

The German Red Cross were doing a great job, but they were followed by German journalists. One approached Janet.

'I see you haf a mobile phone. Can I use it to call Germany?'

'No I'm afraid you can't,' said Janet.

'Why not?'

'Because this is a British Government 'phone and I am a British diplomat. I can't just let anybody use it to call their office.'

'Vell, I sink your attitude is *most uncooperative . . .*'

Maybe national characteristics had not changed so much. The end of Ramadan was approaching, and some of Diyarbakir's more interesting entertainments were due to resume. My colleague Phil Reeves had been filing from the camps themselves, and some of our stories covered the same ground. I heard that the best part of 3 Commando Brigade, including two commandos, 40 and 45, would be coming in to secure sites for 'safe havens' in northern Iraq. The spreading camp at Diyarbakir was getting ready to receive the Marines. Their major conventional units had not played a part in the Gulf War, although the entire Special Boat Service had been deployed, and they were ideally suited to peace-keeping and security in this area. Besides their congenital enthusiasm for mud, rock, mountains and scree, they were more diplomatic than some Army regiments one could think of.

I telephoned Godfrey on Thursday 18th on a military satellite phone from the airfield camp to see if I should stay but it was decided that I should withdraw. That seemed a pity as the Marines were just about to arrive, but I had been there nearly two weeks and the difficulty of filing was becoming a real strain. I was ordered to pull out. Diyarbakir is remote: there was, we discovered, a twice-weekly flight to Ankara on board an ex-Russian Tupolev which had passed its sell-by date. Fortunately, I was able to hitch a ride on an RAF Hercules the next morning.

It flew to Cyprus, and after breakfast there, I caught another one to Lyneham. It was taking a car back to Britain, and if you sit in the car, you get a comfortable seat and cut out most of the noise. It was a slow journey, but I was surprisingly rested when I arrived at Lyneham.

Shortly after I returned from Turkey, there was an incident in which Royal Marines refused to allow the Turkish governor of Semdinli, near the Iranian border, to inspect a food tent. The incident arose because of differences in accepted customs. Robert Fisk, our correspondent, also reported that the Turkish Army had been raiding refugee supplies. The Turks took this as an insult to the Turkish Army. On the night of 2 May, he was arrested in Diyarbakir and held at the central prison. He telephoned Godfrey, while continuing to question the officers about who they were and on whose authority they were acting. Eventually, he was dragged away, and heard saying:

'This is the kind of thing that happens in neighbouring countries, such as *Iraq*!'

Earlier, they had arrested Robert Fox, of the *Telegraph*, and held him for two hours in the belief that he was Robert Fisk, because the names sounded similar.

All the *Independent*'s journalists believed to be in Turkey were declared *persona non grata*: myself and Phil Reeves, as well as Robert. Phil was on his way out, and they may have thought I was still there because I had left with the RAF. I am sure I had done nothing to offend the Turks, but they were making a point. I was in the office as Robert was on the 'phone to Godfrey. Harvey Morris broke the news.

'Chris, you've just been thrown out of Turkey.'

The saga of the Gulf crisis, war and its aftermath, had started nine months before. *Persona non grata*, eh? Some honour to end with.

* * *

The HAVEN plan collapsed less than two months later. By 14 June, the Kurds were begging the Allies not to leave, and thousands of Kurds protested outside the US base at Dihok. Between 21 May and that date, nearly 4,000 Allied troops had pulled out of northern Iraq and southern Turkey, leaving 18,000. The British presence, 3 Commando brigade, peaked at 4,500, but by 14 June there were 3,500 and one of the two Commandos, 45, was withdrawing.

The decision for the British to withdraw was taken on 15 May, according to Tom Hardie-Forsyth, a TA officer and one of the British Army's few Kurdish specialists, who resigned over what many saw as the 'betrayal' of the Kurds. Captain Hardie-Forsyth was Military Liaison Officer to the head of the British relief team. Thousands of Kurdish intellectuals and professional people advised and helped the Allies during 'Operation HAVEN'. Hardie-Forsyth said they would be sitting ducks for Iraqi death squads if the Allies withdrew from northern Iraq. Allied officers made contact with leading Kurdish refugees and persuaded them to give advice and information. British Intelligence interviewed many at length, but would not guarantee their safety, although the camps were riddled with Iraqi agents.

A 'Defence Debriefing Team', based at the Army's intelligence centre at Ashford in Kent was deployed to the area, with the title 'Kurdish Liaison Team' (KLT). Some leading Kurds were employed as '$8-a-day interpreters'. Captain Hardie-Forsyth believed that Iraqi agents in the camps compiled lists of those interviewed, and that to prevent the possible slaughter of leading Kurds on a scale comparable with, say, the Katyn massacre of Polish officers in 1940, a UN military force needed to protect the area for one to three years. In mid-June, Iraqi authorities and Kurdish leaders reached an accord on the future of Kurdistan, but Kurdish intellectuals wanted a UN-backed agreement underwritten by the victorious Coalition promising military intervention if the Kurds were harassed.[4]

The remaining small UN presence would be inadequate to prevent harassment. The policy of eliminating Kurdish identity in northern Iraq began in the mid-1970s. Next to the name of every village on the 1/50,000 maps used by the Allied forces was the word 'destroyed', the legacy of a deliberate policy of bulldozing.

Having decided to support the Kurds in an internal Iraqi struggle, the Allies' withdrawal was bound to be ragged and to create bitterness among Allied officers and soldiers who felt they were betraying people they had promised to help. The war's end was untidy – and is still unravelling.

9

Aftershocks

July 1992–January 1993

In July 1992, Saddam Hussein was still playing games with UN inspectors – a policy called 'cheat and retreat' by some commentators – and the Iraqis were bombarding the Marsh Arabs in the Shi'a area in the south, where the Allies won their great victory, with artillery and ground-attack aircraft.

In late July, 1992 we were again briefed on the situation, following speculation that there might be a 'military strike' against Iraq because it continued to be uncooperative with UN inspectors. A team had been denied access to the Agriculture Ministry in Baghdad, and by the time they were admitted – with no nationals of any of the wartime Allied states as members – any evidence of weapons of mass destruction (probably chemical) would have been spirited away. In the author's view, such a 'strike' would only be of any value if the United States had a very good idea where Saddam Hussein was and high confidence that they could remove him and his immediate entourage. Any other attack would merely kill more innocent or uninfluential Iraqis and would probably rebound politically. There were firm indications of US movements, most significantly an increase in the ability to refuel large bombers in the air, but this was an ideal way of signalling without committing combat aircraft.

However, it emerged that Iraqi military power had been rebuilt to 40 per cent of pre-Second Gulf War levels, with the exception of the Iraqi Navy which had been entirely destroyed in the war (bar one patrol boat) and had not resurfaced.

As I heard the last assessment of Iraqi military strength before this book was finished, five Iraqi Army divisions – maybe 50,000 men with 10,000 in the forward probing patrols – surrounded the Shi'a stronghold in the marshlands of the southern Euphrates. The Iraqis had been flying fixed-wing aircraft since April 1992. Although such flights were prohibited in the March 1991 agreement at Safwan, this was interpreted as a temporary measure to assist the safe disengagement of Allied forces. It was not confirmed in any of the UN Resolutions, notably 687 and 688, though in the author's view it should have been. By mid-July 1992 the only formal prohibition was seen as that prohibiting all flights (helicopter and fixed wing) north of the 36th parallel. Iran's minor air attack on Iraq in early 1992 was widely interpreted as reason to allow the Iraqi Air Force to fly again.

The aircraft attacking the Shi'a area in the south included Swiss PC-7 training aircraft firing rockets – aircraft which the Allies had not even counted as true 'combat aircraft' – and, in the previous few days, Soviet-built Su-25 Frogfoot ground attack planes.

In the north, up to half Iraq's 28 to 30 remaining or rebuilt divisions could launch an attack across 'no-man's land' against the Kurds with very little warning. They were dug in along the southern edge of an ill-defined belt from north-west Iraq (well north of the 36th parallel) to about halfway down the Iranian border (see Figure 9.1). Reports of a continuous fortified line were incorrect, we were told: they were, however, dug in with all the usual trappings of defensive positions.

President Saddam had also established – or re-established – an élite 'Presidential Guard' division, out of the Republican Guard. There were now seven Republican Guard divisions and the one Presidential Guard. In 1980, the 'Republican Guard' had comprised one or two brigades for Saddam Hussein's personal protection. During the war, the designation had been extended to successful army divisions, and the time had clearly come to create a renewed élite as well as enhancing Saddam's personal security. However, we were told there was no firm evidence of any coup attempts or executions. 'I cannot quote you the name of a single general that I even suspect has been shot,' a reliable source told us.

In spite of the efforts of the UN inspection teams, about 100 surface-to-surface missiles – Scud derivations and other types – still remained unaccounted for.

The Iraqi air defences were expected to be able to put up some opposition to the renewed air offensive widely forecast in the press. Although the nerves of the centralised air defence system were largely destroyed in the 1991 war, the individual missile and gun batteries continued to function, probably as effectively as they did in the opening phases of the war. The Iraqis would also get some early warning of an air attack. During the war, they conserved their radars by not turning them on. Some survived unscathed, and others had been repaired. Working radars near the Iraqi border would give some warning of approaching raids. The Iraqi civilian telephone system had been restored, we were told, and intelligence believed that the military communications system had also been rebuilt, though without Russian help (the Soviet Union had ceased to exist seven months before).

Iraqi ground forces were estimated at 350,000 against a pre-Second Gulf War total (see Chapter one, Figure 1.2) of nearly a million. Tanks and artillery totalled 2,000 each against pre-war levels of more than 5,000. Remembering General Colin Powell's reported aim of reducing the Iraqis to perhaps 100,000 men and 1,000 tanks, they retained between two and three times those levels (see Introduction).

At the same time Israeli sources were saying that 115 of the Iraqi aircraft which had fled to Iran were still there. With Gulf War combat losses, Iraq still had 300 aircraft on its territory, however, of which half had flown since military flying re-started in April. These included 50 ground-attack planes: Su-25s and Su-17/20/22

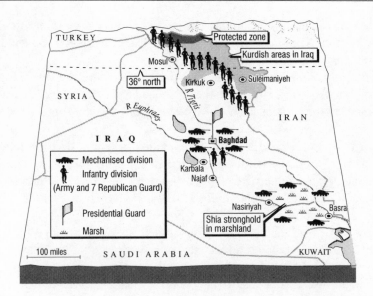

Figure 9.1   Distribution and strength of Iraqi forces, 29 July 1992. Forces have been
reconstituted to 30 divisions, hemming in the Kurds to the north and Sh'ia resistance in the
marshes to the south.
(Published in *The Independent*, 31 July 1992: graphic by Kristina Ferris)

Fighters – and 100 multi-role aircraft including MiG 21s, MiG 23/24 Floggers, MiG-
29 Fulcrums and French-built Mirages.

About two thirds of Iraq's total ground forces strength was in the north of the
country, with 15 divisions hemming in the Kurds. About five Republican Guard
divisions were around Baghdad and two a little further away. Five army divisions
were tightening the noose around the Shi'as in the south.

Shortly before, there had been reports of works to attempt to drain the marshes into
a 'Third River' so they could get in there with armour – as the Allies had been unable
to do.[1] Was the Iraqi penchant for vast geo-strategic projects, like the artificial moat
before Basra, reasserting itself? But intelligence sources said that there had been
plans to build a canal in the area for at least ten years as part of the improvements
to the communications network – which had always depended heavily on waterways.
This might have an 'incidental' effect on the marshes, they said. They added that
Saddam's government had lost control of the marsh areas in the early to mid-1980s,
when tens, perhaps hundreds of thousands of deserters from the Iran–Iraq war had
sheltered there.

Partly for internal political reasons in the United States – President Bush's flagging
election campaign – the US promoted and achieved the enforcement of a second air
exclusion zone over southern Iraq, south of 32nd parallel, on 26 August 1992. This
had a certain geometrical elegance, visibly squeezing Saddam Hussein between two
zones in which no Iraqi aircraft was allowed to fly. Joining hundreds of US aircraft
at Dhahran were three RAF Tornado GR1s with their TIALD pods for reconnaissance
from medium level and three GR1as for low-level reconnaissance, although during

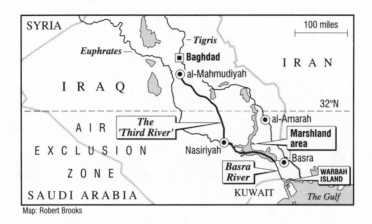

Map: Robert Brooks

Figure 9.2   The 'Third River', September 1992.
(Published in *The Independent*, 9 September 1992: graphic by Robert Brooks)

September only the former were employed.[2] The Americans had been enormously impressed with the GR1a in the 1991 war, and with the low-level attack abilities of the GR1.[3] Now the RAF's mission was to photograph Iraqi activities against the Shi'as in the southern marshes.

Right in the middle of the area of interest lay the vast 'Third River' project. It was completed, on schedule, at the end of August. An article in May by Saddam Hussein's brother-in-law, the Minister for Military Industrialisation, Hussein Kamil Hassan, gave the details of the great canal. It was 565 kilometres long, running from Al-Mahmudiyah, 30 kilometres south of Baghdad, between the two rivers down to near An-Nasiriyah, then through the watery maze of the Hawr-al-Hammar Marsh, to a place called al Gurmah, near Basra. Neither the Hydrographer's Department nor the Royal Geographical Society could find al Gurmah in their gazetteers – Qurna, where the Euphrates met the Tigris, seemed too far north. The RAF said the pictures they had taken had not yet been analysed.[4] But the canal, 90 metres wide at the top, tapering to 36 at the bottom, and eight metres deep, crossed the Euphrates 15 kilometres south-east of An Nasiriyah, where a dam diverted the flow of the Euphrates into it, apparently joined another drainage project, the al-Is-Haqi, and debouched into the Basra 'river' or canal, which flows into the Gulf by Warbah island (see Figure 9.2).

The Iraqi Government continued to insist that the canal's prime role was to carry salt water from the lake area and make the land more suitable for agriculture.[5] By the end of 1992, a substantial portion of the marshes had been drained, as shown in Figure 9.3. The reports continued to be contradictory and confusing – military intelligence, relying mainly on the press, added nothing to what we already knew from other expert sources. Details only emerged in October 1992 when an Iraqi engineer was captured carrying a complete set of maps detailing schemes to drain the Al-Amarah marshes. These included 'Fourth River' or *Umm al-Maarik* ('Mother of Battles') project and the River Banks Project. The former took excess water from the Euphrates which the original Third River, a bona fide project, had not been designed

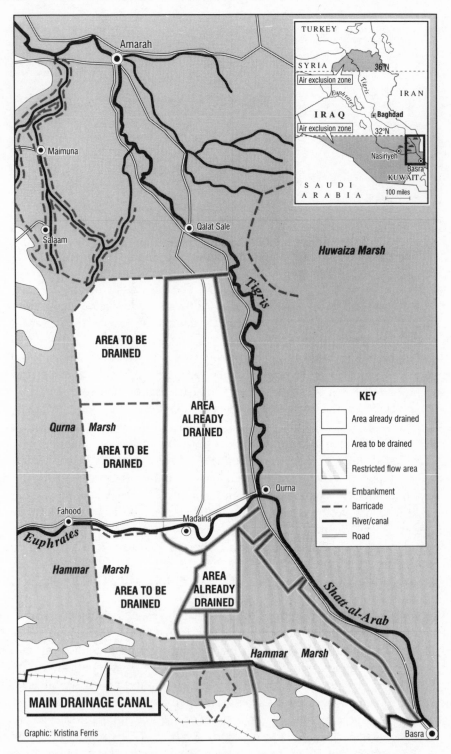

Figure 9.3 Area of the southern marshes drained at the end of December 1992. (Published in *The Independent*, December 1992)

to accommodate. The latter used eight-metre high banks to block off the tributaries from the Tigris and Euphrates into the marshes. These were definitely designed to drain the marshes completely. There were also ominous references to 'Third Anfal' – ominous because Anfal was the name given to genocidal attacks on the Kurds in the 1980s.[6]

Reports from émigré organisations drawing on 'reliable sources' inside Iraq continued to indicate a large-scale offensive, with up to 70,000 troops drawn from ten divisions of three corps – III, IV and VI. III Corps apparently encircled the marshes near An Nasiriyah. The Organisation for Human Rights in Iraq named 19 officers and senior NCOs whom they said had been disciplined for insufficient zeal in prosecuting the campaign. These included Brigadier Anwar Ismael Hentoosh, commander of the 2nd Brigade, 34 Mechanised Division. He was charged with 'neglecting to execute the order to attack the marshes' on 9 July. The same day, a captain commanding a unit of 82 Division was charged with negligence in attacking an objective north of the Hawr-al-Hammar marshes, near Nasiriyah. Two days before, the commander of the medical services of IV Corps, Brigadier A'Amir Rashid Hassoon, was arrested, charged with 'negligence during his tour in al-Amarah marshes.'[7]

The Iraqi achievement in pushing the 'Third River' project to a finish should not be underestimated. Nor should the scale of the campaign against the Marsh Arabs. The Iraqi Army's resilience in the face of colossal defeat in conventional war and of continued internal purges and the constant unwelcome attention of political officers and thought-police mirrors the astonishing resilience of the Red Army before and during the Second World War. The similarity with Stalin's Russia could not be more striking.

Saddam Hussein marked the opening of the Third River with a bizarre token of his favour. He donated another 40 million dinars to plant grass and palm-trees along the dry banks of the great canal, partly to beautify it, partly to prevent erosion. He will go down in history as one of the great survivors of all time.

Although President Saddam could order infantry attacks supported by artillery and air against the Shi'as and the Kurds, he had clearly lost the ability, developed during the First Gulf War of 1980–88, to move armoured formations swiftly. As well as the destruction of thousands of tanks, this was mainly due to the attrition of tank transporters – as important in their own way as tanks themselves. During the second half of 1990, the Iraqis had moved several divisions down into Kuwait: now they only moved 'slowly and raggedly'.[8]

The Iraqi Chief of Staff had apparently published an article on the lessons of the war, from an Iraqi point of view. The author was unable to trace it, but the lessons drawn were apparently rather obvious. A passive defence is a disaster when faced with a technologically superior opponent, and quality beats quantity. Others learned similar lessons, as the final chapter shows. Two years after the war started, Iraq was probably incapable of adventures beyond its borders, though well able to dominate its own people in the centre of the country if not in the northern and southern extremities.

At the end of December 1992, exploiting the last weeks of President Bush's Administration and the hand-over to President-elect Clinton, Saddam Hussein once again tested the west. Fixed-wing aircraft began flying into the no-fly zone declared on 26 August. On 27 December a US F-16 shot down an Iraqi MiG-25. The other aircraft with it fled to Iran. The Iraqi pilots may have been under some threat to make them attack US planes, which they must have known was near-suicidal. At the same time the Iraqis began moving SA-2 and SA-3 anti-aircraft missiles a few tens of kilometres south of the 32nd parallel. On 6 January, 1993 the United States supported by Britain, France and Russia, demanded their withdrawal within 48 hours, as, although obsolete and easily destroyed, they were still something of a threat to Allied aircraft. If the missiles were not withdrawn, the Allies said they would attack – and from my conversations with the Pentagon and the British MoD, I had no doubt they meant it. The British still had six Tornados – now all GR1s with TIALD – at Dhahran. The Americans probably had nearly 200, including 85 on the carrier *Kitty Hawk*, and F-117s, probably again at Khamis Mushait.

The hours ticked by, the Iraqis defiant and apparently determined not to give way. It was their territory, they said, and they could move their hardware anywhere they wanted. At the last minute, they announced a ban on planes carrying UN weapons inspectors landing at Baghdad.

The US authorities were mystified by Iraq's motives. Was it to divert Iraqi opinion from internal troubles? Was Saddam simply testing the resolve of the new administration? I believed it was simpler – even trivial. Saddam Hussein had a *personal* score to settle with President Bush. He wanted to score points in the last days of the Bush presidency – maybe, if he was lucky, bringing down a US plane and capturing the pilot. He did not care if more of his troops or a few old missiles were killed or destroyed in the process. But, at the very last minute, on 8 January, the Iraqis backed down.

I had surmised that renewed Allied action against Iraq was unlikely while the West took its extended Christmas and New Year break. Two years before we had been on tenterhooks as the Gulf War approached, but no action was contemplated until well into January. Heather and I gambled that the same would happen again and took the opportunity to get away on holiday. We returned from America on 6–7 January, as the Iraqi government probed and tested the Allies on the diplomatic front. The timing was perfect.

8 January 1993 was a busy day, a brief but poignant reminder of the events of two years before. We had a briefing on Iraqi strengths and deployments. The missiles were few in number – 'three to five batteries', and did not appear to have been modified. The Pentagon confirmed that three of the twelve US ships in the Gulf had Tomahawk land attack cruise missiles on board, and that there were F-117s in the area. I wrote extensive pieces on the Iraqi dispositions, the Allied forces available and the missiles themselves. There was much speculation about what the Allies might do. I believed it would be a tightly directed strike against the missiles and associated command and control. The Allies had no remit to attack airfields north of the 32nd parallel, where all the aircraft violating the no-fly zone had come from, and, as the British had

Plate 33 Ur of the Chaldees. US troops on top of the Ziggurat, 4 March 1991.
(Photo: Richard Dowden)

Plate 34 Farewell to the Iraqis. Safwan, 3 March 1991.
(*Photo: Author*)

Plate 35 Iraqi revetments in the desert, North Kuwait. The camouflaged vehicles may be part of 1st (UK) Armoured Division in their final position.
(*Photo: Author*)

Plate 36   T-55 and overturned truck in the desert north of Kuwait, 3 March 1991.
(*Photo: Author*)

Plate 37   Looking south from Kuwait City. Allied Chinook helicopters (with recognition signs). On
the horizon – oil wells burn.
(*Photo: Author*)

Plate 38 Blazing oil wells in northern Kuwait (seen from a US helicopter), 3 March 1991.
(*Photo: Author*)

Plate 39 The airport, Kuwait City, 3 March 1991, showing damage done by US cluster bombs.
(*Photo: Author*)

Plate 40 Author and BA Jumbo, trapped at the outbreak of war on Kuwait airport, 3 March 1991.

Plate 41 Consumed by fire. On the Basra–Nasiriyah road, 5 March 1991.
(*Photo: Richard Dowden*)

Plate 42 Just south of Kuwait City, 26 February 1991. Destroyed Iraqi T-55. Note how the turret has been blown upside down.
(*Photo: Richard Dowden*)

Plate 43 Iraqi-MiG-21 on Tallil airbase, near Ur. Flanked by B-52 bomb craters, the aircraft itself is intact, with just a few shards of metal penetrating behind the cockpit, 6 March 1991.
(*Photo: Richard Dowden*)

Plate 44   The mountains of Kurdistan seen from the cockpit of a C-130 Hercules transport aircraft.
(*Photo: Author*)

Plate 45   On the Turkey/Iraq border. A Turkish lieutenant (*left*), conscript soldier (*centre right*) and
Kurdish guerillas, 18 April 1991.
(*Photo: Author*)

Plate 46 Turkish commandos – pale blue berets, turquoise and white camouflage smocks – at Cukurca, Thursday 18 April 1991.
(*Photo: Author*)

Plate 47 Kurdish refugees gather rations delivered by a British Chinook helicopter.
(*Photo: Author*)

learned early in the Gulf War, the main Iraqi airfields were so big it would be virtually impossible to close them down without massive attacks.

I was home in time for the 10 pm news. The 22.15 deadline passed. A few minutes later, a reporter who should have been shot said excitedly that 30 aircraft had recently flown from the *Kitty Hawk*: F-14s, F/A-18s, A-6s (he said '16s'), surmising that they might have gone to gain more information on the missile movements.

Although there were reconnaissance variants of the F-14 and F/A-18, it did not sound like a reconnaissance package to me. They were air-to-air fighters and ground-attack.

I telephoned the newsdesk and warned them that an attack might be underway. Then, I had the sense to check with the Pentagon. They said it was an old report – several hours old – from a news agency on board the *Kitty Hawk*. The aircraft were obviously not associated with an attack on Iraq which was just getting underway.

'It might be an exercise,' I said.

'It might be anything,' said the Pentagon.

I cursed the television for sensationalising out-of-date wire reports. Then, at about 23.30, we heard that Saddam had once again backed down. The Pentagon said there was 'no attack imminent'. I called the office again, and stood down.

No attack imminent. Not until the next aftershock from the 1991 Gulf War, anyway . . .

Late on Sunday night, 10 January, I was woken up with the news that earlier in the day hundreds of Iraqi workers had swarmed across the border into Kuwait near Umm Qasr to recover weapons – including four six-metre long HY-2 Silkworm anti-ship missiles – left there after the 1991 war. I was sceptical, believing, in my semi-conscious state that missiles of that type, if they had been taken by the Allies, would have been destroyed by now. As I dimly remembered, orders had been given to destroy them, in August, but I later learned the UN and Kuwait had argued over who would disarm them and they remained in the bunkers where the Iraqis eventually recaptured them.[9] A raid had clearly taken place, however, and we ran the story. The next day it emerged that the Iraqis were systematically removing the equipment to meet the UN deadline for withdrawal of 15 January.[10]

Kuwait's border with Iraq had been a constant source of argument and one of the proximate causes of the 1991 war. The line shown on most maps was that of the boundary according to the British interpretation of December 1951, which ran south of the original town of Umm Qasr. During the 1980s the town had expanded southwards with the construction of Iraqi naval facilities, across the ill-defined border. As Iran was then perceived as the main enemy and Kuwait was giving aid to Iraq, nobody bothered about it. After the 1991 war, a demilitarized zone was established five kilometres south of the border and 10 kilometres north of it. A boundary commission was to carry out a detailed survey to fix key points on the boundary. From what one could see on a 1/250,000 scale map, the boundary had not changed as far as the coast: Umm Qasr had just got bigger. Once it hit the coast, it was to follow the low water mark – not the median line of the channel of the Hawr-al-Hammar, or the Thalweg line, that is, the middle of the deepest channel. The latter

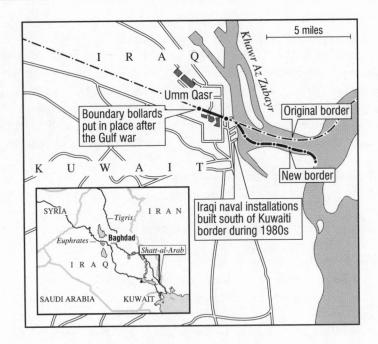

Figure 9.4   Boundary between Kuwait and Iraq in the vicinity of Umm Qasr.
(Published in *The Independent*, 12 January 1993)

decision gave Iraq the whole navigable course of the Hawr-al-Hammar, so it was a decision very favourable to Iraq – a point often missed.[11] The boundary is shown in Figure 9.4.

Robert Fisk arrived on the scene and reported that the boundary had been moved, slightly in the Kuwaitis' favour. At first there was an embarrassing contradiction between Robert reporting from Kuwait that the boundary had moved and my insistence that it had not. In practice, of course, a line on a small-scale map has to be interpreted. You cannot just bulldoze lanes through buildings in order to put in boundary bollards. In interpreting the boundary, the commission had moved it slightly north in places. But Iraq still had secure access to its port of Umm Qasr and out from there into the Gulf – something about which they could hardly complain.[12]

On 11 January, four permanent UN Security Council members: the US, Britain, France and Russia – protested to Saddam Hussein and warned that further violations would lead to serious consequences. On 13 January, Iraq said it would allow UN inspectors to fly into Iraq in their own aircraft and that it would also stop the expeditions across the border to retrieve stockpiled weapons. They had misjudged the West again. It was too late. 114 Allied aircraft took off to attack the air defence network protecting the no-fly zone south of 32nd parallel.

On 12th we started getting indications that something was likely to happen and I cancelled other appointments for 13th. Much of the day was spent preparing a detailed order of battle showing all the Allied aircraft in the region and a table showing outlines and details of the Allied arsenal. It was much like the 'glass' queue

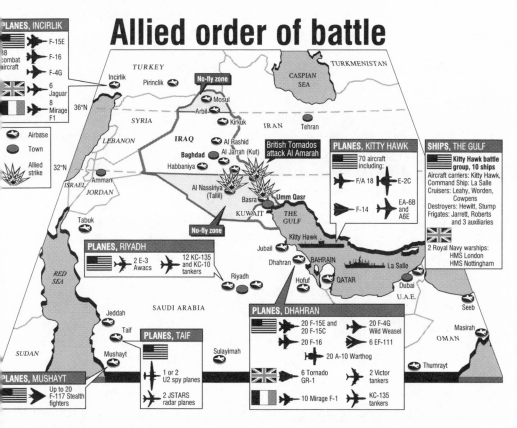

Figure 9.5 Allied Order of Battle for the strike on 13 January 1993, as known at the time. (Published in *The Independent*, 14 January 1993)

before the 1991 war. The Order of Battle, with, later additions showing the first reported strikes, is reproduced as Figure 9.5. We agonised over what to call the diagram. 'Allied forces available for attack on Iraq . . .' too long. 'Crisis in the Middle East . . .' too imprecise. 'What about "order of battle"?' I said.

'Doesn't that refer to soldiers and tanks . . .'

'You can have an "Air Order of Battle",' I said. '"AOB". And it sounds sort of . . . military.'

'Is it *right*?' said Bob Williams, who was masterminding the front page.

'It is right.'

Order of Battle it was, as shown in Figure 9.5.

A Bush Administration official described the attack as a 'spanking for Saddam, not a real beating'. US military sources had been saying it would be a 'short, sharp shock' or, as British officials described it that night, a 'short, sharp and telling lesson'.[13]

The first reports came in at about 17.30 that Wednesday afternoon. The American operation *Jural* had begun. The British component was called *Ingleton* – the next twee village on the MoD's list of codewords. The AWACS and tankers were tracing their elliptical paths south of the Iraqi border, while the strike and support aircraft had taken off. At about 18.15, the strike aircraft began their attacks, all passing over their targets in the space of about 15 minutes.

The Pentagon confirmed that an attack was underway. The British MoD seemed to have forgotten everything they had learned in the 1991 Gulf War.

'We can confirm that a strike is taking place.'

'Are British aircraft involved?'

'We can confirm that a strike is taking place . . .'

We learned that British planes – six Tornados from Dhahran, all GR1s, were involved. From the Americans. Local witnesses said aircraft had taken off at about 19.00 local (16.00 GMT). With scant information being provided, one knew enough of the background to piece together what was happening.

There were about 80 combat aircraft on board the USS *Kitty Hawk*, one of twelve ships of the carrier battle group in the Gulf: 20 F-14s, 20 F/A-18s, EA-6 Prowlers and A-6E Intruders. 35 carrier aircraft took off carrying 2,000 lb Laser Guided Bombs and HARM anti-radar missiles. More aircraft were at Dhahran, an estimated 20 F-16s, 20 F-15E Strike Eagles and 20 F-15C fighters, plus F-4G Wild Weasel defence suppression and EF-111 jamming aircraft. Between 12 and 20 F-117 Nighthawks were in their old lair at Khamis Mushait, E-3 AWACS warning and control aircraft, KC-135 and KC-10 tankers, U-2 spyplanes and E-8 JSTARS were also involved, plus six British Tornados with two Victor tankers, and 10 French Mirage 2000s providing top air cover. Of the 114 aircraft that we were later told had taken part, about 30 did the attacking. The rest were covering or in support. The British attacked one of the eight targets with four Tornados. Two more were designating the TIALD pods and the other two were each carrying three 1,000 lb laster-guided bombs (LGBs) in reserve.

Some analysts had been saying that this time the Allies would try to remove Saddam Hussein from power. This would mean targeting command bunkers, secret police barracks and communications centres – many of them in or near Baghdad. But attacking Baghdad was politically risky, not least because of the probability of civilian casualties and of downed pilots being captured and paraded by Saddam just as President Bush was about to leave office. It was a high-risk strategy, and unless carried out with overwhelming force, unlikely to achieve the commensurate high gains.

A more limited aim, destroying the surface-to-air missiles covering the no-fly zone, the radars without which they were useless, and supporting infrastructure, was therefore preferred. Later, it was described as 'proportional' and 'appropriate'. Iraq had violated the conditions attached to the no-fly zone: let the punishment fit the crime.

The SA-2 and SA-3 missiles were antiquated, having been brought into Soviet service in 1957 and 1961, respectively. The SA-2 had brought down Gary Powers' U2 spy-plane over Russia in 1960. They were not really much of a threat – General Powell, the US Chief of Staff had said so. People sensibly asked why, if they were a threat to the aircraft over the no-fly zone, had they been so easy to destroy. A fair point. But if you attack something head-on, it is less of a threat to you than if it sneaked up behind you. While they remained intact, they were a worrying nuisance.

We later learned the Allied planes had attacked four fixed sites at An Nasiriyah (Tallil), As Samarah, Al Amarah and An Najaf, and four mobile sites near Basra and An Nasiriyah. They attacked at night, which was not supposed to make any difference to accuracy, but they only struck about half their individual targets, according to the White House. Some were very difficult targets – missiles on launch rails or trucks, very small, and well dispersed over large sites. Individual large high explosive bombs, even if delivered with pinpoint accuracy, were not necessarily the best weapons for such an attack. Many of the targets were command and control facilities. The British Tornados attacked a headquarters and an intercept control centre near Al Amarah, about a kilometre apart.

The Pentagon described the damage as 'moderate' but said of the air defence network in the southern zone – 'major parts do not work'. The assessment followed the usual pattern for estimates of battle damage (see Chapter four): the first report saying an event had taken place, the second that 'you maybe haven't done as well as you thought'. The words of the US Colonel in Riyadh came back to me. One of the four anti-aircraft missile batteries had been destroyed, two put out of operation and one was unscathed.[14]

As reports of the attacks came in, I kept in touch with the Ministry of Defence. At some stage in the evening I was asked

'Have you a car and are you sober?'

'I haven't a car here,' I said. Sensible people don't take them to work in London.

'There's a briefing at 10.30 tonight – at High Wycombe', – the Primary Static War Headquarters and Headquarters of RAF Strike Command. There was some logic in holding a briefing there but there was no way that any of the defence correspondents could leave their offices, where they were attempting to form a picture of what was happening and ensure it was transmitted in some sensible form. Wandering around the Buckinghamshire countryside at that time of night in search of a bunker – and for what?

A briefing at 22.30 might be filed by 23.30. Our third edition went to press about then – I might only make the fourth and final edition, assuming there was anything new to say anyway.

I and most of my colleagues on the other papers declined to attend. There was more than enough to do ensuring that the two pages of detailed coverage was complete and accurate.

The next day, aircraft returned to the targets to get pictures for bomb damage assessment. The Americans showed pictures of the pilots returning to the *Kitty Hawk* and, later, to bases in Saudi Arabia as well. Although the RAF's attack on the two targets near Al Amarah was the only completely successful strike, there were no pictures until 48 hours after the raid. Then they released a short and very blurred video showing one strike. Whenever cine or video film is converted to still, it loses quality still further, and the video was useless for our purposes.

I made the point strongly that the public was, in the main, still behind the strikes against Iraq and that people wanted to see what the RAF had done. For PR purposes, the services and the MoD were preoccupied with the television, at the expense of the print media. But even the television news reporters were unhappy. David Shukman of the BBC explained to me that the footage shown on television was fourth-hand. They took the 'gun camera' film, copied that, flew the copy back to Britain where another copy had to be taken with all the graticules and technical markings round the picture masked out, and so on. The TV news folk were discussing ways of working directly with the RAF, to help in the declassification process.

As for photographs of returning pilots, there was nothing. The British MoD blamed it on Saudi sensitivities, but the US Air Force did not seem to have any problems. One official said the Saudis had been angry at the release of the US Air Force film, but I was not sure whether to believe him.

One of the main lessons drawn from the 1991 war was the disproportionate value of attacks with precision guided bombs (see Chapter four). It had been widely enunciated in the military analysis of the war. So how was it that only 50 per cent of the targets had been hit, according to the White House. The Pentagon refused to give a figure. It dismissed Iraqi claims that civilian areas had been hit in the attack but admitted that they had hit a structure near Basra which was not a target. I asked what proportion of the ordnance delivered had been precision-guided. 'We are not going to discuss ammunition' was the reply. I assumed that it was virtually all 'smart' weaponry: the 2,000 lb LGBs carried from the *Kitty Hawk* and HARM anti-radiation missiles, for example.

It seemed that the Iraqis had been wrong-footed. But the question was asked more and more: 'Where do we go from here: where is it all leading?' The aim was clearly not to unseat Saddam or, if so, the action taken was quite inappropriate. The Allies should have attacked the mechanisms and organs keeping him in power, not dispensable, out-of-date missile sites. Or they should have aided the Kurds and Shi'as specifically and obviously, by attacking the Iraqi forces threatening them, and Iraqi supply lines leading south and north. In that way, the Allies might have encouraged and assisted rebellion. But this policy of tit-for-tat, it seemed, could go on forever, and only strengthen Saddam, not weaken him.

My timing was getting better, however. On Sunday 17th we had been visiting relatives. As I returned to the house, at about 17.00, the telephone rang. It was the office.

'We have it on good authority it's cruise missiles this time. Everything you've got on cruise missiles.'

That made sense. There were 72 hours to go until President Bush left office. The last thing he wanted was a US pilot killed or captured and paraded. In the last three days, that would give Saddam the last laugh.

The attack took place under two hours later, at 18.40 GMT. About 40 missiles were fired from the cruiser USS *Cowpens* and the destroyers *Hewitt* and *Stump* in the Gulf, and the USS *Caron* in the Red Sea. They headed for the Zaafaraniyah factory in southern Baghdad. It had been a nuclear installation, although David Kyd, of the UN's International Atomic Energy Agency said it 'was not, in and of itself, a high-value installation'.

Baghdad was lit up by anti-aircraft fire, and the Iraqis claimed to have shot down several of the low-flying missiles. An explosion at the Rashid hotel – where the foreign press corps were based – killed two women: a receptionist and a guest, and injured 31 other people. It was not clear whether the damage was done by one of the missiles, having gone inexplicably off course, or by anti-aircraft rounds falling back to earth. Later, the US said it was one of their cruise missiles. It surprised me that they could be sure. There was no way the missile would have been that far off target normally, and it seemed unlikely that its flight path would have been over the city when they were flying from south-east or south-west – see Figure 9.6. If the missile with its half-ton warhead had detonated 'as advertised' it would have done much more damage to the hotel. Presumably it had been knocked off course by anti-aircraft fire and glided several miles to the hotel, where it had exploded, imperfectly but tragically. Even so, to this day, it seemed an extraordinary coincidence that it had landed right in front of the foreign press, giving rise to speculation that there might be a bunker in the hotel basement which was a high-value target.[15]

The raid was another piece of military history. The initial attacks in the Gulf War had been with cruise missiles and manned aircraft. But this was the first all-robot attack. The first attack just to use the 'smart' missiles – though their intelligence was, as it turned out, limited – to attack a target without endangering pilots' lives. The impact of this little piece of history was lessened, however, by another manned

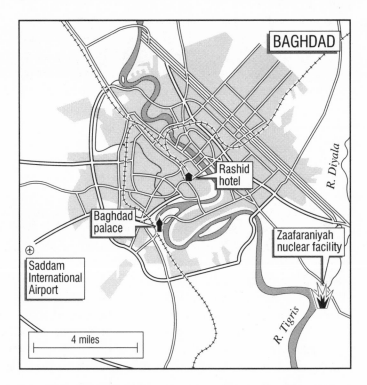

Figure 9.6 Metropolitan Baghdad, showing cruise missile strikes, 17 January 1993. (Published in *The Independent*, 18 January 1993)

aircraft attack the next day – this time, returning to the anti-aircraft system.

The next morning the Allies attacked again, at 06.35 GMT (09.35 local). Some 43 Allied aircraft took part, 29 in attack roles and 14 in support. They went for the targets at An-Najaf, As-Samawah and An-Nasriyah, not completely destroyed in the earlier (13 January) raid. The RAF again sent four Tornados in two pairs, one plane in each pair carrying three 1,000 lb LGBs, the other plane acting as the designator. Their target was the interceptor operations centre at An-Najaf, which had a command and control function for air defences, both aircraft and surface to air missiles, which could threaten Allied aircraft over the no-fly zone.

An-Najaf is a religious centre, and was the scene of some resistance to Saddam's forces immediately after the 1991 war. The mosque was of particular significance: the target was over 5 kilometres from it. Apparently, a minimum distance from civilian or religious sites for targets is laid down, though the RAF, understandably, declined to give details.

The first pair of Tornados failed to identify the target positively. The second pair were more successful, and delivered their bombs. The first pair tried again, still could not identify the target, and brought their bombs home. The RAF emphasized this action as an indication of the lengths to which they went to avoid collateral damage, particularly where an important religious site was concerned.[16]

The Tornados landed safely at 10.10 GMT. We were told there would be a briefing at 16.00 – 'at High Wycombe'.

16.00 would have been difficult if it had been in Whitehall. High Wycombe was, again, out of the question. A number of my colleagues later had a meeting with the MoD to try to ensure that information was released sooner and in a more convenient fashion. We agreed that it might be possible to have some information released sooner, and in London – that the RAF had been involved, what had been hit, had all the planes returned – but the detailed operational briefing would still have to be done by the Joint Headquarters. Nevertheless, the release of film from this second raid was handled better.

As the Allied aircraft had taken off on 18 January, there was a missile attack alert at Dhahran. Some press reports claimed that the Iraqis were about to fire Scud-type missiles in retaliation. Here was the test – did Iraq have any left, or not? Since 1991, UN experts had been combing Iraqi military sites. At the al-Taji camp, near Baghdad, they had found 62 al-Hussein missiles and six mobile launchers, which they had crushed and cut up. In 1992 the CIA claimed that Iraq still had about 200 missiles, either basic Scuds or the extended-range al-Hussein. The arithmetic was complicated by uncertainty about how many Scuds you needed to convert into an al-Hussein (see Chapter one). The UN believed it had accounted for most of the Scuds supplied to Iraq by the former Soviet Union although Iraq might still be hiding missiles from North Korea. Most experts reckoned there were very few missiles left. If Saddam Hussein did have any, it was in his interest to hide them, rather than advertise their existence by firing them. If he did, he would invite heavier attack from the Allies and more intrusive inspections afterwards. As expected, the press reports were wrong – no surface-to-surface missiles were fired.

By now, people were getting anxious about the raids, their purpose and consequences. Russia demanded a new mandate from the UN Security Council before further raids were carried out. There was a report that the Kuwaitis had requested British and French troops to join the 1200 Americans, although the Defence Secretary, Malcolm Rifkind, later told us there had been no formal request. It was not so much a fear that we might again be dragged into ground involvement, but more a correct scepticism about what these actions were to achieve. It seemed the last Allied attacks had more to do with the imminent handover from President Bush to President Clinton than with any coherent strategy for attacking Saddam Hussein. As David Howell, the chairman of the Commons Select Committee on Foreign Affairs, said, 'Something more is needed here in the way of longer-term strategy.'[17]

Then, unexpectedly, Saddam offered an 'unconditional ceasefire', to begin at 08.00 local (05.00 GMT, midnight EST) on 20 January, the day of President Clinton's inauguration. Mr Clinton's initial reaction was circumspect. He neither wanted to cede the initiative to Iraq, nor give any signal that he would take a less tough stance than President Bush. The Iraqis said they hoped the 'ceasefire' would give Mr Clinton the chance to assess the legitimacy of the two no-fly zones. Interestingly, they had been declared by the Allies, but were not specifically authorised by the UN. The no-fly zone over Bosnia was specifically authorised by the UN, but was not being enforced. Accusations of 'double standards' began to fly.

But at least the ceasefire offered the chance of a respite in the hostilities that had flared a week before. Gulf War Two-and-a-Half, I called it. Iraq had been unable to mount any effective opposition to the renewed Allied strikes, but they had done no really significant damage to Iraq. If the Allies wanted to remove Saddam Hussein, they would need to take action of a different order, which so far they had declined to do. Dreaming that a disaffected colonel with a Kalashnikov would do the job was a pious hope. Iraq had shown astonishing resilience in reconstructing its armed forces and its air defence network. If it learned the lessons of the Second, 1991 Gulf War – notably the need for much better quality forces able to engage in manoeuvre warfare – and if states desperate for hard currency were allowed to re-arm Iraq, we might yet see a Third Gulf War.

10

Some Conclusions

All wars are unique and the Second Gulf War was more unique than most. There will never be another like it, which makes drawing lessons very dangerous. As Brigadier Cordingley said, 'We must be careful about the lessons we take from a war where we defeated a technologically inferior enemy on featureless terrain and met very few reverses.'[1]

The open terrain of the Arabian Peninsula favoured using the Coalition's technological lead in reconnaissance, electro-optics and precision bombing. The Allies established command of the air and the electro-magnetic spectrum. It was always clear that the next war would be won by the side which best used the electromagnetic spectrum. *In that environment* the advantage enjoyed by the power(s) with superior technology over a slightly inferior adversary has probably increased.

The Allies also had unhindered communications to and within the Peninsula. As a naval officer said to me afterwards: can you imagine the effect if, instead of a few hundred tanks, Saddam Hussein had just two submarines?

The Saudis also had enormous wealth and, to use the jargon of the first British official lessons, 'exceptional host-nation infrastructure' – huge, well developed but empty ports and bases.[2]

Although technology was obviously very important, too much emphasis tends to be put on it. Iraq did, after all, possess much modern equipment. As stated in the Introduction, the Allies won by brain-power, in every area. The planning and deception which completely fooled the Iraqis as to the direction of the surface attack owed much to technology, and to the lack of any air opposition, which permitted the Allies to deploy in secret once the air campaign started (but not before). But they were also dead cunning. The logistics of the left flanking move were a grandiose, ambitious and – if Wellington's definition of genius as 'an infinite capacity for taking pains' is accepted – a brilliant piece of staff work and number crunching.

Nor, as the chapters have told, was the Allied victory as complete as it at first seemed. Playing devil's advocate, Major General Viktor Filatov, editor of the former Soviet *Military Historical Journal*, said the 'Americans' (Allies)

> Did not fulfil a single one of the aims put before their army and the Allied armies. The Iraqi Army was not destroyed, their regiments were not driven from Kuwait in disorganized flight. The Iraqi Army left Kuwait of its own volition, having accomplished a regular military manoeuvre: an organized withdrawal, preserving personnel, arms and military equipment. President Hussein was not overthrown, he is alive and well. The ruling Ba'ath Party has not been deposed, the régime has not been destroyed.[3]

General Filatov's views cannot be sustained with regard to the Iraqi Army in Kuwait, but they can for the Republican Guard north of Kuwait. VII Corps objective, it will be recalled, was *to destroy the RGFC*. It did not. As far as the RGFC was concerned, General Filatov's remarks are sustainable. As for the Iraqi Army, Saddam did not care about them. They were expendable.

The Russians' views on the war are very interesting. Having invested much intellectual capital in the study of future war, they were gratified to see many of their predictions coming true, even in a one-sided way. In the pages that follow, I have drawn fairly extensively upon contemporary Russian thinking about the Second Gulf War, for two reasons. First, because, nationally, they have put so much effort into the study of modern warfare on a big scale and secondly, because there is no other nation that can match their experience in the organisation and handling of really large forces of all arms and, probably, their intellectual approach to their studies of the character of future war. Even if we do not always agree entirely with their views and feel that they may have been influenced to some degree by the fact that the Iraqis were using a high percentage of Soviet equipment and had been trained by Soviet advisers, it would be an act of intellectual arrogance to ignore them.

On the day of the ceasefire, 28 February, an article in the conservative paper *Sovetskaya Rossiya* said:

> The final stage in the assault on the Republican Guard should be the capture of Basra. Communications tying the main forces of the Iraqi military intersect there, which determines the strategic significance of that city. One imagines that the completion of an inner noose of encirclement will also be important.[4]

The Russian Colonel was absolutely right (see Chapter 7). He expected the operation to last several days more. But maybe the Russians were not yet so aware of the fragile nature of public opinion, fanned by instant news coverage.

The Russians also had some doubts about the air campaign. According to the then Soviet Air Force Chief of Staff, industrial and administrative targets were attacked 'mechanistically' – regardless of the influence that their destruction would have on the outcome of the war. Iraqi camouflage and deception was very effective and many of the 'first line' targets – mobile ones, for example, mobile Scuds, were not identified. The Allies did not 'fully utilise the possibilities of precision guided munitions'. Fires in the target area confused infra-red and TV guided munitions. The simplest and shortest range air defences – AAA – proved a serious problem, forcing the Allied air forces to fly high.[5] There is some truth in all of that.

Iraqi operational and tactical deception impressed the Russians. They painted holes on Hardened Aircraft shelters and lit fires to make the Allies think they had hit targets when they had not. Advancing British armour ran into dummy tanks. This is probably why the Allies overestimated the amount of armour destroyed.

The Russians strongly refute any suggestion that their equipment was at fault. Most of that encountered by the Allies was old. Some of the Republican Guard tanks had been buried in sand to minimise damage from air attack. If you dig a tank out of the sand after two months and it starts – which theirs did – that is a tough tank. 'As far as Soviet combat equipment is concerned, it is not so much the problem, I think, as the people operating it,' said Lieutenant General Gorbachev on 21 January 1991. However, they acknowledged the primitiveness of the Scud. 'If the Iraqis instal a small jamming station, the Scud's invulnerability will increase tenfold,' said Major General Kostin.

On 1 April 1991, Colonel General Nikolay Chervov identified seven key Iraqi weaknesses and one strength. Weaknesses were: no unified military doctrine, no defined war plan, no unified air defence, misplaced emphasis on the political factors of the war, poor training, poor unit and service interaction (units not firing in mutual support, complete unawareness of what was going on) and poor night fighting ability. The strength was operational and tactical camouflage and deception (*maskirovka*).

The Soviet Union, now succeeded by Russia, was in the process of developing a new doctrine of 'defensive sufficiency' relying on a period of defence prior to launching a counter-attack. The Gulf War's clearest military lesson was probably the massive failure of a strategic defensive posture using Soviet equipment (if not military art) when confronted by new technology weapons. Major General Slip-chenko, one of the more progressive senior officers, said 'A counterattack [under defensive sufficiency] requires us to wait too long in this era of high-technology weapons.... A defensive doctrine does not equal a defensive strategy.' Marshal Losik, a tank warfare expert, added 'staking everything on a retaliatory strike is only possible at all given a fortified, stable and efficient system of early detection and warning of a military attack and high mobilization and combat readiness.'[6] Fortified it was, efficient it was not. The Iraqis were expecting an attack; their mobilisation was high, their combat readiness was lamentable.

The 'preponderant' role of the air campaign in the victory certainly struck the Russians. 'The Gulf War supports the fact that air strikes can themselves form the basis of victory,' said General Slipchenko.

> By the year 2000 ground forces will no longer be the primary force ... the forces of the future are the strategic rocket forces [now part of the strategic deterrence forces], the air force and navy, and air defence. We have discussed the diminishing role of ground forces for years but now we have proof.[7]

The newspaper *Red Star* chose its words carefully. 'The modern level of technological development makes it possible with air strikes, if not to conclusively crush the enemy, then, at least, to inflict on him a decisive defeat.'

The choice of a Marshal of Aviation, Yevgeniy Shaposhnikov, as Soviet Defence Minister after the successive falls of Marshal Dmitry Yazov and General Mikhail Moiseyev, may have owed something to both the discussions of the previous years and the Gulf War.

Major General I.N. Vorob'ev, one of Russia's most profound if esoteric writers on 'future war' during the late Soviet period reappeared in print in early 1992, after due reflection, to give his authoritative judgment on the 1991 Gulf War:

> Military operations were not conducted on the classical model. They do not lie within the parameters of established canons, accepted stereotypes. Without exaggeration one can say that this war, which was abnormal in character, necessitated looking at certain aspects of military theory afresh. Unfortunately, in our [Russian] publications, no detailed work analysing its operational–tactical peculiarities from all sides has appeared. There is the impression that the military experience gained does not apply to us. That is explained in some measure by some authors' tendency to underline the fact in their descriptions of military operations that they took place in close to text-book conditions, and that one's attitude to them must be very critical. But there is another side to the coin: the wish to cut ourselves off from the paralysing defeat of our former Allies – the Iraqi Army. You see, the operational–tactical concepts of the Soviet military school supported the Iraqi military–political command for a long time. In addition, therefore, the Western press considers the Persian Gulf War [sic.] to be a "mirror image" of future operations with the Armed Forces of the Commonwealth of Independent States.[8]

General Vorob'ev nonetheless thought the Gulf War marked a major revolution in military affairs comparable to the 1870–71 Franco–Prussian War, which he cited as the paradigm bringing together revolutions in small arms, open-order infantry tactics, the use of the railway and the telegraph. Similarly, he said, the Persian Gulf War, as the Russians call it, was a watershed.

> It draws an invisible line, as it were, under classical wars, which were fought with the participation of multi-millioned armies, and opens an era of wars at a higher technological level with the involvement of a new sphere – space – in active operations and also [operations] on a wider scale – the ether. Its character, determined by many factors, is sharply distinguished from all preceding wars.[9]
>
> In preceding 'local' wars, including the 1973 Middle East War and the 1982 Falklands Conflict, only certain new types of technology were employed. But in the Gulf, he continued, we saw the use of 'ultra-modern armaments and munitions [stealth and precision guidance, for example] *on a mass scale*'. The other side lacked the means to counter the new weaponry. This led to the 'one-sided' nature of the conflict, 'a game with one goal'.[10]

Other commentators mirrored General Vorob'ev's views: Lieutenant General A.V. Politsyn, for example, writing in the grandiose Russian tradition on 'A glimpse at the war of the new epoch'. Prefacing a translation of a US analysis, he reiterated that the Gulf War differed from both the two World Wars and the 'local wars' – Korea,

Vietnam, 1973 – which had preceded it. The 'one-sidedness' meant that the key issue in going to war was not the terrible uncertainty as to who would win but the price that would have to be paid. The price to the victors turned out to be trivial compared with the Soviet Union's 50 million dead (military and civilian) in the Great Patriotic War, a newly revised figure. He warned against the resulting 'euphoria' – which might tempt politicians to resort to 'surgical' military means when politics had failed.[11]

Vorob'ev said the Gulf War was also marked by a redistribution of the traditional 'spheres of influence' of the component parts of what the Russians call Military Art – Strategy, Operational Art and Tactics.

> If in all preceding wars Tactics – the contact of fighting infantry and tank formations with the support of artillery and air – played the leading role in defeating the enemy, then here the most important place was occupied by strategic and operational assets. These were represented by strategic, tactical and carrier-borne aviation, and also rockets and missiles. There were tactical battles, but it was not they which determined the 'face' of the operation, its course and outcome. From this, one can conclude that *in the new conditions battle has ceased to be the only means of securing victory ...* the dependence of tactics on strategy and operational art has increased, but this does not form a basis for rejecting tactics. Tactics, as the art of fighting the battle is not fading away, but its role in the new conditions is changing fundamentally.[12]

Operation DESERT STORM was therefore 'an operational electronic-fire battle [*èlektronno-ogenvoye srazheniye*] – the sum of a range of massed, prolonged air-space, missile and electronic strikes in concert with strikes by naval forces.'[13] The Gulf War also forced military theorists to look again at the interaction between manoeuvre and positional forms of warfare. Previously they had alternated in a rough balancing act.

> Here, manoeuvre dominated. In Operation DESERT STORM, in order to overcome a well-fortified, deeply echeloned defence they did not use the classical form of offensive action – the breakthrough [an extraordinary statement as there were classic breaching operations, but the author goes on to explain himself]. Breaching the defence's operational integrity was achieved by other means – by a prolonged and unbroken massed electronic-fire offensive in concert with a subsequent double envelopment of his forces – on the ground and through the air – and by forming in the enemy rear an active front by means of air, air-mobile and naval attacks [*desanty*]. I suggest that, on the basis of this experience, the prognosis could be a significant reduction in the specific gravity of such an important attribute of the First and Second World Wars, as the breakthrough.[14]

Of course there were breaching operations, but General Vorob'ev distinguishes these from the more grandiose and costly breakthrough operation. Those breaches proceeded so swiftly and in such text-book fashion, he is saying, because the enemy was already largely incapacitated by the 'double envelopment' taking place through the air and the ether.

His comments mirror Russian and Soviet terminology from the first two decades of this century, when warfare was described as the 'alternation of manoeuvre and positional war in time and space'.[15] And General Schwarzkopf's operation, with its air and electronic strikes against the enemy nervous system, exemplified in new dimensions what the military theorists of the 1920s and 30s had sought to achieve. As the prescient Soviet theorist G.S. Isserson put it, in 1938, manoeuvre in modern war 'lay not in front of the enemy's forward line of troops, as it had in time and space before World War I, but behind it, and in the enemy depth'.[16] General Schwarzkopf said the same. Only when his forces were beyond the enemy front could they start fighting the manoeuvre war – their kind of war.

The Iraqis, General Vorob'ev concluded, were the 'prisoners of outmoded stereotypes'. They learned a cruel lesson, which was 'instructive for other nations' – like his own. The lessons of the Gulf War, unsurprisingly, permeate the new draft Russian military doctrine, published in May 1992.[17]

In their highly academic way, the Russians acknowledge what Western commentators also recognise – that this *was* a completely new kind of war, in the political sense, a novelty made possible by technology. Since the Industrial Revolution – the American Civil War was probably the first – wars have tended to totality, overriding the impulses which started them and careering off with their own logic, like un-guided missiles. The Gulf War, perhaps, marks the return to the limited war, *even if* fought with 'unlimited means'. Wars have once again become 'precision guided' – a bizarre mirror, on a vast scale, of the technology they contain.

This account of the Gulf War has neglected the unseen but minatory force of sea power and its ever-present influence on operations. It is difficult to define the direct way in which sea power brought victory about, apart from the significant participation of carrier-based aircraft and sea-launched cruise missiles in the initial Allied attack, and the effect of a genuine amphibious force at sea in deceiving the Iraqis. But had the Allies not ruled the waves totally, the operations could never have taken place as they did. The Navy gets no credit for winning, but if they lose, everybody loses. There is much in the conviction that in a contest between an oceanic power and a continental one, the oceanic power always wins in the end. Napoleon's France and Germany in two world wars found that. That realisation was behind Admiral Sergey Gorshkov's build-up of the Soviet Navy. He did not want to be the continental power that lost.

Sea lines of communication were vital to the Allied build up and sustaining the Allied effort. Two Iraqi submarines would have multiplied the effort to keep supplies flowing inordinately, and diverted Allied ships from other tasks. The 16th century Francis Bacon's comment that 'he that commands the sea is at great liberty and may take as much and as little of the war as he will' still stands.[18] The strength of the US and Western reaction when, in September 1992, Russia looked set to deliver two submarines to Iran, underlines this point. Such a minute force, deployed in the Gulf itself or, more likely, the Arabian Sea, would transform the balance of power in the area. The US blocked the Russian sale – temporarily, anyway. And in addition to the sea's disproportionate value as the most cost-effective means of transporting oil from the region, it is of growing importance in a broader, strategic sense. With the increase in the importance of satellites and other space-based assets, the military importance of the oceans, which cover 71 per cent of the earth's surface, can only increase also.

The Iraqi sea-mines exercised a considerable influence. The only Iraqi success at sea was when mines inflicted severe damage on the USS *Tripoli* and *Princeton*. Little advertised, the mine-sweepers, an area in which the UK leads the world, made it possible for the great American battleships to approach the Kuwaiti coast. Since it started in the American Civil War, mine warfare has always been a cost-effective option for the weaker side. A key lesson of the Gulf War is that a relatively small investment in mines – and, therefore, in Mine Counter-Measures Vessels – goes a long way.

The sea was also the slithery platform for some very effective weapons systems, notably the 16-inch guns of the US battleships. These are to be retired, because their giant crews are not cost-effective. Although modern high precision guidance and missiles gained much publicity, the oldest long-range high precision weapon – the battleship gun, proved very useful. Take a 16-inch gun and put a 12-inch saboted round inside it and you can get 50 miles range. Various replacements for the battleships are under discussion, and some sort of sea-based multiple-launch-rocket system combined with accurate cruise missiles might do the job. But watching the tragic events in Dubvrovnik, on the Croatian coast in 1991–92, one wondered what the effect of a US battleship, which can put a one-ton shell in a target the size of a tennis court 15 to 20 miles inland, on the besieging bullies would have been, physically and psychologically.

The old B-52 Stratofortress bomber also proved most effective. The Iraqi ground forces were not, by and large, defeated by precision bombing. They were stunned, paralysed, crippled by the terrifying weight of heavy bombing. An Iraqi general confirmed that this was what broke his troops. If the Allies had only had a small number of high-precision attack aircraft, the ground forces would have had a far harder job.

On the ground, the most spectacular and revolutionary device was the Global Positioning System (GPS). For the first time, ever, forces operating in featureless terrain knew exactly where they were, every few seconds. Without it the giant but, at the same time, intricate manoeuvres in the desert would have been just impossible. In any other war, the units and formations would have got hopelessly lost, bumped into each other, and integration of air and ground forces would have resulted in frequent friendly fire incidents. GPS meant that supplies could just be dumped on Exchange Points (XPs), miles from anywhere, and units could move to pick them up.

Next, the battle-winning contribution of artillery was re-emphasized. The Multiple-Launch Rocket System exemplified the disproportionate amount of firepower that artillery produces for a given amount of manpower, and took the trend further. Everyone who witnessed the Allied fireplans described them as 'awesome'. Brigadier Durie described the effect [on the enemy] seen by advancing infantry and armour as 'overwhelming'.[19] Whole Iraqi companies, hundreds of men, were wiped out at a time.

Major General Rupert Smith listed four battle winners: the GPS; the ability to fight at night; 'simple little boxes we got to strap on the radios' which automatically coded and decoded the messages, doing away with complex and time-consuming codes; and the lethality and accuracy of artillery systems.[20] General de la Billière said two pieces of equipment were 'potential war winners' – the GPS, again, and the TOGS (Thermal and Optical Gunsight), which enabled tank crews to see in the dark. The former gave vehicle commanders their accurate position to a ten-figure grid reference, or to within about 15 metres – enough for very accurate indirect fire gunnery, while the latter enabled them to see anything, including small rodents – out to about 2,500 metres, while the Iraqis could see nothing. All the Allied commanders understood that for over half of any 24-hour period – night – the enemy was totally at their mercy.[21]

But General Smith described the presence of generations of equipment spanning thirty years, from the 1950s to the 1980s, as 'mad'. When the reconnaissance was slower than the main forces for whom they were supposed to be reconnoitring, that was, indeed, insane. The official British 'lessons' recognised this point.[22]

Means of recognising friendly ground forces were grotesquely primitive compared with the other technology employed and the Identification Friend or Foe system long in use in the air. Inverted black vees and plastic sheeting were not enough. By the end of the ground campaign, Allied tanks were sprouting brilliantly coloured flags – Union Jacks, lions rampant, the cross of St Andrew – for further identification. Some of the US journalists thought that there might at least be something in the composition of the paint that showed up on Allied targeting systems. There was not, although the British found that the black paint of the vees did show up quite well in their TOGS sights. Following the tragic attack on two Warriors by US A-10s which killed nine British soldiers, leading to a verdict of 'unlawful killing' by a British inquest, the UK is working with the US to identify technical ways of minimising the risk of fratricide. The Defence Research Agency was also reported to be undertaking a research programme to assess short- and long-term solutions.[23] The US air commander, Lieutenant General Horner, said the same. 'Rapid battlefield movement requires improved capabilities for the identification of friendly forces. It is critical that we acquire systems that will allow pilots attacking forces on the ground to quickly distinguish friend from foe.'[24]

In a fast moving battle, formations cannot rely entirely on timely intelligence from higher echelons. They need their own intelligence gathering and dissemination. The classic example of failure here is when 1st (UK) Armoured Division had to discontinue the 'depth battle', because they could no longer find depth targets.

When NATO faced a cohesive and largely one-directional 'threat' from the Warsaw Pact, planning was comparatively straightforward. In the uncertain world which follows the welcome end of the Cold War, as the Second Gulf War demonstrates, power will have to be projected far and fast. General Horner concluded that time had become a critical factor. 'Airlift, sealift and pre-positioning makes this kind of operation possible. Future conflicts will require forces to get there in a hurry, creating tremendous logistic requirements. What cannot be stored in theater will have to be moved in a quickly, and in an orderly manner.'[25] Early air supremacy, he continued, is critical. 'With the freedom to fly at will, the rest falls into place.'[26]

Stealth technology proved worth every penny. Operating at night against targets protected by 3,000 anti-aircraft guns and 60 SAM batteries without a single loss, or even a scratch, was held to have proved the value of stealth technology, although means of detection will inevitably catch up. Also, the stealth aircraft needed less electronic combat support than earlier generation aircraft, freeing specialised EW aircraft to support other missions.

Precision guided munitions clearly minimise collateral damage around targets. Their greater efficiency also reduces aircraft exposure and, consequently, aircraft losses.

Another lesson, taken on board by all Western Armed Forces was the overwhelming importance and battle-winning dominance of logistics. This was not new, of course. Field Marshal Lord Wavell (1883–1950), the British Second World War commander, said that the more he saw of war, the more he realised it boiled down to organisation, and transport – what the Americans and now the British also call logistics. It was relatively simple, he said, requiring little imagination. It involved deciding where you want to put an Army and then by what routes you are to resupply and sustain it. And a respected adversary of Wavell's knew the same – and lost, because he was let down. 'The battle is fought and decided by the Quartermasters before the shooting begins.' So wrote Field Marshal Erwin Rommel.[27]

During the one-dimensional stand-off between NATO and the Warsaw Pact, those positions and routes were known or, at least, utterly predictable. But the Gulf War marked a new era, requiring forces to be deployed to an unexpected area with unfamiliar climatic and terrain conditions. Even so, the Allied forces had the benefit of months in which to prepare their campaign, uninterrupted, and of the superb – even opulent – infrastructure 'in Theatre'. In future operations, the distances could be even longer, the routes circuitous and the support infrastructure uncertain or virtually non-existent.

The role played by reserves provides an important lesson. Smaller, high-tech armed forces will, inevitably, have to rely more on reserves to fulfil certain tasks. The US called up and used reserve units and even formations – the 'total force' concept. The 142 Field Artillery Brigade, which fired in support of the British division's insertion, was a National Guard Unit. The British, on the other hand, were suspicious of reserve units and only called up a relatively small number of specialists. This was a problem because Queen's Order, mobilising reserves, is an all-or-nothing device. New procedures, enabling swift but selective call-out of reserves while giving them statutory protection, are a must.

In addition, there will be severe problems in recruiting and keeping reserves if they do not believe that in the event of a crisis they will be used.

This was a limited war, with defined political objectives. That makes the small print of ceasefires and its scrupulous observance even more important. It was a strange, some would say tragic, twist that the talks at Safwan allowed the Iraqis to continue to fly helicopters, which they promptly did. For some reason, no-one foresaw what the result of that would be. Having nailed down the opposition at the conference table, it is also important to insist on absolute compliance, and to respond swiftly, even disproportionately, to any violation. It is like a suspended jail sentence. Saddam Hussein continued to weave, attacking the Kurds, moving air defence systems north of the 36th parallel: just enough to get away with. The occasional punitive strike – 'I said *don't* do that' – would have been in order. Eventually, the Allies realised that with the attacks of 13–18 January 1993.

Returning to the conduct of the war itself, the crucial role of the Allied Special Forces – highly trained troops operating in small groups inside enemy territory – is another key difference from earlier major wars. Many commanders, including General Schwarzkopf, were perhaps rightly suspicious and dismissive of Special Operations Forces (SOF, in the US forces, SF in the British). As Michael Howard, the military historian observed of their contribution to the Second World War, they were seen as 'luxuries sustained by the patient and unspectacular efforts of their more self-effacing colleagues, and their activities did not appear to make much contribution to the massive and collective destruction of which war now inevitably consisted.'[28] General Schwarzkopf was certainly of this view. His air campaign and violent, swift ground campaign *were* spectacular and, he thought, could achieve anything the Special Forces could. General de la Billière said he 'steam-rollered' General Schwarzkopf into agreeing that the British Special Forces should be allowed into Iraq. Yet even he then repeatedly wondered whether they would find a worthwhile role inside Iraq.[29]

But when the British Special Forces crossed the border on 20 January, scoring their first big success on 23rd and joined by their US colleagues on 8 February, their contribution was immediately felt in the most crucial area. There was an immediate drop in the number of Scud launches, which helped keep Israel out of the war and the Coalition intact. Air strikes alone could not knock out the evasive missiles, and sometimes when the British SAS used lasers to designate the targets for air attack, they had to wait up to 50 minutes for the aircraft to arrive, so they attacked them directly instead.[30] There could be no clearer example of the new tendency, also noted by the Russians, for the boundaries of tactical, operational and strategic responsibilities to shift. Small patrols were attacking operational-strategic targets.

It seems that the more 'political' a war – the more its military progress is intimately entwined with political considerations at every level – the more important Special Forces become. In future operations, it seems likely that the importance of Special Forces will increase. As armed forces get smaller, and the operations in which they are expected to be involved become more politically delicate – partly on account of the reactions of the populations of the belligerent countries, the case for having a higher proportion of Special Forces looks persuasive.

This leads to the possibility of targeting commanders-in-chief – specifically, Saddam Hussein. The Allied commanders assumed they were targets themselves, and Iraq had stressed terrorism as part of its psychological warfare campaign. General de la Billière said 'Saddam himself was not a coalition target but, as Commander-in-Chief of the enemy forces and the man running the war against us, he inevitably became a military target from time to time' – a nice distinction.[31] There is no doubt that the Allies would have been delighted to get Saddam if they could but, as Prince Khalid pointed out, that would probably have turned him into a martyr and placed someone equally ruthless and perhaps even more formidable on the throne. It would be necessary to destroy a large slice of the ruling élite – something which the Allied command may have attempted (see Chapter four).

The fact remains that heads of Government have a mutual interest in discouraging open season of their own kind. There remain unwritten rules – sometimes ambiguous, but rarely crossed. No doubt there were plans to kill both Hitler and Churchill in the Second World War, but heads of Government are well protected. General de la Billière said two Allied air raids came close to killing Saddam. In both cases the objective was a legitimate 'military target', although Saddam was thought to be there. The first was a convoy, attacked by US aircraft. Either Saddam was in one of the few cars which escaped, or he was not travelling with them. The second was a mobile caravan headquarters, where, according to General de la Billière, the Allies had received information that Saddam was to spend the night. The target was destroyed but, again, he was not there.[32] Like Churchill and Hitler, Saddam makes extensive use of doubles, and this may have been responsible for the Allied errors.

The final but crucial operational lesson is that while intelligence from 'national technical means' – spy satellites, and high-flying aircraft was very good and had an unprecedented effect on the outcome of the war, humint – human intelligence – was lamentable. The paralysing effect of fear on the population of Iraq was a powerful factor, making it virtually impossible for an enemy agent to operate. The British Commander admitted after the war that 'we had no live sources in Baghdad or anywhere else in Iraq'.[33] There were reports from defectors and the Kuwaiti resistance, but the West had few people who could interpret them satisfactorily. Having spent 45 years concentrating on the Soviet Union, there were few Arabists in the Western forces. When visiting the Navy in the Gulf in November, 1990, I asked an officer on one of the major warships – a destroyer or frigate – whether there were any Arabic speakers on board. 'Can't say. That's an operational capability,' he said. Too right it was. The provision of a smattering of competent linguists across the Armed Services is one area where a little investment, especially in reservists, goes a long way.

* * *

Forty years of Cold War and of reliance upon the United States nuclear umbrella had allowed the British Armed Forces to become dangerously eroded. Despite an impressive 'shop window' in Germany, the plain fact was that there was nothing behind it and even the goods on view would not stand too close an inspection. Twice in under ten years the BAOR had to be reduced to near impotence because its resources had been plundered to put a small force into the field. As for war reserves, even such plundering was not enough – some items, such as artillery ammunition were simply not available in sufficient quantity for even a divisional battle in a short war. As for the supply of trained units, ready for battle – there were virtually none.

Regiments and supporting services had to be scratched together and trained on arrival in the theatre. Two things saved the day – a six months breathing space and the sheer quality of the commanders and all who served under them, a quality that enabled those commanders to get maximum value out of the training organised in the God-given gift of time they had been granted.

As for the logistic build-up, the cold hard fact is that no matter how ready a nation may be to respond to an operational call, that build-up will always take time, even given the sort of host nation support available for the defensive and offensive phases of the campaign. Nevertheless, readiness will ensure that that time is kept to a minimum. So, the principal lesson to emerge from the Second Gulf War is quite simply this. With the Cold War a thing of the past and the influence of the nuclear umbrella no longer a dominating factor, like a sort of strategic camouflage, national defence policies can no longer be founded on bluff. Hence, foreign policy too must take full account of the limitations imposed by reality and coats must be cut according to a limited quantity of cloth – albeit of the highest quality and durability. In recent months, *Operation Grapple*, the British contribution of 2,400 troops in support of UN Aid operations in Bosnia, has required the deployment of far greater numbers overall than the combat forces seemed to justify and, once again, stretching the British Army's resources to the limit.

* * *

It will have become clear from this book that, throughout, the defence ministries and Allied forces in theatre made a terrific effort to keep the media informed and educated. This was, as noted, crucial because maintaining public interest and confidence and commitment is crucial to any war effort by a democracy. The presence of direct, live coverage of events through satellite dishes meant that the public were informed as never before on what was happening. This made it even more important for the briefers to explain why it was happening and what the results of it happening might be. The Americans were slightly better at this than the British, because they used operational soldiers, not specialised Public Information staff, whether service or civilian, to brief and organise the media. Brigadier General Neal was particularly successful because he was Deputy Director of Operations. He knew exactly what was going on, what was likely to be of value to the enemy, and what he could say. Group Captain Irving, for the British, was also in on all the operational briefings.

Outside the war itself, the press were sometimes exasperated by the interference of civilian press officers who just did not know the answers. It was not that they were being devious or secretive: they just didn't know. In many countries, also, a uniform goes a long way: civilian press officers were treated as journalists, as I discovered in Turkey. Military officers enjoy a certain, cosmopolitan status.

There is also a tendency to assume that the public do not like military detail and military hardware. They do. They find it absolutely fascinating. Brigadier Cordingley recalled how he wanted to bring out a giant array of armour, which was promptly interfered with by press officers who selected one vehicle of each type.[34] Nor does this only apply to 'nuts and bolts'. People are very interested in tactics, operational art and strategy, I discovered. When I described the land operation in geometrical terms – a quadrilateral and a triangle – people found that fascinating. The so-called 'general reader' was intrigued by the style and vocabulary of, for example, AirLand battle doctrine. Our syndication department received particular requests for detailed and technical articles on military subjects from many foreign newspapers. 'Background' briefings proved exceptionally useful in this regard. Several other journalists, surveying the handling of the press during the war, noticed the same thing. Give the media something to write about, and they go away happy. If you do not, they tend to speculate.

Now that public support and interest are even more vital for maintaining any military effort, commanders must be made responsible for their own PI. PI is one of the principles of war. Access to front line formations can obviously be restricted, but at the higher levels, it is part of a commander's responsibility to maintain public interest and support. Get rid of the civilian press officers, and make it part of the chain of command.

There were also disasters. The reason why the friendly fire incident when A-10s destroyed the two Warriors became such a *cause célèbre* was not that it happened. Everybody knew that such things happen in war. People were angry because the initial explanation that it had happened in the heat of battle in bad visibility was just untrue. They had stopped, and visibility was good. It took months to find out what really happened. At the time, 4th Armoured Brigade was still fighting through objectives. But if a full and accurate statement could have been made just a few days later, the acrimony surrounding that sad event would have dispersed. If you make a mistake, you have to advertise it. It sounds bizarre, but with media coverage as it is, and media organisations' pathological desire to find 'cover-ups' and conspiracies where none exist, you have to be very up-front about your mistakes.

The RAF realised this brilliantly. When bombs went astray at Fallujah, they spent most of a day getting the video of it occurring. They showed it, and everybody shrugged their shoulders. Okay, thanks for being honest. These things happen. . . .

Two years later, these lessons in handling the media had been forgotten. The time taken to give the barest details of the attack on 13 January 1993, and then to release pictures, was too great in the last decade of the twentieth century. The British Defence Ministry and the RAF, in particular, seemed oblivious to the RAF's own doctrine. Military operations cannot be conducted by a democracy 'in the face of public hostility or indifference' (see Introduction). As in 1991, the Americans handled it better. If, as looks likely, the 'new world order' means many more military operations, conducted while Western states are notionally at peace – what the Americans are now calling 'peacetime engagement' – then Governments must address this question. If military strikes are to be effective tools to enforce international order in peacetime, they have to be advertised. Maybe not in detail before they happen, but certainly afterwards.

It was not so long since military operations were expected to take place only in the context of total war, an atmosphere of secrecy in which normal peacetime attitudes to information were suspended. It is not surprising that defence ministries still cling to that attitude, whatever they say to the contrary. In this respect, as in many, the Gulf conflict and the aftershocks, were radically new. For most of the soldiers, sailors, airmen and officials on the Allied side in 1991 it was not only their first experience of this kind of limited war, but of any war. That is perhaps what is most extraordinary. That you can take a military machine devised in peace, set it down in western Asia, and for it to function so smoothly, is little short of a miracle. For many of the journalists, it was their first war too. We all made some mistakes. But, as an American Admiral said,

> To inquire if and where we made mistakes is not to apologize. War is replete with mistakes because it is full of improvisations. In war we are always doing something for the first time. It would be a miracle if what we improvised under the stress of war should be perfect.[35]

Chapter Notes

Prelims

1. T.E. Lawrence, *Seven Pillars of Wisdom*, (Penguin, in association with Jonathan Cape, London, 1962), Introductory chapter, p. 22.

Introduction

1. Cited in Peter Paret 'The New Military History', *Parameters, US Army War College Quarterly*, Autumn, 1991, pp. 10–18, this pp. 17–18.
2. Giulio Douhet, *The Command of the Air* (trans. from the Italian by Dino Ferrari), (Faber and Faber, London, 1943). See Chapter 4.
3. Christopher Bellamy, *The Russian and Soviet View of the Military–Technical Character of Future War, 1877–2017*, (2 Vols., PhD, University of Edinburgh, 1991).
4. Leonard Doyle 'Seized documents identify Saddam's nuclear centre', *Independent*, 5 October 1991, p. 1. Harvey Morris and Dr Tom Wilkie, 'Iraq's bomb project back to square two', *Independent*, 21 March 1992, p. 17 (with map of Al Atheer).
5. Nick Cohen, 'Radioactive waste left in Gulf by Allies', Nick Cohen and Dr Tom Wilkie, 'Gulf Teams not told of risk from Uranium', *Independent on Sunday*, 10 November 1991.
6. Patrick Cockburn, 'Iraqis violate exclusion zone', *Independent*, 8 April 1992, p. 1 and 'Allies face new challenge from Iraqi air power', *Independent*, 9 April 1992, p. 2.
7. Patrick Cockburn, 'Iraqi dead in Gulf War no more than 15,000', *Independent*, 5 February 1992.
8. John Heidenrich, article in *Foreign Policy*, Spring 1993, previewed by John Boatman, 'Report puts Iraqi dead at 1500' [oversimplification], *Jane's Defence Weekly*, 13 March 1993, p. 5; author 'Gulf War body count drops to 1500 Iraqis', *Independent*, 11 March 1993, p. 1.
9. David Rew, MA, MChir, FRCS, RAMC(V), letter to the author, 12 March 1993. Mr Rew,

senior registrar in surgery of the Southampton University hospitals, was with the British medical team.

10. John Heidenrich, cited in Jane's.
11. See the chapter in Edward Mead Earle, *Makers of Modern Strategy. Military Thought from Machiavelli to Hitler*, (Princeton University Press, 1944); Lt Col F.E. Whitton, Moltke, (Makers of the Twentieth Century, Constable, London, 1921).
12. The term was first used in the German Army in World War I, but the idea was developed further by the Soviet Union. It entered the US and UK military vocabulary in the 1980s. See Bellamy, *The Evolution of Modern Land Warfare: Theory and Practice*, (Routledge, London and New York 1990) ,pp. 57, 60–65.
13. Brigadier Ian Durie, '1st Armoured Division Artillery in Operation Granby', *Journal of the Royal Artillery*, Vol. CXVIII No. 2, September 1991, pp. 16–29, this pp. 19–21.
14. David Black, 'Punching a path through enemy defences', *Independent*, 25 February 1991, p. 4. At this stage we did not know that 1st Armoured would be passed through 1st Infantry, but such an operation seemed probable, so we took a diagram of a Soviet OMG penetration, doctored it by inserting Allied flags and substituting Allied equipment, and put it in the newspaper on the night of 24th. 1st Armoured Division passed through the 1st Infantry breach as the paper went to press that very morning, 25th, and was ready to break out from phase line New Jersey at 1515. See Chapter 6.
15. The Russian Military attaché, Colonel Nikolay Uvarov, to the author, 1 April 1992.
16. Maj Daniel P Bolger, 'The Ghosts of Omdurman', *Parameters*, Autumn 1991, pp. 28–39, this p. 29.
17. Bellamy, *The Evolution* . . ., pp. 2, 242.
18. For Frederick and his renewed relevance see Christopher Duffy, *Frederick the Great. A Military Life*, (Routledge, London, 1988).
19. John Bulloch, 'How Bush lost the Gulf war', *Independent on Sunday*, Sunday Review, 8 December 1991, citing the testimony of General Tom Kelly, the US Director of Operations during the war.
20. Clausewitz, *On War*, trans. Howard and Paret, introductory chapter 'The genesis of On War', p. 21 citing *Strategie aus dem Jahr 1804*, p. 51.
21. Ibid., p. 22; Clausewitz's own 'Note of 10 July 1827', p. 69.
22. *Air Power Doctrine, AP 3000*, (Published under the direction of the Chief of the Air Staff, 1991), p. 1.

PART I – THE STORM CLOUDS GATHER

Chapter 1: Three Campaigns to the Sun

1. Lt Gen Sir Aylmer Haldane, *The Insurrection in Mesopotamia 1920*, (William Blackwood, Edinburgh and London, 1920), p. 312.
2. *BR 524* (Restricted) *Iraq and the Persian Gulf*, (Geographical handbook series, Naval Intelligence Division, September, 1944), p. 1; Lt Col Peter Boxhall, 'The Iraqi claim to Kuwait', *Army Quarterly and Defence Journal*, Vol. 121, No. 1, January 1991, pp. 33–37; David Munro and Alan Jay, *A World Record of Major Conflict Areas*, (Edward Arnold, London, Melbourne and Auckland, 1990), p. 122.
3. Haldane, *The Insurrection* . . ., p. 8.
4. *Ibid.*, p. 9.

5. Algernon John Insall, 'Events leading up to the assumption of military control in Iraq by the RAF', *The Fighting Forces*, (London, 1927), pp. 242–51, this p. 242; Air Marshal Sir John Salmond, 'The Air Force in Iraq', *Journal of the Royal United Services Institute (RUSI)*, Vol. LXX, 1925, pp. 483–98; Mark Jacobsen, '"Only by the sword": British counter-insurgency in Iraq, 1920', *Small Wars and Insurgencies*, Vol. 2, August 1991, No. 2, pp. 323–63; Philip Towle, *Pilots and Rebels: the use of aircraft in unconventional warfare*, 1918–88, (Brassey's (UK), London, 1989), pp. 13–23.

6. Insall, p. 243.

7. Boxhall, p. 36; Cdr Charles Koburger, Jr., 'The Kuwait Confrontation of 1961', *United States Naval Institute Proceedings*, January 1974, pp. 42–49, this p. 45.

8. Koburger, p. 45.

9. *Ibid.*, p. 49.

10. Efraim Karsh, *The Iran–Iraq War: a Military Analysis*, (Adelphi Paper 220, International Institute for Strategic Studies, London, Spring 1987), p. 7; Francis Tusa, *A Chronology of the Iran–Iraq War*, RUSI/Brassey's Defence Yearbook 1989, pp. 279–89.

11. *Ibid.*, pp. 6–7, 10–11.

12. See the author's *The Future of Land Warfare*, (Croom Helm, Beckenham, 1987), pp. 19–26 and 'Space Age Verdun', *RUSI Journal*, March, 1981, pp. 57–60.

13. Conversations with Colonel Derrick Turner, former British Military Attaché in Baghdad, 1979–83, 8 August, 1990.

14. Munro and Jay, pp. 126–27; Karsh, *The Iran–Iraq War . . .*, pp. 20–30.

15. Bellamy, *Future of Land Warfare*, pp. 19–26.

16. W Seth Carus, 'Missiles in the Middle East: a New Threat to Stability', *Policy Focus*, Washington Institute for Near East Policy, 6(June)/1988; Ron Matthews, 'Dangerous New Twists in the Middle East's Arms Race Spiral', *RUSI*, Winter 1990, pp. 31–38; Anthony Cordesman, *Weapons of Mass Destruction in the Middle East*, (RUSI Study, Brassey's (UK), London, 1990).

17. Karsh, p. 61.

18. Conversation with Col Turner, 8 August 1990. Same conclusion drawn by Karsh, pp. 26, 56; Cordesman, pp. 84–93.

19. *Ibid.*, pp. 44–47; Matthews, p. 32; table is based on *The Military Balance* for 1980–81 through to 1990–91 and, post-war, 1991–92.

20. Christopher Bellamy, 'Self-sufficiency is a key to rise of a frightening military power', *Independent*, 4 August, 1990, p. 8; J.M. Abdughani, *Iraq and Iran: the years of crisis*, (Croom Helm, London, 1984), pp. 156–57.

21. Matthews, p. 35.

22. Special report by Harvey Morris, Andrew Higgins, Tom Wilkie, *The Independent on Sunday*, Sunday Review, 19 and 26 April, 1992.

23. The author visited the IAEA in Vienna on 19 May 1992: briefing by Messrs. Kyd, Zifferero and Von Baeckmann. They showed a video of the 11th inspection, which brings home the vast size of the Iraqi installations. IAEA has also produced a most useful pamphlet, *IAEA Inspections and Iraq's Nuclear Capabilities*, (IAEA, Division of Public Information, Vienna, 1992).

24. *Ibid.*

25. Preceding 9 paragraphs: Cordesman, pp. 65–73, Morris and Wilkie, 'Iraq's bomb project back to square two'.

26. International Institute for Strategic Studies, London, *The Military Balance 1980–81 to*

1991–92. The *Balance* 1990–91 gives the position in June 1990, just before the Iraqi invasion of Kuwait: pp. 97, 105–06. On artillery, Christopher F Foss, ed., *Jane's Armour and Artillery* 1989–90, (Jane's Information Group, Coulsdon, 1989), pp. 588–90, 623–5, 780–81.

27. Col Atchison, USAF, background briefing on Battle Damage Assessment, Hyatt, 26 Jan 1991.

28. See Bellamy, *The Future of Land Warfare* . . .; also 'How the Desert Sword would strike', *Independent*, 20 September 1990, p. 18 and 'Baptism of fire for air–land strategy', *Independent*, 1 March 1991, p. 8.

29. See Bellamy, *The Evolution* . . ., pp. 193–99, esp. p. 197 and 'Heirs of Genghis Khan. The Influence of the Tartar Mongols on the Imperial Russian and Soviet Armies', *RUSI*, March, 1983.

30. Christopher Bellamy, 'Red Star in the West: Marshal Tukhachevskiy and East–West Exchanges on the Art of War', *RUSI*, December 1987.

31. *FM 100–5*, HQ, Department of the Army, Washington DC, 20 August 1982, pp. 1–1.

32. *Ibid.*, pp. 1–3, 2–1.

33. *Ibid.*, pp. 8–1 to 8–2.

34. *Ibid.*, pp. 3–11 to 3–12. More detailed discussion of how to fight in desert areas is in *FM 90–3*.

35. *Ibid.*, pp. 7–1, 7–13.

36. See for example Col David Glantz, *Soviet Military Operational Art. In Pursuit of Deep Battle*, (Frank Cass, London, 1991). This work had its Genesis in *Towards Deep Battle, the Soviet Conduct of Operational Manoeuvre*, (US Army War College, Carlisle Barracks, Pa, 1985).

37. Dwight L Adams and Clayton R Newell, 'Operational art in the Joint and Combined Arms Arenas, *Parameters*, June, 1988, pp. 33–39; British – General Sir Martin Farndale, *Counterstroke – Future Requirements*, address to the Royal United Services Institute for Defence Studies, London, 15 October 1985; see also author, *The Future* . . ., pp. 145–46.

38. Maj-Gen Rupert Smith, lecture to the Royal United Services Institute, 7 November 1991. The division had to 'fight in depth, not breadth. Only I could reinforce success. The British Army had to be in at the kill, therefore I had to fight in such a way that we could endure – lots of little fights, fast . . . [there would be] no lateral reinforcement from another division or corps . . . force ratios were such that the Allies should concentrate on a few axes and go in deep . . . therefore, I would focus the power of the division rather than mass it . . . [we would have to] conduct business on a very narrow frontage.'

39. *Design for Military Operations – The British Military Doctrine*, D/CGS/50/8 (Prepared under the direction of the Chief of the General staff, 1989), p. vii.

40. Brigadier (retd.) Richard Simpkin, *Race to the Swift. Thoughts on Twenty-First Century Warfare*, (Brassey's (UK), London, 1985).

41. US analysts first noticed references to Soviet World War II Mobile Groups in Polish articles in 1981. Christopher Donnelly, 'The Soviet operational manoeuvre group: a new challenge for NATO', *International Defense Review*, 9/1982, pp. 1177–86 brought the OMG into the public eye. On the chronology, context and vast bibliography on the subject, see Bellamy, *The Evolution* . . ., pp. 121–190, 266–77.

42. G.A.B Dewar and Lt Col J.H. Boraston, *Sir Douglas Haig's Command*, December 19, 1915 to November 11, 1918, (2 Vols., Constable, London, 1922); John Terraine, *White Heat, the New Warfare*, 1914–18 (Sidgwick and Jackson, London, 1982).

43. Attributed to Helmuth von Moltke, 'the Elder', Robert Debs Heinl Jr., *Dictionary of*

Militry and Naval Quotations, (US Naval Institute Press, Annapolis, 1984), p. 239.

44. Dr Rajendra Persaud, 'Saddam, sanity and the age old traits of the dictator', *Guardian*, 18 January 1991.

45. 'The man who stopped the world: Saddam Hussein, the new threat to peace', Profile, *The Independent*, 11 August 1991.

46. *Ibid.*

47. John Bulloch, 'Profile: A tyranny based on blood, oil and tears', *Independent on Sunday*, 18 March 1990.

48. Erika Cheetham, ed. and trans., *The Prophecies of Nostradamus*, (Neville Spearman, London, 1973). The other references occur in I.50, II.28, II.89, VIII.77 and X.72. This one is VI.33, p. 261. Nostradamus describes a plague that kills both humans and animals, which is unusual. But Anthrax, a known biological warfare agent, was probably available to the Iraqis and Allied troops were inoculated against it.

Chapter 2: *Don't* Go Home

1. 'Customs detain "biggest gun in the world",' *Independent*, 12 April 1990, p. 1; 'MoD backs "supergun" claim', *ibid.*, 13 April, p. 1; 'Rocket may be losing out in battle with the gun', *ibid.*, p. 2; 'Iraq may have aimed to use pipes for satellite launches', *ibid.*, 16 April, p. 2.

2. Christopher F Foss, ed., *Jane's Armour and Artillery* 1989–90, pp. 788–89.

3. Other sources give the time as 01.00 local (23.00 GMT): clearly the operation unfolded over some time. Documents released under the Freedom of Information Act, Defense Intelligence Agency letter of 18 June, 1992, U-4, 547/DSP-1, covering combined message, 021530Z Aug 90, item 00457455.

4. Michael Jempson, 'Hostage scandal of BA 149' [the BA 747] *Independent on Sunday*, 7 March 1993, p. 10; DIA Commonwealth intsum Middle East/Africa, item 00455785, combined message times 021305Z Aug 90, comprising three messages times 0400Z, 0600Z and 0930Z, this the first, para. 3. My thanks to Mike for letting me have copies of these signals.

5. Item 00455785, 0600 report, para. 1.

6. *Ibid.*, 0930 report, para. 1.

7. Item 00457004, 021030Z Aug 90, para. 7; 00457455, 021530Z report.

8. Testimony of Col Bruce Duncan, Commanding Officer of the British liaison team and RSM Michael Haynes, at a press conference, 14 December 1990. The most concise account of the war as a whole from the British side is probably the official Despatch by Air Chief Marshal Sir Patrick Hine, Joint Commander of the UK Operation *Granby*, *Second Supplement to the London Gazette of Friday 28th June, 1991, G37–52*, (HMSO, London, 1991). On the US side, *Final report to Congress. Conduct of the Persian Gulf War. 102–25*, (US Government Printing Office, Washington DC, April 1992).

9. UK operational codenames are issued by a department in the basement of the Ministry of Defence. Recent ones have all been the names of villages. Thus, the operation to put a fence around Molesworth was called *Yelstead*, then there was *Granby*, and the operation to provide medical support for UN troops in Croatia in 1992 was called *Hanwood*, and that for Cambodia, *Lecturer*. Since the names are not usually remotely secret, one wonders why they should not be more colourful, like the American ones.

10. Conversation with John Hines of the Rand Corporation and Lt-Gen Gerhard Berkhof of the University of Leiden, 10 August, 1990.

11. *Supplement to the London Gazette*, p. G38; 'Blockade to last at least to Christmas', *Independent*, 14 August 1990, p. 8.

12. Col James W Pardew, Jr, 'The Iraqi Army's Defeat in Kuwait', *Parameters*, Winter 1991–92, pp. 17–23, this pp. 19–20. Col Pardew was the US Army's Director of Foreign Intelligence and, during Operations *Desert Shield* and *Desert Storm* was involved in US Army, US Government and Joint (coalition) assessments of Iraqi forces in the KTO.

13. 'Chemical Strike prowess of Iraq over-estimated', *Independent*, 23 August 1990, p. 7; Iraqis may have Scud missiles with chemical warheads', *Independent*, 3 November 1990, p. 8.

14. 'Iraq building a second defence line in Kuwait', *Independent*, 16 October 1990, p. 10.

15. Interview with Staff Officer in Net Assessment, the Pentagon, October 1990.

16. *Ibid.*

17. 'US Marines to stage landing near Kuwait', *Independent*, 14 November 1990, p. 12; Gen Schwarzkopf's briefing, Riyadh, 27 February 1991 (Appendix A); interview with Net Assessment.

18. Christopher D Bellamy and Joseph S Lahnstein, 'The new Soviet defensive policy: Khalkhin Gol 1939 as case study', *Parameters: US Army War College Quarterly*, September 1990, pp. 19–32.

19. John Erickson, *The Soviet High Command, 1918–1941*, (Macmillan, London, 1962), p. 522.

20. *Independent*, 16 October 1990, p. 10.

21. *Ibid.*, 18 October 1990, p. 10.

22. *Ibid.*, 20 October 1990, p. 8.

23. *Ibid.*, 1 November 1990, p. 11.

24. *Ibid.*, 10 November 1990, p. 10; 12 November 1990, p. 1.

25. *Ibid.*, 2 January 1991, p. 8.

26. *Ibid.*, 27 December 1990, p. 8; 28 December, 1990, p. 14.

Chapter 3: Ticket to Riyadh

1. Mohammed A Seraj, Abdulaziz Saddique, *Brief Notes and Guidelines on 'Toxic Chemicals and their Effects', 'Air Raids and Siren Instructions'*, (2nd ed., Safir Press, Riyadh, December 1990).

2. Procurement Research Sub-Committee of the House Armed Services Committee, 16 April, 1991, reported in 'The pros and cons of US Patriots', *Independent*, 29 April 1991, p. 10.

3. The preceding 17 paragraphs are the text of the author's report, with tenses changed and references to places and distance from the front inserted. The description of the A-10s behaving aggressively is as filed during the first week of February, 1991.

PART II – THE STORM BREAKS

Chapter 4: The Decisive Field: The Undivided Sky *January–February 1991*

1. Gen Giulio Douhet, *Il dominio dell'Aria*, first published by Italian War Ministry, 1921, trans. Dino Ferrari, *The Command of the Air*, (Faber and Faber, London, 1943), p. 24. A second edition, adding a second part from 1926, was published in 1927. Original in *Il Dominio dell'Aria. Probabili aspetti della guerra futura e gli ultimi scritti del Gen. Giulio Douhet con prefazione di Italo Balbo*, (A Mondadori, Rome, 1932). The Ferrari translation contains *Command of the Air* (to p. 118), *Probable Aspects of Future War*, a monograph from 1928 (pp. 119–167), *Recapitulation*, published in *Rivista Aeronautica* in November, 1929 (pp. 168–232) and *The War of 19 . . .* published in *Rivista Aeronautica* in March 1930, shortly after Douhet's death (pp. 233–316). 'Undivided Sky' is from translation, p. 191, but not in Italian: 'Decisive Field' is, trans., p. 199.
2. Ferrari trans., p. 204, from *Recapitulation*.
3. *TIALD: The Gulf War*, (GEC Ferranti, Edinburgh, 1991), pp. 8–9, 51.
4. 'US Air Force Performance in Desert Storm', US Department of Defense document reproduced in *Military Technology* 6/1991, pp. 146–56, this p. 150.147.
5. John Zugschwert, 'Vertical Flight Comes of Age', *Military Technology*, Vol. XV, 6/1991, pp. 28–32, this pp. 28–29; 'Desert Storm Almanac', *ibid.*, pp. 118–44, this p. 123.
6. *We Own the Night*, Special Edition of *Lockheed Horizons*, No. 30, May 1992, (Lockheed, Calabasas, Calif., 1992), pp. 2–3, 54.
7. 'US Air Force Performance . . .' p. 147.
8. *Ibid.*
9. *We Own the Night*, pp. 8–9, 33–35. The initial analysis was based on century-old Maxwell, Sommerfeld and Ufimtsev equations but those had been considered too cumbersome to be applied to anything except simple, geometric forms. Bill Schroeder, a retired Lockheed mathematician, had the idea of reducing the complex shape of a traditional aircraft to a finite set of two-dimensional surfaces that could be analysed using these calculations. It was therefore built as a series of triangular panels or facets. Every possible measure was taken to minimise the three key cross-sections: radar, infrared and electromagnetic emissions. All doors and removable panels on the aircraft have saw-toothed forward and trailing edges. The aim was the get the cross-sections down until the plane could not be detected until it could also be heard, by which time it would be too late for the defence to react: the military definition of surprise. Even traditional 'nose art' was banned: that would negate the value of the radar absorbent covering – instead, the pilots painted their sensuous mascots on the inside of the bomb bay doors. The F-117 would carry two 2,000 lb bombs or a combined bombload of 5,000 lb.
10. *Ibid.*, pp. 51–57.
11. *Ibid.*, pp. 55, (analysis) 57.
12. 'Desert Storm Almanac', p. 123.
13. *London Gazette*, 28 June 1991, pp. G41–42.
14. Wg Cdr Jerry Witts, cited in Charles Allen, *Thunder and Lightning: the RAF in the Gulf: Personal experiences of War*, (HMSO, London, 1991), p. 54.
15. Phrase from 'US Air Force Performance . . .' p. 151. Data on aircraft from pp. 147–49, *London Gazette*, p. G40.
16. Flt Lt Angus Elliott, cited in Allen, p. 53.

17. AVM Wratten to press conference, 25 March 1991; 'RAF Chief tells how war strategy changed', *Independent*, 26 March 1991.

18. 'US Air Force Performance ...' p. 148.

19. Allen, pp. 74–75.

20. *London Gazette*, p. G42; British Aerospace Defence, *The Gulf War: Second Edition, a Report on British Aerospace Products in Combat*, (BAe, Kingston-upon-Thames, 1991), p. 50.

21. Lt Col A. Ya Manachinskiy, Lt Col V.N. Chumak, Col (retd.) E.K. Pronkin, '*Operatsiya "Burya v pustine": itogi i posledstviya*' ('Operation "DESERT STORM"; conclusions and consequences'), *Voyennaya Mysl' (Military Thought) (VM)*, 1/1992, pp. 88–92, this p. 88.

22. Author interview with Glen Galvin before his retirement as SACEUR, RUSI, Whitehall, London, 1 June 1992.

23. Col. V.V. Romanov, Col. V.P. Chigak, '*O primenenii kosmicheskikh sredstv v rayone Persidskogo zaliva*', ('On the use of space assets in the Persian Gulf region'), *Voyennaya Mysl'*, 3/1991, pp. 76–80, diagram on p. 77.

24. Unattributable briefing, Saturday 26 January 1991, Hyatt, Riyadh.

25. 'Strategic Air War in the Gulf: conflicting views: Strategic Campaign focused on targets and cut casualties, Pentagon maintains', *Aviation Week and Space Technology*, 27 January 1992, pp. 64–65, this p. 64.

26. Unattributable briefing, 19 February 1991, Hyatt.

27. Gen Schwarzkopf briefing, Saudi oil briefing, Sunday 27 January 1991, Hyatt.

28. *The Military Balance*, 1991–92, p. 100.

29. *Ibid.*, p. 101; *London Gazette*, p. G43.

30. *TIALD: The Gulf War*, pp. 15, 26, 33.

31. Gen. Schwarzkopf wore the Saudi insignia of a full general: crossed swords, *two* stars and a crown, as well as his US four stars. Saudi insignia, like all Arab armies', was based on the British, but those of the general officer ranks were more logical. Thus, a major-general had a *crown* and crossed swords – 'major-general', unlike the British pip and crossed swords. A Lieutenant-general, the next rank up, then had a crown, pip and swords – 'lieutenant-*colonel* general', not a crown and swords, and a full general became a 'full-colonel general'. Some middle eastern armies, including Iraq, substitute an eagle for the crown.

32. 'Iraqi weapons "cut by a fifth"', *Independent*, 9 February 1991; 'Cheney reports to Bush on timing of ground offensive', *ibid.*, 11 February 1991.

33. 'Iraq "has lost 1,300 tanks in air raids"', *Independent*, 15 February 1991.

34. *Ibid.*

35. 'Tactical Bombing of Iraqi Forces outstripped Value of Strategic Hits, Analyst Contends', *Aviation Week and Space Technology*, 27 January 1992, pp. 62–63, this p. 62.

36. 'Strategic Campaign ...' *AW&ST*, 27 January 1992, p. 65.

37. *Ibid.*, p. 64.

38. 'A bold plan in the most cerebral of campaigns', *Independent*, 25 February 1991; *Desert Storm Almanac*, p. 128.

39. *Statement on the Defence Estimates 1992, Cmnd 1981* (HMSO, London, 7 July 1992), p. 74 para 420, in 'Operation GRANBY: Lessons for the Future', pp. 68–79; 'Strategic Campaign ...' *AW&ST*, 27 January 1992, p. 65.

Chapter 5: Reconnaissance by Battle *January–February 1991*

1. Zaki M.A. Farsi, *National Guide and Atlas of the Kingdom of Saudi Arabia*, (Zaki M.A. Farsi, publisher, Riyadh, 1989), p. 1–1.
2. Most figures from Lt Gen Prince Khalid briefing, Hyatt, 8 February 1992. Also pool reports 31 January, from Tom Ferraro, *UPI*; Jim Michaels, *San Diego Tribune*; Patrick Bishop, *Daily Telegraph*; Carlyle Murphy, *Washington Post*. 1 February from Storer Rowley, *Chicago Tribune*; Malcolm Browne, *New York Times*; Ray Wilkinson, *Newsweek*. Also Col Michael Dewar, *War in the Streets, the Story of Urban Warfare from Calais to Khafji*, (David and Charles, London, 1991), pp. 81–84.
3. Robert Fisk, 'Crisis in the Gulf: tanks bogged down in unmapped mud and confusion', *Independent*, 23 January 1991.
4. Dick Cheney briefing, 10 February 1991, Hyatt.
5. 'Desert Storm Almanac', *MT*, 6/1991, p. 124; 'ATACMS Operational', *MT* 11/1990, p. 1211.
6. Trevor N. Dupuy, *How to Defeat Saddam Hussein: Scenarios and Strategies for the Gulf War*, (Warner Books, New York, 27 January 1991), pp. xi, 61–95. Previously titled *If War Comes, How to Defeat Saddam Hussein*, (Hero Books, McLean, VA, 11 January 1991).
7. Bellamy, *The Evolution of Modern Land Warfare*, pp. 184–87.
8. Maj William L Brame, 'From Garrison to Desert Offensive in 97 days', *Army*, February 1992, pp. 28–35; Joe A Fortner, Capt Jules T Doux, USA, Capt Mark A Peterson, 'Bring on the HET [Heavy Equipment Transporter]. Operational and Tactical Relocation of Heavy Maneuver Forces', *Military Review*, January 1992, pp. 36–45; Andrew E Gibson and Cdr Jacob L Stanford, USN, 'Desert Storm and Strategic Sealift', *Naval War College Review*, Spring 1991, pp. 6–19; Air Marshal Sir Kenneth Hayr, 'Logistics in the Gulf War', *Command in War: Gulf Operations*, (Whitehall paper, RUSI, London, 1991, pp. 71–79; Brig Gen Charles C Kulak, 'CSS [Combat Service Support] in the Desert', *Marine Corps Gazette*, October 1991, pp. 22–25 *and* 'A War of Logistics', *US Naval Institute Proceedings*, November 1991, pp. 55–57; Col Peter Langenus, USAR, 'Moving an army: Movement control for Desert Storm', *Military Review*, September 1991, pp. 40–51; Lt Col John A O'Donavan, 'Combat Service Support During Desert Shield and Desert Storm: from Kibrit to Kuwait', *Marine Corps Gazette*, October 1991, pp. 26–31; Lt Gen William G ('Gus') Pagonis, 'Good Logistics is Combat power: the Logistics Sustainment of Operation Desert Storm', *Military Review*, September 1991, pp. 28–39; Lt Gen Jimmy D Ross, 'Victory: the Logistics Story', *Army*, October 1991, pp. 128–138; Capt Vincent C Thomas, Jr., USN, 'The Sea Services' Role in Desert Shield/Storm, *Sea Power*, September 1991, pp. 26–33; Capt Alan B Will, 'Supply Support during Desert Storm: A Field Perspective', *Marine Corps Gazette*, October 1991, pp. 42–43.
9. Pagonis, 'Good Logistics . . .', pp. 33–34.
10. Gen Sir Peter de la Billière, *Storm Command: a personal account of the Gulf War*, (Harper/Collins, 1992), pp. 92–94, 151–52; Ben Brown and David Shukman, *All Necessary Means: Inside the Gulf War*, (BBC Books, London, 1991), p. 124. Briefings after the war repeatedly denied any particular concern about the US Marines but stressed the need to use the division at a level and over terrain where its abilities could be given free rein. Gen de la Billière said he had thought, privately, that if used in the frontal attack on Kuwait the British might suffer 17 per cent casualties, as against an average of about five per cent across the whole front.

11. De la Billière, pp. 92–94, 151–52; Brig Ian Durie, to the Royal United Services Institute, 1 April 1992; Gen Sir Peter de la Billière to House of Commons Defence Committee, 8 May 1991.
12. Langenus, 'Moving an Army . . .', pp. 46–47.
13. *Ibid.*, p. 50.
14. *Ibid.*, pp. 50–51.
15. *Ibid.*
16. Philip Longworth, *The Art of Victory. The Life and Achievements of Generalissimo Suvorov*, (Constable, London, 1965).
17. Pagonis, 'Good Logistics . . .', pp. 35–37.
18. Krulak, 'CSS . . .' pp. 22–24, quote p. 24.
19. We were introduced to the term 'berm' in one of the first UK MoD briefings in summer 1990. In fact, 'berm' originally meant a flat shoulder between the top of a fortress moat and the bottom of an earthen rampart (to stop the latter sliding into the former), but was disliked as it gave troops climbing out of the ditch a foothold before assaulting the rampart. If *only* these people would study their Vauban . . .
20. Krulak, 'CSS . . .', p. 24.
21. Brame, 'From Garrison to Desert Offensive . . .', pp. 31, 34.
22. Hayr, 'Logistics in the Gulf War', pp. 77, 79.
23. Army General G Forray, French Chief of Staff, 'The Eight lessons of Success', in feature on Operation Daguet, *Military Technology* 8/1991, pp. 23–35, this pp. 26, 35.
24. Pearce, *The Shield and the Sabre* . . . p. 80; author's encounter with Naval EW unit, 1 February.
25. De la Billière, *Storm Command*, pp. 220–27. On pp. 235–49, Gen de la Billière gives a graphic account of an SAS corporal's escape from western Iraq after his patrol was 'bounced' by the Iraqis. On the Iraqi claim that the Special Forces accounted for no missiles at all, *Newsnight*, BBC2, Monday 29 June 1992, previewed by Mark Urban in the *Daily Telegraph*, same day.
26. Durie, '1st Armoured Division Artillery in Operation GRANBY', *RA Journal*, pp. 22–23.
27. Zugschwert, 'Vertical Flight . . .', pp. 29–30.

Chapter 6: Desert Cannae *24–28 February 1991*

1. Cited in 'The Eight Lessons of Success', in feature 'Operational Daguet' *Military Technology*, 8/1991, pp. 23–35, this p. 27.
2. Oliver Latremolière, 'Objective White: the Battle for As Salman', in *ibid.*, p. 29.
3. Pool report by Jeffrey Ulbrich, Associated Press, 0700, 24 February 1991.
4. 7th Armoured Brigade operational order 11.00 19 February 1991, copy no 16 of 16 (Secret), 71 pp. Op orders always contain the outline plan several levels above that to which they refer in detail; Brig Patrick Cordingley (commander 7th Armoured Brigade), 'The Gulf War – a Personal Account', *Seaford House Papers: Selected theses written by members of the course at the Royal College of Defence Studies*, 1991, pp. 13–23.
5. Latremolière, pp. 29–30; 'Les Compagnies Montées: Le GMLE', *Kepi Blanc* (Journal of the French Foreign Legion), June 1991, pp. 22–26.
6. Quotations from pool report of John Balzar, AP, with 18th Aviation Brigade, XVIII Corps; also John Pomfret, AP, 23.00, 24 February.

7. *Operation Granby. An Account of the Gulf Crisis 1990–91 and the British Army's Contribution to the Liberation of Kuwait*, (71512, Inspectorate General, Doctrine and Training, MoD, London, 1991) (Restricted), p. 5–5.
8. Pool report, Kirk Spitzer, Gannett News Service, 21.00, 24 February 1991.
9. Latremolière, p. 30; Gen Schwarzkopf 24 and 27 February briefings, see Appendix A.
10. Maj Gen Rupert Smith, to RUSI, 7 November 1991.
11. *Ibid.*
12. Durie, '1st Armoured Division Artillery . . .', p. 21; Maj Gen Smith lecture to RUSI, 7 November 1991.
13. Latremolière, pp. 30–31.
14. Operation Granby . . . p. 5–8.
15. Unattributable briefing, 3 March 1991; pool report from John Balzar, *Los Angeles Times*, 26 February 1991.
16. Pool report from XVIII Airborne by Jaffrey Ulbrich, AP, 19.30, 27 February.
17. Pool report 1252 by Bill Gannon, *Newark Star Ledger*, undated.
18. *Statement on the Defence Estimates 1992, Cmnd 1981* (HMSO, London, 1992), p. 73; Maj Gen Smith to RUSI, 7 November 1991.
19. Durie, p. 27.
20. Pearce, pp. 116–17.
21. Durie, p. 27.
22. *Operation Granby . . .* pp. 5–19 to 5–20; Cordingley, 'The Gulf war . . .' pp. 21–22.
23. Durie, pp. 27–28.
24. *Ibid.*; Maj G.W. Berragan, letter in *JRA*, in response.
25. 'Victor of Kuwait reveals his strategy', *Independent*, 28 February 1991, p. 2.

Chapter 7: Field of the Cloth of Gold *March 1991*

1. Cordingley, 'The Gulf War . . .', p. 22.
2. Brown and Shukman, pp. 155–57; conservation with Mark Laity, BBC Radio, who spoke to Brig Gen Neal.
3. Unattributable briefing, 27 February.
4. Thomas Ferraro, UPI, pool report, 2 March 1991; Desert Storm Almanac, p. 134.

PART III – 'SUCH A VICTORY AS THIS'

Chapter 8: Midnight Express *March–April 1991*

1. *Washington Post*, 18 March 1991.
2. *'Desert Storm Almanac'*, pp. 134–35.
3. Resolution 687, Adopted by the Security Council at its 2981st meeting, 3 April 1991, recorded in *'Desert Storm Almanac'*, pp. 140–44.
4. Interview with Capt Tom Hardie-Forsyth, Sunday 16 June 1991; 'Kurds beg allies not to pull out of haven', *Independent*, 15 June 1991; 'Major's haven plan in tatters', *Independent*, 17 June 1991; 'Kurds need help beyond call of duty', *Independent*, 19 June 1991.

Chapter 9: Aftershocks

1. Barbara Stapleton, 'Arabs flee Iraq's deadly marshes', *Independent on Sunday*, 19 July 1992, p. 17.
2. *Independent*, 27 August 1992; Archie Hamilton, Minister of State for the Armed Forces, testimony to House of Commons Defence Committee, 22 September 1992.
3. Lt Gen Buster Glosson, USAF (USAF Chief of Staff during the war), to RAF Air Power Conference, held under the auspices of the Chief of the Air Staff, Queen Elizabeth Conference Centre, London, 4 September 1992. Lt Gen Glosson said Gen Schwarzkopf had asked him what the Allied Command might most usefully request from the British. 'GR1s, Sir.' 'We've got GR1s,' said Gen Schwarzkopf. 'I want 'em *all*,' he is alleged to have replied.
4. I am grateful to Adrian Halliwell, of the Hydrographer's Department, Taunton, Somerset, and Francis Herbert, of the Royal Geographical Society, for all their help on this and other geographical questions.
5. 'Hussein Kamil Hassan puts cornerstone to the "General Drainage" project next week', *Al Juhmuriah*, 20 May 1992, plus map 'The course of the "General Drainage"'.
6. Barbara Stapleton, 'Saddam's deadly aim in the marshes', *Independent*, 29 December 1992, p. 8. Also by Barbara Stapleton, *The Shi'as of Iraq. An historical perspective on the present human rights situation.* (A report to the Parliamentary Human Rights Group, March 1993). Captured engineer and details of projects, p. 29.
7. Organisation for Human Rights in Iraq, 'The massacres in the Marshlands, the south of Iraq, 1992' and 'Disappeared Officers in Iraq', 24 August 1992; 'Iraqi officers arrested on negligence charges', *Independent*, 9 September 1992, p. 12.
8. Unattributable briefing, 29 July 1992.
9. 'Saddam's double snub for UN', *Independent*, 12 January 1992, p. 10; Robert Fisk, 'Showdown threat to Saddam', *Independent*, 15 January 1992, p. 1.
10. *Ibid.*
11. Gulf Centre for Strategic Studies, *The GCC Border Disputes Seminar*, (GCSS, August 1992), pp. 41–43, 49. I am grateful to Professor Ewan Anderson, head of the Geography Department of Durham University, to whom I spoke at the GCSS on 11 January 1993, for his help and advice.
12. *Ibid.*; Fisk, 'Showdown threat to Saddam' and 'Iraqis remove police posts', 18 January 1993, p. 10: 'the new Iraqi–Kuwaiti frontier'.
13. *Independent*, 14 January 1993, p. 3.
14. *Independent*, 15 January 1993, p. 10.
15. *Independent*, 18 January 1993, p. 1.
16. Transcript of the briefing at High Wycombe, 18 January 1991. I am grateful to the RAF desk, MoD Press Office.
17. 'MPs uneasy about new raids on Iraq', *Independent*, 19 January 1993, p. 1.

Chapter 10: Some Conclusions

1. Cordingley, 'The Gulf War . . .', p. 23.
2. 'Operation Granby: Lessons for the Future', *Statement on the Defence Estimates*, 1992, p. 68.

3. *Voyenno-istoricheskiy zhurnal (VIZh)*, March 1991.

4. Col D. Belskiy, *Sovetskaya Rossiya*, 28 February 1991.

5. Lt Gen A.I. Malyukov, in '*Pervye uroki voyny*' ('First Lessons of the War'), to a 'round table' conference, in *Voyennaya mysl*' (*VM*) (*Military Thought*), 5/1991, pp. 60–71.

6. Marshal Losik, 5 March 1991. Unless otherwise identified by publication, quotations were collated in a Pentagon briefing on Soviet lessons from the war made available to the author.

7. Slipchenko, 13 March 1991.

8. Maj Gen (Reserve) I.N. Vorob'ev, Doctor of Military Science, '*Uroki voyny v zone Persidskogo zaliva*' ('Lessons of the War in the Persian Gulf'), *VM* 4–5/1992, pp. 64–74, this p. 67.

9. *Ibid.*, p. 68.

10. *Ibid.*

11. Lt Gen A.V. Politsyn, '*Vzglyad po voynu novoy epokhi*', *VM* 3/1992, pp. 69–79, this p. 69. See also Col A.N. Ionov, '*Nekotorye uroki malen'koy voyny*' ('Certain lessons of a small war'), pp. 79–80.

12. Vorob'ev, '*Uroki . . .*', p. 69.

13. *Ibid.*, p. 70.

14. *Ibid.*, p. 71.

15. Aleksey Gutor (1868–1938), '*Kharakter sovremennoy voyny*' ('The character of contemporary war'), *Voyennoye delo (Military Affairs)*, 21/1918, pp. 3–6, this p. 3 col. 1 and 6 col. 1.

16. G.S. Isserson (1898–196?), '*Operativnye perspektivy budushchego*' ('Operational perspectives of the future'), *VM* 8/1938, pp. 14–26, quotation on p. 23.

17. The draft doctrine was not formally published but disseminated in Moscow. I am grateful to Charles Dick of the Sandhurst Research Centre (formerly Soviet Studies Research Centre) for drawing this to my attention. The draft doctrine contains many elements of discussion in previous issues of *VM*.

18. Francis Bacon, *Of the True Greatness of Kingdoms and Estates*, 1597.

19. Durie, '1st Armoured Division . . .', p. 25.

20. Maj Gen Smith to RUSI, 7 November 1991.

21. De la Billière, *Storm Comand*, pp. 286–87.

22. 'Operation Granby . . .', in *SDE* 1992, para 417, p. 73.

23. *Ibid.*, para 428, p. 76.

24. Lt Gen Charles A Horner, 'The Air Campaign', *Military Review*, September 1991, pp. 16–27, this p. 26.

25. *Ibid.*, p. 25.

26. *Ibid.*, p. 26.

27. Gen Sir Peter Inge, Chief of the General Staff, to a presentation marking the launch of the British Army's new Royal Logistic Corps, Andover, 23 September 1992. The RLC, formed on 5 April 1993, comprises the Royal Army Ordnance Corps, Royal Corps of Transport, Royal Pioneer Corps, Army Catering Corps and the Postal and Courier Service of the Royal Engineers.

28. Michael Howard, 'War and Technology', (based on the Roskill Lecture given at Churchill College, Cambridge on 18 February 1986), *RUSI Journal*, September 1987, pp. 17–22, this on p. 19.

29. De la Billière, *Storm Command*, pp. 220–21.

30. *Ibid.*, pp. 222–23, 224, 266–67. Le Gen 'Buster' Glosson to RAF Air Power Conference,

4 September 1992, Queen Elizabeth Hall, London (on effect on Scud launches).

31. De la Billière, pp. 259–60.
32. *Ibid.*
33. *Ibid.*, p. 74.
34. Cordingley, 'The Gulf War . . .', p. 13.
35. Vice Admiral H.G. Rickover, USN, Testimony before House Military Appropriations Sub-committee, April 1964.

Glossary of Military Terms and Acronyms

Note: The Arabic definite article al- (the) is omitted.

AA	Anti-Aircraft
AAA	Anti-Aircraft Artillery
Aabed	(Worshipper) Three stage Iraqi space-launch vehicle
AAM	Air-to-Air Missile
AAR	Air-to-Air Refuelling
AB	Airborne (used of parachute troops)
Abbas	Iraqi modification of SS-1 'Scud' missile. Maximum range 900km
ABCCC	Airborne Battle Command and Control Centre
ABD	Airborne Division
ABM	Anti-Ballistic Missile
AD	Air Defence (against aircraft)
AEW	Airborne Early Warning
AFB	Air Force Base
AIFV	Armoured Infantry Fighting Vehicle (US Bradley, UK Warrior, Russian BMP – all carry armament of more than 20 mm calibre and designed to be fought from if necessary)
ALARM	Air-Launched Anti-Radiation Missile (for destruction of enemy radars)
ALCM	Air-Launched Cruise Missile
APC	Armoured Personnel Carrier (lightly armoured vehicle for carriage of troops in battle but with lighter armament than AIFV and not designed to be fought from)
Arty	Artillery. (Defined as a system of 100 mm calibre or over designed to engage ground targets, usually by indirect fire)
ASM	Air-to-Surface Missile(s)

ATACMS	Army Tactical Missile System (US). Surface-to-surface missile with a range of about 150 km and mounted on modified Multiple Launch Rocket System (see MLRS))
ATGW	Anti-Tank Guided Weapon(s)
ATO	Air Tasking Order (now normally computer generated planning document. In the Gulf Air Campaign, 200 pages (approx) daily)
AWACS	Airborne Warning and Control System (in E3 'Sentry' aircraft)
BB	Battleship (US only. Refers to heavily armoured ships with massive guns eg. USS *Missouri* and *Wisconsin* in the Gulf)
BDA	Battle Damage Assessment
Bde	Brigade. Smallest complete military formation embodying all arms and services. Normally some 5,000 troops
Bn	Battalion. (Up to 8 or 900 troops of one arm. In British Army applies to infantry only. In US and Russian applies also to artillery, engineer, tank and medical units)
BMP	*Boyevaya Mashina Pekhoty* (Russian AIFV)
BTR	*Bronetransportër* (Armoured Transport (Russian). Wheeled armoured vehicle)
Bty	Battery. (Artillery minor unit of, usually, 6 or 8 guns. Normally 100–150 troops)
C-	US indicator for transport aircraft (eg. C-130 Hercules, C-141 Starlifter)
CAFMS	Computer Assisted Force Management System
CAS	Close Air Support (used of ground attack aircraft)
CBA	Combat Body Armour (In the Gulf a general issue to troops for the first time since the 17th Century. Provides protection against shrapnel but lighter than the Flak Jacket with its heavy ceramic inserts worn in situations such as Bosnia)
CET	Combat Engineer Tractor (UK)
CG	Commanding General (US) or naval cruiser equipped with surface to air missiles
CIS	Commonwealth of Independent States (replaced USSR 8 December 1991)
CNN	Cable News Network (US 24-hour news operation based in Atlanta, Georgia)
CONUS	Continental United States
Coy	Company. (Minor unit of 100–150 troops, normally infantry)
CRA	Commander Royal Artillery (UK) (Senior artillery officer in a British division)
CV	Aircraft Carrier (US)
CVBG	Carrier Battle Group (US) (Includes Carrier, escorts and support ships)
CVN	Nuclear-powered CV (US)
CVR(T)	Combat Vehicle Reconnaissance (Tracked) (UK) (Includes a family

	of Alvis vehicles all on the same chassis: Scorpion (76mm), Scimitar (30mm), Sultan (command), Samaritan (ambulance), Samson (Engineer), Spartan (APC))
CW	Chemical Warfare
DD	Destroyer
DFC	Distinguished Flying Cross (UK)
Div	All arms formation. Iraqi divisions had a 'paper' strength of 12–15,000 troops (less in practice). Allied divisions were up to twice that size.
DLB	*Division Légère Blindée* (FR) (Light Armoured Division)
DRA	Defence Research Agency (UK)
DSO	Distinguished Service Order (UK)
E-	US indicator, added to other aircraft indicators to indicate that the aircraft has been modified for the Electronic Warfare role
ECCM	Electronic Counter Counter Measures
ECM	Electronic Counter Measures
ECR	Electronic Combat and Reconnaissance
ELINT	Electronic intelligence
EOD	Explosive Ordnance Disposal (UK) ('Bomb Disposal')
EPW	Enemy Prisoner(s) of War
ESM	Electronic Support Measures
EST	Eastern Standard Time (Washington) (During the war, 5 hours behind GMT and 8 hours behind Riyadh)
EW	Electronic Warfare
F-	US indicator for fighter or tactical bomber aircraft
FAC	Forward Air Controller
FF	Frigate
FGA	Fighter Ground Attack
Fao	210mm self-propelled gun (Iraqi) (Designed by Dr Gerald Bull and shipped to Iraq in April 1988. Named after Fao Peninsula on the Gulf coast)
FM	Field Manual (US) (FM 100-5 was the principal framework document for Operations *Desert Shield* and *Desert Storm*: others dealt with specialised aspects of military operations)
G-5	Towed 155mm gun (South African) (Range about 40km)
GA	Tabun (nerve gas)
GB	Sarin (nerve gas)
GHN-45	Gun Howitzer Noricum (Austrian) (Towed 155mm artillery piece with range about 40km)
GMLE	*Groupement de Marche de la Légion Etrangère*. Tactical grouping of the French Foreign Legion (Formed the western group of the 6th *Daguet* ('Gazelle') Division (DLB))
GW	Guided Weapons
HACV	Heavy Armoured Combat Vehicle (Weighing more than six metric

	tons and with organic direct fire armament of at least 75mm and not falling within the definitions of APC, AIFV or MBT)
HAS	Hardened Aircraft Shelter
HUMINT	Human Intelligence. (Reports from first-hand observers on eg. deployment, equipment, organisation and morale)
IAEA	International Atomic Energy Agency (based in Vienna)
ID(M)	Infantry Division (Mechanised)
IFF	Interrogation – Friend or Foe (Automated means of identifying enemy or friendly aircraft – but can be used for fighting vehicles (rarely))
Il-	Ilyushin (Russian aircraft manufacturer)
INF	Intermediate Range Nuclear Forces (500–5,000km range)
IRBM	Intermediate Range Ballistic Missiles (range as for INF)
IZ	Iraqi Forces (indicator)
JCS	Joint Chiefs of Staff (US)
JFC(E)	Joint Forces Command East (Allied formation (Corps equivalent) comprising Saudi, Kuwaiti, Omani and UAE units)
JFC(N)	Joint Forces Command North (Allied corps equivalent comprising 3rd (Egyptian) and 9th (Syrian) Divisions. Operated on western flank of Kuwaiti southern border)
JIB	Joint Information Bureau (UK)
JP 233	RAF airfield denial weapon
JSTARS	Joint Surveillance Target Attack Radar System. (Mounted in E8 Boeing 707 derivative aircraft. Provides radar picture of movement on the battlefield.
KIA	Killed in Action
KKMC	King Khalid Military City
KTO	Kuwait Theatre of Operations
LAMPS	Light Airborne Multi-Purpose System (USN) (Helicopter)
LANTIRN	Low Altitude Targeting and Navigation Infra-Red System Night
LGB	Laser Guided Bomb
LPD	Landing Platform Dock (Assault ship)
LPH	Landing Platform Helicopter (ie. Carrier devoted to helicopter operations – usually for amphibious assault purposes)
LSW	Light Support Weapon (UK) (Light machine-gun version of 5.56mm SA-80 rifle)
LZ	Landing Zone (for helicopter operations)
Majnoon	155mm self-propelled gun, shipped to Iraq April 1988. Named after island in Iraqi southern marshes: scene of a victory in 1980–88 war.
MBT	Main Battle Tank (Now defined as an armoured tracked vehicle weighing at least 16.5 metric tons with main armament of not less than 75mm calibre and 360 degrees traverse)
MCMV	Mine Counter Measures Vessel
MEF/B	Marine Expeditionary Force(s)/Brigade(s) (US). (In the Allied

attack against the Iraqi positions in Kuwait, the two US Marine divisions of the MEF were deployed between JFC(N) and JFC(E)

MIA	Missing in Action
MICV	Mechanised Infantry Combat Vehicle
MiG	Mikoyan-Gurevich (Russian aircraft manufacturer)
MLRS	Multiple Launch Rocket System
MMAS	Master of Military Art and Science (US)
MoD 108	Identity document for war correspondents accompanying an armed force (complies with conventions on the laws of war)
MP	Military Police
MRE	Meals Ready to Eat (US) (Field ration which requires no cooking)
MRL	Multiple Rocket Launcher (generic term, covering MLRS, Soviet-built BM-21 and Astros II in service with Iraq)
MRT	Media Response Team(s). (Teams of journalists attached to forward troops)
MSR	Main Supply Route
MTI	Moving Target Indicator
NBC	Nuclear, Biological and Chemical
NCO	Non-Commissioned Officer (below the rank of Sergeant Major)
OMG	Operational Manoeuvre Group (originally Russian). Mobile formation inserted through a weak point in the enemy's defences to attack objectives in depth, vulnerable areas (eg. headquarters and communications centres) and so throw the enemy off balance)
OTH	Over-the-Horizon
OTHR	Over-the-Horizon Radar
OTHT	Over-the-Horizon Targeting
PGM	Precision Guided Munition(s)
PLOD	Pipeline Over the Desert
POMCUS	Prepositioning of Material Configured to Unit Sets (US)
PWHQ	Primary War Headquarters (UK) (located near High Wycombe, Buckinghamshire)
RAS	Replenishment at Sea
RGFC	Republican Guard Force Command (separate from the Iraqi Army and better trained and equipped)
RL	Rocket Launcher(s)
RPV	Remotely Piloted Vehicle (unmanned aircraft)
SAM	Surface-to-Air Missile
SAR	Search and Rescue (for downed pilots, either at sea or on land) *or* Synthetic Apperture Radar
SAS	Special Air Service (Army) (UK)
SBS	Special Boat Service (Royal Marines) (UK)
'Scud'	NATO codename for Soviet-built SS-1 tactical surface-to-surface missile, range 300km. Also used loosely in the Gulf War to refer to longer range *Hussein* and *Abbas* Iraqi-built or modified derivatives)

SF(UK) *or* SOF (US)	Special Forces/Special Operations Forces. Highly trained specialist troops operating behind enemy lines
SIGINT	Signals Intelligence (interception and analysis of enemy communications)
SLCM	Sea-Launched Cruise Missile
SRBM	Short-Range Ballistic Missile
SSM	Surface-to-Surface Missile
Su-	Sukhoi (Russian aircraft manufacturer)
TA	Territorial Army (UK)
TACC	Tactical Air Control Centre
TAPIO	TA Public Information Officer (UK)
TCN	Third Country National (Non-Western immigrant worker in Arab country)
TD	Tank Division
TFW	Tactical Fighter Wing (US)
TIALD	Thermal [and TV] Imaging Airborne Laser Designator (UK) (fitted to Tornado GR1 bombers and used in the Gulf from 10 February 1991)
TOGS	Thermal and Optical Gun Sight (UK)
TRADOC	Training and Doctrine Command (US)
Tu-	Tupolev (Russian aircraft manufacturer)
UNIKOM	United Nations Iraq/Kuwait Observer Mission
UNIIMOG	United Nations Iran/Iraq Military Observer Group
USA	US Army
USAF	US Air Force
USN	US Navy
USSR	Union of Soviet Socialist Republics (Disintegrated and dissolved 8 December 1991. Replaced by the Commonwealth of Independent States)
VX	Highly toxic nerve agent
WIA	Wounded in Action
XP	Exchange Point (Point in the desert to which supplies were delivered for collection by units)
'Zulu'	Greenwich Mean Time

Appendix 'A'

CENTCOM News Briefing
General H Norman Schwarzkopf, USA
Riyadh, Saudi Arabia
Wednesday, February 27, 1991 – 1:00 p.m. EST

General Schwarzkopf: Good evening, ladies and gentlemen. Thank you for being here.

I promised some of you a few days ago that as soon as the opportunity presented itself I would give you a complete rundown on what we were doing, and more importantly, why we were doing it – the strategy behind what we were doing. I've been asked by Secretary Cheney to do that this evening, so if you will bear with me, we're going to go through a briefing. I apologize to the folks over here who won't be able to see the charts, but we're going to go through a complete briefing of the operation.

(Chart)

This goes back to 7 August through 17 January. As you recall, we started our deployment on the 7th of August. Basically what we started out against was a couple of hundred thousand Iraqis that were in the Kuwait theater of operations. I don't have to remind you all that we brought over, initially, defensive forces in the form of the 101st, the 82nd, the 24th Mechanized Infantry division, the 3rd Armoured Cavalry, and in essence, we had them arrayed to the south, behind the Saudi task force. Also there were Arab forces over here in this area, arrayed in defensive positions. That, in essence, is the way we started.

(Chart)

In the middle of November, the decision was made to increase the force because, by that time, huge numbers of Iraqi forces had flowed into the area, and generally in the disposition as they're shown right here. Therefore, we increased the forces and built up more forces.

I would tell you that at this time we made a very deliberate decision to align all of those forces within the boundary looking north towards Kuwait – this being King Khalid Military City over here. So we aligned those forces so it very much looked like they were all aligned directly on the Iraqi position.

We also, at that time, had a very active naval presence out in the Gulf, and we made sure that everybody understood about that naval presence. One of the reasons why we did that is it became very apparent to us early on that the Iraqis were quite concerned about an amphibious operation across the shores to liberate Kuwait – this being Kuwait City. They put a very, very heavy barrier of infantry along here, and they proceeded to build an extensive barrier that went all the way across the border, down and around and up the side of Kuwait.

Basically, the problem we were faced with was this: When you looked at the troop numbers, they really outnumbered us about three-to-two, and when you consider the number of combat service support people we have – that's logisticians and that sort of thing in our armed forces, as far as fighting troops, we were really outnumbered two-to-one. In addition to that, they had 4,700 tanks versus our 3,500 when the buildup was complete, and they had a great deal more artillery than we do.

I think any student of military strategy would tell you that in order to attack a position you should have a ratio of approximately three-to-one in favor of the attacker. In order to attack a position that is heavily dug in and barricaded such as the one we had here, you should have a ratio of five-to-one in the way of troops in favor of the attacker. So you can see basically what our problem was at that time. We were outnumbered as a minimum, three-to-two, as far as troops were concerned; we were outnumbered as far as tanks were concerned, and we had to come up with some way to make up the difference.

(Chart)

I apologize for the busy nature of this chart, but I think it's very important for you to understand exactly what our strategy was. What you see here is a color coding where green is a go sign or a good sign as far as our forces are concerned; yellow would be a caution sign; and red would be a stop sign. Green represents units that have been attrited below 50 percent strength; the yellow are units that are between 50 and 75 percent strength; and of course the red are units that are over 75 percent strength.

What we did, of course, was start an extensive air campaign, and I briefed you in quite some detail on that in the past. One of the purposes, I told you at that time, of that extensive air campaign was to isolate the Kuwaiti theater of operations by taking out all the bridges and supply lines that ran between the north and the southern part of Iraq. That was to prevent reinforcement and supply coming into the southern part of Iraq and the Kuwaiti theater of operations. We also conducted a very heavy bombing campaign, and many people questioned why the extensive bombing campaign. This is the reason why. It was necessary to reduce these forces down to a strength that made them weaker, particularly along the front line barrier that we had to go through.

We continued our heavy operations out in the sea because we wanted the Iraqis to continue to believe that we were going to conduct a massive amphibious operation in this area. I think many of you recall the number of amphibious rehearsals we had, to include Imminent Thunder, that was written about quite extensively, for many reasons. But we continued to have those operations because we wanted him to concentrate his forces – which he did.

I think this is probably one of the most important parts of the entire briefing I can talk about. As you know, very early on we took out the Iraqi Air Force. We knew that he had very, very limited reconnaissance means. Therefore, when we took out his air force, for all intents and purposes, we took out his ability to see what we were doing down here in Saudi Arabia. Once we had taken out his eyes, we did what could best be described as the "Hail Mary play" at football. I think you recall when the quarterback is desperate for a touchdown at the very end, what he does is he sets up behind the center, and all of a sudden, every single one of his receivers goes way out to one flank, and they all run down the field as far as they possibly can and into the end zone, and he lobs the ball. In essence, that's what we did.

When we knew that he couldn't see us any more, we did a massive movement of troops all the way out to the west, to the extreme west, because at that time we knew that he was still fixed in this area with the vast majority of his forces, and once the air campaign started, he would be incapable of moving out to counter this move, even if he knew we made it. There were some additional troops out in this area, but they did not have the capability nor the time to put in the barrier that had been described by Saddam Hussein as an absolutely impenetrable tank barrier that no one would ever get through. I believe those were his words.

So this was absolutely an extraordinary move. I must tell you, I can't recall any time in the annals of military history when this number of forces have moved over this distance to put themselves in a position to be able to attack. But what's more important, and I think it's very, very important that I make this point, and that's these logistics bases. Not only did we move the troops out there, but we literally moved thousands and thousands of tons of fuel, of ammunition, of spare parts, of water, and of food out here in this area, because we wanted to have enough supplies on hand so if we launched this, if we got into a slug fest battle, which we very easily could have gotten into, we'd have enough supplies to last for 60 days. It was an absolutely gigantic accomplishment, and I can't give credit enough to the logisticians and the transporters who were able to pull this off, for the superb support we had from the Saudi Government, the literally thousands and thousands of drivers of every national origin who helped us in this move out here. And of course, great credit goes to the commanders of these units who were also able to maneuver their forces out here and put them in this position.

But as a result, by the 23rd of February, what you found is this situation. The front lines had been attritted down to a point where all of these units were at 50 percent or below. The second level, basically, that we had to face, and these were the real tough fighters we were worried about right here, were attritted to some place between 50 and 75 percent. Although we still had the Republican Guard located here and here, and part of the Republican Guard in this area – they were very strong, and the Republican Guard up in this area strong, and we continued to hit the bridges all across this area to make absolutely sure that no more reinforcements came into the battle. This was the situation on the 23rd of February.

I shouldn't forget these fellows. That SF stands for special forces. We put special forces deep into the enemy territory. They went out on strategic reconnaissance for us, and they let us know what was going on out there. They were the eyes that were out there, and it's very important that I not forget those folks.

(Chart)

This was the morning of the 24th. Our plan initially had been to start over here in this area, and do exactly what the Iraqis thought we were going to do, and that's take them on head-on into their most heavily defended area. Also, at the same time, we launched amphibious feints and naval gunfire in this area, so that they continued to think we were going to be attacking along this coast, and therefore, fixed air forces in this position. Our hope was that by fixing the forces in this position and with this attack through here in this position, we would basically keep the forces here, and they wouldn't know what was going on out in this area. I believe we succeeded in that very well.

At 4:00 o'clock in the morning, the Marines, the 1st Marine Division and the 2nd Marine Division, launched attacks through the barrier system. They were accompanied by the U.S. Army Tiger Brigade of the 2nd Armored Division. At the same time, over here, two Saudi task forces also launched a penetration through this barrier. But while they were doing that, at 4:00 o'clock in the morning over here, the 6th French Armored Division, accompanied by a brigade of the 82nd Airborne, also launched an overland attack to their objective up in this area, As Salman Airfield, and we were held up a little bit by the weather, but by 8:00 o'clock in the morning, the 101st Airborne Air Assault launched an air assault deep into enemy territory to establish a forward operating base in this location right here. Let me talk about each one of those moves.

First of all, the Saudis over here on the east coast did a terrific job. They went up against the very, very tough barrier systems; they breached the barrier very, very effectively; they moved out aggressively; and continued their attacks up the coast.

I can't say enough about the two Marine divisions. If I used words like brilliant, it would really be an under-description of the absolutely superb job that they did in breaching the so-called impenetrable barrier. It was a classic, absolutely classic military breaching of a very, very tough minefield, barbed wire, fire trenches type barrier. They went through the first barrier like it was water. They went across into the second barrier line, even though they were under artillery fire at the time – they continued to open up that breach. Then they brought both divisions streaming through that breach. Absolutely superb operation, a textbook, and I think it will be studied for many, many years to come as the way to do it.

I would also like to say that the French did an absolutely superb job of moving out rapidly to take their objective out here, and they were very, very successful, as was the 101st. Again, we still had the special forces located in this area.

What we found was, as soon as we breached these obstacles here and started bringing pressure, we started getting a large number of surrenders. I think I talked to some of you about that this evening when I briefed you on the evening of the 24th. We finally got a large number of surrenders. We also found that these forces right here, were getting a large number of surrenders and were meeting with a great deal of success.

We were worried about the weather. The weather was going to get pretty bad the next day, and we were worried about launching this air assault. We also started to have a huge number of atrocities of really the most unspeakable type committed in downtown Kuwait City, to include reports that the desalinization plant had been destroyed. When we heard that, we were quite concerned about what might be going on. Based upon that, and the situation as it was developing, we made the decision that rather than wait the following morning to launch the remainder of these forces, that we would go ahead and launch these forces that afternoon.

(Chart)

This was the situation you saw the afternoon of the 24th. The Marines continued to make great progress going through the breach in this area, and were moving rapidly north. The Saudi task force on the east coast was also moving rapidly to the north and making very, very good progress. We launched another Egyptian/Arab force in this location, and another Saudi force in this location – again, to penetrate the barrier. But once again, to make the enemy continue to think that we were doing exactly what he wanted us to do, and that's make a headlong assault into a very, very tough barrier system – a very, very tough mission for these folks here. But at the same time, what we did is continued to attack with the French; we launched an attack on the part of the entire 7th Corps where the 1st Infantry Division went through, breached an obstacle and minefield barrier here, established quite a large breach through which we passed the 1st British Armored Division. At the same time, we launched the 1st Armored Division, and the 3rd Armored Division, and because of our deception plan and the way it worked, we didn't even have to worry about a barrier, we just went right around the enemy and were behind him in no time at all, and the 2nd Armored Cavalry Division. The 24th Mech Division was also launched out here in the far west. I ought to talk about the 101st, because this is an important point.

Once the 101st had their forward operating base established here, they then went ahead and launched into the Tigris and Euphrates Valleys. There are a lot of people who are still saying that the object of the United States of America was to capture Iraq and cause the downfall of the entire country of Iraq. Ladies and gentlemen, when we were here, we were 150 miles away from Baghdad, and there was nobody between us and Baghdad. If it had been our intention to take Iraq, if it had been our intention to destroy the country, if it had been our intention to overrun the country, we could have done it unopposed, for all intents and purposes, from this position at that time. That was not our intention, we have never said it was our intention. Our intention was truly to eject the Iraqis out of Kuwait and destroy the military power that had come in here.

So this was the situation at the end of February 24th in the afternoon.

(Chart)

The next two days went exactly like we thought they would go. The Saudis continued to make great progress up on the eastern flank, keeping the pressure off the Marines on the flank here. The special forces went out and started operating small boat operations out in this area to help clear mines, but also to threaten the flanks here, and to continue to make them think that we were, in fact, going to conduct amphibious operations. The Saudi and Arab forces that came in and took these two initial objectives turned to come in on the flank heading towards Kuwait City, located right in this area here. The British UK passed through and continued to attack up this flank. Of course, the VII Corps came in and attacked in this direction shown here. The 24th infantry Division made an unbelievable move all the way across into the Tigris and Euphrates Valley, and proceeded in blocking this avenue of egress out, which was the only avenue of egress left because we continued to make sure that the bridges stayed down. So there was no way out once the 24th was in this area, and the 101st continued to operate in here. The French, having succeeded in achieving all their objectives, then set up a flanking position, a flank guard position here, to make sure there were no forces that could come in and get us from the flank.

By this time we had destroyed, or rendered completely ineffective over 21 Iraqi divisions.

(Chart)

Of course, that then brings us to today. Where we are today, is we now have a solid wall across the north of the 18th Airborne Corps consisting of the units shown right here, attacking straight to the east. We have a solid wall here, again of the VII Corps also attacking straight to the east. The forces that they are fighting right now are the forces of the Republican Guard.

Again, today we had a very significant day. The Arab forces coming from both the west and the east closed in and moved into Kuwait City where they are now in the process of securing Kuwait City entirely, and ensuring that it's absolutely secure. The

1st Marine Division continues to hold Kuwait International Airport. The 2nd Marine Division continues to be in a position where it blocks any egress out of the city of Kuwait, so no one can leave. To date, we have destroyed over 29 – destroyed or rendered inoperable. I don't like to say destroyed because that gives you visions of absolutely killing everyone, and that's not what we're doing. But we have rendered completely ineffective over 29 Iraqi divisions. The gates are closed. There is no way out of here, there is no way out of here, and the enemy is fighting us in this location right here.

We continued, of course, high level air power. The air has done a terrific job from start to finish in supporting the ground forces, and we also have had great support from the Navy – both in the form of naval gunfire and in support of carrier air.

That's the situation at the present time.

(Chart)

Peace is not without a cost. These have been the U.S. casualties to date. As you can see, these were the casualties we had in the air war; then of course, we had the terrible misfortune of the SCUD attack the other night which, again, because the weapon malfunctioned, it caused death, unfortunately, rather than in a proper function. Then, of course, these are the casualties in the ground war, the total being as shown here.

(Chart)

I would just like to comment briefly about that casualty chart. The loss of one human life is intolerable to any of us who are in the military. But I would tell you that casualties of that order of magnitude considering the job that's been done and the number of forces that were involved is almost miraculous, as far as the light number of casualties. It will never be miraculous to the families of those people, but it is miraculous.

This is what's happened to date with the Iraqis. They started out with over 4,000 tanks. As of to date, we have over 3,000 confirmed destroyed – and I do mean destroyed or captured. As a matter of fact, that number is low because you can add 700 to that as a result of the battle that's going on right now with the Republican Guard. So that number is very very high, and we've almost completely destroyed the offensive capability of the Iraqi forces in the Kuwaiti theater of operations. The armored vehicle count is also very, very high, and of course, you can see we're doing great damage to the artillery. The battle is still going on, and I suspect that these numbers will mount rather considerably.

(Chart)

I wish I could give you a better number on this, to be very honest with you. This is just a wild guess. It's an estimate that was sent to us by the field today at noon time, but the prisoners out there are so heavy and so extensive, and obviously, we're not in the business of going around and counting noses at this time to determine precisely what the exact number is. But we're very very confident that we have well over 50,000 prisoners of war at this time, and that number is mounting on a continuing basis.

I would remind you that the war is continuing to go on. Even as we speak right now there is fighting going on out there. Even as we speak right now there are incredible acts of bravery going on. This afternoon we had an F-16 pilot shot down. We had contact with him, he had a broken leg on the ground. Two helicopters from the 101st, they didn't have to do it, but they went in to try and pull that pilot out. One of them was shot down, and we're still in the process of working through that. But that's the kind of thing that's going on out on that battlefield right now. It is not a Nintendo game – it is a tough battlefield where people are risking their lives at all times. There are great heroes out there, and we ought to all be very, very proud of them.

That's the campaign to date. That's the strategy to date. I'd now be very happy to take any questions anyone might have.

Q. I want to go back to the air war. The chart you showed there with the attrition rates of the various forces was almost the exact reverse of what most of us thought was happening. It showed the front line troops attritted to 75 percent or more, and the Republican Guard, which a lot of public focus was on when we were covering the air war, attritted less than 75. Why is that? How did it come to pass?

A. Let me tell you how we did this. We started off, of course, against the strategic targets. I briefed you on that before. At the same time, we were hitting the Republican Guard. But the Republican Guard, you must remember, is a mechanised armor force for the most part, that is very, very well dug in, and very, very well spread out. So the initial stages of the game, we were hitting the Republican Guard heavily, but we were hitting them with strategic-type bombers rather than pinpoint precision bombers.

For lack of a better word, what happened is the air campaign shifted from the strategic phase into the theater. We knew all along that this was the important area. The nightmare scenario for all of us would have been to go through, get hung up in this breach right here, and then have the enemy artillery rain chemical weapons down on troops that were in a gaggle in the breach right there. That was the nightmare scenario. So one of the things that we felt we must have established is an absolute, as much destruction as we could possibly get, of the artillery, the direct support artillery, that would be firing on that wire. That's why we shifted it in the very latter days, we absolutely punished this area very heavily because that was the first challenge. Once we got through this and were moving, then it's a different war. Then we're fighting our kind of war. Before we get through that, we're fighting their kind of war, and that's what we didn't want to have to do.

At the same time, we continued to attrit the Republican Guard, and that's why

I would tell you that, again, the figures we're giving you are conservative, they always have been conservative. But we promised you at the outset we weren't going to give you anything inflated, we were going to give you the best we had.

Q: He seems to have about 500–600 tanks left out of more than 4,000, as just an example. I wonder if in an overview, despite these enormously illustrative pictures, you could say what's left of the Iraqi Army in terms of how long could it be before he could ever be a regional threat, or a threat to the region again?

A: There's not enough left at all for him to be a regional threat to the region, an offensive regional threat. As you know, he has a very large army, but most of the army that is left north of the Tigris/Euphrates Valley is an infantry army, it's not an armored army, it's not an armored heavy army, which means it really isn't an offensive army. So it doesn't have enough left, unless someone chooses to rearm them in the future.

Q: You said the Iraqis have got these divisions along the border which were seriously attritted. It figures to be about 200,000 troops, maybe, that were there. You've got 50,000 prisoners. Where are the rest of them?

A: There were a very, very large number of dead in these units – a very, very large number of dead. We even found them, when we went into the unit ourselves, we found them in the trench lines. There were very heavy desertions. At one point we had reports of desertion rates of more than 30 percent of the units that were along the front here. As you know, we have quite a large number of POW's that came across, so I think it's a combination of desertions, of people that were killed, of the people that we've captured, and of some other people who are just flat still running.

Q: It seems you've done so much, that the job is effectively done. Can I ask you, what do you think really needs more to be done? His forces are, if not destroyed, certainly no longer capable of posing a threat to the region. They seem to want to go home. What more has to be done?

A: If I'm to accomplish the mission that I was given, and that's to make sure that the Republican Guard is rendered incapable of conducting the type of heinous acts that they've conducted so often in the past, what has to be done is these forces continue to attack across here, and put the Republican Guard out of business. We're not in the business of killing them. We have psy ops aircraft up. We're telling them over and over again, all you've got to do is get out of your tanks and move off, and you will not be killed. But they're continuing to fight, and as long as they continue to fight, we're going to continue to fight with them.

Q: That move on the extreme left which got within 150 miles of Baghdad, was it also a part of the plan that the Iraqis might have thought it was going to Baghdad, and would that have contributed to the deception?

A: I wouldn't have minded at all if they'd gotten a little bit nervous about it. I mean that, very sincerely. I would have been delighted if they had gotten very, very nervous about it. Frankly, I don't think they ever knew it was there. I think they never knew it was there until the door had already been closed on them.

Q: I'm wondering how much resistance there still is in Kuwait, and I'm wondering what you would say to people who would say the purpose of this war was to get the Iraqis out of Kuwait, and they're now out. What would you say to that public that is thinking that right now?

A: I would say there was a lot more purpose to this war than just get the Iraqis out of Kuwait. The purpose of this war was to enforce the resolutions of the United Nations. There are some 12 different resolutions of the United Nations, not all of which have been accepted by Iraq to date, as I understand it. But I've got to tell you, that in the business of the military, of a military commander, my job is not to go ahead and at some point say that's great, they've just now pulled out of Kuwait – even though they're still shooting at us, they're moving backward, and therefore, I've accomplished my mission. That's not the way you fight it, and that's not the way I would ever fight it.

Q: You talked about heavy press coverage of Imminent Thunder early on, and how it helped fool the Iraqis into thinking that it was a serious operation. I wondered if you could talk about other ways in which the press contributed to the campaign. (Laughter)

A: First of all, I don't want to characterize Imminent Thunder as being only a deception, because it wasn't. We had every intention of conducting amphibious operations if they were necessary, and that was a very, very real rehearsal – as were the other rehearsals. I guess the one thing I would say to the press that I was delighted with is in the very, very early stages of this operation when we were over here building up, and we didn't have very much on the ground, you all had given us credit for a whole lot more over here. As a result, that gave me quite a feeling of confidence that we might not be attacked quite as quickly as I thought we were going to be attacked. Other than that, I would not like to get into the remainder of your question.

Q: What kind of fight is going on with the Republican Guard? And is there any more fighting going on in, Kuwait essentially out of the action?

A: No. The fight that's going on with the Republican Guard right now is just a classic tank battle. You've got fire and maneuver, and they are continuing to fight and shoot at us as our forces move forward, and our forces are in the business of outflanking them, taking them to the rear, using our attack helicopter, using our advanced technology. I would tell you that one of the things that has prevailed, particularly in this battle out here, is our technology. We had great weather for the air war, but right now, and for the last three days, it's been raining out there, it's been dusty out there, there's black smoke and haze in the air. It's an infantryman's weather – God loves the infantryman, and that's just the kind of weather the infantryman likes to fight in. But I would also tell you that our sights have worked fantastically well in their ability to acquire, through that kind of dust and haze, the enemy targets. The enemy sights have not worked that well. As a matter of fact, we've had several anecdotal reports today of enemy who were saying to us that they couldn't see anything through their sights and all of a sudden, their tank exploded when their tank was hit by our sights. So that's one of the indications [we look for].

Q: Are you saying . . .
A: A very, very tough air environment, obviously, as this box gets smaller and smaller, and the bad weather, it gets tougher and tougher to use the air, and therefore, the air is acting more in an interdiction role than any other.

Q: Can you tell us why the French, who went very fast in the desert in the first day, stopped (inaudible) and were invited to stop fighting after 36 hours?
A: That's not exactly a correct statement. The French mission on the first day was to protect our left flank. What we were interested in was making sure we confined this battlefield – both on the right and the left – and we didn't want anyone coming in and attacking these forces, which was the main attack, coming in from their left flank. So the French mission was to go out and not only seize As Salman, but to set up a screen across our left flank, which was absolutely vital to ensure that we weren't surprised. So they definitely did not stop fighting. They continued to perform their mission, and they performed it extraordinarily well.

Q: The Iraqi Air Force disappeared very early in the air war. There was speculation they might return and provide cover during the ground war. Were you suspecting that? Were you surprised they never showed themselves again?
A: I was not expecting it. We were not expecting it, but I would tell you that we never discounted it, and we were totally prepared in the event it happened.

Q: Have they been completely destroyed? Where are they?
A: There's not an airplane flown. A lot of them disappeared throughout civilian communities in Iraq. We have proof of that.

Q: How many divisions of the Republican Guard now are you fighting, and any idea how long that will take?
A: We're probably fighting on the order of . . . . There were a total of five of them up here. One of them we have probably destroyed yesterday. We probably destroyed two more today. I would say that leaves us a couple that we're in the process of fighting right now.

Q: Did you think this would turn out, I realize a great deal of strategy and planning went into it, but when it took place, did you think this would turn out to be such an easy cake walk as it seems? And secondly, what are your impressions of

Saddam Hussein as a military strategist? (Laughter)

A: First of all, if we thought it would have been such an easy fight, we definitely would not have stocked 60 day's worth of supplies on these log bases. As I've told you all for a very, very long time, it is very, very important for a military commander never to assume away the capabilities of his enemy. When you're facing an enemy that is over 500,000 strong, has the reputation they've had of fighting for eight years, being combat-hardened veterans, has a number of tanks and the type of equipment they had, you don't assume away anything. So we certainly did not expect it to go this way.

As far as Saddam Hussein being a great military strategist, he is neither a strategist, nor is he schooled in the operational art, nor is he a tactician, nor is he a general, nor is he a soldier. Other than that, he's a great military man. I want you to know that. (Laughter)

Q: I wonder if you could tell us anything more about Iraqi casualties on the battlefield you said there were large numbers. Are we talking thousands, tens of thousands? Any more scale you can give us?

A: I wish I could answer that question. You can imagine, this has been a very fast-moving battle, as is desert warfare. As a result, even today when I was asking for estimates, every commander out there said we just can't give you an estimate. It went too fast, we've gone by too quickly.

Q: Very quickly, the special operations folks – could you tell us what their front role was?

A: We don't like to talk a lot about what the special operations do, as you're well aware. But in this case, let me just cover some of the things they did. First of all, with every single Arab unit that went into battle, we had special forces troops with them. The job of those special forces was to travel and live right down at the battalion level with all those people to make sure they could act as the communicators with friendly English-speaking units that were on their flanks, and they could also call in air strikes as necessary, they could coordinate helicopter strikes, and that sort of thing. That's one of the principal roles they played, and it was a very, very important role. Secondly, they did a great job in strategic reconnaissance for us. Thirdly, the special forces were 100 percent in charge of the combat search and rescue, and that's a tough mission. When a pilot gets shot down out there in the middle of nowhere, surrounded by the enemy, and you're the folks that are required to go in and go after them, that is a very tough mission, and that was one of their missions. Finally, they also did some direct action missions, period.

Q: General, there have been reports that when the Iraqis left Kuwait City they took with them a number of the Kuwaiti people as hostages. What can you tell us about this?

A: We've heard that they took up to 40,000. I think you've probably heard the

Kuwaitis themselves who were left in the city state that they were taking people, and that they have taken them. So I don't think there's any question about the fact that there was a very, very large number of young Kuwaiti males taken out of that city within the last week or two. But that pales to insignificance compared to the absolutely unspeakable atrocities that occurred in Kuwait in the last week. They're not a part of the same human race, the people that did that, that the rest of us are. I've got to pray that that's the case.

Q: Can you tell us more about that?
A: No sir, I wouldn't want to talk about it.

Q: Could you give us some indication of what's happening to the forces left in Kuwait? What kind of forces are they, and are they engaged at the moment?
A: You mean these up here?

Q: The ones in Kuwait, the three symbols to the right.
A: I'm not even sure they're here. I think they're probably gone. We picked up a lot of signals with people, there's a road that goes right out here and goes out that way, and I think they probably, more than likely, are gone. So what you're really faced with is you're ending up fighting the Republican Guard heavy mech and armor units that are there. Basically what we want to do is capture their equipment.

Q: They're all out of Kuwait then?
A: I can't say that. I wouldn't be the least bit surprised if there are not pockets of people all around here who are just waiting to surrender as soon as somebody uncovers them and comes to them, but we're certainly not getting any internal fighting going on across our lines of communication or any of that sort of thing.

Q: General, not to take anything away from the Army and the Marines on the breaching maneuvers . . .
A: I hope you don't.

Q: But many of the reports from the pools we've gotten from your field commanders and the soldiers were indicating that these fortifications were not as intense or as sophisticated as they were led to believe. Is this a result of the pounding that they took that you described earlier, or were they perhaps overrated in the first place?
A: Have you ever been in a minefield?

Q: No.
A: All there's got to be is one mine, and that's intense. There were plenty of mines out there, plenty of barbed wire. There were fire trenches, most of which we set off ahead of time. But there were still some that were out there, the Egyptian forces had to go through fire trenches. There were a lot of booby traps, a lot of

barbed wire – not a fun place to be. I've got to tell you probably one of the toughest things that anyone ever has to do is to go up there and walk into something like that and go through it, and consider that while you're going through it and clearing it, at the same time you're probably under fire by enemy artillery. That's all I can say.

Q: Was it less severe than you had expected? You were expecting even worse, in other words.

A: It was less severe than we expected, but one of the things I contribute that to is the fact that we went to extensive measures to try and make it less severe. We really did. I didn't mean to be facetious with my answer, but I've just got to tell you that that was a very tough mission for any person to do, particularly in a minefield.

Q: Is the Republican Guard your only remaining military objective in Iraq? I gather there have been some heavy engagements. How would you rate this army you face – from the Republican Guard on down?

A: Rating an army is a tough thing to do. A great deal of the capability of an army is its dedication to its cause and its will to fight. You can have the best equipment in the world, you can have the largest numbers in the world, but if you're not dedicated to your cause, if you don't have the will to fight, then you're not going to have a very good army.

One of the things we learned right prior to the initiation of the campaign, that of course contributed, as a matter of fact, to the timing of the ground campaign, is that so many people were deserting, and I think you've heard this, that the Iraqis brought down execution squads whose job was to shoot people in the front lines. I've got to tell you, a soldier doesn't fight very hard for a leader who is going to shoot him on his own whim. That's not what military leadership is all about. So I attribute a great deal of the failure of the Iraqi Army to fight, to their own leadership. They committed them to a cause that they did not believe in. They all are saying they didn't want to be there, they didn't want to fight their fellow Arabs, they were lied to, they were deceived when they went into Kuwait, they didn't believe in the cause, and then after they got there, to have a leadership that was so uncaring for them that they didn't properly feed them, they didn't properly give them water, and in the end, they kept them there only at the point of a gun.

The Republican Guard is entirely different. The Republican Guard are the ones that went into Kuwait in the first place. They get paid more, they get treated better, and oh by the way, they also were well to the rear so they could be the first ones to bug out when the battlefields started folding, while these poor fellows up here who didn't want to be here in the first place, bore the brunt of the attack. But it didn't happen.

Q: Can you tell us something about the British involvement, and perhaps comment on today's report of ten dead through friendly fire?

A: The British, I've got to tell you, have been absolutely superb members of this coalition from the outset. I have a great deal of admiration and respect of all the British that are out there, and particularly General Sir Peter [de la Billière] who is not only a great general, but he's also become a very close personal friend of mine. They played a very, very key role in the movement of the main attack. I would tell you that what they had to do was go through this breach in one of the tougher areas, because I told you they had reinforced here, and there were a lot of forces here, and what the Brits had to do was go through the breach and then fill up the block, so the main attack could continue on without forces over here, the mechanized forces over here, attacking that main attack in the flank. That was a principal role of the British. They did it absolutely magnificently, and then they immediately followed up in the main attack, and they're still up there fighting right now. So they did a great job.

Q: The 40,000 Kuwaiti hostages taken by the Iraqis. Where are they right now? That's quite a few people. Are they in the line of fire? Do we know where they are?

A: No, no. We were told, and a lot of this is anecdotal. We were told that they were taken back to Basra. We were also told that some of them were taken all the way back to Baghdad. We were told 100 different reasons why they were taken. Number one, to be a bargaining chip if the time came when bargaining chips were needed. Another one was for retribution because of course, at that time Iraq was saying that these people were not Kuwaitis, these were citizens of Iraq and therefore, they could do anything they wanted to with them. So I just pray that they'll all be returned safely before long.

Q: The other day on television, the Deputy Soviet Foreign Minister said, they were talking again already about re-arming the Iraqis. There's some indication that the United States, as well, needs to have a certain amount of armament to retain a balance of power. Do you feel that your troops are in jeopardy finishing this off, when already the politicians are talking about re-arming the Iraqis? How do you feel about that?

A: I certainly don't want to discuss (inaudible) because that's way out of my field. I would tell you that I'm one of the first people that said at the outset that it's not in the best interest of peace in this part of the world to destroy Iraq, and I think the President of the United States has made it very clear from the outset that our intention is not to destroy Iraq or the Iraqi people. I think everyone has every right to legitimately defend themselves. But the one thing that comes through loud and clear over, and over, and over again to the people that have flown over Iraq, to the pilots that have gone in against their military installations, when you look at the war machine that they faced, that war machine definitely was not a defensive war machine, and they demonstrated that more than adequately when they overran Kuwait and then called it a great military victory.

Q: Before starting the land phase, how much were you concerned by the Iraqi planes coming back from Iran? And do we know what happened to the Iraqi helicopters?

A: As I said before, we were very concerned about the return of the Iraqi planes from Iran, but we were prepared for it. We have been completely prepared for any type of air attack the Iraqis might throw against us, and oh, by the way, we're still prepared for it. We're not going to let down our guard for one instant, so long as we know that capability is there, until we're sure this whole thing is over.

The helicopters are another very interesting story, and we know where the helicopters were – they traditionally put their helicopters near some of their other outfits, and we tracked them very carefully. What happened is despite the fact that the Iraqis claim that we indiscriminately bombed civilian targets, they took their helicopters and dispersed them all over the place in civilian residential areas just as fast as they possibly could. Quite a few of them were damaged on airfields, those that we could take on airfields, but the rest of them were dispersed.

Q: You mentioned about the Saudi armed forces. Could you elaborate about their role on the first day?

A: The Saudi Army, as I said, the first thing they did we had this Marine attack that was going through here, and of course we were concerned about the forces over here again, hitting the flanks. That's one of the things you just don't want to have happen to your advancing forces. So this force over here, the eastern task force, had to attack up the coast to pin the enemy in this location. The Saudi forces in this area attacked through here, again, to pin all the forces in this area because we didn't want those forces moving in this direction, and we didn't want those forces moving in that direction. It's a tough mission because these people were being required to fight the kind of fight that the Iraqis wanted them to fight. It's a very, very tough mission. I would point out, it wasn't only the Saudis, it was the Saudis, the Kuwaitis, the Egyptians, the Syrians, the Emiris from United Arab Emirates, the Bahrains, and Qataris, and the Omanis, and I apologize if I've left anybody out, but it was a great coalition of people, all of whom did a fine job.

Q: Is there anything left of the SCUD or chemical capability?

A: I don't know, but we're sure going to find out if there's anything left. The SCUDs that were being fired against Saudi Arabia came from right here. So obviously, one of the things we're going to check on when we finally get to that location is what's left.

Q: Could you tell us in terms of the air war, of how effective you think it was in speeding up the ground campaign. Obviously, it's gone much faster than you ever expected. As a second part of that, how effective do you think the air/land battle campaign has been?

A: The air war, obviously, was very, very effective. You just can't predict about things like that. You can make your best estimates at the outset as to how quickly you will accomplish certain objectives, but of course, a lot of that depends on the enemy and how resilient the enemy is, how tough they are, how well dug in they are. In the earlier phases we made great progress in the air war. In the latter stages we didn't make a lot of progress because frankly, the enemy had burrowed down into the ground as result of the air war. That, of course, made the air war a little bit tougher, but when you dig your tanks in and bury them, they're no longer tanks. They're now pill boxes. That, then, makes a difference in the ground campaign. When you don't run them for a long time they have seal problems, they have a lot of maintenance problems and that type of thing. So the air campaign was very, very successful and contributed a great deal.

How effective was the air/ground campaign? I think it was pretty effective myself. I don't know what you all think.

Q: Can you tell us what you think as you look down the road would be a reasonable size for the Iraqi Army, and can you tell us roughly what the size is now if the war were to stop this evening?

A: With regard to the size right now, at one time Saddam Hussein was claiming that he had a seven million man army. If he's got a seven million man army, they've still got a pretty big army out there. How effective that army is, is an entirely different question.

With regard to the size of the army he should have, I don't think that's my job to decide that. I think there are an awful lot of people that live in this part of the world, and I would hope that is a decision that's arrived at mutually by all the people in this part of the world to contribute to peace and stability in this part of the world. I think that's the best answer I can give.

Q: You said the gate was closed. Have you got ground forces blocking the roads to Basra?

A: No.

Q: Is there any way they can get out that way?

A: No. (Laughter) That's why the gate's closed.

Q: Is there a military or political explanation as to why the Iraqis did not use chemical weapons?

A: We had a lot of questions about why the Iraqis didn't use chemical weapons, and I don't know the answer. I just thank God they didn't.

Q: Is it possible they didn't use them because they didn't have time to react?

A: You want me to speculate, I'll be delighted to speculate. Nobody can ever pin you down when you speculate. Number one, we destroyed their artillery. We went after their artillery big time. They had major desertions in their artillery, and that's how they would have delivered their chemical weapons. Either that or by air, and we all know what happened to the air. So we went after their artillery big time. I think we were probably highly, highly effective in going after their artillery.

There are other people who are speculating that the reason why they didn't use chemical weapons is because they were afraid if they used chemical weapons there would be nuclear retaliation.

There are other people that speculate that they didn't use their chemical weapons because their chemical weapons degraded, and because of the damage that we did to their chemical production facilities, they were unable to upgrade the chemicals within their weapons as a result of that degradation. That was one of the reasons, among others, that we went after their chemical production facilities early on in the strategic campaign.

I'll never know the answer to that question, but as I say, thank God they didn't.

Q: Are you still bombing northern Iraq? If you are, what's the purpose of it now?
A: Yes.

Q: What's being achieved now?
A: Military purposes that we.... Exactly the same things we were trying to achieve before. The war is not over, and you've got to remember, people are still dying out there. Those people that are dying are my troops, and I'm going to continue to protect those troops in every way I possibly can until the war is over.

Q: How soon after you've finally beaten the Republican Guard and the other forces that threaten you, will you move your forces out of Iraq – either into Kuwait or back into Saudi?
A: That's not my decision to make.

Q: Are you going to try and bring to justice the people responsible for the atrocities in Kuwait City? And also, could you comment on the friendly fire incident in which nine British were killed?
A: I'm sorry, that was asked earlier and I failed to do that. First of all, on the first question, we have as much information as possible on those people that were committing the atrocities, and of course, we're going through a screening process. Whenever we find those people that did, in fact, commit those atrocities, we try and separate them out. We treat them no differently than any other prisoner of war, but the ultimate disposition of those people, of course, might be quite different than the way we would treat any other prisoner of war.

With regard to the unfortunate incident yesterday, the only report we have is that two A-10 aircraft came in and they attacked two scout cars, British armored cars, and that's what caused the casualties. There were nine KIA. We deeply regret that. There's no excuse for it, I'm not going to apologize for it. I am going to say that our experience has been that based upon the extremely complicated number of different maneuvers that were being accomplished out here, according to the extreme diversity of the number of forces that were out here, according to the extreme differences in the languages of the forces out here, and the weather conditions and everything else, I feel that we were quite lucky that we did not have more of this type of incident. I would also tell you that because we had a few earlier that you know about, that we went to extraordinary lengths to try and prevent that type of thing from happening. It's a terrible tragedy, and I'm sorry that it happened.

Q: (Inaudible)

A: I don't know, I'm sorry. I don't believe so because I believe the information I have that a forward air controller was involved in directing that, and that would indicate that it was probably during the afternoon. But it was when there was very, very close combat going on out there in that area.

Q: The United Nations General Assembly was talking about peace. As a military man, you look at your challenge, and you can get some satisfaction out of having achieved it. Is there some fear on your part that there will be a cease fire that will keep you from fulfilling the assignment that you have? Is your assignment as a military man separate from the political goals of the ...

A: Do I fear a cease fire?

Q: Do you fear that you will not be able to accomplish your end, that there will be some political pressure brought on the campaign?

A: I think I've made it very clear to everybody that I'd just as soon the war had never started, and I'd just as soon never have lost a single life out there. That was not our choice. We've accomplished our mission, and when the decision-makers come to the decision that there should be a cease fire, nobody will be happier than me.

Q: We were told today that an A-10 returning from a mission discovered and destroyed 16 SCUDs. Is that a fact, and where were they located?

A: Most of those SCUDs were located in western Iraq. We went into this with some intelligence estimates that I think I have since come to believe were either grossly inaccurate, or our pilots are lying through their teeth, and I choose to think the former rather than the latter, particularly since many of the pilots have backed up what they've been saying by film and that sort of thing. But we went in with a very, very low number of these mobile erector launchers that we thought the enemy had. However, at one point we had a report that they may have had ten times as many. I would tell you, though, that last night the pilots had a very, very successful afternoon and night as far as the mobile erector launchers. Most of them in western Iraq were reportedly used against Israel.

Q: You've said many times in the past that you do not like body counts. You've also told us tonight that enemy casualties were very, very large. I'm wondering with the coalition forces already burying the dead on the battlefield, will there ever be any sort of accounting or head counts made or anything like that?

A: I don't think there's ever been, ever in the history of warfare, been a successful count of the dead. One of the reasons for. . . . That's because it's necessary to lay those people to rest, for a lot of reasons, and that happens. So I would say no, there will never be an exact count. Probably in the days to come you're probably going to hear many, many stories – either over-inflated or under-inflated, depending upon who you hear them from. The people who will know best, unfortunately, are the families that won't see their loved ones come home.

Q: If the gate is indeed closed, as you said several times, and the theories about where these Kuwaiti hostages are – perhaps Basra, perhaps Baghdad, where could they be? A quick second question, was the timing for the start of the ground campaign a purely military choice, or was it a military choice with political influence on the final choice of dates?

A: When I say the gate is closed, I don't want to give you the impression that absolutely nothing is escaping. Quite the contrary, what isn't escaping is heavy tanks, what isn't escaping is artillery pieces, what isn't escaping is that sort of thing. That doesn't mean that civilian vehicles aren't escaping, that doesn't mean that innocent civilians aren't escaping, that doesn't mean that unarmed Iraqis aren't escaping – that's not the gate I'm talking about. I'm talking about the gate that is closed on the war machine that is out there.

The timing for the beginning of the ground campaign, we made a military analysis of when that ground campaign should be conducted. I gave my recommendation to the Secretary of Defense and General Colin Powell, they passed that recommendation on to the President, and the President acted upon that recommendation. Why, do you think we did it at the wrong time? (Laughter)

Q: I'm wondering if your recommendation and analysis was accepted without change.

A: I'm very thankful for the fact that the President of the United States has allowed the United States military and the coalition military to fight this war exactly as it should have been fought, and the President in every case has taken our guidance and our recommendations to heart, and has acted superbly as the Commander-in-Chief of the United States.

Thank you very much.

Appendix B

Gulf Crisis: Coalition Forces Order of Battle
(excluding forces of Gulf Cooperation Council[a])

GROUND FORCES

(Source: The International Institute for Strategic Studies, The Military Balance 1991–92)

		Equipment	
Country	Tanks	Artillery	Attack Helicopters
Deployed for *Operations Desert Shield, Desert Storm, Desert Sabre*			
UNITED STATES			
HQ 3rd Army			
HQ XVIIIth Airborne Corps (from CONUS)			
82nd Airborne Division	–	54	18
101st Air Assault Division	–	54	70
1st Cavalry Division (two brigades only)	216	56	18
24th Mechanised Infantry Division	270	72	26
(with 197 separate brigade under command)			
3rd Armoured Cavalry Regiment	129	42	26
XVIII Corps Artillery (one brigade)	–	72	–
HQ VII Corps (from USAREUR)			
1st Armoured Division	324	80	44
3rd Armoured Division	324	80	44
1st Infantry Division (from CONUS)	270	72	26
(with one brigade 2nd Armoured Division under command)			
2nd Armoured Cavalry Regiment	129	42	26
VII Corps Artillery (three brigades)	–	240	–
11th Combat Aviation Brigade	–	–	36
III Corps Artillery (two brigades)	–	144	–
7th Air Defence Artillery Brigade	–	–	–
11th Air Defence Artillery Brigade	–	–	–

12th Combat Aviation Brigade	–	–	18
5th Special Forces Group	–	–	–
1st Marine Expeditionary Force			
1st Marine Division (reinforced to four regiments)			
with under command one brigade 2nd Armoured			
Division	248	144	–
2nd Marine Division (two regiments)	140	120	–
Marine Aircraft Group – 16	–	–	24
Marine Aircraft Group – 26	–	–	24
Afloat			
4th Marine Expeditionary Brigade			
Regimental Landing Team – 2	ε50		–
Marine Aircraft Group – 40	–	–	8
5th Marine Expeditionary Brigade			
Regimental Landing Team – 5	ε50		–
Marine Aircraft Group – 50	–	–	8
13th Marine Expeditionary Unit	ε20		4

UNITED KINGDOM

1st Armoured Division			
7th Armoured Brigade	117	24	–
4th Armoured Brigade	60	24	–
Divisional Artillery	–	40	–
Divisional Aviation	–	–	18
Armoured Reconnaissance Regiment	–	–	–
Special Forces: Elements 22nd Regiment SAS.			
Elements SBS Royal Marines			

FRANCE

6th 'Daguet' Light Armoured Division	40	18	70
(one tank, two armoured reconnaissance, two			
infantry, one artillery, one engineer,			
two aviation regiments)			

EGYPT

3rd Mechanised Division	200	70	–
4th Armoured Division	250	40	–

SYRIA

9th Armoured Division	300	54	–
Special Forces Regiment	–	–	–

CZECHOSLOVAKIA

Chemical Defence Unit	–	–	–

Deployed for *Operation Desert Shield* only

BANGLADESH (some 5,000 men) one infantry brigade and engineers.
MOROCCO (some 2,000 men) including Special Forces Unit
NIGER (some 500 men) infantry battalion
PAKISTAN (some 10,000 men) Two brigades (one equipped from Saudi Arabian stockpile)
SENEGAL (some 500 men)

Non-Combat Units deployed in Saudi Arabia

AUSTRALIA Medical Team (on board USNS *Comfort*)
HUNGARY Medical Team
NEW ZEALAND Two Medical Teams
POLAND Medical Unit
SIERRA LEONE Medical Unit
SINGAPORE Medical Team (with UK medical services)
SWEDEN Field Hospital

AIR FORCES
(excluding transport aircraft)

Deployed for *Operations Desert Shield, Desert Storm and Desert Sabre*

Country	Aircraft	Totals
UNITED STATES		
US Air Force		
Fighters	F-15C/D *Eagle*	120
Fighter Ground Attack	F-15E *Eagle*	48
	F-16 *Fighting Falcon*	249
Close Air Support	A-10	144
Fighter-Bombers	F-111E	80
	F-117A	44
Bombers	B-52	32
Electronic Warfare	EF-III *Raven*	18
	F-4G *Wildweasel*	48
AWACS	E-3A *Sentry*	5
Reconnaissance	RC-135	16
	U-2R	6
	RF-4C	2
	E-8A (JSTARS)	2
Tankers	KC-135	256
	KC-10	46
Special Forces	AC/EC/MC/HC-130	
	MH-53J *Pave Low*	50+
US Navy		
6 Air Wings embarked on USS *America, John F Kennedy, Midway, Ranger, Saratoga, Theodore Roosevelt*		
Fighters	F-14E *Tomcat*/F/A-18A *Hornet*	144
Fighter Ground Attack	F/A-18A *Hornet*/A-7E *Corsair*	144
	A-6E *Intruder*	60
Electronic Warfare	EA-6B *Prowler*	24
AEW	E-2C *Hawkeye*	24
Tanker	KA-6D	24
US Marine Corps		
3rd Marine Aircraft Wing (reinforced)		
Fighter Ground Attack	FA-18 *Hornet*	132
	AV-8B *Harrier*	100
	A-6E *Intruder*	20
FAC	OV-10 *Bronco*	18
Electronic Warfare	EA-6B *Prowler*	15
Tanker	KC-13	n.k.
UNITED KINGDOM		
Fighters	*Tornado* F-3	18
Fighter Ground Attack	*Tornado* GR-1	42
	Jaguar	12
	Buccaneer	6
AEW (MR)	*Nimrod*	3
Tankers	VC-10	8
	Victor	6
	Tristar K-1	2
CANADA		
Fighters	CF-18	26
Tanker	CC-137	1
FRANCE		
Fighters	*Mirage* 2000C	14
	Mirage F-1C	8
Fighter Ground Attack	*Jaguar* A	28
Reconnaissance	*Mirage* F-1CR	6
ITALY		
Fighter Ground Attack	*Tornado* 1DS	8

NAVAL FORCES

(excluding Amphibious Forces and Underway Support Vessels)

Deployed for operations 1 January – 3 March 1991 (cease-fire)

(Only ships of the US and UK Navies and the French DD *Jean de Vienne* took part in offensive operations in direct support of *Operations Desert Storm* and *Desert Sabre*.

UNITED STATES

Carrier Battle Groups: (6)

USS *America* Battle Group: CV *America*; CGN *Virginia*; CG *Normandy*; DDG *William V Pratt, Preble*; FFG *Halyburton*.

USS *Kennedy* Battle Group: CV *Kennedy*; CGN *Mississippi*; CG *Thomas S Gates, San Jacinto*; DD *Moosbrugger*; FFG *Samuel B Roberts*.

USS *Midway* Battle Group: CV *Midway*; CG *Bunker Hill, Mobile Bay*; DD *Fife, Oldendorf* FFG *Curts, Rodney M Davis*.

USS *Ranger* Battle Group: CV *Ranger*; CG *Princeton, Valley Forge*; DD *Paul F Foster, Harry W Hill; Francis Hammond*.

USS *Roosevelt* Battle Group: CVN *Theodore Roosevelt*, CG *Leyte Gulf, Richard K Turner*; DD *Caron*; FFG *Hawes*; FF *Vreeland*.

USS *Saratoga* Battle Group: CV *Saratoga*, CG *Belknap* (Flagship 6th Fleet) *Biddle, Philippine Sea*; DDG *Sampson*; DD *Spruance*; FF *Thomas C Hart, Elmer Montgomery*.

Other Forces

Command Ships: *La Salle, Blue Ridge*

Battleships: *Missouri, Wisconsin*

Cruisers: *Antietam, England, Horne, Worden*

Destroyers: DDG *Kidd, Macdonough*; DD *David R Ray, Leftwich*

Frigates: FFG *Rentz, Robert G Bradley, Taylor, Vandergrift; Ford, Jarret, Mcinerney, Nicholas*; FF *Barbey*

Submarines: SSN *Louisville* plus about 5 others

Hospital Ships: *Comfort, Mercy*

UNITED KINGDOM

Destroyers: *Cardiff, Gloucester, Manchester, Exeter.*

Frigates: *Brazen, London, Brilliant, Brave.*

Helicopter support/hospital ship: *Argus.*

Submarines: *Otus, Opossum.*

(UK force was in process of relief as *Desert Storm* began)

Deployed to enforce UN sanctions

ARGENTINA

Destroyer: *Almirante Brown/La Argentina*[b]

Frigate: *Spiro/Rosales*[b]

AUSTRALIA

Destroyer: *Brisbane*

Frigate: *Sydney*

BELGIUM

Frigate: *Wandelaar/Wielingen*[b]

CANADA

Destroyer: *Athabaskan*

Frigate: *Terra Nova*

DENMARK

Frigate: *Olfert Fischer*

FRANCE

Destroyers: *Du Chayla, La Motte-Picquet*

Frigates: *Commandant Bory, Doudart de Lagree, Premier Maître L'Her, Protet*

GREECE

Frigate: *Elli*

ITALY

Destroyer: *Orsa/Audace*[b]

Frigates: *Libeccio, Zeffiro/Lupo, Sagittario*[b]

NETHERLANDS

Frigates: *Jacob Van Heemskerck*
Philips Van Almonde

Fast combat support ship: *Zuiderkruis*

NORWAY
Armed Coast Guard ship: *Andenes*
POLAND
Hospital ship: *Wodnik*
Rescue ship: *Piast*
SPAIN
Frigate: *Numancia/Victoria*[b]
Corvettes: *Diana, Infanta Cristina/Vencedora, Infanta, Elena*[b]

Mine Countermeasures Forces (deployed in the Gulf operational area during *Desert Storm* and *Desert Sabre*)

UNITED STATES
MCO: *Avenger*; MSO: *Adroit, Impervious, Leader* plus squadron six MH-53 helicopters
UNITED KINGDOM
Ocean Survey Ship (HQ): *Herald/Hecla*[b]
MHC: *Atherstone, Cattistock, Dulverton, Hurworth, Ledbury/Brocklesby, Bicester, Brecon*[b]

Mine Countermeasure Forces (deployed to Gulf operational area after 28 February 1991)

BELGIUM
MHC: *Iris, Dianthus, Myosotis*
Support ship *Zinnia*
FRANCE
MCM: *L'Aigle, Pégase, Orion, Sagittaire*
Diving spt ship: *Pluton*
GERMANY
MHC: *Koblenz, Göttingen, Marburg*
MSC: *Schleswig, Paderborn* with (*troika* minesweeping drones)
Support ship: *Donau*
ITALY
MHC: *Milazzo, Sapri, Vieste*
Support ship: *Tremiti*
NETHERLANDS
MHC: *Haarlem, Harlingen, Zierikzee*
AUSTRALIA
Support Ship: *Westralia* with diving team on board
JAPAN
MCC: *Yurishima, Hikoshima, Awashima, Sakushima*
Support ship: *Hayase*

Notes:
[a] The GCC is made up of representatives from Bahrain, Kuwait, Oman, Qatar, Saudi Arabia and the UAE. For forces see under individual country listings in 'Countries' Section.
[b] Ship reliefs took place from January to February.

Gulf Crisis: Main Financial Contributions

(to the cost of the war, and as compensation for economic loss caused by the war)

Pledged by	Financial Aid (in $bn) to				Aid In Kind
	US	UK	Turkey/Egypt[a]	Other	
Saudi Arabia	16.80	0.56	2.85	1.77	ε6.0[b]
Kuwait	16.01	1.32	2.50	2.18[c]	–
UAE	3.50	0.50	0.85	0.62	0.14[b]
EC	–	–	0.80	–	–
France	–	0.175	0.20	0.03	–
Germany	6.57	0.60	1.19	0.94[d]	0.53
Italy	0.45	-	0.65	–	–
Other EC	–	0.02	0.19	–	–
Japan	10.74	–	2.13	0.10	0.46
South Korea	0.37	–	0.10	0.02	0.02
Norway	–	–	0.02	0.08	–
Switzerland	–	–	0.12	–	–
Other	–	–	0.17	–	–

Notes:
[a] Does not include debt forgiveness to Egypt worth est $7bn from Arab countries and $7bn from US.
[b] Cost of supply for petrol, water and other services to Coalition forces.
[c] Includes $1bn aid to France.
[d] Includes $800m aid to Israel.

Index

Factual information in the figure captions and footnotes, not included in the main text, is indexed. Thus, footnote 4 to chapter 9, appearing on page 201, is indexed 201.9.n.4. Figures are prefixed f and plates p.

The Arabic definite article 'al-', 'as-', 'an-', 'az-', which often prefixes place names, is generally omitted. So, for Al-Amarah, look under Amarah, for Az Zubayr, under Zubayr, and so on.

Individual corps, divisions and brigades are listed under 'Corps ...' etc. IZ is the Allied designator for Iraqi forces.

As a reference aid, the latitude and longitude of some important places in the Theatre of War are given.